Appreciation for *The Combat Trauma Healin*
from Military Ministry Press

D1312006

"The Combat Trauma Healing Manual is a superb body of work
this subject I have ever read. Beginning with Nate Self's moving
wartime experiences and his "war within," the manual provides insight and practical
steps that leaders, counselors, and family members can take to help. Paula and
I only wish we would have had this earlier because it has greatly added to our
understanding and compassion for those suffering. The best 'counseling manual' on
the subject I have ever read! God inspired. Reinforces that there is hope for those
suffering!!"

Lieutenant General R. L. VanAntwerp, U.S. Army

"America's Warriors returning from deployments and from combat will be affected
by their experiences in a myriad of ways – as are their families. Many will seek care,
counseling, or assistance, but many will not. Our Lord told us in Mark 12:30 to 'Love
the Lord your God with all your heart, with all your soul, with all your mind, and
with all your strength' – reminding us that we human beings have to pay attention
to our emotional, spiritual, and mental, as well as our physical needs. This manual
is a superb resource in helping our Warriors and families, and helping counselors
and caring communities to assist them, especially in dealing with their unseen
wounds and in ministering to their emotional and spiritual needs."

Major General (Retired) Kenneth L. Farmer, Jr., M.D., U.S. Army

"This outstanding manual provides a wealth of material for the care of our
military Reserve Components warriors who often return home without the ready
infrastructure of a military base. It needs to be in the hands of every religious
congregation across America as they seek to serve those in their communities who
suffer PTSD as a result of serving their country in war."

Chaplain (Brigadier General, Retired) Douglas E. Lee, U.S. Army

"I wish I had this (The CTHM) 15 years ago."

Arizona National Guard Desert Storm Veteran

"I have used the Combat Trauma Healing Manual in the past with great success. Not
only does it describe the 'what' and 'why' that surrounds stress and combat stress,
but also details a focused Christ-centered plan of 'how' to overcome. This positive
and inspiring manual is one of the only tools that I've seen be successful in helping
to overcome the effects of PTSD."

Major, Company Commander, U.S. Army

"I was sent a copy of The Combat Trauma Healing Manual. This is the best
workbook that I have seen in my thirteen years of ministering to veterans."

State Coordinator for Point Man International Ministries

Returning Warriors Need Spiritual Healing

"My husband will soon be deploying for his 3rd time in 5 years. He is suffering from PTSD so PLEASE send anything you can to help him, myself, and our 3 girls. Thank you for what you're doing!"

"My daughter-in-law is currently serving in the Army in Baghdad & having both PTSD & marital problems. I want to know how to help her."

"My brother has recently returned from Afghanistan and is suffering from PTSD, I want him healed."

"I am a military wife of 16 years, and my husband has served in the Canadian Army for 20 years. He returned from his second tour in Afghanistan Sept. '07 and has had a tour to Bosnia and Cyprus. He came home physically but mentally he died in that desert. We finally asked our church Elders to pray for us. We shared our story about PTSD and what it was doing to us. They laid hands on us and prayed for us both. WOW what a difference that made. Are we there yet, No but we are on the right path to healing with God's help."

"My son returned from Iraq last year and has lost everything. His wife, his son and he is now living with us. We are struggling to find a way to help him. Our hearts break for him each day. My mother has been listening to you this week and I know that this is an answer to our prayers. So thank you for caring for our young men and our families. May God bless this ministry the need is great!"

"I am a disabled Army Vet who thanks you for your ministry. God is using you to start the healing process in my life also. Thanks."

"Thank you for your ministry. Being a disabled vet from the Vietnam era myself I have interest in helping others find comfort in Jesus Christ."

"We started a prayer support group in our church when our son joined the Marine Corps in 2004. We have had many ministry opportunities, and have wonderful testimonies of Gods protection over the warriors we pray for. We would like to be trained in PTSD healing, as we now have two military families struggling in our church family, and more are coming our way. Thanks in advance for the video."

"Wow! I am a combat vet from Iraq. I too have been struggling with the effects of P.T.S.D. The Lord has put it on my heart and my family's heart to reach out to service members coming home from these hostile areas in my community. I am attending a church that I think is very willing to help me and my family take on this great challenge we have in our communities."

WHEN WAR COMES HOME

CHRIST-CENTERED HEALING FOR WIVES OF COMBAT VETERANS

by

Rev. Chris Adsit, Rev. Rahnella Adsit and

Marshéle Carter Waddell

MILITARY
MINISTRY PRESS
NEWPORT NEWS, VA

When War Comes Home: Christ-centered Healing for Wives of Combat Veterans is part of the **Bridges to Healing Series**, a publication of Military Ministry Press.

Also in the series: *The Combat Trauma Healing Manual: Christ-centered Solutions for Combat Trauma*

Coming in October 2008: *Care and Counseling for Combat Trauma.* A 30-hour video training series and certification program jointly produced by Military Ministry and the American Association of Christian Counselors.

Coming in 2009: *The Bridges to Healing Leaders Guide for Group Discussion; The Bridges to Healing Bible Study*

Published by Military Ministry Press, a communications initiative of Military Ministry, P.O. Box 120124, Newport News, VA 23612-0124. Military Ministry is a division of Campus Crusade for Christ International, Orlando, FL. For more information about Military Ministry, please visit our web site at www.militaryministry.org or call 1-800-444-6006. For specific information about our ministry to those suffering from Combat Trauma and Post-traumatic Stress Disorder, please visit www.ptsdhealing.org.

All Scripture quotations, unless otherwise indicated, are taken from the New American Standard Bible.
Copyright © 1960, 1962, 1963, 1968, 1971, 1972, 1973, 1975, 1977 by the Lockman Foundaton. Used by permission.

Other versions of The Bible used are:

AMPLIFIED = THE AMPLIFIED BIBLE, Old Testament. Copyright © 1965, 1987 by the Zondervan Corporation. *The Amplified New Testament.* Copyright © 1958, 1987 by the Lockman Foundation. Used by permission. All rights reserved.

CEV = *Contemporary English Version.* Copyright © 1995. Used by permission of the American Bible Society, New York, NY. All rights reserved.

ESV = *The Holy Bible, English Standard Version.* Copyright © 2001 by Crossway Bibles, a division of Good News Publishers. All rights reserved.

LB = *The Living Bible.* Copyright © 1971. Used by permission of Tyndale House Publishers, Inc., Wheaton, IL 60187. All rights reserved.

NCV = *New Century Version.* Copyright © 2003 by Word Publishing, a division of Thomas Nelson, Inc. Used by permission. All rights reserved.

NIV = the *Holy Bible, New International Version*®. Copyright © 1973, 1978, 1984 by International Bible Society. Used by permission of Zondervan Publishing House. All rights reserved.

NKJV = the *New King James Version.* Copyright © 1979, 1980, 1982 by Thomas Nelson, Inc. Used by permission. All rights reserved.

NLT = the *Holy Bible, New Living Translation.* Copyright © 1996. Used by permission of Tyndale House Publishers, Inc., Wheaton, IL 60189. All rights reserved.

RSV = the *Holy Bible, Revised Standard Version.* Copyright © 1952. Used by permission of Zondervan Publishing House, Grand Rapids, MI.

TM = THE MESSAGE. Copyright © 1993, 1994, 1995 by Eugene H. Peterson. Used by permission of NavPress Publishing Group. All rights reserved.

DISCLAIMER

This book is not a substitute for appropriate medical or psychological care for those experiencing significant emotional pain or whose ability to function at home, school, or work is impaired. Chronic or extreme stress may cause a wide assortment of physical and psychological problems. Some may require evaluation and treatment by medical or mental health professionals. When in doubt, seek advice from a professional.

Cover design: Sensa Business Communications
Interior design: Karen Watkins, Military Ministry
Illustrations: Teresa Lee, Campus Crusade for Christ
Publisher: Mike McCandless, Military Ministry Press

ISBN 978-1-4392-0890-8
Printed in the United States of America

She answered God by name,
praying to the God who spoke to her,
"You're the God who sees me!"

Yes! He saw me; and then I saw him!

— Genesis 16:13 (TM)

God sees you.

You are not alone.

Table of Contents

ACKNOWLEDGEMENTS

Authors

Reverend Christopher B. Adsit

Chris is a graduate of Colorado State University in Biological Sciences and has been on the staff of Campus Crusade for Christ since 1974. For his first fifteen years he ministered with Athletes in Action, competing in the decathlon and achieving All-American honors. In 1991 he founded "Disciplemakers International," a Campus Crusade ministry dedicated to training disciplemakers worldwide. During that period he wrote *Personal Disciplemaking* and *Connecting With God*, publications used by many Bible colleges and seminaries. Since 2005 he has been the Military Ministry's Associate National Director of Disciplemaking. Drawing on his training and experience in research and writing he wrote *The Combat Trauma Healing Manual* in 2007 (with the research assistance of his wife, Rahnella) for troops returning from war zones with traumatic stress – a companion manual to *When War Comes Home*.

Reverend Rahnella Adsit

Rahnella attended Biola College majoring in Christian Education and Bible and has been on the staff of Campus Crusade for Christ since 1978. Her passion has always been in the area of pastoral counseling – especially in helping those who have been severely traumatized by ritual abuse, childhood abuse and sexual abuse. She has maintained a private counseling practice for many years, and upon joining the staff of Military Ministry in 2005, she has been their Associate National Director of Staff & Troop Care. She was further tasked with launching the Military Ministry's PTSD ministry in 2006, helped design their "Bridges To Healing" training conferences, and was asked to draw upon her trauma counseling background to help write *When War Come Home*.

Chris and Rahnella are both ordained by the Evangelical Church Alliance – an accrediting agency that examines and ordains ministers of independent churches and parachurch organizations. They live in Eugene, Oregon, have been united in marriage since February 11, 1978, and have four mostly-grown children. Their youngest son David will be commissioned in the U.S. Army in 2009.

Marshéle Carter Waddell

Marshéle served with her husband, Commander (ret.) Mark Waddell, a career U.S. Navy SEAL, for 24 years. Together with their three children, the Waddells have endured over two decades of lengthy separations and eleven deployments for combat duty, special operations training and real world conflicts. Mark is now battling Posttraumatic Stress Disorder with Marshéle at his side. Her son, Joshua was recently commissioned as a 2nd Lieutenant in the Marines. Marshéle's first two books, *Hope for the Home Front: Winning the Emotional and Spiritual Battles of a Military Wife* and it's companion Bible study, *Hope for the Home Front Bible Study* arm other military wives with God's promises of His presence, power and protection. She is the founder of One Hope Ministry based in Monument, Colorado where she is an almost-empty-nester with her husband and three children. She is also a popular national and international speaker and has written numerous articles for both Christian and military publications. God has blessed her with a love for His Word and the enjoyment of communicating His heart through her pen and her life. www.hopeforthehomefront.com.

Review, research and editing assistance

The following people provided significant review, professional insight, feedback, correction and editing of this manual:

Suzanne Best, Ph.D. – Iraq War Veteran Posttraumatic Stress Disorder (PTSD) therapist, San Francisco VA Medical Center; co-author of *Courage After Fire: Coping Strategies for Troops Returning from Iraq and Afghanistan and Their Families*

Karen Blehm – Co-author of *Angel of Death* with husband Sergeant First Class John Blehm, highly decorated Vietnam War veteran and PTSD victor

Ruth A. Collins – Independent business owner/consultant, mother, wife of Vietnam veteran William E. Collins (1966-68, 3/506, 101st Airborne), PTSD victor

LaDonna Cutshall – Mother of two soldiers (Jim and Jeremiah), wife of former Army National Guard Medical Platoon Sergeant Bruce Cutshall (Operation Iraqi Freedom (OIF): April 2004 to March 2005), PTSD victor

Paul Davis, Ph.D. – Colonel (USAF, retired) Military Ministry associate staff member, Williamsburg, VA.

Kathie S. Green – Military Ministry staff member, Newport News, VA

Glenn Gritzon, M.A., M.A.B.C., and wife Jo – Church Relations Representatives, FamilyLife Ministry, Campus Crusade for Christ

Chaplain Robert Hicks – Air Force Reserve Specialist on traumatic stress issues; cofounder of Life Counseling Services in Philadelphia; Professor of History at Belhaven College/Orlando; Wing Chaplain for the 187th Fighter Wing of the Air National Guard; Consultant for the Air Force Air University

Benjamin Keyes, Ph.D., Ed.D. – Professor and Program Director for the Masters in Counseling Programs as Regent University, Virginia Beach, VA

Patti Kowalchuk – Military Ministry staff member, Newport News, VA

Shirley Lawing – Military Ministry associate staff member, Poquoson, VA

Martha A. Mills, Ph.D. – Program Director, PTSD Center, Veteran Affairs Medical Center, Martinsburg, WV

Amy Renslow-Nuttall – Continental Airlines, mother, wife of former Army Reserve Military Police Major Robert Nuttall (OIF: February 2003 to September 2003), PTSD victor

Dr. Bruce D. Perry, M.D., Ph.D. – Teacher, clinician and researcher in children's mental health and the neurosciences; Senior Fellow, Child Trauma Academy, Houston, TX

Karen D. Watkins – Special Projects Coordinator, Military Ministry, Eugene, OR

Andrea J. Westfall – Military Ministry staff member, former U.S. Army Reserves Staff Sergeant and combat zone flight medic (OIF: August 2002 to May 2003), PTSD victor

❧ ❧ ❧ ❧

Artwork

The charcoal illustrations of our four veterans' journaling wives are by **Teresa Lee**, Campus Crusade for Christ, Campus Ministry staff member, Eugene, OR, daughter of Major Albro L. Lundy, Jr., USAF, Vietnam War casualty, missing in action (MIA) until 2004.

A special thanks to Terry's models for helping us put faces on the issues in this manual: Cory Alverts, Linnea Alverts, Lydia Alverts, Lindsay Black, Kevin Broadous, Ann Christianson, Ashley Gilchrist, Lois Klune, Josh Lee, and Ella Slaughter.

❧ ❧ ❧❧ ❧ ❧

BEFORE YOU BEGIN

If you are the wife of a war zone veteran struggling with Combat Trauma, we want you to know that we of the Military Ministry are very grateful – not only for your husband's sacrificial service to our country, but also for *yours*. Our hearts go out to you because of the difficulties you are currently experiencing due to your husband's trauma. We, and many others in our global network, have prayed for you and are continuing to do so.

We know that one of your primary objectives in life right now is to establish stability, peace, joy and strength in your home once again. We are certain that the One who created you, Who has walked by your side your whole life (whether you knew it or not) and Who loved you enough to offer Himself sacrificially on Calvary stands ready to help you.

Many people think that Christianity is merely a "religion." We're sorry to say that it has degenerated to that in many parts of the country and the world. But at its core, Christianity is meant to be a *relationship* with the living God made possible through His Son, Jesus Christ. Many of us in the Military Ministry were "religious people" for years before we understood how to enter into an actual relationship with Jesus Christ. Others of us were very far from Him most of our lives before we discovered this vital truth.

In either case, from the day we made the decision to invite Christ into our lives as Lord and Savior our relationship with God became personal and alive! And most importantly, each of us has seen that as we pursued this relationship with God we were able to experience His specific guidance, comfort, healing and joy. We're not saying our lives became a moonlight cruise on calm seas from then on. But we *are* saying that with Him now at the helm, He has brought us through every storm we've encountered, and brought us through *better* and *stronger* each time.

God is many things, but one of His primary characteristics is that He is our *Healer*. Your husband needs healing, and in many respects so do you. There are many approaches to traumatic stress therapy that can be beneficial for you and your husband. They can equip you with coping strategies, behavior modification and cognitive therapy. But God wants to go beyond that: He wants to bring about *healing* in you both.

In the companion to this publication written specifically for war zone veterans entitled *The Combat Trauma Healing Manual*, we integrated strategies endorsed by most mental health professionals in the military and private practice. But underlying it all are the strategies endorsed by God Himself right out of His message to mankind: the Bible. In *this* manual we include many of those same strategies – both clinical and biblical – and present them along with a number of other suggestions which address the unique needs of wives whose husbands struggle with Combat Trauma.

If you have not yet begun a relationship with Jesus Christ, then you won't be able to experience the most effective benefits from this manual. If that's the case, we urge you to first take a few minutes to read through **Appendix A**, starting on page 217 to learn how to enter into a personal relationship with your Healer. It – and He – will make all the difference in the world.

> *For whatever is born of God overcomes the world; and this is the victory that has overcome the world – our faith. Who is the one who overcomes the world, but he who believes that Jesus is the Son of God?*
>
> **– 1 John 5:4,5**

INTRODUCTION

Dear Wife of a Warrior,

I have often heard an Army expression that says, "*There is nothing harder than loving a Soldier.*" A familiar T-shirt says "*Marine Wife – Toughest Job on Earth!*" Most certainly these statements apply to wives and families of all Services. You are amazing women, you military wives, you wives of warriors. You, in fact, are warriors yourselves … warriors in defense of your family, yourself and your very nation. On behalf of those who truly understand this reality: I thank you, honor you, and affirm your selfless service and amazing contributions.

In my mind's eye, I also see families – "the great stroller brigades" which you command – those throngs of youthful cheerleaders, intermingled with extended family and faithful supporters. Yes, those great "bakers of cookies and senders of letters" arrayed with balloons … cheers … hand-crafted signs of adoration … ready to sprint across the tarmac to their returning warriors. "Welcome home, Daddy!" What joyful reunions!

Yet … many of the eagerly anticipated reunions are replaced by dashed hopes and expectations. Some warriors do not return at all. "Goodbye, Daddy," and TAPS resound as the last tragic farewell to a warrior lost in battle. Or … the beloved husband and father does not return home "the same" because of emotional, psychological and spiritual wounds of war. As we well know, the tough reality is that war often "comes home" with the warrior. When this war does come home to the home front, wives of warriors often find themselves in a tsunami of confusion, potential violence and dark despair.

In an effort to help wives of warriors have "Hope on the Home Front," Military Ministry brings you a complementary volume to the *Combat Trauma Healing Manual*. In equally relevant and practical ways, *When War Comes Home – Christ-centered Healing for Wives of Combat Veterans* speaks to the wife of a combat veteran who is struggling with the hidden wounds of war, ranging across the entire Combat Trauma spectrum from reintegration challenges to the severity of Posttraumatic Stress Disorder (PTSD). *When War Comes Home* offers Christ-centered solutions for the "Secondary Trauma" she is experiencing – when *his* trauma symptoms impact the family, and even begin to show up in *her*. Insights from the medical and counseling community wrapped in biblical principles, combined with the shared experiences of wives who are veterans of their own husbands' PTSD struggles, guide the wife of a warrior to …

- understand what happened to her husband – spiritually, psychologically and physiologically
- understand how her husband's trauma symptoms are affecting her
- learn how to deal positively with grief, loss and forgiveness issues associated with her husband's PTSD
- learn how to build her own "healing place," develop her support network and know when and how to find physical safety
- understand and focus on her true identity in Christ
- recognize the real enemy and how to fight the spiritual war she and her family are engaged in
- learn how she can contribute to her husband's healing environment
- learn how to construct a safe, healthy environment for her children
- understand the process of moving on to a "new normal"

We will begin our journey together through the eyes and journal entries of a military wife like you. She asks the desperate questions:

"Where is my husband?
Who is this man that they sent home to me?
There must be some mistake!"

Just maybe you are or will soon be asking the same questions. Just maybe you likewise need a healing touch, wise counsel, an encouraging word, and strength to adapt and conquer. If so, let me encourage you to "go for it" as you begin *When War Comes Home*. There *is* HOPE, there *is* light at the end of the tunnel, there *is* a path to higher ground far above the valley in which you may now feel trapped. Just as the great warrior woman Deborah in the Bible, may you likewise proclaim:

O my soul, march on with strength.

Judges 5:21*b*

Yes, dear sister, may you likewise "march on with strength" to support your warrior husband in this latest battle, to fight for your family, to experience personal restoration, and to enter into a hopeful future that will be far brighter than you can now imagine.

With my great respect for your incredible service as a military wife,

Robert F. Dees
Major General, U.S. Army, Retired
Executive Director, Military Ministry

PROLOGUE

Barefoot on the beach, my husband and I staked out a spot to call our own. The cool tide kissed our sand-sugared toes as we waited for the Fourth of July oceanfront celebration to start. It seemed the perfect salute to honor Mark's recent return from Operation Iraqi Freedom. With precision and punctuality any military town would be proud of, the fanfare began.

Bright bouquets of red, white and blue fireworks burst into bloom against the black Virginia Beach sky. Like tall candles on a white sand birthday cake, the strand's resorts lit up by American pyrotechnic patriotism and pride. One after the other, rockets hissed and whistled over our heads. Plumes of gray smoke clouded the clear horizon and veiled the stars. The man-made thunderstorm and cheering crowds drowned out the lullaby of the gently rolling waves.

Tiny crabs scurried sideways to take cover in underground bunkers. Seagulls screeched, took flight and soared inland. Between one oblivious *ooooohhhh* and one mesmerized *aaaahhhhh*, I turned to smile at the man I had missed for months.

"Mark?" I called out.

No answer. Missing in action.

I scanned the shoreline. No husband. I pushed upstream through an army of sky-gazers away from the sonic booms to a quieter, darker stretch of the beach. A lone figure stood facing the ocean with his back to the flag-waving festivities.

"Mark?"

There was no response, but I knew it was the man who shared my bed. He just stared into black water that swallowed black sky. I tried unsuccessfully to snuggle into an embrace that his rigid arms wouldn't allow. With tear-filled eyes and trembling voice, he made his quiet request, "Can we just go home?"

If I had known then what I know today, I would have understood. I would have realized that my husband, like the coastline crabs and gulls, was in a cold-sweat search for safety, desperately looking for a hiding place for his painful memories of a war far from these shores.

When my U.S. Navy SEAL husband returned from Iraq with only a broken leg, I praised God that he was home safe and sound. In the months that followed his homecoming, I sensed that his leg was the least of our concerns. Although he was recovering physically, his soul still walked with a limp. His unseen wounds, caused by war zone experiences, went unmentioned, unnoticed and untreated. Slowly but surely, these invisible injuries infected our marriage, our children and our family life. He was home with us in body but in his spirit a war still raged. From irritability and irrationality to nightmares and emotional paralysis, it became very clear to me that my veteran husband was suffering from posttraumatic stress. For two years my husband denied any need for help and unintentionally led our family into a land of silent suffering.

Medical studies, military surveys and the media are now reporting that our family is not alone. I am grateful that the government and other organizations are putting forth their best efforts to help vets with acute stress and its potential result: Posttraumatic Stress Disorder (PTSD). **The aftermath of war is a battle fought on the home front.** Spouses and families who love and live with these vets day in and day out are fighting from unfamiliar foxholes against an enemy no one prepared them to face. The homes of our nation's heroes are being ambushed by the fallout of posttraumatic stress. Military marriages, extended families and even churches are caught in the crossfire of the flying shrapnel of stress caused by their loved ones' wartime experiences.

We, the spouses, children, family and friends of U.S. service members today urgently need to understand the soldier's heart and to arm ourselves with biblical truth to weather the storm of combat-related stress at home.

I authored two books for military families, launched a ministry for military wives, published countless articles, and spoke across the U.S. and internationally before I was invited to be a co-writer for this book. For more than two decades, our marriage had survived everything that a special operations career could throw at us: frequent deployments, long separations for training and real world conflicts, serious injuries and surgeries as well as multiple overseas family moves. The stress of my husband's job was nothing new for either of us. That may explain why my husband's frustrations and underlying anxieties caused me no new concerns at first. It was "all systems normal" and "steady as she goes," or so I thought. *Hope for the Home Front: Winning the Emotional and Spiritual Battles of a Military Wife* and its companion Bible study were penned before I knew anything about the beast that would raise its ugly head when Mark returned from the front lines. Military Life 101 was a cakewalk compared to the challenges that came home in Mark's mental rucksack.

I thank God for the privilege of being on the writing team of **the first and only Christ-centered, evangelical book available today for the military family warring against the effects of posttraumatic stress**. While physicians write prescriptions and psychologists try therapies, *When War Comes Home* speaks to the souls of our nation's unsung heroes, the wives of combat vets. I look back now and see that the bittersweet blessing of writing with honesty and transparency about our family's journey through the nightmare of combat stress has been God's hand leading me toward a deeper healing than I could have imagined. *When War Comes Home: Christ-centered Healing for Wives of Combat Veterans* will help readers connect the dots and draw a trail map for those not too far behind me. It is my prayer that with good information posted at the trail head, a military family's journey from combat-related pain to Christ-centered healing will be smoother.

I have made up my mind not to let combat trauma define me. While PTSD is a deep, dark valley, I have decided not to allow this shadow of death to determine the outcome of my life and marriage. I will not let this journey be the end of my joy. Satan's lie is that a vet's wife will never get out of this darkness, that her new, permanent address is in the valley of the shadow of PTSD. God's Word tells us the opposite. His Word says we are traveling *through* the valley, not building our homes there.

I invite you to travel with me, to keep moving across this lonely, frightening stretch of life. You are not alone. We will get to the other side by locking arms and taking brave steps together. Which will you allow to define you … your trauma or your testimony of a defiant, fearless celebration of faith as you walk through this valley? God's Word will be a light to our path and a lamp to our feet as we walk according to His promises to us. *When War Comes Home: Christ-centered Healing for Wives of Combat Veterans* is a lantern that holds the Light we need to make it safely across.

Jesus invited the one who doubted to touch His hands and side. The nail prints in His hands and the scar under His heart were wounds of warfare in the ultimate battle He fought for our souls. Jesus said, "*Put your finger here; see my hands. Reach out your hand and put it into my side. Stop doubting and believe.*" (John 20:27 NIV). His words were an invitation to believe, to trust the only One whose battle wounds can heal those of all others. Jesus extends the same invitation today to scarred soldiers and their families: to reach out in faith and touch the Christ who bore in His body on the cross all the casualties we cause one another, both seen and unseen.

"*The LORD is a warrior; the LORD is his name*" (Exodus 15:3). He knows a warrior's heart and can make it whole again. He also recognizes the cry of the warrior's wife because He has a Bride Himself whom He knows intimately and loves dearly – us.

He is able to care for His Bride's needs and to present her to God one day complete and spotless. He can do the same for this earthly warrior's wife in His perfect time.

Marshéle Carter Waddell

1 WHAT HAPPENED TO MY HUSBAND?
Understanding Combat Trauma

Lauren's Journal ...

Where is my husband? Who is this man that they sent home to me? There must be some mistake!

I pick up the morning paper and read the names of the fallen. I ache for their loved ones. Jason's name is not listed among the dead, and for this I am eternally grateful. Yet, I ache for myself. My heart breaks for both of us.

Sometimes I feel like my marriage died for my country. Jason is not the man who deployed. We are not the same couple who tearfully said goodbye all those months ago.

God protected Jason, but God didn't protect him. I prayed Psalm 91 for Jason every day, many times a day, believing God would shield him, cover him, even make him bulletproof. I prayed for him the minute I awakened, as I got our kids ready for school, as I stood in bank lines, as I waited in traffic, as I washed the dinner dishes, then outside looking up into the stars and the rising moon, and finally as I lay in our bed alone ... over and over I prayed for his safety. I never knew to pray for Jason's mind.

I just assumed that if he returned to me physically whole, then everything would be fine. I was wrong. The war has come home with Jason. The war has walked right through our front door uninvited. It sits on our sofa, rides in our car with us, and eats our meals with us. The war is here 24/7.

Jason's pain seems to be contagious. He's been home for a while and we are all hurting now. We stand back and can only watch as Jason wrestles an unseen monster, day after day, night after night. Sometimes he seems pretty normal, but then something happens, and this mysterious beast emerges breathing fire, vomiting the contents of its wounded soul all over everyone. The children and I stand speechless, afraid, confused, angry - sometimes at Jason, sometimes at the beast that this war conceived in my beloved's soul, writhing in its personal agony, imprisoned in its own pain and anchored to this war.

Why? Why Jason?

I'm out of answers. I'm even out of questions.

How could God have allowed this to happen?

When an individual experiences a horrific event where evil triumphs and good people are harmed, or when a random, unexpected event results in destruction and death, it is a natural human tendency to ask, "Where was God? Why didn't He prevent this?" Lauren's questions are natural and *normal*. If you've been asking similar questions, don't feel bad about it. God knows the motivation behind your questions is pain. He's eager to comfort you, strengthen you, and help you better understand what you are experiencing.

There are two things we know about God: He is "supremely good" and He is "supremely powerful." But wait a minute. If God is supremely good, certainly He wouldn't want bad things to happen. And if He's supremely powerful, He certainly would be able to do what He wants – and keep bad things from happening.

So … why do so many bad things happen in a world ruled by a God who is so good and so powerful?

Here's why …

"For God so loved the world ..." You've heard that line before, right? God loves the world, God loves *you,* and God loves *your husband* – at a depth and with an intensity that exceeds our understanding by infinity. His love isn't the sentimental, syrupy love that we see in the movies or daydream about. It's a love that is wise, selfless and freeing. It has eternity in mind, not just the here-and-now.

"Control freaks" are also characterized by depth and intensity. But they don't care about you – they have their own agenda. God is the opposite of a control freak. Because He loves you, He's not going to force you to do anything. He's not interested in a race of puppets that will do what He says when He pulls the right strings. He *loves* you, and what He passionately longs for is *your* love, sent back to Him of your own free will. If we are forced, it's not love at all. It's *physics*: simple action and reaction.

So from the very beginning God has deeply desired that we would decide on our own to respond positively to His loving overtures. Love cannot be coerced.

❄ ❄ ❄❄ ❄ ❄

"We do not want this man to reign over us!" That is what Jesus reported as He told a story in Luke 19 about how He was going to be rejected as King.

The story came true a few days later. *"Away with Him! Away with Him! Crucify Him! We have no king but Caesar!"* The people didn't want God – or His Son – as their ruler, so they killed Him. But this was nothing new. People have been rejecting God's rule in their affairs since the time of Adam and Eve. Mankind said "No" to God at the first opportunity and we've been saying "No" ever since. But God still reaches out in love and says, "May I be your Covering, your Guide, your Guardrails, your Sustainer, your Companion, your Comforter?" But every one of us at one time or another has said, "No, You may not. I would prefer to be the Captain of my own soul. Leave me alone. I'll do as I please."

God didn't change His mind about respecting our free will. He granted our wish. He backed off. But not very far. Always there, always ready to respond, always reaching out – but out of our way. "We don't need Him – we can handle things just fine by ourselves."

According to historian Will Durant, there have only been 268 of the past 3,421 years when a major war wasn't raging somewhere on Earth.[1] Mankind has been doing a truly bang-up job of handling things. Apart from God our history has been one of selfishness, war, conquest, and oppression. These facts lead us to the following very important conclusion:

Your husband's condition is due to the sinful actions of men – not God.

But you may still ask, as Lauren did, "Where *was* God, then? Where was He when my husband was in combat? I was praying so hard! Why didn't He listen? Did He go AWOL? Is God a deserter?" It might seem like that, but He was right there with him, ready to act and stepping in at just the right moment. He wept over your husband's friends who died just like He wept at the tomb of His friend Lazarus. He grieved for your husband's wounds, physical, mental and spiritual. He is biding His time until the day He will judge and eliminate all evil and those who practice it. But in the meantime He has been walking beside your husband and you, anguishing over the pain you are experiencing. He hasn't kept evil from touching your lives, but He has preserved you both alive in the midst of it.

He was in combat with your husband, perfectly harmonizing his will, his attacker's will, God's will, and the circumstances to keep your soul mate alive, equip you both for eternity and bring glory to Himself. It was a supernatural juggling act.

But why did some of your husband's friends – and some of *your* friends' husbands – die? We'll never know this side of heaven. There are too many variables for us to try to figure it out. It's like an ant trying to understand a computer. Just like the ant, we simply do not have the equipment to comprehend such eternal matters.

We keep on trying, however. That's our nature. The Bible says that God put eternity in our hearts (Ecclesiastes 3:11). Because of this, we *know* there's something beyond this crazy life. We *long* for that something. That mysterious, soul-deep longing for an uninterrupted life of peace and harmony makes us conclude that the evil and suffering of this world are *not right;* yet, we're utterly immersed in it. And not getting any answers as to why our experiences don't match with what we long for frustrates the heck out of us.

In the meantime, if we ask, God can give us a gift of faith to trust Him that the answers will eventually come. We're not talking about putting on rose-colored glasses and denying the pain you're experiencing. Your pain is legitimate and intense. But God wants to help you sort it out and conquer it. As you progress through this manual, our hope and prayer is that He will give you clear direction regarding exactly how to do that.

 How do you feel toward God right now? You may never have thought very deeply about this question before, but getting in touch with your innermost thoughts about God is an important exercise. Put an "X" on the line below that best describes your feelings.

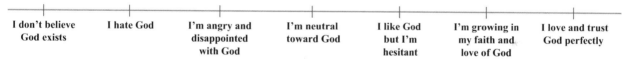

I don't believe God exists	I hate God	I'm angry and disappointed with God	I'm neutral toward God	I like God but I'm hesitant	I'm growing in my faith and love of God	I love and trust God perfectly

If you find that you placed your X more toward the left end of the line, that's okay! We applaud your honesty! God knows the distress you are currently experiencing. Your anger, doubt and disappointment are things He can lovingly deal with, and He will, over time, if you let Him. If your X is more toward the right end, count on God to build on your faith.

The past and the present

Take a few moments and think about the way things were. Ask God to help you remember, and then write down a few descriptive terms that express your husband's positive traits prior to deployment.

_____

_____

_____

As you remember these things, how does it make you feel right now?

_____

_____

_____

Take a moment and write about your grief, anger or sense of loss in a prayer to God. If you need an example of how to do this, look at *Lauren's Prayer* at the end of this chapter.

_____

_____

_____

_____

_____

_____

❀ ❀ ❀❀ ❀ ❀

How combat has affected your husband

"Combat Trauma" (officially called "Deployment-Related Stress" by the Army) describes a spectrum of distressing reactions a troop may have to the trauma of combat. These reactions could include anything from the normal, relatively mild tensions associated with the transition from deployment back to home and family life (Reintegration Issues), all the way up to severe conditions known as Acute Stress Disorder (ASD) and Posttraumatic Stress Disorder (PTSD). ASD and PTSD occur in those who have been exposed to a traumatic combat-related event (or series of events) which involved actual or threatened death or serious injury and caused an emotional reaction involving intense fear, panic, helplessness or horror. The symptoms for both disorders are: (1) a persistent re-experiencing of the event(s) through nightmares, intrusive thoughts or dissociative episodes, (2) obsessive avoidance of any stimuli associated with the event(s), and (3) feeling "keyed-up" (aroused, angry, sleepless, jumpy) at all times.[2] The difference between these two disorders is how long the symptoms persist: one month for ASD, no time limit for PTSD.

By the way, your husband didn't have to experience direct combat to develop Combat Trauma symptoms. He may have been a logistics officer, a truck driver, a mail deliverer, never experienced a firefight, and still came back traumatized – which could be very puzzling to both of you. In most modern wars, *there is no safe place!* Your husband was conscious of the fact that any moment could be his last. Mortar rounds frequently fell inside the Green Zone in Baghdad. Improvised Explosive Devices (IEDs) killed many truck drivers and mailmen. Seemingly friendly civilians or their vehicles could be wired to explode at an opportune time. He knew this, and for months he was constantly on edge and on high alert, 24/7. This accumulation of stress and anxiety can result in Combat Trauma.

The following graphic presents this **spectrum of Combat Trauma**:[3]

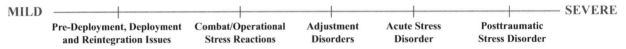

MILD					SEVERE
Pre-Deployment, Deployment and Reintegration Issues	Combat/Operational Stress Reactions	Adjustment Disorders	Acute Stress Disorder	Posttraumatic Stress Disorder	

Combat Trauma sufferers toward the left end of the spectrum usually exhibit fewer symptoms and typically improve without significant treatment. Those at the right end of the spectrum exhibit profound symptoms which persist for at least a month, maybe years, and – if untreated – a lifetime. These symptoms may not begin to surface for months or years after the traumatic event(s).

❀ ❀ ❀❀ ❀ ❀

? Put an "X" on the spectrum above representing where you feel your husband is right now. You don't have to know the definitions of each designation on the line – just estimate where he fits on the "mild" to "severe" continuum.

❀ ❀ ❀❀ ❀ ❀

Posttraumatic Stress Disorder (PTSD) has been called the "signature injury" of Operation Enduring Freedom (OEF) in Afghanistan and Operation Iraqi Freedom (OIF). This is the disorder most people have heard about, and it is probably the one you are most worried about. This manual addresses the most difficult issues that develop if you are married to a man with full-blown PTSD. But even if your husband is more to the left end of the "Combat Trauma Spectrum" line, you *will* be helped by applying the principles shared in this manual.

PTSD isn't new

PTSD has been called many different names over the centuries, which makes it clear that it's a disorder not unique to modern wars, but common to all wars. During the latter half of the 1600s, the Swiss observed a consistent set of symptoms in some of their solders and called it "nostalgia." German doctors of the same period used the term *Heimweh,* and the French called it *maladie du pays,* both terms roughly translated as "homesickness." The Spanish called it *estar roto,* "to be broken." During America's Civil War it was called "soldier's heart." The disorder was called "shell shocked" in World War I, "combat fatigue" in WWII, and "war neurosis" during the Korean war. In the 1970s psychiatrists coined the phrase "Vietnam Veterans Syndrome."

Each of these terms shows facets of the disorder. The soldier's heart *does* get profoundly altered by war. Nostalgia and homesickness describe the desperate longing of a PTSD sufferer to leave the chaos of the battle and return to the safety of home. Emotionally, something is indeed broken inside these wounded warriors resulting in various psychological neuroses – a familiar, persistent syndrome of symptoms. You can probably see many of these facets in your husband.

It wasn't until 1980 that the American Psychiatric Association formally identified, named and defined Posttraumatic Stress Disorder, and it's been in the official diagnostic manuals of the medical profession ever since. More research is constantly being done on this mystifying disorder.

But here is the first thing you need to know – which *all* the experts agree on:

Posttraumatic Stress Disorder is a *common* reaction to an *uncommon* event.

Common. It may be difficult for you to imagine that your husband's new anxiety-riddled behavior is common, but that's exactly the case. His symptoms are what would be *expected* from someone who experienced what he did. They are common to hundreds of thousands – perhaps millions – of other courageous men and women who have fought in wars down through the centuries.

But compared to how he used to be, he's probably acting very *uncommonly*. No doubt, he's different from his pre-war self and different from his friends who never experienced combat. But for someone who saw, smelled, felt, heard and tasted the things he did, it's common.

It is estimated that over 400,000 Vietnam War veterans suffer from PTSD – undiagnosed and untreated. Some put the number as high as one million. In a recent report by the Veterans Health Administration 38 percent of OIF/OEF veterans (100,580 troops) who have sought care were diagnosed with PTSD or other mental health issues.[4] This doesn't include the ones who *haven't* sought care (it is estimated that only 23 percent seek treatment[5]). You and your husband are most definitely *not* alone.

If this is new information to you, let us spell it out:

- PTSD is not rare or an aberration – it's a common response to an uncommon stressor.
- Hundreds of thousands of men and women are in the same boat as you and your husband.
- It is *normal* to be affected by combat.
- It is *normal* to be affected by threat, trauma, pain, atrocity, horror and gore.
- Facing death changes a person.
- It would be *abnormal* if he *weren't* affected.
- It shows that he is human, and what happened downrange matters deeply to him.

Here is the next thing you both need to know:

He is not weak, weird or cowardly. He has been *wounded*.

What can cause a wound? We normally think of physical implements, like a knife or a bullet. But one can receive "soul wounds" that are as bad as or worse than physical wounds, affecting a person deeper and lasting longer than anything a gun could produce. And we're not talking sentimental psychobabble here – this is as real as it gets. You know. You've seen and experienced your husband's woundedness.

The word "trauma" is from a Greek word which means "a wounding." When applied to the physical realm, it refers to an event in which some external force has damaged a part of your body. The normal defense mechanisms (such as the skin, muscle, skull, internal bone framing, etc.) were unable to prevent the injury. Even non-military persons know how difficult it is to function the way you're used to after a wounding. Your strained back keeps you from bending over and picking up your child. The cast on your leg prevents you from walking normally.

In a similar fashion, a person can receive psychological wounds that are incapacitating. Events can get past our normal defenses and severely disrupt our emotions, our souls and spirits, our faith, our self-identity, our confidence, our trust in other humans, our sense of security and even our will to live. After this we will have difficulty coping, thinking, reacting, planning and functioning the way we used to – at least for a while.

Let's say your husband had been a track star in school. If he came home with a severely damaged foot, you wouldn't expect him to simply "get over it" and start running as fast as he used to right away. Time and treatment would be needed to generate healing. If he tried to get on the track and run too early, it would only worsen and prolong his convalescence. The same principles hold true with the very real wounding of PTSD.

❀ ❀ ❀❀ ❀ ❀

? If your husband were physically injured, it would be important for you to be able to tell certain people about it – such as a doctor, family member or a good friend. Take a few minutes to think about how to describe his "soul wounds" and write it below.

_____

_____

_____

_____

_____

❀ ❀ ❀❀ ❀ ❀

What causes PTSD?

Not just combat. Any kind of horrific event that makes a person think they could be severely injured or killed *can* trigger PTSD. We emphasize *can* because it doesn't mean it necessarily will. One study determined that approximately 75 percent of Americans have had a traumatic experience significant enough to cause PTSD, but only about 10 to 25 percent of those actually develop the disorder.[6] Experts do not fully agree as to why some do and some don't, but it seems that the *intensity* of the experience or multiple experiences has a lot to do with it. In addition, if a person has been traumatized at a younger age (physical or sexual abuse, abandonment, kidnapping, assault, etc.) it increases their likelihood of developing PTSD as an adult.

Experiences that can produce PTSD are combat, sexual and physical assault, being held hostage, terrorism, torture, natural and man-made disasters, accidents, receiving a diagnosis of a life-threatening illness, violating one's conscience by engaging in mutilation or other violations of the Law of Armed Conflict or the killing of innocents (accidentally or on purpose) in life-threatening situations. Even witnessing threatening, mutilating or deadly events or hearing about them happening to a family member or other close associate can cause

PTSD. It can be especially severe or long-lasting when the trauma comes from an intentional human act, rather than from an accident or a natural disaster.

? Prior to deployment, did your husband ever experience any of the events, besides combat, described in the previous two paragraphs? If so, list them here:

_____

_____

_____

_____

_____

❈ ❈ ❈❈ ❈ ❈

The physiology, psychology and theology of PTSD

One of God's top design priorities when He created us was that we be equipped to defend ourselves and survive in a wide variety of dangerous situations. To this end, He equipped us with an amazing set of response mechanisms in our brain.

Our brain is divided into two halves. The left side is our analytical side. It scrutinizes incoming information logically, thinks rationally, explicitly and in concrete terms. It's on this side of the brain that practical information, our ability to speak, read, write, spell and do math is stored. This side remembers names and craves precision.

> *I will praise You, for I am fearfully and wonderfully made; marvelous are Your works, and that my soul knows very well.*
> **– Psalm 139:14** (NKJV)

If our left side is more like a "computer," our right side is more like a "photo album." This side remembers faces and craves rapport and relationship. It's our emotional side. It's intuitive, spontaneous, experience-oriented, artistic and creative. It stores emotions. We dream on this side of our brain. And very importantly, this is the "alarm" side of our brain.

Beneath these two halves is our "lower brain" or brain stem. This part of our brain controls all automatic life functions, such as our breathing, digestion and heartbeat. The lower brain always trumps the two halves of our higher brain. For instance, it doesn't matter how logical it may seem, or how passionately you might want to do it, you can't make your heart stop beating just by thinking about it. You can hold your breath for a while, but before long your lower brain once again asserts its dominance and forces you to breathe.

The Science of Trauma Reactions. When we encounter something that we feel threatens our life, a cascade of hormonal reactions is triggered. A nerve shoots a message to our adrenal glands to dump adrenaline and noradrenaline into our bloodstream, causing our heart to beat faster, our lungs to pump harder, getting the rest of the body ready to either fight, fly or freeze. Our pupils dilate, giving us tunnel vision so we can focus on the threat and not be distracted by peripheral action. Thousands of small muscles in our arms and legs constrict, sending blood away from our skin and into our muscles for quick movement so that if our extremities are wounded, we won't bleed as badly. Our blood sugar and free fatty acids instantly ramp up, giving us more energy. At the same time, up to 70 percent of our brain-bound oxygen is quickly shunted into our muscles so we can run, kick or punch like we never had before. Additional hormones give us uncommon strength and quickness. Our perception of time is altered – a ten-minute firefight seems like it only took a minute.

But something happens deep inside our brains, too. Our right-brain alarm goes off, and drowns out the logical analysis of our left brain. It screams, "Less thinking, more action!!" It also starts taking pictures like mad – the noradrenalin heightens the emotional aspects of the situation making it more vivid and notable. Very strong and clear memories are being recorded, probably so we will remember this event and avoid it in the future.[7]

At this point, our lower brain takes over. It's live-or-die time. With this organ in control, nothing else matters. It automatically directs the rest of the body in very complex but focused ways to do whatever it takes to survive.

Patience Mason, who is married to a Vietnam War veteran and has written extensively on PTSD describes this behavior eloquently and realistically …

> Whatever it takes! This is not a polite, well-behaved part of us. It [urinates] and [defecates] in its fear. It scratches and bites and goes berserk, beating people to death with the rifle-butt when the bullets are gone. It kicks and gouges. It runs out on its friends, trampling whoever gets in its way. It cowers, unable to get up or to fight, unable to protect those it loves. It may freeze or follow orders that are against all the survivor personally believes in. Survivors may feel shock or shame over what this part of them did.[8]

Research has shown that your body will exhibit these built-in survival techniques no matter what your race or gender is, whether you come from a privileged background or the ghetto, whether you are mentally slow or highly intelligent, whether you come from a happy family or a broken one, whether you're a cheerful person or a total pessimist, whether you're young or old. But it's important to know two things:

1. God gave us this reactive pathway so that we would be able to do whatever was necessary to survive. It kept your husband alive. God knows that when our lives are threatened this behavior needs to come out or we could die. At that point, all the rationality, dignity, intelligence and decorum in the world is absolutely useless.

2. No matter how hard your husband might have tried, he couldn't have stopped this reaction. Can a person stop his heartbeat? No. Neither are we able to control ourselves when our brains have clicked into this mode.

❊ ❊ ❊❊ ❊ ❊

? Has your husband talked about one or more of these "automatic" reactions while he was deployed? If so, place an "X" on the line below indicating how severe it was.

Mild ┼—————————————————————————————————————┼ **Severe**

Has he had any of these reactions since he came home, in the form of a flashback? If so, indicate how severe it was on the line below.

Mild ┼—————————————————————————————————————┼ **Severe**

❊ ❊ ❊❊ ❊ ❊

PTSD persistence — getting "stuck"

"Okay," you say, "The crisis is over now. He survived and made it home. So why can't he move on? Why does he keep reliving what happened?"

Often, a trauma survivor can go through a short period of decompression and processing, and return pretty close to "normal." But if the traumatizing event was exceptionally violent and life-threatening, or if there were multiple episodes, the brain stays "stuck" in this crisis-alert mode.

Think of it in terms of walking across a frozen lake. As you walk, you feel confident and enjoy sliding along on the ice. You might even do a few aerial leaps and spins like the skaters on TV, just for fun. Suddenly you hear a loud pop, and you notice the ice is cracking under your feet. You instantly freeze. Your arms reflexively shoot out from your sides for balance and your feet spread wide to distribute your weight. Your muscles are now tight, your shoulders bunched up, your eyes are the size of softballs and you begin to take very small, careful steps back the way you came. You hardly breathe. After about twenty yards, you are beyond where the cracks are. Do you think you'll now go bounding merrily the rest of the way to shore? You'll probably remain on high alert the rest of the way, because you are now aware that the ice *could* give way beneath you at any time.

After a traumatic event, your brain knows that it just had an incredibly close call, and it is determined to be ready to react if the danger comes by again. Good idea – except if it gets stuck in that mode, which is essentially what PTSD is. It's like the ice-walker tiptoeing down the two miles of sidewalk to get home.

The shock physically alters parts of your brain. Your reactive pathways modify and your brain chemistry changes becoming hypersensitive, quickly overreacting to normal stimuli. Your hippocampus – the part of your brain that interprets and calms your emotional responses – shrinks and works less effectively. Your left and right brain hemispheres have trouble communicating and balancing each other – so you're either emotional and unordered, or you're emotionless, cold, withdrawn and not much fun to be around. Sometimes each of these can happen inside of five minutes.

And whenever your brain senses that it's getting near the "scene of the crime" via some sensory trigger (a smell, a sound, a sight, a memory), it quickly opens up the photo album it created during the earlier traumatic event and puts on an intense slide and video show to re-instruct you that you don't want to go there again! "Are you *nuts!??* We almost *died* when we were there last time!! Get away!!" The technical term for this is "re-experiencing."

The opening of the photo album can also have another function. It's a flare being sent up by the trauma survivor's inner self alerting the outside world that he's been through more than he can handle, and he needs help dealing with it. We humans aren't meant to suffer our traumas alone and not bother anybody else about them. We are an *interdependent* species, ordained so by our Creator. We need each other. And if our "outer self" won't take action, our "inner self" will keep up the pressure until we do. By the way, it seems to work. More PTSD sufferers finally decide to seek help due to their re-experiencing symptoms than for any other reason.

❀ ❀ ❀❀ ❀ ❀

? **Three questions:** (1) Has your husband talked much with anybody about his combat experience(s)? (2) If not, why not? (3) Do you think he would be open to talking more about it if the right person were willing to listen?

_____

_____

_____

_____

❀ ❀ ❀❀ ❀ ❀

PTSD *symptoms*

Since the American Psychiatric Association defined Posttraumatic Stress Disorder in 1980, and with additional research done after that, experts seem to agree that there are three classic categories of symptoms that characterize this disorder. Read through the list that follows and put an "X" in the box of any symptoms that your husband has experienced in the past, or is currently experiencing. If his experience of a symptom is mild or very infrequent, give it a light, small "X." The more intense or more frequent the symptom, enlarge and darken the "X."

Symptoms

1. Re-experiencing Symptoms
Memories and images of the traumatic events may intrude into the minds of those with PTSD. They occur suddenly without obvious cause. They are often accompanied by intense emotions, such as grief, guilt, fear or anger. Sometimes they can be so vivid the sufferer believes the trauma is actually recurring.[9]

In the past but not now	Currently experiencing	
☐	☐	Nightmares, night terrors
☐	☐	Sleepwalking, sleep fighting
☐	☐	Unwanted daytime memories, images, thoughts, daydreams
☐	☐	Flashbacks, feeling like he's reliving the traumatic event
☐	☐	Somatic flashbacks (physical pain or a medical condition emerges, linked to the feelings or bodily states associated with the traumatic event)
☐	☐	Fixated on war experience, living in the past
☐	☐	Spontaneous psychotic episodes (the world vanishes, and he's suddenly somewhere else, experiencing some sort of trauma)
☐	☐	Panic attacks, undefined dread or fear
☐	☐	Phobias (What kind does he experience?)_____

2. Avoidance Symptoms
Traumatized individuals attempt to avoid situations, people or events that remind them of their trauma. They feel numb, emotionless, withdrawing into themselves trying to shut out the painful memories and feelings. Friends and family feel rejected by them, as they are unable to show appropriate affection and emotion.

In the past but not now	Currently experiencing	
☐	☐	Avoiding anyone or anything that reminds him of the traumatic event
☐	☐	Physical/emotional reaction to things that remind him of the traumatic event
☐	☐	Self-isolating, dread of social interaction
☐	☐	Anxiety in crowds, traffic
☐	☐	Despair, depression, sadness, emptiness, loneliness
☐	☐	Inability to trust others
☐	☐	Very reluctant to talk about his traumatic event(s)
☐	☐	Lack of interest or motivation regarding employment, recreation, former hobbies, sex, exercise
☐	☐	Relationships that were once close and even intimate are now strained, cold, distant, requiring too much energy to maintain
☐	☐	Emotional numbness, flat, can't get happy or sad, "dead" inside
☐	☐	Substance abuse to "numb" himself and escape
☐	☐	Suicidal thoughts
☐	☐	Suicide attempts
☐	☐	Physical fatigue
☐	☐	Neglect/abandon personal care, hygiene, nutrition, exercise

3. Arousal Symptoms
Fearing further trauma, PTSD sufferers are always on the alert, on guard, jumpy, unable to sleep, angry, irritable. Many also have concentration and memory problems.

In the past but not now	Currently experiencing	
☐	☐	Anger, irritability, "short fuse," fits of rage
☐	☐	Hypervigilance (always on guard), always needs to be armed with knife or gun
☐	☐	Easily startled, reacts to loud noises, jumpy
☐	☐	Substance abuse to "un-numb" himself and stay sharp, ready to react
☐	☐	Reduced cognitive ability (slow thinking, confusion, problem-solving, concentration)
☐	☐	Poor memory
☐	☐	Trouble falling asleep or staying asleep, insomnia
☐	☐	Night sweats

❏ ❏ Accelerated heart rate, rapid breathing, heart palpitations for no good reason
❏ ❏ Questions/abandons faith, feeling of being betrayed or abandoned by God, mad at God
❏ ❏ Fear of becoming violent
❏ ❏ Becoming violent, provoking fights
❏ ❏ Homicidal thoughts
❏ ❏ Anniversary reaction (becomes anxious nearing the monthly or yearly anniversary of the traumatic event or events)
❏ ❏ Adrenalin junkie (taking risks, getting hyped-up)
❏ ❏ Self-mutilation, cutting, excessive tattooing

If you found yourself checking more than two or three of the boxes in the "Currently experiencing" column of each of the three major categories, it is likely that your husband is struggling with some level of Combat Trauma. If you checked fewer in that column than you did in the "In the past but not now" column, this would indicate that he's made some positive progress. If there are more in the second column than the first, his Combat Trauma may still be developing. This is not cause for despair, but it is cause for you to take action – not only for him, but for yourself as well. Whatever the case, it's good to have a realistic grasp of your situation.

❀ ❀ ❀❀ ❀ ❀

? What do you miss most about how your life was before your husband was deployed?

_____

_____

_____

_____

❀ ❀ ❀❀ ❀ ❀

Traumatic Brain Injury

Medical professionals treating those who have been wounded in the recent conflicts in the Mideast tell us that many troops coming home with a diagnosis of PTSD actually have *Traumatic Brain Injury*. According to Amber Nicodemus, Executive Director of the Cognogenesis Brain Center in Colorado Springs, Colorado, these conditions exhibit many of the same symptoms, hence the confusion.

Traumatic Brain Injury (TBI) is usually the result of a sudden, violent blow to the head. The skull can often withstand a forceful, external impact without fracturing – but a blow such as this can launch the brain on an internal collision with the skull. The result, an injured brain inside an intact skull, is known as a "closed-head injury."

A brain injury may also occur when a projectile, such as a bullet, rock or fragment of a fractured skull, penetrates the brain. The severity of brain injuries can vary greatly, depending on the part of the brain affected and the extent of the damage. A mild brain injury may cause only temporary confusion and headache, but a serious one can be fatal.[10]

Regarding war-related instances of TBI, the Brain Injury Association of America says:

> Shock wave blasts from improvised explosive devices, rocket propelled grenades and land mines are the leading cause of TBI for active duty military personnel in combat zones. In prior military conflicts, TBI was present in 14-20 percent of surviving casualties. Reports indicate 12,274 service members have sustained a TBI in Operation Iraqi Freedom (OIF) and Operation Enduring Freedom (OEF) as of March 24, 2007, but that number could grow as high as 150,000.[11]

Read over the list of TBI symptoms below, and you will see how some troops could be misdiagnosed with PTSD. The symptoms in bold print are the same ones you'll find on lists of PTSD symptoms.

TBI Signs & Symptoms[12]

1. headaches
2. dizziness or vertigo
3. **memory problems**
4. balance problems
5. ringing in ears
6. **sleep problems**
7. **poor word recall**
8. difficulty reading
9. **difficulty concentrating**
10. visual disturbances
11. **irritability or anger outbursts**
12. **impulsivity**
13. lack of forethought
14. obsessive/compulsive behavior
15. inflexible in thought
16. **anxiety**
17. sensitivity to light, touch, sound
18. gets lost or becomes misdirected
19. **depression**
20. **negative attitude**
21. **antisocial or isolated**
22. slowed or impaired motor skills
23. **poor judgment**
24. speech problems
25. balance problems
26. seizures
27. loss of sense of taste or smell
28. **change in sexual drive or ability**
29. **avoidance behavior**
30. **restricted range of affect (e.g., unable to have loving feelings)**

Though we don't have the space to go into the subject of TBI in this manual, it's important for both you and your husband to be aware of this alternative diagnosis. Only a healthcare professional can properly assess your husband to determine if he has TBI or PTSD, but if his symptoms seem to match the above list more closely than the previous list of symptoms for PTSD, you may want to investigate it. The treatment for the two disorders is *different*!

What's ahead for me ... for us?

Undoubtedly, this is one of the most difficult times you and your husband have ever experienced. Neither of you ever expected him to come back from war so different. It's important to understand that this turn of events has not taken God by surprise. He knew in advance what your husband was going to encounter. He knew how your husband was going to be affected, and He also knew how he was going to oppose the debilitating effects of his trauma. God specializes in working all things together for the good (Romans 8:28). He is the eternal expert in exchanging "beauty for ashes" (Isaiah 61:3). It won't be an easy process, but if you follow His lead, He'll guide you and your husband through it.

It's also important to understand that God is the healer, and you aren't. We're sure that you desperately desire to bring healing, respite, stability, *normalcy* back to your husband and to your household. But that job is too big for you. It's too complex. Only the infinite mind of God can get a handle on your situation and bring about the conclusion you desire. But He *will* use you in the process. You could be the most significant "bridge" that God will use to create the environment that will give Him optimal access to your husband's body, soul and spirit. Keep your mind open to the partnering God wants to forge with you. Parts of this manual will give you practical ways to do that.

But there's one more important thing you need to understand: the necessity of taking care of *yourself*. As drill sergeants tell their recruits, "You're no good to anybody dead." When someone is obviously wounded, caregivers flock to the victim and render aid. The VA and the Department of Defense are unleashing tons of resources to try to help our wounded warriors. But who's helping you? We recognize that you are wounded too and also need the caregivers' attention. If you don't take care of yourself, who will? How can you do it? That's what *most* of this manual is about.

So you're *both* wounded. What's the prognosis? Frankly, it's not that positive – if we look at the track records of so many couples who have split up because of the veteran's PTSD. But that doesn't have to be *your* story. If you will cooperate with God in the process that He has in mind, both of you will experience healing. You may not end up "as good as new" and you may never be the same as you were before your husband's trauma. Your experiences have made you both different people – not worse, just different – and with God's contribution, *better* people. There is *much* to be hopeful about!

> For over three decades, I have studied victims of overwhelming stress – concentration camp survivors, POWs liberated from years of captivity, terrorized hostages. Repeatedly, I have been inspired by the countless cases that run counter to "expert" predictions. Instead of a pattern of deficit and defeat, there is one of coping and conquest. Indeed, rather than being devastated by their suffering, many survivors have actually used the experience to enrich their lives ... Human beings have a magnificent ability to rebuild shattered lives, careers, and families, even as they wrestle with the bitterest of memories.
>
> – Dr. Julius Segal[13]

We're not saying this process is going to be a smooth, uninterrupted stroll down the beach. There will be setbacks, slow times and detours. But stick with it! It will be worth it in the end. As Ralph Waldo Emerson once said:

> Our greatest glory is not in never failing,
> but in rising up every time we fail.

And as God said in Proverbs 24:16 (NLT):

> *The godly may trip seven times, but they will get up again.*
> *But one disaster is enough to overthrow the wicked.*

Trauma is a thief. The self-defense mechanisms that God built into your husband were vital at the time his body and mind were attacked, but now – not so much. As a Marine, Soldier, Sailor, Airman or Coastguardsman, he sacrificed. As his wife, *you* sacrificed. But more has been taken from you both than you bargained for. God wants to reimburse you for what has been taken, if you'll let Him:

> *Then I will make up to you for the years that the swarming locust has eaten ... You will have plenty to eat and be satisfied, and praise the name of the Lord your God, who has dealt wondrously with you; then My people will never be put to shame.*
>
> – Joel 2:25,26

? If there's one thing you would like to include in your personal definition of how life will be when you and your husband are "healed," what would it be?

_____

_____

_____

_____

Lauren's Prayer ...

Lord, when my husband returned from Iraq with only a broken leg, I praised You that he was home safe and sound. Now, months later, I sense that his leg is the least of our concerns. He is healing outwardly, Lord, but his soul walks with a limp. I cannot see the wounds caused by his war-zone experiences but You can see them. Only You can heal him. Help me to come to You and to trust You to intercede for us when I cannot find the words. I ask for prayer partners who will remember to pray for us, come what may. I need someone to talk with, Lord, someone who has dealt with this before. Please provide godly counsel and direction.

Dress me in the full armor of the living God as I fight for my marriage and for our family. And as I do my part, Lord, help me then to be still and to know that You are God. I know You have the will and the power to work all of this for our good because we love you and are called according to Your purpose.

You, Yourself, are a warrior, Lord. You know a warrior's heart and can make it whole again. You also recognize the cry of a warrior's wife, because You, too, have a Bride whom You love dearly. You are able to care for Your Bride's needs and to present her to Yourself one day complete and spotless. I believe You can do the same for this earthly warrior's wife in Your perfect time.

Promise from God's Word ...

"For I know the plans I have for you," declares the LORD, *"plans to prosper you and not to harm you, plans to give you hope and a future."*

– Jeremiah 29:11 (NIV)

2 WHAT'S HAPPENING TO ME?
Understanding Secondary Traumatic Stress

Erin's Journal . . .

I got out of bed this morning, shuffled into the kitchen and poured myself a cup of coffee. Scott had already gone to work, and what was left in the pot had boiled down to battery acid strength. I didn't care — I needed something to get me going. I sat at the table, opened my Bible and watched the raindrops run down the window panes. I bowed my head to pray.

That was **20** minutes ago. I can't find any words to pray. My head aches from crying myself to sleep last night. I actually wonder if God is even listening. I hate to admit it, but I'm starting to think God doesn't care anymore about our family, our marriage, or me. Didn't we serve courageously, tirelessly? Haven't we sacrificed enough? Or is this pain the payback for all my past blunders?

Lately life feels like a scary amusement park. A greasy, snaggletoothed carnival worker laughs at my helplessness, refusing to let me off the rickety rollercoaster. The tracks lock and pull me to the shaky precipice, then release me, plummeting to the bottom again and again. The sharp corners and abrupt stops whiplash my heart and mind. I'm freefalling through my days, unable to focus in this blur called combat stress. I want off this terrible ride! Nauseated, I stumble off, only to be startled by nightmarish clowns and by my own twisted reflections in my un-fun house, a home that's been invaded by posttraumatic stress.

I think I'm losing it. Yesterday my neighbor greeted me with a cheerful "How ya doin'?" My throat locked up and I started to cry. Fact is, I'm not doing so well. I can't concentrate on anything. My mind wanders and drifts, searching for a safe place to land. I know others are talking to me, but I don't hear a word they're saying. I read the same sentences over and over, but I don't comprehend much. I'm worried about myself. I find joy in nothing, not even in my favorite people or places or hobbies anymore.

I feel jumpy, irritable, edgy. I worry that I might say or do something to set Scott off. So, we tiptoe around on eggshells, speaking in hushed tones like people do in hospital waiting rooms. How fitting, though. My home has become a hospital ward. And I am growing weary, waiting for Scott to heal.

I'm exhausted today. Come to think of it, I'm exhausted every day. I just want to go back to bed, pull the covers over my head, and pray this has been only a bad dream.

One trauma, two wounds

Erin didn't go to war. She stayed home where it was safe while Scott went bravely into harm's way doing what he had trained to do as a combat medic. He had received the best training on earth and was prepared to work in life-threatening situations, react to deadly violence and defend himself and his buddies. Despite this, he came home to Erin wounded in body, mind and spirit.

> He brought the war home like an STD. He did not mean to, but he never had these problems before the war, and now we both have problems.[1]
>
> -Wife of an OIF veteran

But now Scott's wounds are wounding Erin and she was never trained to defend herself from this surprise attack. She kept the home fires burning. She accomplished both Scott's tasks and hers while he was deployed. She served sacrificially with courage and faithfulness. It wasn't like the horrors of combat he experienced, but somehow *his* symptoms are now showing up in *her*. She felt anxious and even depressed sometimes while he was downrange, and she was so relieved when he came home alive. But now her level of distress has even eclipsed those anxiety-filled deployment days. Her heart screams, "This can't be right!"

Secondary Traumatic Stress — Spousal Combat Trauma

You can probably identify with Erin at some level. She – and you – are experiencing an emotional response that has only recently been identified by mental health professionals. For several decades those in careers that serve the traumatized have noticed that they and their colleagues could sometimes slip into depression and anxiety when they absorb too much of their patients' or clients' emotional overload. Counselors, psychiatrists, nurses, doctors, critical incident responders, social workers, pastors, chaplains and others reported these episodes and were at a loss to explain why they were being affected so deeply or how to avoid it. It wasn't until around 1990 that significant studies began to be conducted on Secondary Traumatic Stress. You can surf the Internet and find tens of thousands of sites and articles that address Posttraumatic Stress Disorder (PTSD) – focusing on the primary survivor of a traumatic event – but you will find precious few that address the needs of those who have been subsequently traumatized by the PTSD sufferers – and almost *nothing* specifically for spouses.

This condition has been identified by several different titles with subtle technical differences between them, such as Secondary Traumatic Stress, Compassion Stress, Vicarious Traumatization, Contagious PTSD, Countertransference, Emotional Contagion, Burnout, etc. For the purposes of this manual, we'll use the term most commonly applied to spouses of Combat Trauma sufferers: *Secondary Traumatic Stress* or STS.

It refers primarily to distressing experiences of people who communicate at a deep level with someone who has been traumatized and become traumatized as well.[2]

Dr. Charles Figley, Founding Editor of the *Journal of Traumatic Stress*, and Founding President of the International Society for Traumatic Stress Studies gives a widely accepted definition of Secondary Traumatic Stress:

> It is the natural, consequent behaviors and emotions resulting from knowledge about
> a traumatizing event experienced by a significant other. It is the stress resulting from
> helping or wanting to help a traumatized or suffering person.[3]

Spouses of Combat Trauma sufferers can experience Traumatic Stress in two ways:

1. Reacting to hearing about his/her spouse's traumatic experiences (*Secondary* Traumatic Stress)
2. Being traumatized directly by his/her spouse's behavior (*Primary* Traumatic Stress)

For instance, a woman could be experiencing Secondary Traumatic Stress because her husband has shared with her his horrific combat memories, and it was more than she was able to handle. In addition, her compassion and empathy has been in overdrive as she's watched her loved one struggle and suffer with his symptoms. But one night the husband could have a vivid nightmare about his time at war, wake up and – thinking his wife is the enemy – physically attack and try to kill her. He comes to his senses before it's too late, but as you can imagine this traumatizes his wife. She could now develop Primary Traumatic Stress, since she has experienced a traumatizing event directly.

In either case – Primary or Secondary – her symptoms can become as intense and debilitating as her husband's and even develop into the most severe form of traumatic stress: Posttraumatic Stress Disorder. This field of study is so new it hasn't yet been formally included in the American Psychiatric Association's Diagnostic and Statistical Manual (their primary authoritative reference). But it is obvious from the formal definition of PTSD in that manual that one can experience all the symptoms of a trauma victim *without actually having experienced the trauma directly*. Note this excerpt from that definition – the italicized sections prove this point:

> … or *learning about* unexpected or violent death, serious harm, or threat of death or injury experienced by a family member or other close associate … Events experienced by others that are *learned about* include, but are not limited to, violent personal assault, serious accident, or serious injury experienced by a family member or a close friend; *learning about* the sudden, unexpected death of a family member or a close friend; or *learning* that one's child has a life-threatening disease.[4]

So, in a very real sense, we have one person going to war, but two (or more) people ending up with Combat Trauma. Clinical psychologist Dr. Mary S. Cerney has written about what happens to therapists who become too empathetic with their patients:

> The affront to the sense-of-self experienced by therapists of trauma victims can be so overwhelming that, despite their best efforts, they begin to exhibit the same characteristics as their patients. That is, they experience a change in their interaction with the world, themselves and their families. They may begin to have intrusive thoughts, nightmares, and generalized anxiety. They themselves need assistance in coping with their trauma.[5]

This is what can happen to highly trained and experienced therapists – so you can imagine how deeply a wife, connected with her husband on so many levels, could be affected. And when the wife becomes the target of abuse by her agitated husband, this adds to her confusion and traumatization and can even lead to her experiencing Primary Traumatic Stress and PTSD.

The following graphic will give you a general idea of the interrelatedness of Secondary and Primary Traumatic Stress, and how the symptoms can fall anywhere along a broad spectrum of severity.

Spousal Combat Trauma

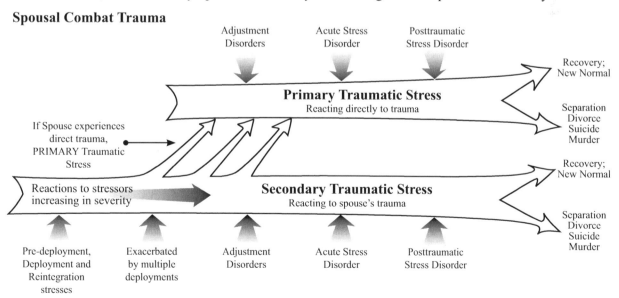

Symptoms

As the wife of a Combat Trauma sufferer, you can actually mirror many of your husband's symptoms. You can also develop other symptoms that he doesn't have. To familiarize you with the possible symptoms that could develop – and to do a personal inventory on specific symptoms you may have – check the boxes next to any symptoms you have experienced within the past six months which you think could be related to your husband's struggles with Combat Trauma. It's important to realize that not all of these symptoms are unique to Secondary Traumatic Stress – even non-traumatized people can manifest many of them. But completing this personal inventory will give you something to consider and pray about concerning your present level of distress.

Symptom Inventory[6]

Cognitive Symptoms

- ❑ Diminished concentration
- ❑ Confusion, spaciness
- ❑ Forgotten appointments
- ❑ Chronic lateness
- ❑ Loss of meaning
- ❑ Decreased self-esteem
- ❑ Preoccupation with trauma
- ❑ Nightmares
- ❑ Flashbacks, intrusive imagery
- ❑ Powerlessness
- ❑ Anxiety
- ❑ Guilt, shame
- ❑ Anger, rage, irritability
- ❑ Survivor guilt
- ❑ Shutting down
- ❑ Numbness
- ❑ Fearfulness, dread, horror
- ❑ Helplessness

- ❑ Apathy
- ❑ Rigid, uncompromising
- ❑ Disorientation
- ❑ Thoughts of self-harm
- ❑ Thoughts of harming others
- ❑ Self-doubt
- ❑ Perfectionism
- ❑ Minimization

Emotional Symptoms

- ❑ Sadness, depression
- ❑ Feeling worthless
- ❑ Hypersensitivity
- ❑ Emotional roller coaster
- ❑ Overwhelmed
- ❑ Depleted
- ❑ Bottled up emotions

Behavioral Symptoms

- ❑ Clingy
- ❑ Impatient
- ❑ Irritable, moody
- ❑ Withdrawn
- ❑ Regression
- ❑ Sleep disturbances
- ❑ Appetite changes
- ❑ Nightmares
- ❑ Hypervigilance

- ❑ Shock
- ❑ Sweating
- ❑ Rapid heartbeat
- ❑ Breathing difficulties
- ❑ Aches and pains

- ❑ Elevated startle response
- ❑ Substance abuse (drugs, alcohol, tobacco)
- ❑ Accident-prone
- ❑ Losing/forgetting things
- ❑ Self-harm behaviors
- ❑ Compulsiveness (eating, gambling, sex, spending, workaholism, self-mutilation, excessive tattooing or piercing, thrill-seeking, etc.)

Physical Symptoms

- ❑ Gastrointestinal distress
- ❑ Dizziness
- ❑ Impaired immune system
- ❑ Poor self-care (i.e., hygiene, appearance)

Interpersonal Symptoms

- ❑ Withdrawn
- ❑ Feeling vulnerable, unsafe
- ❑ Decreased interest in intimacy, sex
- ❑ Mistrust, suspicious of others
- ❑ Isolation from friends
- ❑ Need to control others
- ❑ Loss of personal control and freedom
- ❑ Changes in parenting (overprotective, abusive, critical, disinterested, etc.)
- ❑ Projection of anger or blame
- ❑ Verbally or physically combative
- ❑ Intolerance
- ❑ Loneliness

Spiritual Symptoms

- ❑ Doubt concerning one's values or beliefs
- ❑ Feeling angry or bitter toward God
- ❑ Feeling far from God, unloved, abandoned
- ❑ Feeling God is unresponsive or unconcerned
- ❑ Feeling God is punishing me
- ❑ Pervasive hopelessness; weak or no faith
- ❑ Questioning the meaning of life
- ❑ Neglecting spiritual disciplines (i.e., prayer, Bible study, fellowship, etc.)

❁ ❁ ❁❁ ❁ ❁

? We've shared this long list of symptoms with you *not* to make you feel overwhelmed, but to help you see that your symptoms are a normal response to the stressors you are encountering. From the above list, pick out the three symptoms that bother or concern you the most.

Note: In Chapter 7 we will consider how to deal with these symptoms more extensively. Don't lose this list!

1. _____

2. _____

3. _____

❁ ❁ ❁❁ ❁ ❁

Battle Buddy Assignment

From time to time throughout this manual you will be given a "Battle Buddy Assignment." When your husband was at war he had many Battle Buddies – fellow troops who had gained his trust and whom he knew he could count on to watch his back when they were in dangerous situations together. Now that the war has come home to you, you need a woman friend who can be someone just like that in your life. Ask God to give you a Battle Buddy who has some idea of what you're going through, and with whom you could feel comfortable and safe sharing your frustrations, joys, concerns and prayer requests without fear of judgment or gossip. In Chapter 8 we'll talk more about the characteristics your Battle Buddy should have, but don't wait! Find her soon!

Battle Buddy Assignment: Share your list of checked and unchecked symptoms with your Battle Buddy, and the "Big Three" that concern you the most. Share with her why those three register so deeply with you and listen to her feedback. Then spend some time together in prayer about them.

Here are a few of the psalms of David to help you pattern your prayers. Some Bible scholars believe that King David himself may have been a PTSD sufferer – but one who knew where to go for rescue and relief and didn't hesitate to make the journey.

Psalm 5:1-3 *Give ear to my words, O Lord, consider my groaning. Heed the sound of my cry for help, my King and my God, for to You I pray. In the morning, O Lord, You will hear my voice; in the morning I will order my prayer to You and eagerly watch.*

Note: Avoid the temptation to just repeat David's words without really engaging your mind and heart when you pray. You could use the same words as David, or you could translate them into your own "language." Here's an example of that: "Lord, please listen to me. Listen to my heart because my words can't say what my heart feels. Please hear my cry for help! You are my King. You are my God and You are the only one who can hear and help me. It is a new day with old pain, Lord. I know you are listening, so I'm going to tell you all I am feeling, and I'll keep watch for Your healing peace." Many people prefer to write out their prayers – the writing process can really help crystallize your thoughts.

Psalm 25:15-20 (NLT) *My eyes are always on the LORD, for he rescues me from the traps of my enemies. Turn to me and have mercy, for I am alone and in deep distress. My problems go from bad to worse. Oh, save me from them all! Feel my pain and see my trouble. Forgive all my sins. See how many enemies I have and how viciously they hate me! Protect me! Rescue my life from them! Do not let me be disgraced, for in you I take refuge.*

Psalm 32:7 *You are my hiding place; You preserve me from trouble; You surround me with songs of deliverance.*

Psalm 38:21,22 *Do not forsake me, O Lord; O my God, do not be far from me! Make haste to help me, O Lord, my salvation!*

Psalm 42:1-3,5,8 *As the deer pants for the water brooks, so my soul pants for You. My tears have been my food day and night, while they say to me, "Where is your God?" Why are you in despair, O my soul? And why have you become disturbed within me? Hope in God, for I shall again praise Him for the help of His presence. The Lord will command His lovingkindness in the daytime; and His song will be with me in the night, a prayer to the God of my life.*

Psalm 69:1-3,13-17 *Save me, O God, for the waters have threatened my life. I have sunk in deep mire and there is no foothold, I have come into deep waters, and a flood overflows me. I'm weary with my crying; my throat is parched; my eyes fail while I wait for my God. But as for me, my prayer is to You, O Lord, at an acceptable time. O God, in the greatness of Your lovingkindness, answer me with Your saving truth. Deliver me from the mire and don't let me sink; may I be delivered from my foes and from the deep waters. May the flood of water not overflow me, nor the deep swallow me up, nor the pit shut its mouth on me. Answer me, O Lord, for Your lovingkindness is good; according to the greatness of Your compassion, turn to me, and do not hide Your face from Your servant, for I am in distress; answer me quickly.*

Search through the Psalms on your own and find other prayers there that reflect the cry of your heart and soul. Highlight them, write them out, pray them often.

❀ ❀ ❀❀ ❀ ❀

How bad is it?

Anyone who is ill or injured asks that question. After going through the list of symptoms, you may have recognized your woundedness and wondered how serious your condition might be. Knowing that you're not too bad off could be an encouragement and buoy your spirits. Knowing that it's serious could be distressing at first, but it could also motivate you to take action. For this reason, we're offering the following self-test to give yourself a semi-objective measurement of the Secondary Traumatic Stress (STS) you are experiencing.

A Second Assessment? Why? The "Symptom Inventory" was presented earlier in this chapter to familiarize you with the wide variety of possible symptoms someone in your situation might experience. As you recognized specific symptoms in yourself and realized they were manifestations of your STS, it should have given you some hope and confidence to know that yours is a normal reaction to your abnormal stressors. The next assessment will help you get a better grasp of how serious your STS is.

This test was originally devised by Dr. Charles Figley as a self-test for counselors and therapists to determine how deeply they were being influenced by the trauma of their clients. It was shortened and altered a little later by Figley and two colleagues from Canada's Traumatology Institute, Dr. Anna Baranowsky and Dr. Eric Gentry. We have further adapted it here for use by *you,* the wife of a Combat Trauma sufferer.

PTSD Self-Test for Wives of Combat Trauma Sufferers[7]

Consider each of the following statements about you and your current situation. Write in the number that best reflects your experience using the rating system where "1" signifies rarely or never and "10" means very often. Answer all items, even if they do not seem applicable. Then read the instructions at the end to get your score.

Rarely/Never |———|———|———|———|———|———|———|———|———| Very Often
1   2   3   4   5   6   7   8   9   10

3. _____ I force myself to avoid certain thoughts or feelings that remind me of frightening experiences from my past (any experiences, not necessarily associated with your husband's trauma, but they could be).

4. _____ I find myself avoiding certain activities or situations because they remind me of frightening experiences from my past.

5. _____ I have gaps in my memory about frightening events in my past.

6. _____ I feel isolated and estranged from others.

7. _____ I have difficulty falling or staying asleep.

8. _____ I have outbursts of anger or irritability with little provocation.

9. _____ I startle easily.

10. _____ I have thought about violence against the people who caused my husband's trauma.

11. _____ I have had "flashbacks" about some of the traumatic incidents my husband has shared with me.

12. _____ I have had first-hand experience with traumatic events in my adult life.

13. _____ I have had first-hand experience with traumatic events in my childhood.

14. _____ I have thought that I need to "work through" a traumatic experience in my life.

15. _____ I am frightened by things my husband has said or done to me.

16. _____ I experience troubling dreams similar to those of my husband.

17. _____ I have experienced thoughts that intrude unbidden into my mind about my husband's traumatic incidents (or other traumatic events from my past).

18. _____ I have suddenly and involuntarily recalled a frightening experience from my past while with my husband.

19. _____ I am losing sleep over the traumatic experiences my husband has shared with me.

20. _____ I have thought that I might have been "infected" by the traumatic stress of my husband.

21. _____ I remind myself to be less preoccupied about my husband's well-being.

22. _____ I have felt trapped by my marriage.

23. _____ I have felt a sense of hopelessness about my marriage.

24. _____ I have been in danger from my husband.

25. _____ I have thought that there is no one to talk with about my highly stressful life.

26. _____ I have felt "on edge" about various things and I attribute this to being married to a combat trauma sufferer.

27. _____ My relationship with my husband has made me feel weak, tired and rundown.

28. _____ My relationship with my husband makes me feel depressed.

29. _____ I am not successful at separating my ministry to my husband from my personal life. I feel absorbed by his difficulties.

30. _____ I have a sense of worthlessness/disillusionment/resentment associated with my marriage.

31. _____ I have thoughts that I am a "failure" as a wife.

32. _____ I have thoughts that I am not succeeding at achieving my life goals.

Scoring instructions:

- Be certain you responded to all the questions.
- Add up the values (1 to 10) you wrote next to each of the statements.
- This is your risk of developing PTSD:

Your Score:

  - ➢ 94 or less = Low risk
  - ➢ 95 to 128 = Some risk
  - ➢ 129 to 172 = Moderate risk
  - ➢ 173 or more = High risk

Admittedly, this is not a scientifically or statistically verified test (Figley's original test was, but this wife-specific adaptation has yet to be reviewed). However, it should at least give you some idea of how light or how heavy the stress load you're currently carrying is.

❀ ❀ ❀❀ ❀ ❀

My score is through the roof! What do I do now!?!

First, take a deep breath. Unhunch your shoulders and unfurrow your brow. Relax. Nothing is different now from what it was fifteen minutes ago, except that you are more informed about your present situation. As Sir Francis Bacon wrote, "Knowledge is power." The more you know about yourself and the difficulties you and your husband are experiencing, the more empowered you are and the more you can take action to improve your situation.

One thing you *can* do is to keep working through this manual! Most of your questions will be addressed in later chapters. In addition, we'll be taking you through various exercises, Scriptures and thought-processes that *will* make a difference for you.

❀ ❀ ❀❀ ❀ ❀

Keeping the STRESS from becoming the DISORDER

Summarizing what we wrote earlier, "Secondary Traumatic *Stress*" (STS) is the normal emotional response to learning about the traumatization of a client or significant other and/or being targeted for abuse by the struggling PTSD sufferer. The symptoms may persist for more than a month, but with proactive care – and with a decrease in the ongoing traumatizing by the significant other – they will eventually subside.

A caregiver, therapist or wife's Secondary Traumatic *Stress* (STS) can develop into Posttraumatic Stress *Disorder* if they continue to experience stress-filled interaction with their client or husband, and don't seek help or relief. When the *Stress* gives way to the *Disorder*, a person can get stuck in that condition and have difficulty pulling out of it without a great deal of intentional care. Of course, God provides a huge advantage to a PTSD sufferer seeking help, but it would be best to reverse the trend toward the *Disorder* as soon as possible.

What can you do?

Dr. Eric Scalise, Vice President of the American Association of Christian Counselors and a leading authority on secondary trauma, shares nine elements of a "Personal Stress Prevention Plan" that you can begin to employ immediately! You don't even have to wait to get to the end of the manual! Put an asterisk (*) next to each element that you feel you need to do something about and come up with an action plan.

Personal Stress Prevention Plan[8]

1. **Don't forget your First Love.** In Revelation 2:1-4, Jesus addresses the church in Ephesus and commends them for their perseverance and faithfulness in the face of great difficulty. But He has one gentle criticism: "*You have left your First Love,*" referring to Himself. We're not saying that this is necessarily true of *you,* but search your heart and see if you're allowing the turmoil in your life – even your heroic, sacrificial efforts to support your husband or protect your kids – to crowd out your relationship with God. Given the difficulties you've had to endure, it's understandable if you have. But it's not a condition that you want to let persist. Christ's desire is to *help* you, but He can't if you're not paying attention to His lead. "*Without Me,*" Jesus instructs us, "*You can do nothing*" (John 15:5 NKJV).

[?] Do you need to make Christ your first love again? If so, what will you do to bring this about?

_____

_____

❀ ❀

2. **Learn to rest.** Physical and emotional respite is vital for you – even if you *weren't* so stressed out. It's interesting to note that in the Ten Commandments God spends more time delivering Commandment #4 – keeping the weekly Sabbath – than on any other one. He designed us to work hard, play hard, fight hard, but then to *rest* in order to restore our body, mind and spirit. We're not trying to "put you under the law" and advocate that you observe the Sabbath exactly the way it's prescribed in the Old Testament; but the principle of getting a regular rest break – daily, weekly, monthly, yearly – is one that you will ignore at your peril.

[?] Write one change you can make in your schedule in order to get more rest:

_____

_____

❀ ❀

3. **Learn to be silent and learn to be still.** This is a practice that 21st century mankind has virtually forgotten. Where can you go where there is no noise? Who's got time to be still? If you snooze, you lose! GO, GO, GO!! But David wrote, "*I have stilled and quieted my soul; like a weaned child with its mother, like a weaned child is my soul within me.*" (Psalm 131:2 NIV) Like a weaned child rests contentedly against his mother, no longer seeking her for what he can get out of her, so God desires us in that condition. "*Be still,*" the psalmist writes, "*and know that I am God.*" (Psalm 46:10) Intentionally seek out times when you can be still and quiet your soul, remembering just how big God is.

[?] Write down a place you can go to be silent and still, and set a date to do it:

_____

_____

❀ ❀

4. **Seek to give your burdens to God each day.** You don't have to carry them alone. Jesus said, "*Come to Me, all you who are weary and burdened, and I will give you rest. Take My yoke upon you and learn from Me, for I am gentle and humble in heart, and you will find rest for your souls. For My yoke is easy and My burden is light.*" (Matthew 11:28-30 NIV) At the beginning of each day, come before God and

think about the issues that are weighing you down. Then ask Him to take them one by one. He has broad shoulders and is an awesome Burden-Bearer!

? Write down one or two burdens that you're going to intentionally give to God today:

_____

_____

❀ ❀

5. **Learn to triage the events of your day and life.** Life is probably coming at you really fast right now. Kids, groceries, bills, housework, friends, church, broken dishwasher, laundry – it's a flood! And your husband's diminished capacities aren't helping matters. Just like a combat medic who is being overwhelmed by incoming wounded, you need to make some decisions about what to give your time and energy to. You can't try to do *everything!* Set priorities and boundaries, making sure that you're keeping the main things *main!* If you can accomplish just two or three important things in a day, declare victory and re-read #2 above! As the Apostle Paul said in Philippians 3:13, "*This one thing I do* ..." (KJV). Not, "These 20 things I go crazy trying to scratch the surface of." Simplify! Streamline!

? What are two things you were thinking of doing tomorrow that you can put off?

_____

_____

❀ ❀

6. **Learn to have realistic expectations of yourself and others.** We know how desperately you want to return to your pre-deployment capacities. You want your husband to act and react the way he did before he went to war. You want your kids to be as calm and well-behaved as they used to be. But things have changed. For *this season,* you must lower your expectations a bit, and give yourself permission to be less productive, less perfect, less spectacular. This season won't last forever, but if you keep pushing too hard you may prolong it.

? List one unrealistic expectation you have for yourself, and one for your husband:

_____

_____

❀ ❀

7. **Seek to resolve those things that can be attended to easily and quickly.** Every little victory is just that: a *victory!* You may look at that kitchen floor and think, "We really need new tile ..." Are you really ready for all the hassle, inconvenience and frayed nerves of a remodeling project? Right now? You could mop that floor in a few minutes, classify your flooring deficiencies under #4 above, remember #1 and go do #3 instead! The boy's room needs paint? Forget about it! Screw in a lower watt bulb and join your kids in the pool! By following this philosophy, you'll satisfy your desire to accomplish *something* and leave room for more of the truly therapeutic activities you need.

? Write down one quick-and-easy thing you can accomplish tomorrow:

_____

_____

❀ ❀

8. **Learn to manage your time or your time will manage you.** One can never stockpile time. It has to be used as it goes by. Once it's gone, it's gone. Ask God to give you wisdom so that you can invest your time in the things that you and He feel are true priorities in your life. As the Bible says, "*Therefore be*

careful how you walk, not as unwise men but as wise, making the most of your time, because the days are evil" (Ephesians 5:15,16). As you deal with a husband who is draining you of an increasing amount of time and energy, it's vital that you reserve some of those precious commodities and expend them in ways *you* decide.

? What activity should you be saying "no" to so you'll have time do something more important?

_____

_____

❀ ❀

9. **Learn to delegate to others whenever, wherever, however it's appropriate.** When your husband was deployed you had to carry his load of household responsibilities as well as your own. It wasn't easy, but you adapted and learned how to do it – all by yourself. Now that he's back, and the chaos of the war is here with him, it's time for you to recognize that you need some help. Give your kids chores if they don't already have them. Look for ways your husband can pitch in. His capacities may be diminished, but he can still do some things. And he wants to, too! If friends or church members offer help, accept it. Don't let your pride get in the way. Besides, it'll make them feel useful – you'll be ministering to *them* as you let them help *you!*

? Write down one thing you're doing that someone else could do for you:

_____

_____

❀ ❀ ❀❀ ❀ ❀

Wrap up

This has been a chapter that has led you to conduct a lot of introspection. We know it hasn't been easy, but it's been necessary. You've catalogued your trauma symptoms, prayed through them with a Battle Buddy, assessed the severity of your condition and thought through some proactive steps to keep your "stress" from becoming a "disorder." But there is one last thing we want you to think about …

? What do you want God to do for you?

Visualize it. Think deeply about it. Long for it. Jesus encourages us to "*ask … seek … knock*" in Matthew 7:7,8. "*For everyone who asks receives, and he who seeks finds, and to him who knocks it will be opened.*" He loves to work in answer to our prayers. It builds our faith and delights His heart. So … what do you want God to do for you? Think about it for a few moments, and then write it down here:

_____

_____

_____

_____

_____

Battle Buddy Assignment: Share this request with your Battle Buddy, and the two of you begin to pray for it regularly. Sometimes God answers our prayers simply because we've been persistent about our request (read Luke 11:5-10 and 18:1-5).

Erin's Prayer ...

Lord, You tell me in Your Word to come to You and that You will give me rest. Only You know how tired and burdened I am. All I can manage to do today is barely crawl into Your throne room. I ask You for the faith I lack. I ask You for the strength to keep believing that You are not only Scott's Healer, but You are mine, too. Thank You that You see me. You see my tears. You see our family, our home, our hurts. Thank You that Your Holy Spirit prays for us and for me, when I cannot. I can't crawl any closer, Lord. Thank You that You meet me where I am.

Promise from God's Word ...

God's loyal love couldn't have run out,
His merciful love couldn't have dried up.
They're created new every morning.
How great Your faithfulness!

- Lamentations 3:22,23 (TM)

3 WHY AM I SO SAD?
Dealing With Loss and Grief Issues

Danielle's Journal ...

I heard the kids talking and giggling today in the family room. It was music to my ears. I was curious to know what held their attention there on the couch. They had several scrapbooks spread open on their laps - photo albums I had put together when marriage and family were fresh and new.

They laughed and squealed with the turn of each page, pointing at Michael's outdated sunglasses and my hairdo. I slid in beside them and let their joy wash over me. They finished all too soon and flitted away to another adventure. The scrapbooks and I sat alone. I sank into the sofa and studied the photos in silence ... Michael in uniform, his arms around me, pulling me close, the schoolgirl smile across my blushing face as he kissed my cheek ... Michael holding our newborn daughter to his chest, a beaming, doting father ... our happy family in new, red pajamas around the tree on Christmas morning ... summer fun on the beach, building sandcastles together on the coast.

Suddenly I sensed that I was sitting in a cemetery. The photos are now eerie memorials not only to dead hair styles, but to dead people, dead relationships and dead dreams. Something has snuffed out the sparkle in our eyes and stolen the ease of our smiles. Passionate bear hugs have become tentative touches. Laughter has dissolved into a fragile and sad silence that thickens the air like gloomy fog in a graveyard.

It seems that most of the things we hold dear hang dying on the cross of combat stress. Our innocence as sweethearts, my image of him as my strong shield and leader, the kids' image of him as invincible, stable and safe. Our circle of friends is critically injured too. The soldiers Michael trained with _and their wives_ have inner wounds none of us dare mention. Even our future plans and dreams as a couple are suffocating in the stress.

Sometimes I wonder - God forgive me - if Michael's physical death would have been easier to bear than this death we keep dying every day. No, of course I don't want that ... I just want things to be how they were before!

Death, loss and grief

Michael isn't dead, but because so much has changed, Danielle feels like he is and someone else has replaced him. So many hopes, dreams and relationships seem to have died as well. They feel irretrievable.

"Grief is love not wanting to let go," wrote Rabbi Earl A. Grollman.[1] This is why Danielle's heart hurts so much. At the root of her pain is love – the strongest force on earth. If love had not been present, she would not be feeling such pain, loss and grief born from the dark changes that occurred in Michael downrange. The strength of the pain over her losses is as deep as the strength of her love for Michael and all that he has represented in her life. Solomon wrote in Song of Solomon 8:6, *Love is as strong as death.*" To Danielle's anguished mind, the finality of Michael's physical death seems almost preferable to trying to deal with this "new" person who is so different from the man she first fell in love with. As Irish writer Frank O'Connor points out, when we feel a great sense of loss "it means that we had something worth grieving for. The ones I'm sorry for are the ones that go through life not knowing what grief is."[2] Danielle had something worth loving – and so did you. The war took that away. Now you know for sure you have something worth grieving for *and* worth fighting for.

> I always thought that if my husband came home from Iraq physically intact, everything would be fine. His only injury was a broken leg, and I was so happy about that! But soon I realized his wounds were psychological – way worse! Now *nothing's* fine.
>
> -Wife of a Special Forces veteran

Compassion Fatigue is one of the names for what you may be experiencing. But you should never feel that your compassion is a door of vulnerability that needs to be slammed shut. The fact that you *have* compassion – and *fatigue* – shows the incredible depth of your love.

> In the New Testament, the Greek word for *compassion* conveys more than an idea of pity. The root word for compassion is *passion.* We know from experience that passion involves more than thought. Instead, passion involves the deepest emotions of the human soul. When you add the prefix *com* to *passion,* you magnify passion and refer to the deepest God-given emotions buried inside each of us – love, sympathy, anger, kindness, hatred, goodness, pity, sorrow, etc.
>
> – Rev. Barrie E. Henke[3]

But right now the emotions you hold may not feel like love. You may feel confused, angry, conflicted, frustrated. He came back alive but in many ways it may seem like he never came back at all. You want your pre-deployment husband back! Your soul vehemently protests your present reality, a common experience for anyone who has lost something precious. Why can't things go back to the way they were?

No one travels through life in this fallen world without experiencing death and loss, which lead to grief. Grief is the means by which we process our losses, celebrate what we had before, mourn the vacuum that now exists, and come to terms with a new world – the one in which our dreams are significantly altered. In this difficult process we gradually and reluctantly turn from the past and once again walk to the future to find new dreams and new joys. It's a vital journey that *must* be taken. You are going to need both hands to embrace the life and love that God has in mind for you – and that will be very difficult if one hand still has a death grip on the past.

Understanding grief

"Chaplain Ray" Giunta writes: **"Grief is the normal process of natural emotions and feelings which are uniquely experienced after any loss of any relationship."**[4] Please note carefully the first characteristic listed: grief is *normal.* It's built into us. God invented it. God experienced it when He walked this earth as a human.[5] *Everybody* experiences it. We all experience grief differently, but we all experience it.

> *Jesus wept.*
> – **John 11:35**

The word "grief" comes from the Latin verb meaning "to burden." That's exactly what grief feels like, doesn't it? A heavy load that you wish you could set down – but you can't.

Grief is always triggered by a **loss** of some sort – losing someone or something we had an attachment to. Grief has different levels and intensities. We grieve a little when a favorite pair of jeans is ruined and we have to throw them away. We grieve a little more when our personal computer crashes and we lose hundreds of cherished photos. Deeper grief comes when a beloved pet dies, a treasured relationship ends, dreams we've held for the future evaporate, or when someone we love passes on.

But, as grief and trauma counselor Dr. H. Norman Wright tells us, "Loss is not the enemy. Not facing its existence is."[6] Loss is the fuse that triggered the bomb. The loss has irretrievably passed – and now comes the process of dealing with the crater that's left.

> Grief is neither a problem to be solved nor a problem to be overcome. It is a sacred expression of love … a sacred sorrow.
>
> – Dr. Gerald May, M.D.[7]

Name your loss. You have suffered many losses throughout your life – as we all have. But since your husband returned from overseas, you have experienced some unique losses, both small and great, that have been difficult to deal with. Write about what you feel you've lost. What did you cherish that seems to no longer exist? What goals and dreams did you share that have evaporated? What characteristics and capacities did you admire in your husband which seem to have been left on the battlefield? By naming your loss, you'll be better able to accomplish the difficult work of grieving over it.

> Give sorrow words; the grief that does not speak whispers to the o'er-fraught heart and bids it break.
>
> – Shakespeare

_____

_____

_____

_____

_____

The purpose of grief

God built the grief response into us for the purpose of mentally, emotionally and spiritually *processing* loss-producing events. Those events are integrated into our altered world, and help us move on to a state of greater strength, resourcefulness, resilience and faith. If we are not willing to face the grieving process, or if we try a short-cut, we'll be left adrift in our sea of pain, never reaching the shores of healing that the Lord intends for us.

As drill instructors repeatedly reminded your husband during basic training, "Pain is simply weakness leaving the body!" In a similar fashion, "Tears are a way God has provided for sadness to leave our body."[8] If we resist this mechanism, our sorrow may never lose its intensity.

King David wrote: "*You have taken account of my wanderings; put my tears in Your bottle. Are they not in Your book?*" (Psalm 56:8) God – in His infinite tenderness and love – not only takes note of your tears, He *stores* them. They are that precious to Him. Down through the ages, mourners would often catch their own tears in tiny bottles called *lachrymatories* and keep them as a memorial for their grief or as a symbol of their love and respect for the person for whom they were grieving. Typically, the mourning period would end when the tears evaporated from the bottle. God sees your tears and feels your sadness. He has a tear bottle with your name on it.[9]

When we grieve,

- we are authentically engaging the emotions that come with loss – rather than stuffing or denying them. As many grief experts say, "You can't heal what you can't feel."
- we are protesting the injustice of the loss – rather than acting like it was okay with us.
- We are expressing that we deeply wish the loss had never occurred – rather than minimizing it.
- we are facing the devastating impact of the loss head on, absorbing it and eventually mastering it – rather than running from it, deflecting it or pretending it didn't happen, only to have its effects hit us again and again.
- we are allowing our brain to replay the tapes of our disturbing and traumatic memories in a safe environment, thereby robbing them of their terror and integrating them into our rebuilding life.
- we are inviting Jesus to enter the dark forest of our pain, experience it with us, comfort us in the midst of it and walk us out the other side of it – rather than sitting passively alone and paralyzed at the edge.

When we refuse to grieve,

- unresolved grief is a factor in the development of a wide range of psychological problems including outbursts of rage, restlessness, depression, addiction, compulsion, anxiety and panic disorders.
- unexpressed grief is linked to the development or worsening of medical problems such as diabetes, heart disease, hypertension, cancer, asthma and a variety of allergies, rashes, aches and pains.[10]
- we are at odds with our body's built-in physiological processes to deal with a traumatic event.
- we are at odds with God's spiritual intentions to meet us in the midst of the fire of our trauma, causing us to miss out on His plans to deepen our faith and strengthen our relationship with Him.

> Heaven knows we need never be ashamed of our tears, for they are rain upon the blinding dust of earth, overlying our hard hearts.
> – Charles Dickens

"Normal" Grief – What you can expect to experience

C. S. Lewis, one of the greatest Christian philosophers and teachers of the past century (author of *Chronicles of Narnia*, among many other works), had his own trek through the dark forest of grief after his beloved wife Joy died of cancer. He kept a journal for many months after her death in which he wrote the following:

> Grief still feels like fear. Perhaps, more strictly, like suspense. Or like waiting; just hanging about waiting for something to happen. It gives life a permanently provisional feeling. It doesn't seem worth starting anything. I can't settle down. I yawn, I fidget, I smoke too much. Up till this I always had too little time. Now there is nothing but time. Almost pure time, empty successiveness.[11]

As you read through the following list of symptoms, **check any that you are experiencing**.

❑ **Fear.** You may fear that you will experience more losses, that your husband won't get any better, that *your* symptoms won't improve or might even get worse, or you won't be able to endure the pressure now existing in your household. You may fear your friends will abandon you in your pain, that your husband might harm you or your children, or that he might leave you.

❑ **Anger.** It doesn't have to be logical. You could be mad at yourself, your circumstances, your husband for coming back so changed, at the military, at God for allowing your husband's trauma, at the paperboy for bringing more bad news about the war, at your neighbor for being intrusively helpful and caring. Your anger might be seething just below the surface for a long time.

❑ **Rage.** You may yell, scream, stomp, slam doors, kick the trash can, kick the dog, pound your pillows, throw things, yank things off walls or out of the ground. Sometimes you feel better afterwards. Usually you don't.

- ❑ **Weeping.** You may cry. Then cry some more. And more. And just when you think you couldn't possibly have any more tears to cry, you cry some more. You may wail, scream, or just sit in a chair, tears flowing down your face like a waterfall.
- ❑ **Guilt.** *If only I'd ... What if ... I should have ...* Hindsight and regret could occupy your thoughts for a while. As illogical as it sounds, you may blame yourself for what happened to your husband or for what's happening in your household.
- ❑ **Loneliness.** You may feel that no one can understand what you're going through now – and that no one wants to, either. People may indeed avoid you for a while – not because they don't hurt deeply for you, but because they just don't know what to do or say. So they choose the typical default setting: nothing.
- ❑ **Blaming.** *This is so unfair! Where's the justice? What did we do to deserve this? Somebody has to be held accountable! Why didn't my husband take better care of himself? Why didn't the military protect him better? Why doesn't he get over this?*
- ❑ **Running away/numbing.** You may look desperately for an "escape hatch." *There must be a way out of this!* You may try drugs, alcohol, work, travel, ministry, sex, food, shopping, gambling – anything to get you away from your difficult environment.

Other symptoms may include (check any you are experiencing) ...

❑ **Loss of appetite**	❑ **Frustrated**
❑ **Loss of sexual desire**	❑ **Overly talkative**
❑ **Dehydration**	❑ **No desire to talk**
❑ **Memory lags, mental short-circuits**	❑ **Feeling out of control**
❑ **Unexplained aches and pains**	❑ **Emotionally overloaded**
❑ **Sleepiness, fatigue, lethargy**	❑ **No feelings at all**
❑ **Sleeplessness**	❑ **Others not on the list?** _____
❑ **Nightmares**	_____
❑ **Hyperactivity**	_____
❑ **Feeling abandoned**	_____

Some people might check many or most of the boxes above; while others may have checked only a few. As we mentioned earlier, everyone processes grief and loss differently. If you checked a lot of the boxes, it probably means that you are more fully engaging your grief. If you checked a few of them you may have already worked through a lot of your grief issues – or you might be denying your grief or deferring it – putting it off until later. Only you and God know for sure! In any case, healthy grieving could involve a number of the above symptoms simultaneously. If they persist at a significant level for a long, long time (many months or years) it *could* mean something has "hung up" the process. But for now, it's *okay!* What you feel is normal and you need to embrace and work through these feelings, not try to fend them off!

What about "loss of faith"?

In Chapter 1 (see page 10), we examined the question of how a loving, all-powerful God could allow His children to experience so much pain. You may know the answer to that question. And yet, when your world is crashing down around you, and you're one, huge tangled ball of emotions, excellent theology isn't always the greatest comfort. Doubting God's presence when we're hurting is a pretty common response which is based on a common assumption. As psychologist, educator and author Dr. Larry Crabb writes in his book *Shattered Dreams*:

> In our shallow, sensual way of looking at life, we tend to measure God's presence by the kind of emotion we feel. Happy feelings that make us want to sing, we assume, are evidence that God's Spirit is present. We think a sense of lostness or confusion or struggle indicates His absence.[12]

We can have confidence that the sun continues to exist even when it's hidden by rain clouds. God is still near even when we don't sense His presence in our circumstances. But that doesn't mean we won't have faith struggles – even the best of us! Consider the paragraph written below by C. S. Lewis not long after his wife died. He didn't hesitate to communicate his disappointment with God as he tried to come to grip with the most shattering grief of his life:

> Meanwhile, where is God? … Go to Him when your need is desperate, when all other help is vain, and what do you find? A door slammed in your face, and a sound of bolting and double-bolting on the inside. After that, silence. You may as well turn away. The longer you wait, the more emphatic the silence will become. There are no lights in the windows. It might be an empty house. Was it ever inhabited? It seemed so once.[13]

❀ ❀ ❀❀ ❀ ❀

? How closely can you identify with Lewis' "crisis of faith" expressed above?

_____

_____

❀ ❀ ❀❀ ❀ ❀

C. S. Lewis' crisis didn't last forever. By the end of his journal, we read how he had come out the other side of the dark forest, with more clarity, more love and stronger faith than ever before:

> Turned to God, my mind no longer meets that locked door; turned to Joy, it no longer meets that vacuum … There was no sudden, striking, and emotional transition. Like the warming of a room or the coming of daylight. When you first notice them, they have already been going on for some time.[14]

God's secret work. Dr. Crabb writes: "When God seems most absent from us, He is doing His most important work in us. He vanishes from our sight to do what He could not do if we could see Him clearly."[15]

Remember when Jesus Christ hung on the cross and cried out to His heavenly Father in confusion and despair, "My God! My God! Why have you forsaken Me?" God was silent. But it was at that exact moment that God the Father was closing the transaction which was the *number one reason* the Son had come to earth – reckoning His death as payment for our sins. And this is what brought Jesus the greatest joy of His eternal existence![16]

The late Pastor Ron Mehl describes what God is doing in your life while He seems absent:

> God is aware of your circumstances and moves among them.
> God is aware of your pain and monitors every second of it.
> God is aware of your emptiness and seeks to fill it in a manner beyond your dreams.
> God is aware of your wounds and scars and knows how to draw forth a healing deeper than you can imagine.
> Even when your situation seems out of control.
> Even when you feel alone and afraid.
> God works the night shift.[17]

What you can expect from others

When you have experienced a great trauma or loss and your grief is assumed and evident to all those around, you will be treated differently for a while. This is to be expected – but some treatment you receive is helpful and some you could do without. As C. S. Lewis expressed in his journal, "Perhaps the bereaved ought to be isolated in special settlements like lepers."[18]

The less-than-helpful things. Especially in the Western world, social taboos have been invented that make us try to avoid or deny any discomfort from loss. We look with disdain at the outpouring of grief in other cultures and accuse them of "lack of control." We don't realize *we* are the foolish ones, holding in something that would be better let out.

But it's important to remember that your friends mean well. Their insensitivity is not because they intend to hurt you or prolong your grief – it's just that they're uninformed about what to do and how to help. When the following comments are shared, it's best to see the good hearts behind them. Smile if you can, say thanks and move on. But *don't follow their advice!* Check the ones you've heard ...

- ❑ You need to put it behind you. Time to move on.
- ❑ Don't dwell in the past.
- ❑ You just need a good distraction.
- ❑ Think happy thoughts!
- ❑ Haven't you prayed about this yet?
- ❑ Don't "cave in" to your sorrow. Keep a stiff upper lip!
- ❑ You should be over this by now.
- ❑ What would Jesus do? (counseling by cliché)
- ❑ It's not as bad as it seems.
- ❑ Keep a grip on your emotions. Don't cry in front of *anyone*.
- ❑ Since you're a Christian, you shouldn't be grieving. Don't you know that God works everything out for the good?
- ❑ You'll feel better tomorrow.
- ❑ Hey! Did you see that special on TV last night? (In other words, let's talk about anything else but your grief.)
- ❑ Be strong for your kids – don't let them see you cry.
- ❑ How are you? (But they don't *really* want you to tell them too much.)
- ❑ You think *that's* bad? Let me tell you what happened to *me* ...
- ❑ If you just had a little more faith, this wouldn't seem so bad.

The helpful things. There are going to be a few of your friends who are wise in the ways of grief – either because they've experienced it themselves, have been trained, are particularly intuitive or have read a lot of books! When you find these people, do whatever it takes to keep them around!

- When they ask, "How are you?" they really want to know, and they stick around for the answer.
- They're willing to give you their time; available when you need them.
- They'll sacrifice for you.
- They're good listeners, non-judgmental, won't interrupt you to talk about themselves.
- They take the initiative with you; they reach out to you by calling you up, asking you out, including you in their lives.
- They find out what you need and then go get it for you.
- They'll pray *for* you and pray *with* you.
- They won't mind if you cry, in fact they'll end up crying with you.
- They've got your back.

? Who do you have in your circle of friends like this?

_____

What have they said or done that was especially meaningful?

_____

To whom could *you* be this kind of friend?

! **Prayer Assignment:** If you can't think of anyone who could be your supporter or for whom you could be a support, start asking God to send women like this to you, or to open your eyes to a current acquaintance who can be that kind of a friend. Make this request of Him daily – keep on knocking![19]

How NOT to grieve

Sometimes we will do *anything* rather than undertake the hard work of grief – then think we're accomplishing something. These actions might make us feel a little better temporarily, but they don't allow us to move out of our despairing state. Following is a list of how people attempt to cope with their situation without actually facing their grief – check any you think you might do from time to time.[20]

- ❏ **Act out** – giving in to the pressure to misbehave.
- ❏ **Aim low** – to what seems more achievable.
- ❏ **Attack** – beat down what's threatening you.
- ❏ **Avoid** – stay away from anything that causes you stress.
- ❏ **Compensate** – make up for weakness in one area by gaining strength in another.
- ❏ **Deny** – refusing to acknowledge that the event occurred.
- ❏ **Displace** – shifting an intended action to a safer target (like kicking the dog).
- ❏ **Fantasize** – escaping reality to a world of unachievable wishes.
- ❏ **Idealize** – playing up the good points of a desired action and ignoring downsides.
- ❏ **Identify** – copying others to take on their desirable characteristics.
- ❏ **Intellectualize** – avoiding emotions by focusing on facts and logic.
- ❏ **Passive aggression** – getting your way by pointedly avoiding what is expected.
- ❏ **Project** – seeing your own undesirable characteristics in others.
- ❏ **Rationalize** – creating logical reasons for self-destructive behavior.
- ❏ **Regress** – returning to a child state to avoid problems or responsibility.
- ❏ **Suppress** – consciously holding back unwanted urges while ignoring the root cause.
- ❏ **Trivialize** – making something small when it really is something big.

If you recognize any of these behavior patterns in yourself, you first need to see them for what they are: hoped-for shortcuts to restoration which won't get you there at all.

  Battle Buddy Assignment: Show this list to your Battle Buddy and ask her if she sees you engaging in any of these behaviors. But don't "act out" and punch her if she notices some, and then "rationalize" later. She may move past "passive aggression" and end up "displacing" you! (Look again at the above list if you need a translation of those terms.)

Then, make it a matter of prayer. Ask God to help you realize when you're avoiding your grief work by falling into these habits, and to help you partner with Him in the process.

How to grieve

Be aware of the process. It *is* a process, for sure – but it's not a *precise* process. Each person will grieve a bit differently than the next. However, there are some generalized descriptions that are useful – kind of like milestones along a journey, to let you know that you are making progress – or not.

Elisabeth Kübler-Ross was a Swiss physician who did groundbreaking research in the area of grief. Her book *On Death and Dying* has been a classic for decades. In her studies she found that there is a pattern most people experience when they encounter a life-changing trauma or crisis. Over the years we've come to realize that this cycle applies to just about any kind of significant loss and the resulting grief.

The cycle of emotional states shown on the chart below demonstrates the roller-coaster ride of activity and passivity as the hurting person wriggles and dodges in her desperate efforts to cope with the trauma, avoid change and finally be reconciled to it.

The person starts out in a state of relative stability and then the bomb goes off. Over an unspecified period of time, he or she progresses through these stages:

- **Immobilization stage** – Shock; initial paralysis after being exposed to the crisis or trauma. It takes a while for the enormity to register and sink in. Jaw drops, breath catches, can't decide what to do next.
- **Denial stage** – Trying to avoid the inevitable. *No! This can't be happening!* Or, *It didn't affect me; it's not that bad.* Or even: *It never happened. I just imagined it.*
- **Anger stage** – Frustrated outpouring of bottled-up emotion. *Life sucks!!* Rage seething below the surface at all times; lashing out at anyone for the slightest reason; blaming others; sometimes cold, icy anger; self-isolating to avoid blowing up.
- **Bargaining stage** – Seeking in vain for a way out. Making promises to God if He'll fix things; setting conditions for healing, like: *When my husband returns to normal, then I'll be okay.*
- **Depression stage** – Final realization of the inevitable. A very sad time, but also the turning point, because the griever is finally resolved to the fact that he or she won't be able to restore life to the way it was. It's the staging area for victory.
- **Testing stage** – Seeking realistic solutions. *Maybe I should try getting out more. Maybe I should talk with someone about my situation. Maybe I should start exercising again. Maybe I should join that Bible study I heard about.*
- **Acceptance stage** – Finally finding the way forward. They are now fully acknowledging the trauma or crisis. *It was bad – real bad – but I survived. I'm going to make it. My world changed, but I can live in this new world. I could even prosper.*

The Kübler-Ross Grief Cycle

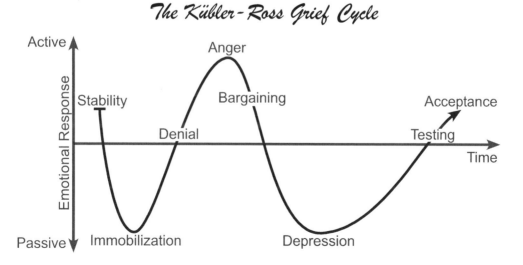

? After you have read the descriptions of the stages on the chart, think about where you are presently in the Grief Cycle. Place an "X" on the appropriate place on the line. Two questions: How do you feel about where you are in the process currently? What do you think it will take to move you beyond your present stage?

_____

_____

_____

_____

A few words about the process. As mentioned before, it's not precise. You may not hit all of these stages. You may skip a stage and then go back to experience it later. You may whiz through one stage and sit in another for a long time. You may find yourself going back and forth between a couple of stages or looping around to various stages willy-nilly. No one can say for sure how you will deal with your unique trauma, given your unique wiring. *Everyone is different!*

Therefore, *don't* give in to the temptation to compare your grief process with someone else's. If you will keep your connections with God strong during this process, He will take you through it in a way that will maximize every stage and bring you through the process as quickly as possible.

How long will it take? Honestly, probably a lot longer than you'll like. In fact, if the trauma you experienced is severe enough, the grief will always be there. It won't be dominating your life like it is currently, but there will always be that hole which the lost person, thing, goal or dream used to occupy. That ache won't go away. But that's not all bad – consider it a memorial to the depth of the love, attachment and value it (or they) held before the loss. And God *will* use it.

> *Blessed be the God and Father of our Lord Jesus Christ, the Father of mercies and God of all comfort, who comforts us in all our affliction so that we will be able to comfort those who are in any affliction with the comfort with which we ourselves are comforted by God.*
>
> **– 2 Corinthians 1:3,4**

❀ ❀ ❀❀ ❀ ❀

How to have a good mourning

When we've experienced a traumatic event, grief is what we *feel*. Mourning is *what we do about it.* It is the action side of grief, the externalizing of our internal pain. And Jesus Christ – who knows *everything* – says that when we do it we are blessed and *will be* comforted. Here are a few principles to keep in mind as you work out your grief through mourning.

> *Blessed are those who mourn, for they shall be comforted.*
> **– Matthew 5:4**

❀ *Remember where God is*

> *The Lord is near to the brokenhearted*
> *And saves those who are crushed in spirit.*
>
> **– Psalm 34:18**

Because of your wound, you hold a special attraction to the Lord. You have His attention. He is a compassionate God, always pulling for the underdog, and ready to aid anyone who will let Him. *Count on that!* You can expect Him to be present and responsive to your needs during this time. He is like your best friend who says, "If you need anything, don't hesitate to ask!" And He means it.

Ask Jesus to enter your pain with you. Close your eyes and feel Him coming up behind you, wrapping His big arms around you and holding on tight. Let Him pull the pain out of your body, soul and spirit into His.

✒ *Remember the past and remain optimistic*

> How hopeless the naked wood of a fruit tree would look to us in February
> if we had never seen the marvel of springtime.

– Lilias Trotter[21]

Though what you are currently enduring may be the worst experience you've ever had to slog your way through, it's not the *only* trauma you've known. Think back to the times God has sustained you in the past. Elisabeth Elliot, whose missionary husband was murdered by primitive natives in Ecuador, wrote: "The death of wintertime is the necessary prelude to the resurrection of springtime."[22] Spring *will* come.

We can make a distinction between the cliché, "Think happy thoughts!" and the admonition from the Apostle Paul to keep our minds focused on positive things:

> *Finally, brethren, whatever things are true, whatever things are noble, whatever things are just, whatever things are pure, whatever things are lovely, whatever things are of good report, if there is any virtue and if there is anything praiseworthy – meditate on these things.*

– Philippians 4:8 (NKJV)

✒ *Put your faith in the right place*

Ask yourself this question: "What do I have faith in?" How did you answer? Assuming you didn't say, "Nothing," perhaps it was like one of these:

- "That God will bring me out of this depression."
- "That my husband's leg will heal."
- "That my husband won't leave me."
- "That I could quit drinking so much."
- "That I can get past my anger."
- "That God will give me a new and lasting love for my husband."

> If you haven't taken that first step of faith yet and invited Christ into your life, go to Appendix A for insight into how to do that.

These are all great faith *goals* and excellent requests to make to God, but they aren't what you put your faith in. If you do – and they don't come about – what happens to your faith? The only answer to the question, "What do I have faith in?" should be "God." Whenever we tie our faith to our circumstances or to a particular desire, we take God off the throne of our life and set ourselves up for great disappointment. We are *lousy* at playing God! David Shepherd is a man of God who had suffered great setbacks when he wrote this letter to his friend, Dr. Larry Crabb:

> Faith, as I am growing to understand it more, is about looking beyond my circumstances to a Person. To have faith in better circumstances, even in God creating better circumstances, is not true faith. I want to be the kind of person who can watch every dream go down in flames and still yearn to be intimately involved in kingdom living, intimately involved with my friend the King, and still be willing to take another risk just because it delights Him for me to do so. And my flesh shivers to think about it.[23]

Thomas Merton, a Trappist monk who authored more than sixty books, wrote: "The real hope is not in something we think we can do, but in God, who is making something good out of it in some way we cannot see."[24] The essence of mature faith is to boldly express our fervent desires to God, and then leave them in His wise and benevolent hands – no matter what. He'll always do what's best.

✒ *Don't try to be the Lone Ranger*

Grief is hard on a person and mourning is difficult work. Effective grief work is not done alone. Don't try to be the pillar of strength to everyone around you. You'll crumble. Be sure to find a few people you know you can count on to be there for you when you need them. Death and grief expert Dr. Harold Ivan Smith writes:

Grievers cannot extricate themselves from their cistern called grief. They need a rope. Grievers need someone on the other end to pull. But they really need individuals to pad the ropes – not with pat answers or spiritual clichés or even Scripture promises but with hope.[25]

✻ *Do something with your anger*

When anger is bottled up indefinitely, it morphs into bitterness. And, as we learned earlier, that bitterness will spread beyond the borders of your life. It's Okay to be angry. It is a normal, reasonable emotion when we are confronted with unjust, hurtful or grievous events. It is recorded in the Bible that Jesus Himself became angry on a few occasions (Mark 3:1-5; Mark 10:14; John 2:13-16). But it's what we *do* with that anger that can lead to sin.

The Bible says in Ephesians 4:26 (NIV) – "In your anger do not sin." When you feel the anger rising up within you, first remove yourself from the physical cause of your anger if you can (e.g., if it's a person, leave the room; a locational trigger, go somewhere else). It's like removing fuel from the fire. No fuel, no fire. Go for a run; work out at the gym, pound the heavy bag for a while; dig a garden; scrub the kitchen floor; swim a few hundred laps; rake some leaves. Or if you're able, do something that will benefit others: go help someone who needs it; build something; go down to the church and see if they need help with anything.

✻ ✻ ✻✻✻ ✻ ✻

? **Plan ahead.** What are some specific things you can do the next time you become angry?

_____

_____

_____

_____

_____

✻ *Keep a grief journal*

Crisis care authority "Chaplain Ray" Giunta and his wife Cathy have assembled a very practical tool for those recovering from trauma called *The Grief Recovery Workbook*. In it they say, "To journal is to heal," and they urge their readers to regularly – daily – record their thoughts. "This may be the biggest favor you do for yourself," they say.

He urges mourners to make this promise to themselves:

> I'm going to get my feelings out. I'm not going to be scared. I'm going to write down how I feel each day. I'm going to express what I'm discovering, how I'm responding to each new idea, how it helps or doesn't help, and where I am right now on the journey. I'll write at least a sentence or two each time I re-read the earlier entries and chapters, because each day is a new day and a new place on the road.[26]

In your journal, you could respond to these three statements that Chaplain Ray suggests:

1. This is how I feel right now.
2. This is what I've discovered today.
3. This is what I still question today.

C. S. Lewis' grief journal, published as *A Grief Observed,* turned out to be extremely therapeutic to him and immensely helpful to all those grievers who have read it down through the years. And David's grief journal – scattered throughout the Psalms – has been a comfort and a guide to millions for centuries. Two great examples!

❀ *Write a lament*

A lament is a special kind of entry that you might find in a grief journal, or you might find it as a literary work all by itself. You find many laments in the Bible – in fact the whole book of Lamentations is a series of long laments by Jeremiah, the weeping prophet.

When a mourner writes a lament, they pour all of their emotion, frustrations, venom, vitriol, sadness, curses – everything *including* the kitchen sink – onto a piece of paper. They rail against their present circumstances. They don't hold back. Like Job (Job 3:11-13 ᴛᴍ):

> *Why didn't I die at birth, my first breath out of the womb my last?*
> *Why were there arms to rock me, and breasts for me to drink from?*
> *I could be resting in peace right now, asleep forever, feeling no pain.*

Or like Jeremiah (Lamentations 1:12):

> *Is it nothing to all you who pass this way? Look and see if there is any pain like my pain which was severely dealt out to me, which the Lord inflicted on the day of His fierce anger!*

Or even like King David (Psalm 22:1,2 ɴʟᴛ):

> *My God, my God, why have You abandoned me?*
> *Why are You so far away when I groan for help?*
> *Every day I call to You, my God, but You do not answer.*
> *Every night You hear my voice, but I find no relief.*

Hey! This is the Bible! So apparently it's okay to talk like that! In a lament, it's "no holds barred." This is your opportunity to express your despair and anger, knowing that no one – not even God – is going to judge you. So let 'er rip!

And when you're done, read it over again. Read it to Jesus, giving Him all that anger, hurt, hate and despair. And He'll appreciate your honesty, absorb your anger and love you just as fiercely as He ever has.

❀ ❀ ❀❀ ❀ ❀

Signs that your mourning is working

As the magnitude of trauma and its effects sink in, a person in crisis asks a lot of *"Why"* questions. *Why did this happen? Why did this have to happen to me? Why now? Why did I do that? Why did he do that? Why did God let this happen? Why won't this pain quit? Why must I suffer so deeply?* These questions are all normal, typical and expected. No one faults you for asking them.

? What were (or are) some of the "Why" questions you have asked?

_____

_____

_____

_____

_____

As universal as they are, the frustration of the "Why" questions is that most of them will never be answered this side of heaven. We don't ask those questions lightly, and we really do expect answers. But they just don't come.

When you start asking the *"How"* questions, that will be a good sign that you are making good progress. *How can I build new dreams? How can I move on? How can I deal with my pain and loss? How can I get back into the swing of things? How can I learn through what I've experienced?* These are all questions that *can* be answered. They look to the future, rather than the past. They spark action, rather than mere contemplation. They invite help from God and from others.

? How can you change some of those "Why" questions you wrote above into "How" questions? What other "How" questions should you be asking?

_____

_____

_____

_____

Grief memorials

Researchers in the field of grief and mourning have learned that memorials play a very important role in starting the grief process and facilitating continued healing.[27] That's why we have funerals and memorial services. That's why we have gravestones. That's why the Vietnam Veterans Memorial Wall is so sacred and meaningful to all who visit it. These things are tangible experiences and symbols of our grief. We need them.

How can you memorialize the grief that's attached to your trauma? What can you do or construct that will provide a touchstone for your pain, something that will symbolize your loss? We're not talking about erecting a shrine in your dining room or anything – or maybe we are. This needs to be a personal gesture you and God decide upon (and something that doesn't annoy your husband too much!). It could be as subtle as a smooth stone that your husband brought back from Afghanistan placed on your dresser, a poem that you write and put up on the wall, or as obvious as the Taj Mahal. You and God decide.

You might even consider having a memorial service of sorts – actually going through a funeral in which you visually, verbally or even literally remember, honor and grieve what you feel you have lost forever. It

> *...To give them beauty for ashes, the oil of joy for mourning ...*
> **– Isaiah 61:3 (NKJV)**

is helpful for some people to name what they lost in order to be able to release it. Perform a burial of some sort, permanently coming to terms with and releasing the dreams, person or relationship you feel has died. Think about gathering some of your Battle Buddies and plan a wake together. Suggestion: write out what you feel you have lost and "cremate" the lists together in a metal container. Bury the ashes and commit them to God – just like in a normal funeral. Place a marker where they are buried. God wants to replace those ashes with His beauty.

Or a more positive approach might be to take your list of losses and tie them to a helium balloon. As you release the balloon, think of it symbolizing the release of your pain and grief to heaven. In the same way that our bodies are transformed in the light of the eternal realm, imagine these losses that you grieve and release being transfigured into new life. This is another ceremony that you might like to share with several of your friends in order to encourage and support each other.

Another idea: write a letter to the parts of your life that have "died" and saying goodbye. Then, after all has been thought through and written, destroy the letter (burning, ballooning, casting it in a river) as a way of ceremonially letting go of your losses and the accompanying grief.[28]

! **Prayer Assignment:** Ask God to give you a specific, creative idea of how you could memorialize what you loved and lost.

Life, death, grief and eternity

Many or most of our experiences in life are joyful and positive, but in the tapestry of every life dark, painful threads are also woven. These threads come from the various storms of life: the death of friends and family, sickness, betrayals, shattered dreams, accidents – not just war. They all have one thing in common: *change.* We need to see all of these life changes as integral parts of the ebb and flow of our existence. Part of growing strong and mature is learning how to fully experience the distressing events of life, embrace them, mourn them, release them and be able to move on. This is the rhythm of the Kingdom of God. Resurrection is preceded by a violent death and a period in the grave. Let's believe that God is working on your personal Easter!

Danielle's Prayer ...

Lord, You know I'm grieving. You know why I'm grieving. You are the God who sees me and You know what I've lost better than I do. You have promised that everyone who has sacrificed family relationships for Your sake will receive a hundred times as much. You say in Your Word that You will repay us for the years the locusts have eaten, that we will have plenty until we are full again.[29]

Lord, thank You that You understand my pain. The One You held most dear hung dying on a cross, too. Lord, just as You raised up Your Son, I believe that You can breathe new life into us, our marriage, our family and our future together. I ask You to open the casket of life and resurrect all that it contains.

Promise from God's Word ...

The Spirit of the Lord GOD is upon Me ...
To console those who mourn in Zion,
To give them beauty for ashes,
The oil of joy for mourning,
The garment of praise for the spirit of heaviness;
That they may be called trees of righteousness,
The planting of the LORD, that He may be glorified.

– Isaiah 61:1,3

4 FORGIVENESS: IS IT POSSIBLE?
The Empowering Nature of Forgiveness

Christina's Journal ...

Maria knows how to push my buttons. She knows just what to say to make me lose my cool. I know she's only eight, but she really gets to me at times. When we can't get on the same page, I can usually keep it together. I've always been the calm, cool and collected one in this family.

Yesterday was an exception. I totally lost my temper with her. I'm positive the whole neighborhood heard me screaming and yelling at my third-grader. The open windows in my house made sure that my tantrum landed on everyone else's front door step. When it was over, Maria and I stared at each other, shaking, stunned and silent. I reached for her, apologizing and asking for a second chance. After a stiff hug, she turned and walked out of the room. I stood there with only my stinging shame and embarrassment to keep me company. I sat on the edge of the bed and tried to catch my breath. A few minutes later, Maria returned and handed me a crinkled index card with her handwriting on it. In bright magic markers she had printed "Second Chance Card." She looked up at me, smiled, and said I could use it any time I needed it.

In that moment, I knew what I had to do. My words and actions toward my daughter had been a replay of my husband's outburst toward me the night before. Angelo's harsh words are still echoing in my heart. His insults and accusations were like daggers flying across the room at me. I know it doesn't make it right, but it's no wonder I exploded today at Maria. My heart is wounded. I'm so angry at Angelo I could burst. But like Maria I need to keep giving him "Second Chance Cards" as we ride out this storm of Combat Trauma. My response to him will have to be a replay of Maria's forgiveness for me. But I have to admit, this is hard for me to do.

Since he returned from the war, he does things he never used to do. His fuse is short on the best of days. He explodes easily, makes irrational comments and places the blame on me for everything around here. He takes no responsibility for his behavior. He's rude in public and refuses to get any help. I know he's hurting, but it's just not fair that we have become his verbal and emotional punching bags. My deck of Second Chance Cards is pretty big - I hope and pray it's big enough!

Putting your pain in context

There is evil in this world. There is an author of evil who wants his deadly poetry to pervade the planet and drown out everything good that God has authored. Angelo went to war because of this evil. His intent was to oppose it and drive it back – and to some degree he probably did. But in the course of the fight, he was wounded by it. His natural defenses were compromised. Christina's courageous warrior husband came back soul-wounded and weakened, and his capacity to fight his own personal evil – spores of which we *all* carry – was diminished.

Now the evil is affecting Christina's household. She wrestles with it almost daily. The evil is assaulting Christina's love for her husband, threatening her family, kidnapping her happiness and killing her dreams. Angelo went to war to confront evil at a very basic level – military combat – but the evil hitched a ride home with him.

We share this insight not to be overly dramatic, but to help put the root and gravity of your difficulty in proper context. This isn't merely interpersonal squabbling. It is part of the determined strategy of your mortal enemy – Satan – to devour you and everything you love. He is ferocious and tenacious, and unless you are prepared to fight for your husband and family with equal ferocity and tenacity, all will be lost. We hope that you'll never lose sight of this truth: your husband isn't the enemy, Satan is.

> *Our fight is not against people on earth but against the rulers and authorities and the powers of this world's darkness, against the spiritual powers of evil in the heavenly world. That is why you need to put on God's full armor. Then on the day of evil you will be able to stand strong. And when you have finished the whole fight, you will still be standing.*
>
> **– Ephesians 6:12,13**

Your husband has been hit by the enemy of your souls. You must take the role of the lioness, defending your wounded mate and your cubs. You can be the strong one – for a season.

God has not left us without weapons. The Bible directs us to *"resist the devil, and he will flee from you"* (James 4:7). It doesn't say you must thrash him to within an inch of his life. Just resist – and God will spring into action on your behalf and make up the difference. You want this evil influence *out* of your house! Resisting your enemy in the way God directs will accomplish that.

When you think of fighting the bad guys, you might see yourself as Wonder Woman with her Lasso of Truth, or Sheena, Queen of the Jungle, with her knives, bows and arrows. Muscles, speed and skill – that's what you need! But those visions of the buff warrioress come from the world's tendency to meet force with force hoping ours is superior. Fight fire with fire, right? But God has a better way. It's found in Romans 12:21:

Do not be overcome by evil, but overcome evil with good.

This is a strategy that doesn't always occur naturally to our minds. But it's like fighting fire with water – which is the preferred medium of most firefighters. Although he might not admit it, much of what is motivating your husband's harmful behavior these days is fear. But God says that *"love casts out fear."* (1 John 4:18) That's it! We need to look for the opposites. The Living Water, goodness and love will defeat Hell's fire, evil and fear. And *forgiveness* will prove to be one of our main weapons in this fight.

When you decide to forgive, you are saying, "I recognize evil is here, and I choose to break the cycle of hurt and violence. Rather than add to the evil, I will contain it, starve it out and kill it – with *good*."

What is forgiveness?

There are several facets to forgiveness. Webster's Dictionary defines forgiveness as "to give up claim to requital [compensation or retaliation]; to cease to feel resentment against an offender."[1] The dominant Greek word for "forgive" in the New Testament is *aphiemi*, which means "to release or set free." Here are some definition components from the International Forgiveness Institute:[2]

- A merciful response to a moral injustice
- The foregoing of resentment or revenge when the wrongdoer's actions deserve it and giving the gifts of mercy, generosity and love when the wrongdoer does not deserve them
- A freely chosen gift (rather than a grim obligation)
- The overcoming of a wrongdoing with good

The Reverend Al Miles of the Queen's Medical Center in Hawaii defines forgiveness as: "The decision on the part of a person who has been abused, betrayed or wronged to let go of or put aside the justifiable anger, bitterness and hurt that arises from being victimized."[3]

❀ ❀ ❀❀ ❀ ❀

Know when to walk away, know when to run: The Issue of Abuse

> *Forgive us our trespasses, as we forgive those who trespass against us.*
> **–Matthew 6:12**
> **(Traditional)**

Before we dive too deeply into the subject of forgiveness, we need to share a few words about your personal safety and its bearing on forgiveness. Any time someone commits an offense against you, you have been given the golden opportunity to act like Jesus and forgive them for what they did. But there is a spectrum of trespasses that needs to be considered. At the mild end are offenses that stem from your husband's more passive "avoidance" symptoms: his unresponsiveness and tendency to self-isolate. These could involve annoying things like oversights, mistakes, gaffs and goofs – things that are relatively easy to forgive because we are all guilty of such things. We understand they stem from his Combat Trauma wounding, and they're not always intentional. At the other end of the spectrum are acts that may manifest from his "re-experiencing" and "arousal" symptoms. Sometimes these become violent, dangerous and directed at *you*. When they do, we would define these trespasses as "abuse."

Abuse occurs whenever a person intentionally uses physical, emotional, sexual or spiritual coercion to demean, humiliate, harm or control another person through the use of threats, profanity, intimidation or physical violence, resulting in the abused person feeling afraid, powerless, dominated or abandoned. An abuser's main objective is to establish his superiority and to secure or maintain his power and control over his victim.

God asks us to forgive those who harm us at *any* level on that spectrum of trespasses. But He doesn't say that we must subject ourselves to chronic abuse and enable the sinful violence of a person intent on harming us. Yes, we can turn the other cheek when we're slapped – but we note that we are not directed to do this more than once (Matthew 5:39). Yes, forgive 70 times 7 (Matthew 18:22), but become a punching bag? No. You are allowed to defend yourself and your children and resist an abuser's efforts to dehumanize and demoralize you. God is definitely opposed to unforgiveness, but He is also *very* opposed to people who commit violence on innocent, defenseless people. When your husband's trespasses against you cross the line over to "abuse," you are not required to stay there and "just keep taking it." You can be forgiving from a distance.

You need to ask God to give you discernment about whether or not your Combat Trauma sufferer husband is someone who is simply difficult to live with and in need of your understanding and a deck of Second Chance Cards, or someone who is subjecting you to abuse and has become a danger to you and your children. If it's the latter, it's probably time to run. Chapter 5 has been written especially for you, and we recommend that you go read it now, before proceeding any farther.

Nine facts about biblical forgiveness

1. Forgiveness is supernatural debt relief

In the Bible, forgiveness can refer to the releasing of a person from a debt he or she owes. When I became a Christian, the debt which I had accrued because of my sin was transferred from my personal ledger to Jesus Christ's. When He died on the cross of Calvary, that debt was paid in full – I don't owe it anymore! Now, when I forgive those who owe me for wrongs they do to me, I am actually moving that debt not to my account, but to Jesus' account. It's as though He buys that debt from me, and the currency He uses is His righteousness and His fruit: *love, joy, peace, patience, kindness, goodness, faithfulness, gentleness and self-control* (Galatians 5:22,23). Now the debtors owe Him – not me – and He can either hold them accountable for the debt or forgive it as they receive His grace.

I could continue to require payment of the debts that others owe me – but I'd have a hard time collecting on them. Forgiving them frees me from the demands of seeking repayment, from the burden of pursuing retribution, and from the grief caused by the unjust treatment. I open my hands to let the debt certificate go, and God fills my empty hands with His great gifts.

☙ ☙ ☙☙ ☙ ☙

? Your husband obviously has many fine qualities, but what are some of the debts he has run up against you since he returned home? What are some of the things he has done that have hurt or offended you (or your kids)?

_____

_____

_____

☙ ☙ ☙☙ ☙ ☙

2. True forgiveness is a process, not a one-time event

Have you ever tried to get inside an onion? After you remove one layer, there's another one waiting for your attention. And another. Forgiveness is very similar. You may forgive your husband for something he did, but the next day the memory of his offense (or some new aspect of it) comes to mind again – followed closely by all the negative emotions of the day before. So you choose to forgive him again, and again the next day. Dr. Lewis B. Smedes, ethicist and theologian from Fuller Seminary wrote:

> Forgiving does not usually happen at once. It is a process, sometimes a long one, especially when it comes to wounds gouged deep. And we must expect some lapses. Some people seem to manage to finish off forgiving in one swoop of the heart. But when they do, you can bet they are forgiving flesh wounds. Deeper cuts take more time and can use a second coat.[4] *[Or a third, tenth or hundredth!]*

Forgiveness may *begin* with a single selfless decision, but that won't be the end of it. This graphic shows the process of forgiveness – and unforgiveness. You can choose which path you want to take:[5]

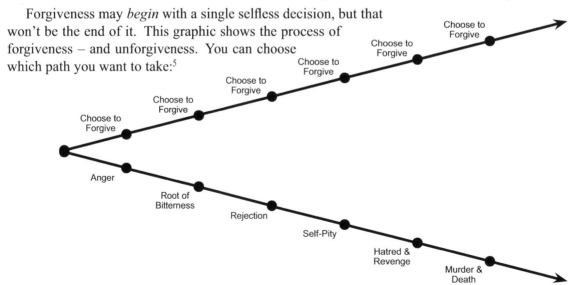

54

Think about your relationship with your husband. How are you doing in the area of forgiveness? Which of these two lines would you say you are on? If you're on the bottom one, how far down that path are you?

3. True forgiveness is costly

Don't think of forgiveness as an easy way out. Some people play a shallow forgiveness card as a way of avoiding conflict: "If I just say I forgive him and don't bring it up again, the storm will blow over and everything will be back to normal." It may bring temporary calm, but the storm will brew again soon. Deciding to set aside our normal tendency toward justice and revenge, not demanding payment of the debt owed, allowing humility to win over pride – these are expensive propositions. Think how much it cost God to forgive us: His only Son! To truly forgive someone is not a cheap grace. Nor is it easy. In the graphic on the previous page, you'll notice that forgiveness is uphill and hard. Unforgiveness is downhill – and downhill always appears easier … as easy as jumping off a cliff, until that sudden stop at the end.

4. True forgiveness can help my husband

When you choose to forgive your husband for his trespasses against you, you are extending an opportunity to him for a positive change of direction. You're untying him from the offense he committed and setting him free. Instead of returning his deadly volleys of vitriol, you are firing back with the most potent weapon of all: love. Your gift of forgiveness establishes

> Forgiveness is the needle that knows how to mend.
> – Jewel, in her song, *Under the Water*

a truce, extends the opportunity for him to lay down his weapons, repent and start anew. We're emphatic when we say your husband is not your enemy, but sometimes he might *seem* like it. This is how the Bible recommends we retaliate against those who have hurt us:

> *But if your enemy is hungry, feed him, and if he is thirsty, give him a drink; for in so doing you will heap burning coals upon his head.*

– Romans 12:20

Now, the picture of heaping "burning coals upon his head" might give you some dark satisfaction if you're currently feeling a little combative. But as biblical scholar and translator Dr. James MacKnight teaches, the illustration actually harks back to the image of the silversmith who would heap burning coals on silver ore in order to purify it through the smelting process. Others make the point that your kind response to his hurtful deeds will produce burning shame and conviction which will lead him to repentance.[7] In any case, by stepping out of the way, not demanding the recompense you deserve, and letting God work on your husband directly, God's purifying influence can flow unhindered through your loving deeds. As theologian and Bible commentator Dr. Adam Clarke wrote:

> So artists melt the sullen ore of lead,
> By heaping coals of fire upon its head.
> In the kind warmth the metal learns to glow,
> And pure from dross the silver runs below.[8]

5. True forgiveness frees me

While forgiving your husband for his offenses *does* benefit him, the Number One Beneficiary is *you*. Many societies in past centuries had "debtor's prisons." If you couldn't pay your bills you went to jail until you could. But there's only one problem: when you're in jail, you can't earn money to repay your creditors. So once the debtor was imprisoned, the one who was owed would seldom get satisfaction. The hope was that friends and family would come up with the money to spring him. But if they couldn't, the creditor's *mind* would be constantly visiting the debtor in prison, becoming more embittered by the day as he waited fruitlessly for payment. The debtor's chains became handcuffs – one end on his wrist, the other on his creditor's.

The principle of imprisonment for indebtedness is still present as a *spiritual* reality. When someone sins against us, that person has incurred a debt that is bound up spiritually in his relationship with us. We can absolve him of that debt – and the prison sentence – by forgiving him. If we decide not to, we end up in jail right beside him, locked in a cycle of action and reaction, offense and outrage, wounding and revenge-seeking. We're desperate to keep the score even – although nobody wins. The present and the future get devoured by the past.

Dr. Beverly Flanigan, clinical professor and therapist specializing on forgiveness issues writes:

> Countless individuals are satisfied to go on resenting and hating people who wrong them. They stew in their own inner poisons and even contaminate those around them. Forgivers, on the other hand, are not content to be stuck in a quagmire. They reject the possibility that the rest of their lives will be determined by the unjust and injurious acts of another person.[9]

Forgiveness frees the forgiver. It gets you out of the offender's prison. As Dr. Lewis Smedes wrote, "To forgive is to set a prisoner free and discover that the prisoner was you."[10]

Exercise: Take a dish towel and get it wet in the sink.[11] Next, wring it out by twisting it as hard as you can. After you've gotten it as twisted as possible, keep your grip on it – squeezing it with all your might. Hold that position for at least thirty seconds. Be aware of your tight muscles – not only in your hands, but your arms, shoulders, back, even your face. How do your hands feel? Stiff? Sore? Now, open your hands and allow the dish towel to drop into the sink. Did you find it difficult to open your hand at first? Did you feel great relief after you let it go? Draw some parallels between this and extending forgiveness to your husband. Can you see the similarity between this and forgiving your husband?

_____

_____

6. *True forgiveness empowers me*

In the same way that removing the handcuffs and escaping captivity empowers us, so forgiveness can give us the power to pursue a more positive path. When we allow another person to hold us hostage to our own growing resentment, it weakens us physically, emotionally and spiritually. Author Malachy McCourt nailed it when he wrote, "Resentment is like taking poison and waiting for the other person to die."[12]

Keep in mind that Satan isn't necessarily planning to use the anger and bitterness in your heart to harm *your husband*. He's stoking that fire to hurt *you*. Releasing resentment, thirst for vengeance, and insistence on "justice" purges us of poison and allows our hearts, souls and minds to function as they were intended – free of the deadly encumbrances of unforgiveness.

7. *True forgiveness keeps me and those around me spiritually healthy*

Poison oak thrives in the Pacific Northwest. If you don't deal with it, it will take over acres of fields and forests making it virtually impossible to enjoy that land. Come in contact with it and you'll be miserable for days. Mowing it down won't help, because as long as the roots are left in the ground it will always come back within a few months, stronger and more widespread than ever. The roots must be pulled up or killed.

That's the spiritual target of this passage of Scripture:

> *Look after each other so that none of you fails to receive the grace of God. Watch out*
> *that no poisonous root of bitterness grows up to trouble you, corrupting many.*
>
> **– Hebrews 12:15** (NLT)

When we have been wounded in some way and feel helpless against the consequences, conditions are ideal for bitterness and resentment to grow. Our hatred for our attacker deepens, our frustration mounts, which makes us more angry and hate-filled – until finally nobody wants to be around us anymore. The bitterness spreads, just like poison oak. The irony is that all this anger and poison does absolutely nothing to the guilty one – only to the one who was wounded. It makes him or her increasingly worse.

Christian educator, counselor and behaviorist Dr. Bill Gothard says,

> In our counseling of troubled youth nowadays, we initially don't even bother about most of the other issues. The first thing we do now is to look for a root of bitterness in the person. In 90 percent of the cases, we find that's the primary reason the person is having psychological, emotional or spiritual problems.[13]

The only way to deal with it is to pull out its root – and that can only be done by forgiving the offender. When we remove that bitter root with God's help, the useless escalation of resentment, hatred and anger toward our offender stops, allowing us to move on to more constructive pursuits.

 Spend a few minutes alone in prayer. Ask God to reveal to you whether or not you are harboring a "root of bitterness" in your heart toward your husband. If the answer is "yes," ask Him to let you know what you can do about it. Then keep your spiritual ears open. He may give you an immediate answer or the solution may become apparent over the next few days or weeks. Once you have an action plan from God about this, write it down here:

_____

_____

8. *True forgiveness forgives the offender but doesn't tolerate the offense*

When you say, "I won't hold this sin against you," you're not saying the sin was no big deal or that it had no effect on you – "So I'll give you a pass." On the contrary, *every* sin against you causes harm at some level. You can forgive the sinner, but still hate the sin and not minimize the damage it does to you.

When Stephen was being stoned to death, he cried out, "*Lord, do not hold this sin against them!*" (Acts 7:60). He didn't follow that up with a lighthearted "But hey, guys! It's okay! No harm, no foul! Really!" In fact, he *died* shortly after that. No one would ever accuse Stephen of condoning murder. How we view the sin and how we view the sinner are two completely different matters. You can love your husband without compromising on being radically opposed to his sins against you. You can embrace him, but set firm boundaries across which you will forbid him to cross. More on that in the next chapter.

9. *True forgiveness is a miracle*

We've made frequent reference to the fact that *all* of us are sinners and fall short of the glory of God (Romans 3:23). If left to our natural tendencies, we would soon be operating at the same depraved level as those who harm us – and perhaps in some areas we already are. Only as we are controlled and empowered by the Spirit of God is it even remotely possible that we can live, walk, act and react the way Jesus did. Here's what one woman, Rebecca, learned about forgiving her husband:

> I [forgive] by extending *mercy* – not by giving him what he deserves: *justice.* By not gossiping or slandering, trying to make things "right" in my own eyes, not exposing his sin to others, not discussing it, living in the past or wallowing in the memories. By not allowing my anger to turn into bitterness, but trading my pain for the beautiful things God wants to do in my life. But all of these things go against my natural self, and *I cannot!* But the Spirit of Christ dwelling in me can, for He has done it before – with those who crucified Him, and with me.

The Apostle Paul put it this way in Galatians 2:20:

> *I have been crucified with Christ; and it is no longer I who live, but Christ lives in me;*
> *and the life which I now live in the flesh I live by faith in the Son of God, Who loved me*
> *and gave Himself up for me.*

❦ ❦ ❦❦ ❦ ❦

? What's the greatest thing you have learned about forgiveness in this chapter so far?

_____

_____

_____

❦ ❦ ❦❦ ❦ ❦

What forgiveness is NOT

Sometimes it's helpful to get a firm grasp on what something *isn't* in order to gain a better understanding of what it *is*. Here are six observations along those lines:

1. Forgiveness is NOT forgetting

Some people like to say, "Forgive and forget. When you no longer remember what he did to you, that means you have truly forgiven him."

The problem is that deep hurts can rarely be wiped out of one's awareness. But it *is* possible to forgive. And by doing so, you empower *yourself*. We have been hard-wired to remember events that have hurt us – and this isn't all bad. By remembering we can avoid negative circumstances in the future, learn from them, be strengthened by them and use them to educate others. The negatives can be turned into positives. Lewis B. Smedes highlights this point:

> Forgiving does not erase the bitter past. A healed memory is not a deleted
> memory. Instead, forgiving what we cannot forget creates a new way to remember. We
> change the memory of our past into a hope for our future.[14]

2. Forgiveness is NOT reconciliation

Reconciliation takes two people. You are only responsible for what's on your side of the ledger. You can offer forgiveness and then hope that your husband will respond positively. And reconciliation is undoubtedly a long-range goal for both of you. But if your forgiveness doesn't lead to an immediate meeting-of-the-minds, that doesn't mean your action was useless.

You can forgive your husband and he may not even know it. He might not agree with your assessment that he even *needs* forgiveness. This is what Jesus Himself encountered on Mount Calvary. The Pharisees thought they were doing God a favor. The Roman leaders were trying to keep the peace. The executioners were just following orders. Jesus still forgave them in spite of – or perhaps even *because of* – the fact that " *... they do not know what they are doing"* (Luke 23:34). Forgiving His murderers didn't precipitate reconciliation – they kept right on murdering Him. But for many of them, their redemption came later.

3. Forgiveness is NOT agreeing with those who hurt you

Some people think, "If I forgive someone his sin toward me, I'm letting him *get away* with his offense. He'll think I'm essentially agreeing with his claim that I don't deserve respect and that what he did was okay." As was mentioned earlier, you can love the sinner but not condone the sin. You can forgive your husband and still make it clear to him that you will not tolerate his hurtful behavior. God doesn't tolerate sin, and neither should you! After Jesus forgave the woman who had been caught in adultery, He said to her, *"Go and sin no more"* (John 8:11). That's the standard and the expectation – though it may not always be achieved by our husbands.

4. *Forgiveness is NOT a free ticket for your husband to keep hurting you*

Abusive husbands will sometimes use the biblical "requirement" of forgiveness as a weapon against their wives, or as leverage to force them to keep quiet about his offenses and be allowed to continue. After an abusive episode he might say something like, "You say you're a Christian, so you have to forgive me. If you don't, God won't forgive you! And you'd better not tell anybody about it either, because that would prove you haven't forgiven me, and it would make you a liar!"

Yes, God wants us to forgive our abusers, but He also wants our abusers to stop abusing! No one can force you to forgive them. That is a decision you must make of your own free will. Your willingness to forgive your husband is one issue, but do not let him link it to the issue of his continuing to abuse you. You'll need to set some boundaries, which will be addressed in Chapter 5.

5. *Forgiveness is NOT a pardon*

A pardon is a legal transaction that releases an offender from the consequences of an action. As such, it can only take place between the offender and the authorities or God. Forgiveness is a personal transaction that releases the one offended from the ongoing pain caused by the offense. You may forgive your husband for his sins against you, but that doesn't mean there won't be subsequent repercussions from the law, from God, or even in his relationship with you.

6. *Forgiveness is NOT a feeling*

Forgiveness is an act of the will. If we have to wait until we *feel* like forgiving someone who has hurt us, we will rarely get around to it. It's a considered, disciplined *choice* to forgive an offender. And the reality is, we may not *feel* any different after forgiving someone. Loss of anxiety and gaining joy may or may not accompany the decision to forgive. Over time this will be the trend, but it's not automatic.

❀ ❀ ❀❀ ❀ ❀

Why should I forgive?

Read the following Scriptures and see if you can discover in each one why it would be a good thing for you to forgive your husband's offenses toward you.

Scripture	I should be forgiving toward my husband because …
"Lord, how often shall my brother sin against me and I forgive him? Up to seven times?" Jesus said to him, "I do not say to you, up to seven times, but up to seventy times seven." **– Matthew 18:21,22**	
If you forgive those who sin against you, your heavenly Father will forgive you. But if you refuse to forgive others, your Father will not forgive your sins. **– Matthew 6:14,15 (NLT)**	
Never take your own revenge, beloved, but leave room for the wrath of God, for it is written, "Vengeance is Mine, I will repay, says the Lord." **– Romans 12:19**	
He has not dealt with us according to our sins, nor rewarded us according to our iniquities. For as high as the heavens are above the earth, so great is His lovingkindness toward those who fear Him. **– Psalm 103:10,11**	

Scripture	I should be forgiving toward my husband because ...
For God was in Christ, reconciling the world to Himself, no longer counting people's sins against them. And He gave us this wonderful message of reconciliation. **– 2 Corinthians 5:19** (NLT)	
Be kind to one another, tender-hearted, forgiving each other, just as God in Christ also has forgiven you. **– Ephesians 4:32**	

How do I forgive? Four Stages of Forgiveness

As we mentioned earlier, forgiveness is a process, not an event. It starts with one pivotal decision (to forgive) which leads to many, many others. If your husband's Combat Trauma is severe and his offenses are ongoing, you might have to be in a constant "state of forgiveness." It's a process that might take a very long time in some cases. That's why you need to look at this as a marathon, not a sprint.

Forgiveness takes place in many ways, at multiple levels and at different intensities. Everyone processes emotional decisions differently. But generally speaking, we can identify four major stages of forgiveness. These stages are not as nice and neat as we will present here, but hopefully this approach will give you some sense of the various facets of forgiving that you might need to be aware of and work through.

First we need to understand the **Four Contexts** of forgiveness – the *where* and *what* of the process.

Four Contexts

Internal: Work done in your heart, with God; focused inward

External: Work done with your husband or a support team; focused outward

Passive: Defensive; in neutral; a longing to let go of the past hurt and find a more positive future; not actively seeking reunion; it's more about you and your mindset, safety and healing

Active: Taking the initiative; positive movement forward; a willed, chosen action; seeking reunion; it's more about your husband and you

In general, you'll need to do the "Internal" work before you'll be ready to do the "External" work. It's the same with Passive/Active contexts. Don't feel anxious or upset if you're stuck in the Internal or Passive stages for a while. You're laying foundations for the later stages.

Four Stages

As you look through the four sections below, you'll notice some statements seem to be very relevant to you and your situation. Others won't seem to apply at all. That's okay! Just disregard the ones that don't fit your circumstances. Your progress through these stages will be varied. If we were only talking about one incident that needed to be forgiven (say, someone stealing something from your home), the steps would be pretty clear. But in all likelihood, the issues that your husband needs to be forgiven for are numerous, and more are being added all the time. You may skip around between various stages, be in different stages on different issues (maybe Stage 4 when it comes to taking out the garbage, Stage 1 concerning the time he hit you).

In addition, you may look at the issues talked about at Stage 4 and think, "There's no way I'll ever get there! It's unimaginable!" We understand your anxiety. But that's why we say it's a marathon. Just think about your current stage and the next few, small steps it will take to get to the next one. It's like how you eat an elephant – one bite at a time.

Notice the boxes next to each statement. Regarding your general sense of forgiveness toward your husband, check each statement that you feel you have already worked into your life.

Stage 1: Working through the pain — Internal, Passive

❑ Recognizing that what he did (or continues to do) is wrong and sinful; blaming him, not yourself

❑ Admitting that what was done hurt you; no minimizing

❑ Trying not to think negatively or wish evil on him

❑ Willing to exercise merciful restraint toward him regarding deserved personal revenge (while not excusing him from legal or moral consequences)

❑ Expressing to God your willingness to forgive him for the offense(s) regardless of your feelings

❑ Recognizing that forgiveness is a process – you may be just peeling off the outermost layers now

❑ Asking God to help you with your anger towards your husband (Ephesians 4:26)

❑ Asking God to help you remove any "root of bitterness" from your heart (Hebrews 12:15)

❑ Adopting an attitude of ongoing forgiveness: "70 times 7" (Matthew 18:21,22)

❑ Letting God comfort you, minister healing to your wounds (Isaiah 61:1-7)

Stage 2: Setting up coping strategies — External, Passive

❑ Being willing to co-exist and communicate with your husband (whether you're still together or not) (Romans 12:18)

❑ Expressing to your husband how he has hurt you

❑ Confronting your husband about his need to get help

❑ Setting boundaries and not allowing them to be violated (verbal, physical, sexual, psychological and spiritual)

❑ Sharing your pain with a trusted Battle Buddy, pastor, chaplain or counselor

Stage 3: Planning for restoration — Internal, Active

❑ Wishing for and praying for blessings for him (Matthew 5:44; Luke 6:28)

❑ Canceling the debt he owes you (Matthew 6:12) and releasing him to God's justice system (Hebrews 10:30)

❑ Asking God to replace with love any anger and bitterness you still have towards your husband

❑ Able to stop meditating on the way(s) your husband hurt you

❑ Letting go of your sense of being victimized and the pain that goes with it

❑ Desiring restoration and a new beginning

❑ Seeing him in a larger context – wounded, as a victim of his earlier (childhood?) traumas, struggling with identity, weak and hurting – just like the rest of us

❑ Considering how to make allowances for his Combat Trauma symptoms

Stage 4: Initiating steps to oneness — External, Active

❑ Exercising generosity towards your husband by giving gifts, time, attention, benefit of the doubt, trust, respect

❑ Going to counseling with your husband

❑ Expressing to your husband face-to-face that you forgive him

❑ Setting times to be alone together; dates

❑ Moving back in together (if separated)

❑ Creating opportunities for cooperation and joint decision-making

❑ Actively seeking his good (Luke 6:27,36)

❑ Getting ongoing reality-checks and feedback from Battle Buddy or other counselors

❑ Discussing how his actions need to change

❑ Talking seriously about restoration with each other; taking steps

Battle Buddy Assignment: Share the list on the previous page with your Battle Buddy. Talk with her about the ones that gave you the most trouble, the ones you felt good about, the ones you didn't understand. Ask her if she thinks you are making accurate assessments of where you are in the forgiveness process.

❀ ❀ ❀❀❀ ❀ ❀

Working through specific points of pain

There may have been some very difficult, abusive experiences you went through with your husband and you're just not sure how to begin Stage 1. Let us suggest an exercise that could help you work through this.

1. **Make a list of your points of pain and trauma.** Do this on a separate sheet of paper, not in this manual. Put down as many points of pain as the Lord brings to your mind – not just the big ones. Don't say, "Oh, that one doesn't matter. That wasn't really *that* big a deal." It may take you a while to accomplish this step, but that's okay. It's important.

2. **Make an act-of-your-will pronouncement of forgiveness for each incident.** You might pray something like this:

   > "Lord, as an act of obedience I choose to forgive my husband for _____.
   > I don't feel like it, but I love You and I know You love me, and I want to obey You. So I hereby release ___(husband)___ from my judgment. I transfer the debt that he owes me over to You. Forgive me if I have hindered Your work in me or in him by my unforgiveness. I now step out of the way so that You can go into action for ___(husband)___ and me."

   It's best if you pray this prayer out loud, rather than silently. Your spoken words have unique power.

3. **Stop at difficult places and take time to see what the Lord wants you to do.** Like what? Depending on what is in your heart and in your past, God will work uniquely with each person according to what he or she needs. He may want you to talk to somebody (Battle Buddy, counselor, pastor), write a letter to your husband, go back to "the scene of the crime" and re-experience the offense with Him at your side, or deal with something in *your* heart. Just keep your spiritual ears open and be willing to do as He directs. It will be for your *good*.

❀ ❀ ❀❀❀ ❀ ❀

A few special questions ...

"How soon after forgiving my husband should I try to establish trust and intimacy?"

Forgiving is the right thing to do, but after you've made the choice to forgive your husband, does God expect you to forget the betrayal and offense you experienced and go right back to business-as-usual? You might think, "When God forgives me, He immediately re-establishes the same level of closeness that we had before. So am I not required to also do this with my husband?"

It's important to remember that forgiveness is a free gift, but trust is *earned*. God doesn't expect you to commit yourself to those who are not trustworthy. Even Jesus knew better than to entrust Himself to just anyone (John 2:24,25). God will re-establish trust with us after we have confessed and repented because He *knows* us and knows exactly what's in our hearts – and how much He can really trust us. You can't know that about your husband. You're stuck with looking at his "outward appearance."

You are commanded to forgive, but you are not commanded to feel safe and secure and able to trust him the next minute. It's okay for you to keep your defenses up for a while. Here's how one wife of a Navy SEAL with PTSD approaches this issue:

> My approach now is that when I wake up, I forgive my husband, even before my
> feet hit the floor. I project it into the future! I am absolutely positive, based on his

track record, that something in our day will require me to forgive him. And even if he is kind *all* day long, the past hurts still echo in my head and shake my heart anew and I have to go through the forgiveness steps in my heart again. I hear what he said last year or the year before or see the way he treated my son or my daughter … or I experience the fear again even though it was months ago.

I've chosen not to re-establish emotional intimacy with him. I do to a degree, but *nothing* like before … and he feels it. But I feel I cannot return to the way I used to handle his antics and patterns. I simply can't live that way. I have truly forgiven, but I am truly guarding my heart and mind from his ways.

"How much abuse should I put up with?"

In terms of how we defined "abuse" early in this chapter: *None*. If you or your children are being abused by your husband, you need to make plans to escape. See Chapter 5 *now*. This will not only ensure your safety, but it should also force a crisis in your husband's mind. It will send a clear message that he needs to seek help if he isn't already, or he needs to better apply what he's learning – or he loses his family. This dramatic action could eventually lead to everything that you both want. But to allow the abuse to continue guarantees the status quo indefinitely.

"But doesn't the Bible say I need to submit to my husband?"

The issue of submission to your husband is a *huge* one that we don't have the space to go into here. But one thing we can say for sure without any fear of contradiction: God *never* expects you to submit to abuse of any sort from your husband – verbal, physical, sexual, emotional, *none!* God abhors violence and all those who practice it. It is characteristic of sinful people and brings the judgment of God (Genesis 6:11,13; Psalm 11:5,6; Proverbs 13:2; 24:15).

The moment you begin to experience abuse from your husband, you can be sure that he is no longer acting in accordance with God's will, and you are not required to submit to his harmful demands. As Peter pronounced to the Jewish High Council, "*We must obey God rather than men.*" (Acts 5:29) Again, you are commanded to forgive, but you are not commanded to submit yourself to abuse. A better move would be to set up clear boundaries.

"How do I set up boundaries?"

We'll be going into this in more detail in the next chapter on "Physical and Emotional Security for You and Your Kids." Boundaries are essential for your safety and well-being. Dr. Grace Ketterman and David Hazard make the point quite clearly:

> To set a boundary is to come into agreement with our own perceptions – wrong was done – and it establishes a barrier to prevent further damage. It is to say, "You've crossed a line and injured me. It stops here."[15]

While oneness in marriage is among the highest ideals we hold as Christians, we can't put that ideal above the sacredness of life itself. God has established the hierarchy within marriage where the man is the head of the household, and the woman is to submit. God's Word also says that husbands are to love their wives as Christ loves the church – which is done by honoring, beautifying and sacrificing for her. Oneness is possible only when *both* parties obey God's commands. By setting boundaries for an abusive husband, you help him to better perform his role so that you can better perform yours.

❀ ❀ ❀❀ ❀ ❀

Look in the mirror

This chapter has focused mainly on how you can go about the costly transaction of forgiving your husband when he has hurt you. But there is one other aspect of forgiveness that must be considered: *your* need for it! None of us is beyond the need for forgiveness. God's Word says *"All of us like sheep have gone astray, each of us has turned to his own way"* (Isaiah 53:6). Jesus made it clear that we need always to be aware of our own sins and humbly seek God's forgiveness for them. Here's one of His teachings on the subject in Luke 18:9-13:

> *And He also told this parable to some people who trusted in themselves that they were righteous, and viewed others with contempt:*
>
> *"Two men went up into the temple to pray, one a Pharisee and the other a tax collector.*
>
> *"The Pharisee stood and was praying this to himself: 'God, I thank You that I am not like other people: swindlers, unjust, adulterers, or even like this tax collector.*
>
> *'I fast twice a week; I pay tithes of all that I get.'*
>
> *"But the tax collector, standing some distance away, was even unwilling to lift up his eyes to heaven, but was beating his breast, saying, 'God, be merciful to me, the sinner!'"*

Jesus' commentary on this parable was that it was the despicable tax collector who ended up forgiven and justified before God, rather than the self-righteous religious leader. Then He said, *"For everyone who exalts himself will be humbled, but he who humbles himself will be exalted."*

Your husband probably has many things for which he needs to be forgiven. But then, so do you. That's why it's so vital that we are intentional about self-examination and keep short accounts with God. As King David asked God,

> *Search me, O God, and know my heart; try me and know my anxious thoughts;*
> *And see if there be any hurtful way in me, and lead me in the everlasting way.*

> **– Psalm 139:23,24**

It has been said that the ten most powerful words in the English language are:

I am sorry. I was wrong. Will you forgive me?

If you can be sensitive to your own sins and hurtful actions and be humble enough to admit them to your husband – becoming adept at using those ten powerful words – you become your husband's teacher, and it could be the switch that eventually turns his lights on.

❀ ❀ ❀❀ ❀ ❀

Spend a little time with God right now and ask Him to search *your* heart and reveal anything in you that is displeasing to Him. We've spent a lot of time considering your husband's various sins against you, but are there some ways that you have been sinning against your husband? The difficulties you and he are experiencing right now may be 90 percent his fault and 10 percent yours, but you still need to take care of your 10 percent. After a time of quiet prayer and reflection, write down anything that God brings to your mind that you need to deal with.

❀ ❀ ❀❀ ❀ ❀

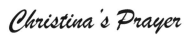

Christina's Prayer

> Lord, I ask you to help me to forgive my husband for his hurtful words and actions against me and our children. I choose to forgive him because You tell me in Your Word that You forgive me to the extent that I forgive others. I know You want me to do good to those who mistreat me.
>
> I know I'm not perfect either. I need Your forgiveness every minute of every day. Help me to forgive myself for behaving badly, for acting compulsively, for being headstrong when I should be soft-hearted. Help me to extend the same grace and patience toward my husband that You have shown me.
>
> Lord, thank You that You are the God of Second Chance Cards. Thank You that You give me third and fourth and fifth chances, too. I am eternally grateful that You paid for all those second chances with the blood of Your Son, Jesus. Strengthen me to be more like You.

Promise from God's Word ...

> *The righteous cry, and the LORD hears*
> *and delivers them out of all their troubles.*
> *The LORD is near to the brokenhearted*
> *and saves those who are crushed in spirit.*
> **– Psalm 34:17,18**

5 I Don't Feel Safe – What Should I Do?

Physical and Emotional Security For You and Your Kids

Lauren's Journal ...

Yesterday was our 10th wedding anniversary. We were actually together for this one. I had so been looking forward to it, coming just one month after Jason returned from his third deployment. Ten years ago, my dashing First Lieutenant promised to have and to hold me, to love and to cherish me from that day forward. Those vows don't mean much to me today. Last night's long-awaited celebration went from sweet to scary in a matter of seconds. I'm still not sure what went wrong.

We were holding hands, happily driving home from the restaurant when another driver sped past and suddenly cut in front of us. Instead of backing off a bit, Jason floored it! He dangerously tailgated the other car at 80 mph, laying on his horn and flashing his brights for what seemed like a mile or more before the other driver finally exited the freeway! Back at the house, I found it hard to catch my breath. The ride home terrified me!

I confronted Jason in the kitchen about his uncharacteristic display of road rage. I let him know that he had frightened me. Instead of apologizing, Jason exploded, yelling in my face about how I know nothing about real fear! Blue veins were protruding across his forehead. Nose to nose with me, he raised his clenched fist above his head. I was silent, too afraid to speak another word. I backed away and braced my body for the blow.

I'm still in shock about what happened next. Jason picked up a plate that was sitting on the kitchen counter and smashed it into bits! Shards of glass and banana bread went everywhere. I've never seen Jason act like that before. From that point on, it was like he didn't even see me or hear me. He was in another place with his men, his mission and his enemy. His eyes were dark. His face was cold and hard as steel. I told him he was scaring me, but he wouldn't calm down. He left the room, still shouting. We stayed in separate ends of the house for the rest of the evening. After he fell asleep on the couch, I swept up the mess and wiped the tears from my cheeks.

Since he's been home, he refuses to sleep without his pistol next to him. He keeps another one in his truck and a third in his desk drawer. His anger escalates at record speeds and to all-time highs these days. I'm beginning to feel uneasy, even unsafe. Next time it might not be the banana bread that gets thrown across the room. I think he is becoming a danger to me, to the children and even to himself.

Who needs this chapter?

While we honor and respect the men and women who went heroically into harm's way overseas to fight for us and protect our land, domestic abuse by returning Combat Trauma sufferers *does* happen. This abuse can be triggered by a variety of stressors and can take many forms. Some veterans seem almost powerless to control their violent actions and reactions, while others are able to stay on top of them. The point is: there are a wide variety of responses and levels of control or violence exhibited by troops returning from war. You may be married to a man at the "controlled" end of the spectrum, which is a great blessing! For you this chapter's main benefit will be to give you warning signs to be aware of in case your husband's stress begins to manifest some of the more violent symptoms of Combat Trauma (as Jason's seemed to in Lauren's journal entry). But if your husband seems to be prone to violent fits of rage, verbal, emotional, sexual or physical abuse, **this chapter is especially for you**.

What makes spousal abuse so horrible?

This Psalm makes it clear why this particular type of abuse wounds us so deeply:

> *My heart is racing fast, and I am afraid of dying.*
> *I am trembling with fear, completely terrified.*
> *I wish I had wings like a dove, so I could fly away and be at peace.*
> *I would go and live in some distant desert.*
> *I would quickly find shelter from howling winds and raging storms.*
>
> *My enemies are not the ones who sneer and make fun.*
> *I could put up with that or even hide from them.*
> *But it was **my closest friend**, the one I trusted most.*
> *My friend turned against me and broke his promise.*
> *His words were smoother than butter, and softer than olive oil.*
> *But hatred filled his heart, and he was ready to attack with a sword.*

– Psalm 55:4-8,12,13,21 (CEV)

How closely can you identify with what the Psalmist wrote? What makes Lauren's experience so heartbreaking – and yours too, if you're experiencing what she did – is that the one person on earth she trusted and loved enough to link herself to for the rest of her life has now turned out to be the exact opposite of what she thought. Her best friend has become her enemy. Trust was broken and she wonders if it can ever be restored. And the question weighing heavily on her right now: Is it going to get worse?

❦ ❦ ❦❦ ❦ ❦

? What is it about your relationship with your husband that makes you feel afraid or not safe?

_____

_____

_____

_____

❦ ❦ ❦❦ ❦ ❦

What is abuse?

Abuse takes place in many contexts, but the one we're interested in here is "domestic violence." *The Domestic Violence Sourcebook* defines it as "abuse by one person of another in an intimate relationship … Any act that causes the victim to do something she does not want to do, prevents her from doing something she does want to do, or causes her to be afraid ... demeaned, humiliated or uncomfortable."[1] C. J. Newton adds, "It's a chronic abuse of power. The abuser tortures and controls the victim by calculated threats, intimidation, and physical violence. Actual physical violence is often the end result of months or years of intimidation and control."[2]

Abuse comes in many forms. In each case the main objective of the abuser is to establish his superiority and to secure or maintain his power and control over the victim. Here are some of the ways abuse can be manifested:[3]

Spiritual Abuse – The misuse of real or perceived spiritual authority to secure superiority, power and control over another or to get their way regardless of the other person's wishes; appealing to biblical precepts (usually out of context) to achieve one's personal agenda with either no thought or a misconception regarding God's actual approval of their action.

Emotional Abuse – An intentional or unintentional attack on another person's character, worth or abilities to gain a position of superiority, power and control through shame, insult, ridicule, intimidation, embarrassment or demeaning. It can also involve:

- Withholding money, limiting access to money or bank accounts, requiring an accounting for every penny, creating debt, not paying child support (also called "Financial Abuse")
- Denying permission to work, see friends or family, make decisions, socialize or keep property ("Social Abuse")
- Threatening abandonment or taking the children away ("Family Threat Abuse").
- Having to prove things to him, mind games, demanding perfection, being made to feel stupid, attacking ideas and opinions, telling the victim she's crazy ("Intellectual Abuse")
- Ridiculing another's valued beliefs, religion, race, heritage or class; forcing another to adopt one's cultural practices; forbidding another to practice his or her cultural beliefs ("Cultural Abuse")

Sexual Abuse – Forcing someone to engage in sexual acts or touching when he or she does not want to; finds it unpleasant, frightening or violent. Forcing someone to have sex with others or watch others (including coerced viewing of video, internet or printed pornography). Threatening to or having an affair; flaunting infidelity. Withholding affection or sex or demanding it as payment. Criticism of sexual performance, sadism, anything that makes the other person feel demeaned or violated.

Verbal Abuse – Intentionally or unintentionally using words to gain a position of superiority, power and control over another through:[5]

- **Withholding** – "I'm in control because I have what you need and you can't have it."
- **Countering** – "I'm right, you're wrong." She doubts herself, so he's in control.
- **Discounting** – "Your opinion is worthless. You don't know what you're talking about."
- **Malicious Joking** – "You can't get mad, I was only joking!"
- **Blocking/Diverting** – Ignoring the subject you bring up and switching to his preferred one.
- **Accusing** – Finding a way to blame all problems on you.
- **Judging/Criticizing** – "You are broken, substandard, defective; I know this because I am superior."
- **Trivializing** – "The things that seem so important to you are actually quite insignificant and should be disregarded."
- **Undermining** – Weakening, marginalizing or denying your authority.

- **Threatening** – Promising harm if you don't perform as directed.
- **Name-calling** – Capsulizing your identity in a derogatory term.
- **Forgetting** – Not remembering various facts that pertain to you in a way that lets you know that you don't count.
- **Ordering/Demanding** – "What you want isn't important. Only what I want is."

Psychological Abuse – Intentionally or unintentionally attacking another person's reality or perspective in order to gain a position of superiority, power and control in a way that is psychologically harmful. Similar to emotional abuse.

Physical Abuse – Any act, physical force or violence that is done to coerce or gain a position of superiority, power and control which results in bodily injury, pain or impairment. It includes (among other things) inappropriate restraint, shoving, hitting, kicking, slapping, grabbing, shaking, manhandling, cutting, biting, burning, blocking, striking with an object, exposure to heat, cold or electrical shock, exposure to a toxic substance or disease, negligence or withholding food or medication.

Physical abuse can also encompass actions that don't *seem* like physical abuse at first glance, but are considered such by legal authorities. These include:[7]

- Refusing to help someone who is sick, injured or pregnant
- Threatening to harm in some way
- Punching walls or doors (message sent: that could have been your face)
- Abandonment in a dangerous or unfamiliar place
- Killing or other abuse of pets (message sent: this could be you)
- Subjecting another to reckless driving
- Locking someone out of the house
- Restraining or blocking a doorway to keep someone from leaving

 As you read through the list of various abuses above, were there any that you feel you have been subject to from your husband? If so, write down which ones:

_____

_____

The Cycle of Abuse

In most cases, the behavior of an abusive husband runs through a predictable cycle known as the Cycle of Abuse. This pattern was identified in the early 1970s by psychologist Lenore Walker, an early pioneer of battered women issues and the Director of the Domestic Violence Institute.[8] Through her research with hundreds of battered women, a three-phased pattern emerged that was fairly common.[9]

During the **Honeymoon** phase, your husband's behavior is positive, affirming, attentive and considerate. He may give you gifts, make promises and behave "normally." He may even help around the house!

Then comes the **Tension Building** phase where he becomes sullen, silent, unpredictable, moody, angry or hostile. This period could last anywhere from minutes to months, during which unbearable tension is placed on your marriage. He may follow you around

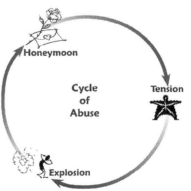

and become very critical of you, or withdraw and appear very disinterested and distant. He may blame his behavior on you or your children, accusing you of "pushing his buttons" or "not being supportive." He may deny the problem completely, insisting there is nothing wrong with his behavior – *you're* the one with the problem. Meanwhile, you're walking on eggshells, doing everything you can to not upset him.

The final phase is the **Explosion** phase and you can probably imagine what this is like. It involves attack-oriented body language (in your face, fists clenched, advancing toward you threateningly, hovering over you, displaying a weapon), throwing, kicking or punching things, yelling, swearing, name-calling, physical assault and battery, rape, etc. The first time your husband entered this phase, it may not have seemed very significant but you noticed it and it bothered you. He may have simply raised his voice, swore at you, slammed a door or gave you the "silent treatment." But the more times he goes around the cycle, the more brutal and frequent the Explosion phase becomes.

Following this, your husband probably moves right back into the Honeymoon phase. He apologizes, promises not to act like that again, expresses remorse, vows to make it up to you, etc. Or he may simply resume behaving in ways that he knows are "normal and acceptable" to you. Since you are a kind and compassionate person, you accept his apologies and are thrilled with this development – your hope is rekindled. You are once again attracted to him and try to resume your role as an understanding, supportive wife. At some level his positive, repentant behavior is probably legitimate and genuine, but it's usually mixed with the ultimate objective of keeping you from leaving him, and giving him an environment where he can continue to maintain superiority, power and control.

It's important to know that *your husband* is in control of the Cycle of Abuse, not you. He uses it to maintain dominance, and all three phases of it are abusive – even the Honeymoon. He may try to blame his behavior on you, and you might even believe him. You, too, may have yelled, swore, thrown things or even hit him and he'll use that to "prove" your guilt. But as battered women experts Jill Cory and Karen McAndless-Davis point out:

> In our experience, women behaving in this way are most often attempting to defend themselves. Women may sometimes behave in ways that seem explosive in an attempt to end the tension phase. If your partner has been increasing the tension for days or is building it to a level that is no longer tolerable for you, you may do something to break the tension phase and move into the inevitable explosion. You may or may not be aware of doing this.[10]

? Can you identify with this "Cycle of Abuse" in your relationship with your husband? _____
If so, to what degree would you say it is characteristic of his interactions with you?
(Place an "X" on the line below that you feel indicates your present experience.)

| Not at all | Rarely | Sometimes | Frequently | All the time |

Are you abused or at risk for abuse?

Many abused women have not had much exposure to a "normal" relationship with a man, and may not even be aware that they are being abused. Your husband may not have actually laid a hand on you up to this point, but if he has an abusive personality or developed one due to his Combat Trauma, then it's only a matter of time. The following is a list of behaviors that are characteristic of the early stages of abuse that often **precede** physical battering. Put a check in the box next to any behavior or characteristic you've observed in your husband.

Personal Abuse Assessment (PAA) — mainly non-physical [11]

❑ 1. Your husband comes from a violent family where he learned that violence is normal.

❑ 2. He tends to use violence to try to solve problems, indicated by a criminal record, quick temper, overreacting, fighting, destructive when angry, cruelty to children or pets.

❑ 3. He abuses alcohol or drugs.

❑ 4. He has a poor opinion of himself and tries to mask it by acting tough.

❑ 5. He is often jealous, not only of other men but also of your friends and family.

❑ 6. He exhibits hypermasculine behavior: feels he should make all decisions, defines your role, considers women second-class citizens and expects you to follow all his orders.

❑ 7. He emotionally attacks you, your children or other women with name-calling, put-downs, humiliation, often in front of others; overly critical of your personality, your physical appearance or your work; tries to destroy your self-esteem.

❑ 8. He isolates you by telling you who you may see or talk to, controls what you do and where you go, even what you read; wants to know where you are at all times.

❑ 9. He intimidates you or your kids through looks, anger, actions, a display of weapons or gestures, destroying your property, hurting your pets; threatens to hurt those who have wronged him. You work hard at trying to keep him from getting angry.

❑ 10. He displays "Jekyll and Hyde" behavior, as though he's two different people: kind versus cruel.

❑ 11. He uses coercion and threats to keep you from leaving, promising to hurt you, leave you or kill you or himself if you do.

❑ 12. He treats you roughly, forcing you to do things you don't want to do (including sexual acts).

❑ 13. He often denies his actions, minimizes his abusive behavior, refuses to take your concerns seriously, mocks them, blames you for his behavior.

❑ 14. He abuses you financially by preventing you from getting or keeping a job, controlling all the household money, concealing his income.

❑ 15. He would never consider being unarmed at any time; always has a weapon close by.

❑ 16. He has battered or stalked a partner in a prior relationship and/or has a history of police encounters for assault, battery, threats or stalking.

❑ 17. When you were dating, he tried to inappropriately accelerate his relationship with you, pressing for a marriage commitment early.

❑ 18. He blames his hostile or violent behavior on his use of alcohol or drugs.

❑ 19. He can't accept rejection, resists change or compromise, is generally inflexible.

❑ 20. He is obsessed with you: always talking about, watching or following you.

❑ 21. He believes others are out to get him, hate him or are jealous of him.

❑ 22. He refuses to take responsibility for his own actions, blames others for problems of his own making.

❑ 23. He is usually moody, sullen, depressed or angry about something.

❑ 24. He tries to enlist your friends, family and church leaders to keep you with him or to get you back.

❑ 25. He becomes destructive when angry: smashing things, throwing things across the room or at you, punching or kicking a hole in the wall, etc.

❑ 26. He has vivid flashbacks and dissociative episodes where he thinks he's back in combat, can't seem to see or hear you, barks orders to his men or yells at his enemies, threatens you as a perceived enemy.

❑ 27. You have an intuitive feeling that you and/or your kids are at risk, and fear he might injure or kill you.

Each of the behaviors or characteristics listed above is a danger sign.

- If you have checked five to ten in the previous list, there is a real cause for concern and you should discuss your situation with your Battle Buddy, a pastor, chaplain or counselor (especially one who is well-versed in domestic abuse issues) and begin devising an emergency escape plan. **We'll be giving you some ideas about how to formulate such a plan later in this chapter.**

- If you have checked more than ten, you are definitely in an abusive relationship, you and your kids are probably in danger, and you *must* discuss your situation with a pastor, chaplain, counselor, your Battle Buddy, perhaps your parents and devise an emergency escape plan.

- If you have checked numbers 11 and/or 12, you should make plans to move out of your home very soon – especially if you also checked number 15.

- If in addition to 11, 12 and 15 you have checked numbers 16, 25, 26, 27, you need to leave *immediately*.

- If in addition to any items you checked in the Personal Abuse Assessment, you have experienced any physical abuse such as shoving, hitting, kicking, slapping, grabbing, shaking, manhandling, biting, burning, blocking your way as you try to move from room to room, then you need to leave *immediately*.

Why is it important that you take such an extreme measure as escaping?

- Like many women, you may be trying to decide between two courses of action: show mercy, patience, longsuffering and courage and *stay*, or consider your own safety and the safety of your kids and *leave*. The intention of the merciful wife in the first course is noble, but if she follows that course despite the obvious danger signs, that courageous, merciful woman could end up dead. The statistics on this are alarming:[12]

  - Each year about 1500 women are murdered by a current or former husband or boyfriend.
  - About one-third of all murders of women in the U.S. are committed by a current or former husband or boyfriend.
  - Up to 6 million women are believed to be beaten in their homes each year. Up to 90 percent of battered women never report their abuse.
  - Battering contributes to one-quarter of all suicide attempts by women in general, and half of all suicide attempts by African-American women.
  - More women are treated in hospital emergency rooms for battering injuries than for muggings, rapes and traffic accidents combined.

- If you won't take action for your own sake, consider it for your kids' sake:

  - Children who watch the victimization of their mothers are five times more likely to exhibit serious behavioral problems than other children.[13]
  - Children who witness violence in their home are six times more likely to commit suicide, 24 times more likely to commit sexual assault, 50 percent more likely to abuse drugs and alcohol and 74 percent more likely to commit crimes against others.
  - Over 60 percent of murderers between the ages of 15 and 21 are incarcerated for having killed their mother's abuser.[14]
  - According to the March of Dimes, battering during pregnancy is the leading cause of birth defects and infant mortality – more than all other diseases combined.[15]

- Most of the behaviors listed in the "Personal Abuse Assessment" above are considered serious enough by civil and military authorities that your husband could be arrested for them.

- According to PTSD and domestic abuse expert Dr. Benjamin Keyes, "If there is already physical abuse taking place in the home, it is *only* going to get worse over time unless there is intervention. It does not get better on its own. Plus, if there is no intervention she's always going to be wondering in the back of her mind if the violence is going to happen again. And if there has not been intervention, it's almost 100 percent that it is going to happen again."[16]

As we mentioned previously, we'll be giving you some ideas about how to formulate an emergency escape plan later in this chapter.

❀ ❀ ❀❀ ❀ ❀

What God thinks about abuse and domestic violence

Dr. Catherine Clark Kroeger, Ranked Adjunct Associate Professor of Classical and Ministry Studies at Gordon-Conwell Theological Seminary writes:

> The Psalms repeatedly denounce violence, bloodshed, lying in wait, stalking, twisting of a person's words, verbal abuse, threats, and intimidation. How strange that we do not understand that these dictates apply as much to domestic abuse as they do to other sorts of violence and mistreatment. Yes, we have been blind to a problem that lies right within our own homes.[17]

God's Word consistently condemns violence and encourages peaceful living. Whenever *anyone* resorts to abuse to achieve his or her own personal ends, they are violating the very heart of God.

Here are some important truths from the Bible about God, abuse and *you*.

1. God hates oppression, cruelty, abuse and violence.

> *The Lord God All-Powerful of Israel hates anyone who is cruel enough to divorce his wife. So take care never to be unfaithful! You have worn out the Lord with your words. And yet, you ask, "How did we do that?" You did it by saying, "The Lord is pleased with evil and doesn't care about justice."*
> — **Malachi 2:16,17** (CEV)

> *Give up your violence and oppression and do what is just and right.*
> — **Ezekiel 45:9** (NIV)

2. You are not the possession of your husband. If you are a Christian, you were bought by God with the blood of Jesus Christ and belong to Him.

> *Or do you not know that your body is a temple of the Holy Spirit Who is in you, Whom you have from God, and that you are not your own? For you have been bought with a price: therefore glorify God in your body.*
> — **1 Corinthians 6:19,20**

3. It is your husband's responsibility to take care of you and provide for your needs, not neglect you and make your life more difficult.

> *But if anyone does not provide for his own, and especially for those of his household, he has denied the faith and is worse than an unbeliever.*
> — **1 Timothy 5:8**

4. If your husband abuses you or treats you disrespectfully, he will experience resistance from God.

> *...You argue and fight and hit each other with your fists. You cannot do these things as you do now and believe your prayers are heard in heaven.*
> — **Isaiah 58:4** (NCV)

The same goes for you husbands: Be good husbands to your wives. Honor them, delight in them. As women, they lack some of your advantages. But in the new life of God's grace, you're equals. Treat your wives, then, as equals so your prayers don't run aground.

– 1 Peter 3:7 (TM)

5. The violence that people practice will eventually backfire.

The trouble he causes recoils on himself;
his violence comes down on his own head.

– Psalm 7:16

6. God forbids verbal abuse and name-calling.

But I promise you that if you are angry with someone, you will have to stand trial. If you call someone a fool, you will be taken to court. And if you say that someone is worthless, you will be in danger of the fires of hell.

– Matthew 5:22 (CEV)

Watch the way you talk. Let nothing foul or dirty come out of your mouth. Say only what helps, each word a gift.

– Ephesians 4:29 (TM)

7. God expects husbands to respect and honor their wives in matters of sex, and will punish those who violate this principle.

God wants you to be holy, so don't be immoral in matters of sex. Respect and honor your wife. Don't be a slave of your desires or live like people who don't know God. You must not cheat any of the Lord's followers in matters of sex. Remember, we warned you that He punishes everyone who does such things. God didn't choose you to be filthy, but to be pure.

– 1 Thessalonians 4:3-7 (CEV)

Setting boundaries

If you are experiencing abuse in your marriage – or if you feel that your marriage is moving that direction – your first step needs to be the setting of personal boundaries.

A boundary describes where one territory stops and another begins. They are usually well-marked, and their function is to let everyone know who has ownership and authority in which territory. Boundaries keep the neighbor's dog out of my garden, his builders from extending his home improvement project onto my property and his kids from building tree forts outside my bedroom window. Boundaries keep order between neighboring cities, counties and states, and keep foreign countries from imposing their laws on our citizens. In each case, the objective is to maintain peaceful relations. Not having clear boundaries opens the door to disputes, strife, harsh words, broken relationships and violence. As the saying goes, "Good fences make good neighbors."

Personal boundaries need to be placed and maintained between you and your husband as well. One of the reasons you are experiencing escalating abuse could be that your husband sees that you have no boundaries or if you do, you don't enforce them. Because of this, he feels little hesitancy about violating your territory, and imposing his will on you.

But here is a very important thing to understand: setting boundaries isn't really about fixing, changing or punishing your husband. It's more about getting *yourself* in a healthy state so that you and he both know what's acceptable and what's not. Dr. Henry Cloud and Dr. John Townsend make the point: "If you aren't in control of yourself, the solution is not learning to control someone else. The solution is learning self-control, one of the nine fruits of the Spirit (Galatians 5:23)." They go on to say that setting boundaries won't make your husband "grow up" or "be more responsible" or "respect me more." More than anything else, it will help you take ownership of your own life so that you are protected, empowered and in a position to love and help your husband without enabling or rescuing him.[18]

The Bible makes it clear that God's will is that you would not be oppressed or in bondage to an abuser. But it will take some determination and action on your part.

> *It is for freedom that Christ has set us free. Stand firm, then, and do not let yourselves be burdened again by a yoke of slavery.*
>
> **– Galatians 5:1**

Anatomy of a good boundary

There are two important aspects of any boundary:

1. It is clear; everyone involved sees it; there is no ambiguity about what it means.
2. The consequences of crossing the boundary are understood by all:
   "If *this* line is crossed, *this* is what will happen."

Here are a few examples of inadequate boundary statements:

- "You shouldn't talk to me that way."
- "Quit spending so much money."
- "Don't hit me."
- "I want you to be nicer to the kids."

Each of the statements above may be a good start, but you can't leave them there. Each is pretty general (although she made it clear what was bothering her), and there were no consequences mentioned. The statements are therefore unenforceable. To an abusive husband they sound like you're nagging, trying to change him, being non-supportive or issuing empty threats. He might think after you make any of those pronouncements: "Or what? What are you going to do about it?"

A good boundary statement really can't be communicated well in the heat of the moment. For one thing, if there is an argument going on, the husband is probably not in an optimal listening mode – and you might not be in the most logical speaking mode. It would be better to wait until things calm down a bit and emotions are less volatile. Then sit down with your husband and set or clarify the boundary. Here's how each of them could be changed into useful statements in a less pressurized context:

- "I need you to know that when you said 'x,' your words hurt me. It's hard for me to believe you love me when you talk like that. I know you're under a lot of stress these days, but I don't think it's right for you to speak to me in such a disrespectful and demeaning way. If you choose to speak to me in that way, I will leave the room until you are ready to take a kinder tone with me."
- "I really appreciate how hard you work to provide for the kids and me. I know that it's one way that you express your love for us. But I don't understand why you are making so many purchases that are getting us further into debt. It's causing me a lot of anxiety. If it keeps up, we could lose our home, cars, savings and good credit. You and I need to sit down and work up a realistic budget, and then hold each other accountable to it. If one of us can't stick to the budget, then that person should give up the checkbook and credit card for a month."
- "I will not tolerate any physical abuse ever again. Not even once. If you push, shove or hit me one more time, or threaten me with a weapon, I will call the police. I will not be intimidated by any verbal threats in that moment. After that, I will leave the house with the kids, go somewhere safe, and I will not be back until you have undergone counseling for spousal abuse. I know it might mean the end of your career or of our marriage, but that's what it will cost you."
- "I've noticed that your patience with the kids has lessened since you came home. I understand that you have a lot on your plate right now and you're doing the best you can, but I want to ask you not to yell or make stinging or insulting comments to them

in your anger and fatigue. When their noise or energy level gets to be too much for you, maybe you could leave the room and have me take over for a while. If you're not willing to do that, and you treat them abusively, the kids and I will leave the house and do something without you until you feel better."

In each case, the husband's unacceptable behavior was clearly stated, the consequences (or alternative plan of action) were outlined, and in many cases, she couched the statement in positive, supportive terms.

Whenever you feel that you are being abused in any of the ways listed earlier in this chapter, it's because he doesn't see or understand a boundary, or you're not enforcing it. You need to establish those boundaries.[19]

Look back at the **Personal Abuse Assessment** (PAA) you completed back on page 72. Choose five of the more serious abuses and write down a boundary statement for each one. The first row is an example of how you could complete the exercise.

PAA List #	Statement of the Abuse	Boundary Statement
7	Critical of my appearance, calls me fat.	It hurts me when you call me names and insult how I look. I may not be Miss America, but I do try to look good for you. If you can't say anything nice about me, then I'd prefer you say nothing at all. The next time you insult me like this, I'll leave the room and not talk with you for the rest of the day or until you apologize.

PAA List #	Statement of the Abuse	Boundary Statement

Feel free to formulate more boundary statements if you need to. By thinking through them and writing them down, you will be in a stronger position to communicate them when the opportunity presents itself.

 Battle Buddy Assignment: Share your list of Boundary Statements from the exercise above with your Battle Buddy. Listen to her feedback and determine together if sharing each statement would be a good move. Have her check each statement for:

- Unacceptable behavior clearly stated
- Consequences clearly stated
- Enforceable
- Positive, supportive aspect

When and how to deliver boundary statements

- **Not in a confrontational manner.** If your husband has been in the military and has PTSD, he has been trained to meet force with force. His knee-jerk reaction to your attack will be to counter-attack – and he's probably better at it than you.
- **At a time when he's calm, rested, open and responsive.** Not right in the middle of an argument. When the abuse occurs, find a way to leave the area and say something like, "I'd like to talk with you about this, but not right now." Then look for a more opportune time later.
- **Specifically.** Be able to site *specific* examples of the abuse. More than likely, he won't remember the incident quite the way you do.
- **Validatingly.** He needs to know that you understand his difficulties and his perspective. Cloud & Townsend: "People have a difficult time changing when their feelings are negated and dismissed. They dig in their heels more, because more is at stake. When they feel misunderstood, they cannot trust that the other person has their best interests in mind."[20]
- **Kindly.** Try to balance what you have to say with something positive about him. Let him know that you want to be helpful and supportive, and that you appreciate all the positive things he does.
- **Fairly.** Make sure you're not crossing *his* boundaries. You can't expect him to respect your territory if you won't respect his. If you can't speak nicely to him, you can't demand that he speak nicely to you.

- **Reasonably.** Don't back the truck up and dump the full load. No one can handle too much correction at once. Just share one or two things at a time.
- **Realistically.** Don't shoot for the moon. Don't ask him to take over all the household chores from now on. Don't ask him to never get angry again. Don't expect overnight changes in multiple areas.
- **Determinedly.** You *must* follow through with the consequences you outlined! If you cave in on the first few tries, he'll know that you're not serious about your feelings of abuse, and he'll pay no attention to any further attempts to communicate them. The abuse that occurs after this could be worse than what you experienced before, as he attempts to "put you in your place" and reaffirm his dominance. Think through what you want to stand firm on, and *do it!*
- **Together.** Revisit the fact with him that the two of you are a *team*. You are Battle Buddies. You aren't each others' enemy. Together, you can make it through this.

Special circumstances

Weapons in the house

If your husband has demonstrated violent, abusive tendencies, if he has ever threatened you or your children with physical harm, or if you checked numbers 11, 12, 16, 25, 26, or 27 in the Personal Abuse Assessment, this needs to be one of the boundaries you set up. The boundary is: All weapons must be taken out of the house and kept with a trusted friend for safe keeping. This is a make-or-break deal. Your statement needs to be, "I don't feel safe when you get angry and have access to weapons. I truly fear that you might use one of them on me or the kids. It has happened to other families, and it could happen to us. Therefore, all of the weapons must be taken out of the house until you are more stable. If you don't agree to this, I will be taking the kids and living elsewhere until such a time as you are willing to do this."

Then, be prepared to make good on your promise. As we've mentioned elsewhere, a common symptom of a PTSD sufferer is the need to be armed at all times, fearing a surprise attack. Nevertheless, this is an issue that you should not compromise on, and he should. If he refuses, move out. Don't hesitate.

Violent flashbacks

If your husband is having a dissociative episode – that is, he thinks he's back on the battlefield, he doesn't recognize that he's home or in a safe place, and he is yelling at his men or his enemies – how you react depends on how he has acted up to this point. If he hasn't exhibited any violent tendencies, it would be good for you to keep your distance from him, but to keep speaking to him in a calm, gentle voice, trying to help him sort out where he is. You might repeat something like, "Bob, it's me, your wife, Jill. You're home, Bob. We're in Iowa. 2355 Western Way. It's June 9th and you're in your home. Everything is okay. There is no enemy here. No battle. I'm right here with you. The kids are just in the next room …" He may not acknowledge you for a while, but keep talking. His ears still work, and what you're saying *is* getting through to him at some level. Eventually, you could talk him back to the here-and-now.

But if he's ever shown any tendencies toward violent behavior, it's important that you get away from him immediately. **Don't hesitate.** It's not worth risking your life.

Teamwork

If your husband has periods where he is calm and supportive (or perhaps during one of the Honeymoon phases), sit down with him and discuss what you should do when he has a violent flashback or dissociative episode. Come up with a plan together so that when those events occur, you can be on the same page or at least be able to refer back to how you acted if he challenges what you did later. "Honey, this is exactly what you and I agreed on together."

Making an emergency escape plan

If your boundary-setting hasn't changed the atmosphere in your home and your husband continues to be abusive, you may need to prepare for the next, more serious step – planning an emergency escape. If you feel your personal safety is jeopardized, the first thing you should do (assuming you have the time and space to do so) is talk over your situation with a counselor who is trained in the area of domestic violence. You should also let your Battle Buddy in on what you're planning, and possibly your parents, pastor, chaplain and a few very close friends.

We are *not* advocating that all women must or should leave an abusive marriage at the first sign of abuse – especially if she has not first tried to establish protective boundaries. But we would *never* suggest that a woman *ought* to remain in a context that puts her life at risk or threatens the safety of her children. All Christians believe in the sacredness of marriage and the need to do everything possible to maintain unity and avoid divorce. But we also believe in the sanctity of life itself and the right of every individual *not* to be abused physically or emotionally. In those cases, it is not only permissible, but *necessary* that a person take measures to preserve their life. For biblical backing of this, do a study of the times David, Paul and Jesus were forced to escape from the civil and religious authorities which had wrongfully targeted them for death.

Here are a number of things you should do *before you are in danger and need to run*:[21]

❑ Pray. Ask God for wisdom, guidance and protection as you consider what to do. Put on your "spiritual armor" every day (more on this in Chapter 10: "Who Is the Real Enemy?"). Pray blessing on your husband (Luke 6:27,28).

❑ Contact a few close friends and relatives who live nearby and find out if they would be willing to take you (and your children) in for a few days if you needed them to.

❑ Let your neighbors nearby know that if they hear any suspicious or violent noises coming from your house, they should feel free to investigate, call your home or call the police.

❑ Choose a place very near your home where you and your children (who are old enough to understand the gravity of the situation) could find each other if you needed to run quickly from your home (a particular neighbor's home, school playground, park, fire station, etc.).

❑ Choose a code word that lets your children and your support system know that you need to escape immediately. Have another code word to indicate that someone should call the police because you are in imminent danger.

❑ Keep a cell phone on you at all times and put trusted people on speed dial who are aware of your situation (including your doctor's office).

❑ Locate a local transition house (domestic abuse shelter) and become familiar with what services they provide.

❑ If your church has an emergency response team, put their leader on your speed dial.

❑ Put your children's school(s) on your speed dial in case you need to contact them quickly.

❑ Contact a counselor who is familiar with domestic abuse issues and let him or her know what you are considering. Run your plan by your counselor.

❑ Get recommendations from friends for a good lawyer who is experienced in domestic abuse and divorce cases, should you need to consult one.

❑ Prepare financially:
  ○ Open a bank account that is only accessible by you.
  ○ Get a credit card in your name.
  ○ Put aside some cash in a safe place.
  ○ Find a program that offers career counseling and training which can help you prepare for and find a job.

❑ Stockpile items you will need when you leave:
- ○ Prescription medications (for you and your children)
- ○ Cash for immediate needs
- ○ Clothing for you and your kids (pack a bag in advance and leave it with a friend or neighbor)
- ○ Important documents (or copies) such as birth certificates, insurance statements, will, legal judgments, mortgages, financial information, medical information, medical insurance cards, vehicle registration and insurance information, credit card statements, etc.
- ○ Extra set of keys to your house and car

❑ Be sure you can access some form of transportation (your car, neighbor's car, public transportation, etc.)

❑ Think through your best escape routes from your house. Run the scenarios in your mind: which is the safest exit; which rooms should I avoid that have no easy escape; what if I'm upstairs when I need to run; what if I'm in the basement, etc. If you live in a high rise apartment building, know where the stairs are.

❑ Keep a diary describing any abuse and dates of the abuse. On the first page of the diary, be sure to write: *For My Lawyer's Eyes Only*. Otherwise, anything you write can be admissible in court and it could be used against you should there be legal proceedings later!

If you don't have a very good support network around you and you feel alone, an excellent contact for you would be the **National Domestic Abuse Hotline**:

1-800-799-SAFE (7233)

1-800-787- 3224 (TTY)

❀ ❀ ❀❀ ❀ ❀

If your husband is still on active duty

If your husband is still on active duty, you should contact the Family Advocacy Program (FAP) on your installation. They will help you determine what your next steps should be. Their aim is to prevent physical, sexual and emotional abuse in military families, protect victims when abuse occurs and treat all family members involved. They help the victim recover and help stop the abuser from attempting to use power and violence to control the victim. The help they provide includes:

- Assessment
- Crisis intervention
- Shelter care
- Support groups
- Individual, couples and group counseling

You need to know that if your husband is discharged from the military due to abuse, you can continue to receive health benefits and up to 36 months of compensation based on his pay level for support while transitioning to civilian life.

The FAP is there for you. Please call them.

The military knows that you may not want to have an official investigation started against your husband. You may be afraid that he will take it out on you or your children in some way. Or you may be concerned about what happens to you afterward. Because of these concerns they have set up a confidential way for you to get help.

This "Restricted Reporting" allows you to report the abuse confidentially without it resulting in an official investigation or the arrest of your husband. In this case, you report the abuse to either a **Victim Advocate** or your **healthcare provider**. Tell them that you want only "Restricted Reporting." (Contact the FAP to get connected to a victim advocate.) They will provide all the services listed above, but confidentially.

You may also talk with your chaplain. Your conversations with him or her may be protected under the Military Rules of Evidence. You should note that if you seek help in a civilian medical facility, their regulations governing release of information will apply.[22]

The Department of Defense prefers that you use the "Unrestricted Reporting" approach. They want to stop the abuse and stop the abuser. If you feel safe enough to do so you can report the abuse to your husband's commander, to the FAP[23] or to law enforcement personnel. This will lead to an official investigation which could affect your husband's military career or result in legal action being taken against him.

If you don't feel safe enough, contact the FAP to get a victim advocate.

If your husband is part of the National Guard or Reserves: Each state has a Family Support Office (FSO) at their state headquarters with representatives in each unit. They can direct you to people who can help you: mental health providers, chaplains, etc. Also, Military One Source is an excellent online resource regarding these matters. Find them at www.MilitaryOneSource.com.

❀ ❀ ❀❀ ❀ ❀

The escape's objective: Restoration

Domestic violence is not a "natural" behavior. It is a learned behavior that takes years of training – usually in a home where the father dominates other family members through intimidation and abuse. It takes time to "unlearn" this sort of behavior. There are a number of excellent men's domestic abuse therapy programs around the country that will help your husband. According to the National Center for Domestic Violence, 68 percent of men who go through a twenty-six or fifty-two week domestic violence course do not repeat their violence again. But most men will never enter such a course until there has been some sort of intervention to break their cycle of abuse. Forcing a crisis through separation or even having the husband arrested, can very often be the first steps to what both the husband and wife truly want: restoration of their marriage.

❀ ❀ ❀❀ ❀ ❀

Lauren's Prayer ...

Father, I'm afraid. This war has stolen so much from me. It has even robbed me of my sense of safety in my own home. My husband's pain has pushed him past his limits. The violence meant for the frontlines has found its way into our family. I pray for wisdom and discernment to know when to speak and when to stay silent, when to stay and when to leave. I pray for trusted friends I can turn to if I need to take cover for a while. I pray for the grace and the ability I need to explain my emergency plan to my children.

Lord, I prayed Psalm 91 for Jason every day of his deployment. Now I'm praying it for both of us. You've been Jason's refuge and fortress. Now I ask You to be mine. I'm putting my trust in You. Let me find safety under Your wings. Let Your faithfulness be my shield. You tell me in Your Word that Your name is a strong tower. I run into that tower and know that You will keep me safe.

Promise from God's Word ...

You are my hiding place!
  You protect me from trouble,
    and You put songs in my heart because You have saved me.
You said to me,
  "I will point out the road that you should follow.
    I will be your teacher and watch over you."

– Psalm 32:7,8 (CEV)

6 WHERE IS MY HEALING PLACE?
Constructing Your Healing Environment

Erin's Journal ...

Abigail was jumping on her bed when I walked into her room this morning. Her blonde ringlets bounced and framed her smiling eyes and laughing mouth. Her joy was contagious. I wanted to jump with her. Instead, I picked up a few toys from the floor and asked her to help me. She bounded across the bed. It was then that she realized she had no wings.

After a hard landing, she grabbed her leg and ran from the room. I found her in the bathroom bent over and squeezing her thigh with both hands. Her blue eyes were saucer-sized, warning me to stay back. She held her breath as tiny tears rolled down her flushed cheeks. I tried to reason with her. She gripped her leg tighter, forcing red blood to seep through her fingers. "You can trust me. I want to help you," I told her. I had to peel her determined grip from her thigh to see what had happened. The sharp edge of the metal bedframe had sliced the back of her leg open on her wingless flight.

One emergency room, three doctors and twelve stitches later, we were able to come home. My exhausted three-year-old slept in my arms on the couch most of the evening. I held her close and replayed in my mind the events of our morning. Why had she been afraid to show me the wound? Why had she hidden from me in her pain? Did she think I would be angry at her for being injured? I closed my eyes to pray for my Abby. She'll have to be still and let the wound heal. I asked God to help Abigail cooperate in the days ahead. Being quiet and still has never been one of her strengths.

The longer I thought about it, the more I saw myself in the events that unfolded today. I felt God reach for my heart. I felt Him ask me to show Him where I was hurt. "You can trust me. I want to help you," He whispered. I sensed His hands move to loosen the death grip I have on my own wounds. Why am I so afraid to show Him my pain, to be transparent with Him? Am I afraid to see the wound myself? Why am I ashamed of my pain? If I ignore it, if I press it down harder and harder, won't it just go away on its own? If I allow God to see the full extent of my heartache, what will He make me do to get well? Will I be strong enough to put up with His prescription?

I pulled away from His touch and tried to press the pain further down. I pressed until my own tears seeped through my grip. I held Abigail closer, kissed her. Abby's childlike faith in me encouraged me to turn to my heavenly Father the same way. I asked God to help me show Him where I'm wounded. I asked Him to show me the way to my own healing, even if it means doing those things that don't come easily for me, like being still.

"For I, the Lord, am your Healer." – Exodus 15:26

If you're like most people, you have had many woundings in your life – probably starting back when you were about Abigail's age. Some required a trip to the Emergency Room and stitches. Some wounds were secret and easier to hide: a friend's betrayal, a parent's hurtful teasing or a crush that turned sour. Some of your wounds may have been more significant, involving severe physical or sexual trauma. Whatever the case, you were hobbled for a while. You may have recovered quickly, but if the wound was deep you may have asked yourself how you could go on in the midst of all that pain. It may have taken a long time before you finally felt strong and stable once again. In fact, some of your childhood wounds may still be unhealed.

Now you are being wounded from a source you *never* anticipated: your best friend, your soul-mate, the one you love and who said he loved you – your husband. As we saw in the previous chapter, these can be some of the deepest wounds a person can ever experience. For some of you, this is something entirely new. For others with painful pasts, this may feel like very familiar territory.

The wounding you are now experiencing since your husband's return may not be new to your relationship. Pain requires healing. And as Erin observed, ignoring or trying to hide your wounds won't make them go away.

The Essence of Healing. When the subject of healing comes up we usually think about doctors. A doctor will *do* something to fix you: stitch you up, set a bone, give you some antibiotic, remove your appendix. But they're not really *healing* you. They are removing or mitigating destructive conditions and impediments in your body and adjusting your environment in such a way that the normal healing processes that God has built into every person can proceed unhindered.

God has set up certain principles that will optimize your physical, emotional and spiritual healing processes. Two things are required: first you need to *know* the principles and then you need to *follow* the principles. They aren't things like, "Go to church three times a week, carry a Bible with you at all times, shower in holy water and live a perfect life." The principles you'll be reading about here have to do **with establishing or deepening your relationship with God**, and how you can cooperate with His healing processes by giving Him optimal access to your wounded soul.

Sometimes God heals in a dramatic fashion – instantly! But usually He takes a more gradual, process-oriented approach. It's like how He would care for an injured sapling: raining down life-giving water and energizing sunlight, bathing it with carbon dioxide for respiration, cool evenings and warm days for an invigorating rhythm, winds to strengthen its trunk. If the sapling wants to heal, it just needs to make sure it remains in the environment God has set up for it. If it decides it doesn't like getting rained on or sun baked, pulls up its roots and takes up residence in a basement, it will never heal.

In the same way, God has set up a healing environment for you. The more you stay in contact with the elements of His "weather," the more healing you will experience.

Building upon the foundation of Jesus Christ being your Lord and Savior (if you're still confused about this, see Appendix A which will describe how to begin a personal relationship with Christ), we want to share **five vital elements** that are crucial to your healing environment:

- **The Holy Spirit** – your divine power source
- **The Word of God** – your divine nourishment
- **Prayer** – vital communication with your Healer
- **The Christian Community** – your divine incubator
- **Mindset** – your spiritual "Battlemind" for divine healing

The effect of these elements probably won't be as sudden as a syringe of adrenalin to a "code blue" heart. But they *will* deepen and strengthen your connection to the Healer, so that He can accomplish His healing work in you.

※ ※ ※※ ※ ※

Element #1: The Holy Spirit – Your divine power source

Who is the Holy Spirit?

The Bible presents God as a "Trinity" – three-in-one. That is, God is affirmed to be the one-and-only God (Deuteronomy 6:4; Isaiah 43:10; John 17:3; 1 Corinthians 8:4), and yet there are three distinct "persons" who are referred to as God:

- **God the Father** – John 6:27
- **God the Son** – John 20:26-28
- **God the Holy Spirit** – 1 Corinthians 3:16

One God presented in three different manifestations, each one with a separate and distinct function. All three Persons of the Godhead have existed as a unit since before time began – never beginning, never ending. But each has a different job.

In a nutshell, the Holy Spirit's function is to reside within us, empower us, comfort us, heal us, transform us, help us communicate with God and enable us to live a righteous and satisfying life.

The indwelling of the Holy Spirit

When you invited Jesus Christ into your life, He took up residence in you in the form of His Holy Spirit. Once there, He's there permanently. This is called the "indwelling" of the Spirit. But what we shared with you in the first chapter about God not violating your free will still holds true. He's not going to *force* you to go His way on any subject. You can choose to disregard His fellowship, His counsel and His offers of help and healing. The Bible says we can "quench" the Holy Spirit by our disinterest (1 Thessalonians 5:19). We can also "grieve" Him through our disobedience (Ephesians 4:30). We can make it so it's *just as if* He wasn't in our life. But He's always there – waiting for you to respond positively to Him.

The filling of the Holy Spirit

 In Ephesians 5:18, God gives us two commands, one positive, one negative. What are they?

1. _____

2. _____

> Don't be drunk with wine, because that will ruin your life. Instead, be filled with the Holy Spirit.
> – **Ephesians 5:18** (NLT)

To "be filled" with the Holy Spirit means to be controlled and empowered by Him. The point of the verse is that, just as alcohol can control us in destructive ways, the Holy Spirit can control us in positive, constructive ways – if we allow Him to do so.

Three kinds of people

The Bible talks about three kinds of people in 1 Corinthians 2:14,15 and 3:1-3:[1]

The Natural Man – "Captain of my own soul!"

S = Self, sitting on the throne or control center of his life

✝ = Christ, outside the life

Circles = Activities, interests, priorities and plans in discord with God's desires

This represents the non-Christian who doesn't have a relationship with God. As he tries to direct his own life in his finite and usually self-interested way, it often results in frustration, despair and discord with God's perfect plans for him.

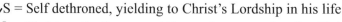

The Spiritual Man – "Walking in faith and obedience."

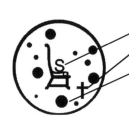

S = Self dethroned, yielding to Christ's Lordship in his life

✝ = Christ on the throne, guiding and empowering the Christian

Circles = Activities, interests, priorities and plans in harmony with God's desires

This represents a Spirit-filled Christian walking closely with God. Since Christ is all-powerful and all-knowing, He can ensure the Christian's life will harmonize with God's plans for him, resulting in love, joy, peace, patience, kindness, goodness, faithfulness, gentleness and self-control (Galatians 5:22,23) – among other things! No guarantee of a problem-free life, only one that is in harmony with God's plans for him or her.

The Carnal Man – "I'll take it from here, thanks."

S = Self back on the throne, trying to direct his life again

✝ = Christ still in the life, but dethroned and not allowed to be Lord

Circles = Activities, interests, priorities and plans in discord with God's desires

This represents a Carnal or Worldly Christian who isn't walking with God. As he ignores or disobeys God's directions, his life falls into disarray. Comparing frustration levels, dead-ends and despair, it's difficult to tell the difference between the Carnal Christian's life and the non-Christian's life.

❀ ❀ ❀❀ ❀ ❀

Study the three diagrams and descriptions above.

Which circle would you say currently represents your life? _____

Which circle would you like to have represent your life? _____

❀ ❀ ❀❀ ❀ ❀

Five steps to filling

If you would say that the top circle best represents your life, read Appendix A and find out how to bring Christ into your life and onto your throne. If you find that the bottom circle represents your life at the moment, and you would rather have it represented by the middle circle, here is a five-step plan that will help you make that move.

1. Desire

Blessed are those who hunger and thirst for righteousness, for they shall be filled.

– Matthew 5:6

What does Jesus say is necessary in order to be "filled"? _____

What would this "hunger and thirst" look or feel like in your life?

_____

_____

Search your heart. Do you "hunger and thirst for righteousness"? Do you truly *want* Jesus Christ as your Lord and the Holy Spirit as your Guide? Are you willing to obey what God tells you to do? Don't expect His power to flow unhindered if you're simply "going through the motions." God looks at the heart, and He knows your heart perfectly.

❀ ❀❀ ❀

2. Confess

If we confess our sins, He is faithful and righteous to forgive us our sins and to cleanse us from all unrighteousness.

– 1 John 1:9

The reason the Holy Spirit may be "quenched" in your life is sin – saying "No" to God and "Yes" to your unrighteous desires. In prayer, ask God to reveal any sins that have been disconnecting you from His plan and power. As He brings them to mind, agree with Him that those choices were wrong (that's the essence of confession). Ask Him to forgive you for each one.

❋ ❋❋ ❋

3. Present

And do not present your members [body parts] as instruments of unrighteousness to sin, but present yourselves to God as being alive from the dead, and your members as instruments of righteousness to God ... For just as you presented your members as slaves of uncleanness, and of lawlessness leading to more lawlessness, so now present your members as slaves of righteousness for holiness.

– Romans 6:13,19 (NKJV)

> Do you think the "presenting" of ourselves mentioned in these verses involves a passive attitude or a purposeful commitment?

Most people associate slavery with demeaning oppression—and in almost every case it is. In the spiritual realm, Satan desires to enslave you to his will, which will lead to destruction. But God wants you to be "enslaved" to *His* will for your *benefit*, leading to freedom from the things that tear you down, and a strong connection to the things that will build you up and bring you satisfaction, healing, fulfillment and joy.

A crucial insight is found in Romans 6:16-18 (TM):

> *You know well enough from your own experience that there are some acts of so-called freedom that destroy freedom. Offer yourselves to sin, for instance, and it's your last free act. But offer yourselves to the ways of God and the freedom never quits. All your lives you've let sin tell you what to do. But thank God you've started listening to a new master, one whose commands set you free to live openly in His freedom!*

❋ ❋❋ ❋

4. Ask

So I say to you, ask, and it will be given to you; seek, and you will find; knock, and it will be opened to you. For everyone who asks, receives; and he who seeks, finds; and to him who knocks, it will be opened. Now suppose one of your fathers is asked by his son for a fish; he will not give him a snake instead of a fish, will he? Or if he is asked for an egg, he will not give him a scorpion, will he? If you then, being evil, know how to give good gifts to your children, how much more will your heavenly Father give the Holy Spirit to those who ask Him?

– Luke 11:9-13

> What astounding, superhuman exploits does this passage say you need to perform in order to "persuade" God to give you what you need?

That was a trick question! Answer: simply *ask*. Remember what was said earlier about our free will? God won't compromise your privilege of choosing. Since each of us makes willful choices to depart from His will, we need to make a willful choice to get "reconnected."

5. Thank Him in faith

Therefore I tell you, whatever you ask for in prayer, believe that you have received it, and it will be yours.

– Mark 11:24 (NIV)

 Notice the past tense used? What does this verse say will happen if you believe that you *have already received* what you prayed for?

_____

If you ask for something and believe you have received it, the normal thing to do next would be to say *thank you!* As Bible teacher Tommy Adkins once said, "Saying thanks is always a sign that you have 'faithed' God."

❀ ❀❀❀ ❀

Asking to be filled

When you pray to God, He isn't as concerned about your specific words as He is with the attitude of your heart. But sometimes it helps to express what is in your heart if someone else supplies the words for you. Here is a suggested prayer:

> Dear Father, I need You. I hunger and thirst for Your righteousness, rather than for the garbage of the world. I want You to be my King and my Guide. But I confess that I have taken the throne of my life from Your control and have sinned against You. I've made many wrong choices. Please forgive me for this. I present myself to You in obedience, desiring to serve You rather than myself or my enemy, the devil. Please fill me with Your Holy Spirit. I step down from the throne of my life and give it back to You. Based on Your promise, I have faith that You have heard my prayer and have filled me with Your Holy Spirit. Thank you! Amen.

Does this prayer express the desire of your heart? _____

If you prayed the above prayer, or something similar, write the date in here: _____

❀ ❀ ❀❀ ❀ ❀

So, am I done with this now?

Well … no. It's an unfortunate but common part of the human condition that we periodically re-take the throne of our lives by asserting our will even when we know it's contrary to God's will. As we grow spiritually, our objective is for this to happen less and less. In the meantime, we must be prepared to recognize when we have slipped into the "carnal" category, and take measures to once again be Spirit-filled. Remember, this doesn't mean we are no longer saved or that the Holy Spirit has left us. It simply means we've temporarily pushed Jesus Christ off the throne of our life and are trying to run things ourselves.

Spiritual breathing

Here is an illustration that will help you understand what to do when you need to be "re-filled." Think of it in terms of breathing. When you exhale, you rid your body of harmful carbon dioxide. When you inhale, you draw life-giving oxygen back into your body. Out with the bad, in with the good, right? A similar thing happens in the realm of the Spirit.

Exhale. When you become aware of sin in your life, it's time to take a spiritual breath. First, you must exhale by **confessing** your sin. The Greek word for "confession" is *homologeo*, which means "to say the same thing as." God's Spirit tells you your action was wrong, and you agree with Him—that's confession. And if you truly agree with Him about it, you will not only say so, you'll quit doing the thing that was grieving Him. That's what **repentance** is: to stop, change your mind, turn around and go back the other way.

Inhale. Now breathe in the life of the Holy Spirit by asking Him to once again take the throne of your life. By faith, ask Him to control, empower and guide you. When you make this request, you can *know* that He will immediately grant it, based on His command in Ephesians 5:18 and His promise in 1 John 5:14,15.

How often do I do this?

As often as you need to. It may be once a week, once a day, once an hour or even once every few minutes! The important thing is to not lose heart and give up in discouragement. As a drowning man will struggle frantically to clear his lungs of water and breathe in oxygen, so we need to recognize the critical need to keep the Holy Spirit on the throne of our lives – confessing our sins, repenting and seeking His filling.

Spiritual breathing should become as natural and automatic as our physical breathing is. Each time you sense the conviction of the Holy Spirit, stop right then and take a spiritual breath. Some Christians have adopted the habit of starting out each day – even before getting out of bed – asking God if there is anything in them that is displeasing to Him, confessing it if there is, and then asking Him to fill them with His Holy Spirit.

❀ ❀ ❀❀ ❀ ❀

Element #2: The Word of God – Your divine nourishment

When you received Jesus Christ into your life, you became a three-dimensional being, composed of a body, a soul and a spirit. We know that our physical bodies need to be fed. Most people are regularly reminded of it by hunger pangs. But our souls and our spirits also need nourishment. Our soul – our will, intellect, understanding, emotions, etc. – is nourished by things like truth, beauty, love, knowledge and friendships. Our spirit – the part of us that relates to God – is

> *Seen on a billboard in the Cleveland area:*
> **Have you read My #1 bestseller? There will be a test. – God**

fed by the words of God: the Bible. As Jesus said in Matthew 4:4, "*Man does not live by bread alone, but on every word that comes from the mouth of God.*" And as Peter wrote in 1 Peter 2:2, "*As newborn babes, desire the pure milk of the word, that you may grow thereby.*" (NKJV)

A Christian who doesn't get a regular diet of God's Word will end up with an emaciated, weak and sickly spirit. Perhaps you've seen photos of people being liberated from Nazi concentration camps at the end of World War II. If we could take photos of the *spirits* of some Christians today, they would probably look very similar to the physical bodies of those poor men and women who had been deprived of proper nourishment for so long. Don't let this happen to you! Be sure that you're getting a steady diet of God's meat and potatoes!

❀ ❀ ❀❀ ❀ ❀

Benefits of reading the Bible

The following passages describe the benefits of studying and applying God's Word to your life. In the box next to each one, write at least one benefit you observe in each passage.

Bible Passage	Benefit(s)
God speaking to Joshua: *Study this Book of Instruction continually. Meditate on it day and night so you will be sure to obey everything written in it. Only then will you prosper and succeed in all you do.* **– Joshua 1:8 (NLT)**	
King David writing: *The law of his God is in his heart; his feet do not slip.* **– Psalm 37:31**	

Bible Passage	Benefit(s)
King David writing: *How can a young man keep his way pure? By living according to Your Word ... I have hidden Your word in my heart that I might not sin against You.* **– Psalm 119:9,11** (NIV)	
Jesus speaking: *If you remain in Me and My words remain in you, ask whatever you wish, and it will be given you* **– John 15:7**	
Jesus speaking: *If you hold to My teaching, you are really My disciples. Then you will know the truth, and the truth will set you free.* **John 8:31,32** (NIV)	

Your personal plan

The following illustration shows that there are five ways a person can get a firm "grasp" on the Word of God. Called the "Word of God Hand Illustration"[2] and created by the Navigators, it demonstrates the importance of getting a balanced input of the different methods of taking the Bible into your life. If you try to grasp it with only one or two fingers, you won't hold it very well. But if you use all five fingers, your grasp of it will be strong.

1. Hearing – Listening to a sermon at church or on tape or CD; listening to audio recordings of the Bible; discussing the Bible with your friends.

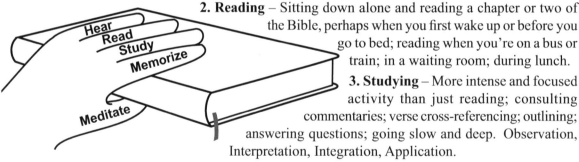

2. Reading – Sitting down alone and reading a chapter or two of the Bible, perhaps when you first wake up or before you go to bed; reading when you're on a bus or train; in a waiting room; during lunch.

3. Studying – More intense and focused activity than just reading; consulting commentaries; verse cross-referencing; outlining; answering questions; going slow and deep. Observation, Interpretation, Integration, Application.

4. Memorizing – Committing key verses of the Bible to memory. After 24 hours, you will remember: 5 percent of what you hear, 15 percent of what you read, 35 percent of what you study, but 100 percent of what you memorize. Running God's Word through your mind can affect your actions and *reactions*.

5. Meditating – Deliberately reflecting on God's Word, praying about it and considering how to apply it to your life. Just as your thumb can touch each of your four fingers, meditate on what you hear, read, study and memorize.

Battle Buddy Covenant: Talk to your Battle Buddy about helping you establish a habit of getting daily spiritual nourishment. Perhaps she'd even consider joining you. While reading the Bible is a desirable and pleasant pursuit, it is also a discipline that each of us needs to work into our lives. And as we all know, any time we want to add a new, positive habit in our lives, we *must* put ourselves into some kind of an accountability structure in order to be successful.

I will commit to a period of personal Bible intake (hear/read/study/memorize/meditate) lasting no less than _____ minutes, _____ day(s) a week, for the next _____ weeks, to start on _____ (date). I will ask _____ to check up on me, give me encouragement, and help me find answers to questions I have.

❀ ❀ ❀❀ ❀ ❀

Here's a good plan to follow as you study the Bible. Read through a chapter (the Gospel of John is a good place to start, if you need a suggestion) and write down your thoughts and observations according to the **SPACE-Q** format:

S: Sins to confess
P: Promises to claim
A: Actions to avoid
C: Commands to obey
E: Examples to follow
Q: Questions I need answered

❀ ❀ ❀❀ ❀ ❀

Element #3: Prayer – Vital communication with your Healer

When two people are in a relationship, talking together strengthens their bond while the silent treatment always weakens it. In your relationship with Christ, *prayer* is your conversation. As Bible teacher Rosalind Rinker wrote, "Prayer is a dialog between two people who love each other."[3] The more time you spend in prayer with the "Lover of our soul," the closer you will grow to Him and the more you will experience His love, power and influence in your life.

Ironically, most Christians don't spend much time at all in prayer. Ask any group of Christians how many of them think they should be spending more time praying, and usually every hand will go up. But you don't have to follow their lead!

❀ ❀ ❀❀ ❀ ❀

? Why do you think so many people are reluctant to spend much time in prayer?

_____

_____

❀ ❀ ❀❀ ❀ ❀

One reason could be that people do not understand prayer's purpose. Though God loves to answer the requests we make of Him in prayer, this isn't its only purpose. God is not a cosmic Santa Claus, existing only to grant us all of our desires and make us happy. We must never forget that Christianity is not supposed to be merely a religion or a philosophy of life. It is a *relationship* with our heavenly Father. And, in any relationship, there must be communication. We don't always benefit directly from the communication itself, but the communication produces a deeper relationship, which opens the door to *all kinds* of benefits.

Healthy couples talk with each other on a regular basis – because they love each other. They can talk about anything and *everything*. There is give-and-take. Sometimes he talks and she listens, sometimes it's the other way around. Sometimes they don't even need words to communicate. This contributes to a relationship that is very deep and satisfying for both partners. These points are all true about our communication with God, too.

❀ ❀ ❀❀ ❀ ❀

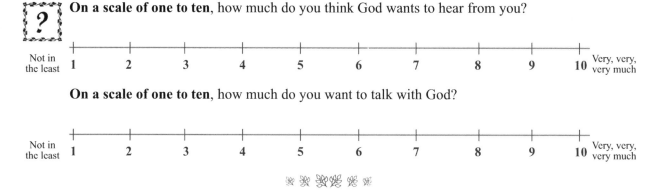

On a scale of one to ten, how much do you think God wants to hear from you?

| Not in the least | 1 | 2 | 3 | 4 | 5 | 6 | 7 | 8 | 9 | 10 | Very, very, very much |

On a scale of one to ten, how much do you want to talk with God?

| Not in the least | 1 | 2 | 3 | 4 | 5 | 6 | 7 | 8 | 9 | 10 | Very, very, very much |

What does God want you to pray about?

God loves you with a love that is more permanent, intense and pure than anything humans can imagine. Proverbs 15:8 says, "*The prayer of the upright is His delight.*" And guess what – because of what Christ did on the cross for you, you are one of the "upright!" Imagine Jesus Christ, sitting by your bed when you wake up, saying, "Good morning! I love you! I can't wait to hear your delightful voice! Say something – anything – please!"

Here are a few verses in the Bible that will give you some insight about what God wants to hear about from you:

Verse	What's being prayed *for* or *about*?
I love You, O Lord, my strength. The Lord is my rock and my fortress and my deliverer, My God, my rock, in whom I take refuge; My shield and the horn of my salvation, my stronghold. **– Psalm 18:1-3**	
In everything give thanks; for this is God's will for you in Christ Jesus. **– 1 Thessalonians 5:18**	
My God, my God, why have you abandoned me? Why are you so far away when I groan for help? **– Psalm 22:1,2 (NLT)**	
If we confess our sins, He is faithful and righteous to forgive us our sins and to cleanse us from all unrighteousness. **– 1 John 1:9**	
Give us this day our daily bread. **– Matthew 6:11**	
Lead us not into temptation, but deliver us from the evil one. **– Matthew 6:13**	
Be anxious for nothing, but in everything by prayer and supplication with thanksgiving let your requests be made known to God. **– Philippians 4:6**	

I want answers!!

God will answer *every* prayer that you pray in faith. Every one. But the thing to keep in mind is that, if we have submitted ourselves to Him as our King and Guide, He gets to decide *how* to answer our prayers. His answers will always be what are best for us and for His Kingdom. And since He's all-knowing, all-powerful and timeless, He ought to know! *His* best is always better than *our* best!

- Sometimes He might answer our prayer, "**No**. It wouldn't be good for you." Like the good mother saying "no" to the toddler who wants to play with the nice, shiny knife.

  For deeper study: Examples of God saying "No" (even to His *Son*!): 2 Samuel 12:15-18; Matthew 26:37-42; 2 Corinthians 12:7-10.

- Sometimes He might answer our prayer, "**Wait**. This would be a good thing for you, but not right now. Be patient. It's on the way." Like the good father saying "wait" to his fourteen-year-old son who wants to borrow the car.

  For deeper study: Examples of God saying "Wait": Genesis 15:2-5; Genesis 50:24,25; Exodus 5:22,23; 6:6-8. In each case, the fulfillment of the promise happened many years later.

- Sometimes God might answer our prayer, "**Yes!** That's a *great* idea!" Like what you say when your twenty-five-year-old son asks, "Can I move out, get a job and pay my own bills?"

  For deeper study: Examples of God saying "Yes": Psalm 32:5; 1 Samuel 1:11,19,20; 1 Chronicles 4:9,10; 2 Kings 6:15-18. In each case, God said "yes" to their request.

Obviously, we would like to increase the percentage of "Yes" answers we get. Psalm 37:4 gives us some great insight on how to do this:

> *Delight yourself in the LORD;*
> *And He will give you the desires of your heart.*

> Prayer is weakness plugged into strength. Prayer is saying, 'I can't, but You can,' and plugging into God's 'I will.'[4]
>
> – Dr. Jack Taylor

When the Lord is our delight, when our attitude toward Him is one of love, acceptance, submission and a quiet confidence that He always knows what's best for us, when we are willing to allow His will to be done rather than what we might prefer, this gives Him unhindered access to our souls and spirits so that our desires will line up with His before we even begin to pray. Then we'll be able to pray boldly the way Jesus prayed:

> *Nevertheless, not as I will, but as You will.*

> **– Matthew 26:39***b* (NKJV)

 Battle Buddy Covenant: Here's another area where you and your Battle Buddy can encourage each other and hold each other accountable …

> I will commit to a period of personal prayer – either by myself or with others – lasting no less than _____ minutes, _____ day(s) a week, for the next _____ weeks, to start on _____ (date). I will ask _____ to check up on me, give me encouragement, and help me find answers to questions I have.

 Prayer Assignment: In Chapter 1, on page 21 you were asked this question: *If there's one thing you would like to include in your personal definition of how life will be when you and your husband are "healed," what would it be?*

Assuming that you wrote something down (or at least, something came to your mind), begin today asking God if He would fulfill that desire for you. Ask Him *every day*.

Element #4: The Christian community — Your divine incubator

You need a safe, comforting place where you can heal and grow stronger. You need a place where wise and friendly people are looking out for you, helping you get the things you need, and keeping the storms and stresses of life at bay for a while – just for a while, so you can rest, regroup and get ready to go back into the battle. This is one of the main reasons God created the Church and, hopefully, has placed a few Spirit-filled friends in your life.

But if your husband is suffering from Combat Trauma, he will tend to self-isolate because he feels "different" and may want to avoid the uninformed who make him feel even more out of sorts. And if you are experiencing some level of Secondary Traumatic Stress, you may have a tendency to self-isolate too. It feels more comfortable at first, and it's easier than trying to deal with people who don't understand. But it's one of the worst moves you can make. Isolating yourself ...

- severely diminishes your support network, who are human conduits to God
- robs you of emotional closeness to people you like and who care about you
- gives you more opportunity to worry and feel lonely, helpless and depressed
- causes you to play into Satan's key tactic – isolate the prey, eliminate all avenues of support, turn up the heat, then offer destructive ways to "fix" problems
- keeps you from experiencing the *good* relationships that are energizing and healing
- makes your environment "encouragement neutral" – no minuses but no pluses either

In addition, this action goes against the basic design objective of our Creator. He made us to be a communal species. Companions were designed specifically *for* this kind of situation.

> *Two people are better off than one, for they can help each other succeed. If one person falls, the other can reach out and help. But someone who falls alone is in real trouble. Likewise, two people lying close together can keep each other warm. But how can one be warm alone? A person standing alone can be attacked and defeated, but two can stand back-to-back and conquer. Three are even better, for a triple-braided cord is not easily broken.*
>
> **– Ecclesiastes 4:9-12** (NLT)

God invented the Church to be like an incubator, a place where His children can grow, get strong, get healed and become stable and independent. And who is supposed to supply this beneficial environment? The Spirit-filled Christians who occupy the church.

We're not necessarily talking about a building here, though that is often where "the Church" will be found. The Church is a living organism composed of Christians all over the world. The Bible refers to this as **"The Body of Christ"** as in, Christ is the head, and we are like His hands and feet, accomplishing His work on the planet. As we cooperate with each other it's much more likely we'll do what He'd like done. The Apostle Paul shows us how it all works in 1 Corinthians 12. Let's look at a few key verses to gain some insight:

> *God's various gifts are handed out everywhere; but they all originate in God's Spirit. God's various ministries are carried out everywhere; but they all originate in God's Spirit. God's various expressions of power are in action everywhere; but God himself is behind it all. Each person is given something to do that shows who God is: Everyone gets in on it, everyone benefits. All kinds of things are handed out by the Spirit, and to all kinds of people! The variety is wonderful:*
>
> - *wise counsel*
> - *clear understanding*
> - *simple trust*
> - *healing the sick*
> - *miraculous acts*

- *proclamation*
- *distinguishing between spirits*
- *tongues*
- *interpretation of tongues.*

All these gifts have a common origin, but are handed out one by one by the one Spirit of God. He decides who gets what, and when.

– 1 Corinthians 12:4-11 (TM)

The Main Point: The Holy Spirit gives every person – including *you* – some kind of a gift (or gifts) that he or she can use to help others. He knows exactly which gifts each of us would be best suited for, and He expects us to use them for the good of His body! He distributes them, but He also continually energizes them. So, though the Spirit will accomplish a lot in your life by direct contact with you, He will also work on you through other gifted people.[5]

※ ※ ※ ※

I want you to think about how all this makes you more significant, not less. A body isn't just a single part blown up into something huge. It's all the different-but-similar parts arranged and functioning together. If Foot said, "I'm not elegant like Hand, embellished with rings; I guess I don't belong to this body," would that make it so? If Ear said, "I'm not beautiful like Eye, limpid and expressive; I don't deserve a place on the head," would you want to remove it from the body? If the body was all eye, how could it hear? If all ear, how could it smell? As it is, we see that God has carefully placed each part of the body right where he wanted it.

– 1 Corinthians 12:14-18 (TM)

The Main Point: What do you think it is?

_____

_____

※ ※ ※ ※

The way God designed our bodies is a model for understanding our lives together as a church: every part dependent on every other part, the parts we mention and the parts we don't, the parts we see and the parts we don't. If one part hurts, every other part is involved in the hurt, and in the healing. If one part flourishes, every other part enters into the exuberance.

– 1 Corinthians 12:25,26 (TM)

The Main Point: What do you think it is?

_____

_____

※ ※ ※※ ※ ※

So *Church* is simply a community of Christians. In America, its most resourceful and pervasive version would be a local congregation based in a building, providing a wide variety of Spirit-filled people and helpful programs for its members. *Church* can also be a small group of people who meet regularly in a home. Or it could simply be a collection of your Christian friends who are looking after you and each other in love, motivated and directed by the Holy Spirit. Whatever its configuration, it is crucial that you be vitally connected with a group of believers who know and love you.

Here are a few verses that describe what should happen when Christians form a community that is determined to make a place where God can help and heal. Write down what you observe in each verse:

Verse	What Should Happen
As iron sharpens iron, so a friend sharpens a friend. **– Proverbs 27:17** (NLT)	
Laugh with your happy friends when they're happy; share tears when they're down. Get along with each other; don't be stuck up. Make friends with nobodies; don't be the great somebody. **– Romans 12:15,16** (TM)	
Those of us who are strong and able in the faith need to step in and lend a hand to those who falter, and not just do what is most convenient for us. Strength is for service, not status. Each one of us needs to look after the good of the people around us, asking ourselves, "How can I help?" **– Romans 15:1,2** (TM)	
But encourage one another day after day, as long as it is still called "Today," so that none of you will be hardened by the deceitfulness of sin. **– Hebrews 3:13**	
Let's not merely say that we love each other; let us show the truth by our actions. **– 1 John 3:18** (NLT)	

❀ ❀ ❀❀ ❀ ❀

What happens underground?

Have you ever spent time in northern California and walked among the majestic redwood trees in the various parks there? These are the tallest and most massive trees on the planet, some of them ascending over 350 feet. Some have been around for 2,000 years. You can't help but to be awestruck by their strength, endurance and tenacity.

But think for a minute. Have you ever seen a redwood tree growing all by itself in the middle of a field? Probably not – unless the area around it was recently cleared by man. And if so, it won't stand there for long. God has ordained that redwood trees must always live in groves, because He is aware of their secret: *shallow root systems.*

Unlike many trees that have deep taproots, redwood root systems grow laterally, and cover a huge area to efficiently absorb the small amount of rain that falls on their often rocky habitat. So, in order to keep from being blown over, redwoods *interlace* their roots below the surface, forming a solid platform that stretches for acres – even miles. When the storms blow through their valleys, they remain standing because they hold each other up!

This is an excellent picture of how the Christian community is supposed to be. The world can be a stormy place from time to time. As a combat veteran, your husband has been in some of the worst storms in history. The storms *you* have endured as his wife have been horrendous too. Any Christian who tries to "go it alone" is vulnerable. It won't be long before difficulties are encountered that are more than they were designed to handle. This is why it is *crucial* for Christians to get involved in each other's lives, interlace their "roots," and hold each other up during the storms that hammer them.

※ ※ ※※ ※ ※

Element #5: Mindset – Spiritual "Battlemind" for divine healing

The Army has a plan for training its soldiers to have self-confidence, courage and mental toughness so they can face fear and adversity in combat with courage. It's called "Battlemind Training." This training involves a mindset that helps them survive and succeed in their mission. As the wife of a Combat Trauma sufferer, you also need a mindset – a *spiritual* Battlemind based on what God's Word recommends.

The Bible makes it clear that our mindset is foundational for survival and success:

> *Be careful what you think, because your thoughts run your life.*
>
> **– Proverbs 4:23 (NCV)**

> *For the mind set on the flesh is death, but the mind set on the Spirit is life and peace.*
>
> **– Romans 8:6**

The word "flesh" in the verse above refers to our indwelling sinful nature[6] – the part of us that is self-centered, impure, angry and ready to fight (for a full list of the "deeds of the flesh," see Galatians 5:19-21). For many wives of Combat Trauma sufferers who are just trying to negotiate the eggshells, landmines and despair of day-to-day living with an angry, moody, soul-wounded veteran, it's hard *not* to focus on the things that are not from God. You're surrounded by them! That's why we have to make an intentional effort to shift our mindset from the negative aspects of our lives to the positive ones that God supplies.

> *Finally, brethren, whatever is true, whatever is honorable, whatever is right, whatever is pure, whatever is lovely, whatever is of good repute, if there is any excellence and if anything worthy of praise, dwell on these things.[7]*
>
> **– Philippians 4:8**

A Spirit-focused mindset includes numerous elements – far more than we have space to include here. But there are five that we see as very important. If they are present, you will heal faster; if they're absent, it gets a bit iffy. No one can give them to you – no one but God, that is. If these elements are not already a part of your personality, or if they were burned out of you in the weeks or months since your husband came back, start asking God to supply them for you. God says in His Word that we often have not because we ask not (James 4:2*b*). He has freely given us salvation through His Son, so why would He not also freely give us all things necessary to help us to survive and prosper (Romans 8:32)? It's as simple as saying, "Lord, give me courage." He'll give you what you need for today. But follow Jesus' advice to "*keep on asking.*"

Mindset #1: Courage

The wife of a Combat Trauma sufferer must make up her mind to be courageous. In the Bible, God *commanded* Joshua to be strong and courageous. He said, *"Haven't I commanded you? Strength! Courage! Don't be timid; don't get discouraged. GOD, your God, is with you every step you take."* (Joshua 1:9 TM)

- You need courage every hour of every day to face the facts about traumatic stress and its effect on your husband, on you, on your family and on your community.
- You need courage to continue to learn more about traumatic stress and to apply what you learn to your relationships and to your own healing.
- You need courage to seek help.
- You need courage to communicate with others honestly about what's really going on in your life, in your marriage and in your home. Being transparent requires being brave because you have no guarantee how your husband or others will respond to your bare heart.

Being the kind of wife you believe God wants you to be takes a big dose of courage. In order to be Christ-like in your current circumstances, you must first be courageous in believing that God's ways are best when it comes to interacting with, loving and serving your husband. Handling challenges with the love of Christ leaves no room for you to be timid or afraid.

Mindset #2: Truth

Posttraumatic stress is a dark place. The wife of a Combat Trauma sufferer needs the light of God's truth to shine into her darkness every day. God has a lot to say about the challenges you face. However, you will never know His perspective unless you read His Word, hide it in your heart and obey it. He promises that when you do this, His Holy Spirit will bring to your mind all that He has said to you (John 14:23-26). Your enemy the devil is a liar and the father of all lies (John 8:44) – he would much rather you *not* seek this mindset.

Combat Trauma sufferers don't always see situations as they really are. They do not always speak the truth. They frequently see the present and the future as overwhelming, full of doom and gloom, hopeless. Therefore, you need to make up your mind to listen to God's truth and to speak His truth to yourself at all times. God never intended for His children to wander around in a thick fog of lies, confusion and anxiety. Setting your mind on what is pure and true and trustworthy frees you from the darkness Combat Trauma drags around with it. The first piece of spiritual armor God tells us to put on is truth: *"Stand firm then, with the belt of truth buckled around your waist ..."* (Ephesians 6:14) Strap it on first thing every day!

Mindset #3: Gratitude

The darkness of PTSD is constant and heavy; therefore, those touched by it need to develop hearts that are consistently grateful for the good that remains and a hope for the good that is a result of the struggles. The path of least resistance invites a vet's wife to become bitter and hopeless. The path less traveled invites her to look for her blessings in the mess.

"Give thanks in all circumstances, for this is God's will for you in Christ Jesus." (1 Thessalonians 5:18) *"All circumstances"* includes the challenges of PTSD. This takes *courage.* So return to Mindset #1, do not pass GO and do not collect $200.

Mindset #4: Forgiveness

In Matthew 6:12 Jesus taught us to pray, *"Forgive us our debts, as we also have forgiven our debtors."* Remember the words of the vet's wife in Chapter 4: "My approach now is that when I wake up, I forgive my husband, even before my feet hit the floor. I project it into the future! I am absolutely positive, based on his track record, that something in our day will require me to forgive him." As the wife of a wounded warrior, you are wise to develop and maintain a constant attitude of forgiveness and grace toward your husband. This mindset softens the sharp edges of daily life with someone who suffers from PTSD.

Mindset #5: Joy

"Be joyful always." (1 Thessalonians 5:16) Spend some time remembering what brings you joy. This can be a tiring mental exercise due to the weight of your circumstances. Do it anyway. Next, surround yourself with reminders of these things: a photo of a loved one or a favorite pet, a card from your best friend, a vase full of your favorite flowers. Listen to music that lifts your spirit and infuses you with energy and hope and faith. Take a walk on your favorite neighborhood loop or country road. Make a list of those things that soothe your nerves and help you breathe more easily. Do at least one of those things each day. Cultivating a mindset of joy will help push out the sorrows PTSD brings to your marriage, family and home.

❁ ❁ ❁❆ ❆ ❆

Erin's Prayer ...

Lord, I feel You loosening the grip I have on my wounded heart one finger at a time. You already know how deep the cuts go. The sharp edge of war has sliced through my soul, and I need Your help if I'm ever going to heal.

Thank You, Jesus, that You pray for me all the time. Thank You that You've been praying for my healing even before I knew I was wounded. Help me to rest while You protect me in green pastures. Help me to drink from the quiet waters You provide.

Thank You that You are walking with me on this difficult path. Thank You that all this is not pointless, but that all I am experiencing will bring honor to Your name one day. I ask You to restore my soul, to heal my emotions, and to stir up my spiritual gifts that have been riddled with the shrapnel of war. And though I hate the uphill, painful path I'm on these days, help me to remember that You call it a path of righteousness.

Help me to cooperate with Your plan for my healing. Thank You that my future with You is bright and sure. Fear, confusion and heartache will not always nip at my heels. You've promised that goodness and mercy will follow me all the days of my life. Thank You that I can have an eternal perspective through this earthly pain. Thank You that health and wholeness are mine for the asking. In Jesus' name, I pray, Amen.

Promise from God's Word ...

> He used his servant body to carry our sins to the Cross so we could be rid of sin, free to live the right way. His wounds became your healing.
>
> – **1 Peter 2:24** (TM)

Nurturing Your Spirit, Soul and Body

Christina's Journal ...

I don't know much about marathons. I don't know much about endurance running at all. I'm a sprinter. I loved the 100M dash, the 200M dash and running anchor in the 400M relay in high school. I loved exploding out of the starting blocks, pumping my arms and legs as fast as they could go, and leaning across the finish line in a blaze of glory.

Even though I'm way past high school and I haven't worn my spikes in forever, I still do life as a sprinter. Doing my days as all-out dashes must be in my DNA. I wake up and explode out of the starting blocks into my day. I move as fast and as furiously as my arms and legs will take me through my long list of things to accomplish. Then, at bedtime, I lean across the finish line and collapse onto my mattress. And while there isn't a stadium full of cheering fans, I applaud myself for giving life my personal best once again.

Yesterday I had almost made it to my finish line when I ran out of gas. Literally. I had gotten up late, rushed Maria to school and had been sprinting all day at work. After a frantic trip to the grocery store I was racing to pick up Maria from soccer practice when my car sputtered, spit and slowed to a stop on a lonely stretch of road. After I called a friend to pick up Maria and called the roadside assistance guys to come rescue me, I sat alone in my car and waited. It was so quiet I could hear the ice cream melting in the back seat.

I considered calling my friend back to pass the time, but opted to cry instead. Frustrated and so very, very tired, I leaned my forehead against the steering wheel and wept. Why this? Why now? Didn't God know how much I still had to do? Didn't He realize that running out of gas was not on my schedule? My stomach growled, reminding me I had forgotten to eat lunch. My dull headache told me I was dehydrated, too. With Angelo still TDY, I had no choice but to be still and wait. The sun streamed in through the window and warmed me. I fell asleep like a contented cat on a sofa. Several pleasant dreams later, a knock on the window awakened me. The roadside assistance guy had finally found me. I was startled and disoriented for a minute, but so happy to see the bright red gas can he had with him.

With my tank refilled and an unscheduled nap under my belt, I was able to pick up my daughter at my friend's house and make dinner in a much better frame of mind. I didn't even mind so much when Maria asked for help with her math homework. As I put my head on my pillow last night, it occurred to me that life is more like a marathon than a sprint. I have a lot to learn about pacing myself as I try to cope with Angelo's Combat Trauma and my reactions to him. I have to make time to take better care of myself. I want to go the distance. I want to reach the finish line and to know I've run the race well. If I'm running on fumes, I know I may not be able to finish this marathon.

A man once asked Jesus, *"Teacher, what is the most important commandment in the Law?"* Jesus gave him two for the price of one – not only the most important, but the second most important too:

> *"'You shall love the Lord your God with all your heart, and with all your soul, and with all your mind.' This is the first and foremost commandment. The second is like it, 'You shall love your neighbor as yourself.' On these two commandments depend the whole Law and the Prophets."*
>
> **– Matthew 22:37-40**

It's not too hard to catch Jesus' main point. If we were to love God and love our neighbors with everything we had, we really wouldn't need any other laws – they'd all be covered! But what many people miss is the standard of measurement He placed on "*love your neighbor.*" How are we to love them? *In the same way we love ourselves.*

For a lot of people that's not a very high standard – especially for those who are experiencing depression, stress and anxiety. Their self-esteem is in the toilet. They are discouraged with how little they are accomplishing each day, and they feel they are failing on so many fronts. "Besides," wives of hurting veterans often reason, "my husband's needs are greater than mine. My kids need me now more than ever. My needs aren't as important." And so the needs of the wife are continually stuffed, marginalized and neglected until she is running on fumes and unable to give anything to anybody anymore.

If we don't love ourselves, does that let us off the hook regarding the second commandment? It's probably more accurate to say that if we don't love ourselves, we won't be able to love others either, and thereby back-burner that second commandment. Dr. Barbara de Angelis makes a good point when she writes,

> If you aren't good at loving yourself, you will have a difficult time loving anyone, since you'll resent the time and energy you give another person that you aren't even giving to yourself.[1]

Maybe you've heard the saying that goes like this: "**J**OY comes when you put **J**esus first, **O**thers second, and **Y**ourself last." The sentiment is admirable and it certainly represents a humble attitude. But many people make that the guiding philosophy of everything they do, wearing it like a crown of thorns – to the profound neglect of their own basic needs. Even Jesus made sure His body, soul and spirit were maintained during His very rigorous earthly ministry. Yes, it is a godly trait to put the needs of others before your own – but *not* to the detriment of your physical, mental and spiritual health. Some of the biggest "givers" on the planet – combat medics – have this philosophy hammered into them throughout their training: "You're no good to anybody dead!" Neither are you, wife. Neither are you, mother. You and the medics *must* be sure your needs are being met, and then you can take care of others.

Gerontological Consultant Katherine Karr simplifies the matter for us:

> Meeting our needs is not selfish. How could it be? If we are rested, relaxed, and making absolutely certain our needs are met on a regular, ongoing basis, we are more tolerant, less frustrated, in better humor, and have considerably more of ourselves to give to those who need us."[2]

Who am I really?

Many people confuse self-love with self-centeredness or selfishness. Those latter traits are at the center of what the Bible calls "pride" and they *will* lead to destruction (Proverbs 16:18). But to love yourself is to simply give yourself the same dignity, worth and respect that God affords you. How worthy does *He* think you are? Worthy enough to die for.

In God's eyes you are beautiful, lovable, incredible, amazing and worth every drop of blood He shed for you. That's His opinion, even if it isn't yours at present. He honors you by making your body the temple of His Holy Spirit and by calling you His daughter and His friend. He enriches you with spiritual gifts, sanctification, blessed plans and eternal life. You may feel like a slave to your household, your duties and your circumstances and it may be hard to see past the pile of dirty laundry, dirty dishes and dirty windows, but you are one of God's most unique and majestic creations. As philosopher Teilhard de Chardin once wrote: "We are not human beings having a spiritual experience, we are spiritual beings having a human experience."[3] [Chapter 9 will take you deeper into this truth.]

We expend a tremendous amount of energy settling for and maintaining the status quo without realizing that if that energy were harmonized with God's truth and refocused on who He wants us to become, we would eliminate a lot of the friction and drag we currently battle.

This chapter will give you some ideas and practical tools that will help you take care of yourself, reduce the load of stress you are currently carrying and increase your level of energy, resiliency and contentment. We've arranged these ideas in three categories, relating to the three basic components of our being: **spirit**, **soul** and **body**.

> *Now may the God of peace Himself sanctify you entirely; and may your **spirit** and **soul** and **body** be preserved complete, without blame at the coming of our Lord Jesus Christ.*
>
> *– 1 Thessalonians 5:23*

Spirit-Nurture

It's difficult to make absolute pronouncements as to what exactly the "spirit" is, and how it differs from a person's "soul." Sometimes the Bible seems to use the terms interchangeably (Matthew 5:3; Matthew 11:29; Matthew 26:38; Matthew 26:41), while in other places they are spoken of as being distinct (1 Corinthians 15:45; Hebrews 4:12). For the purposes of this manual, we'll refer to the "spirit" as the part of us that relates to and responds to God. It deals with the "vertical," God-oriented aspects of our lives (Luke 1:47; Romans 8:16; 1 Corinthians 14:14). We'll refer to the "soul" as the part of us that involves our will, intellect, understanding and emotions. It's the essence of *you*. It deals with the "horizontal" aspects of our lives including relating to our environment and to other people. More on "soul" at the beginning of the **Soul-nurture** section following this one.

John 3:1-8 records an interchange between Jesus and a Pharisee named Nicodemus. Jesus told him that he needed to be "*born again*." This puzzled Nicodemus – "*How can a man be born when he is old?*" he asked. Jesus explained to him that He wasn't talking about a second physical birth, but of a spiritual birth. Everyone alive has been born "*of the water*" (physically), but to enter the Kingdom of God a person also needs to be born "*of the Spirit*" (spiritually – verse 5). Whether our spirit is created, gained, accessed, activated or cleaned up when we receive Christ as our Savior, it's obvious from numerous scriptural passages that we are spiritual "newborns" at that point. We're just as immature, vulnerable and unfamiliar with the new realm of the Spirit as we were with the physical world when we first showed up in the delivery room. So the part of us that relates to God – our spirit – needs to grow. In this section we want to pass on five important principles and activities that will help you to nourish and nurture your growing spirit.

1. Stay in your healing place

Chapter 6 talked about how you can cooperate with God to construct an environment that will facilitate your healing. Five important elements of that environment were expanded upon:

- **The Holy Spirit – your divine power source**
- **The Word of God – your divine nourishment**
- **Prayer – vital communication with your Healer**
- **The Christian Community – your divine incubator**
- **Mindset – your spiritual "Battlemind" for divine healing**

Those same five elements are also vital to an environment that will facilitate your *growth*. The more time you spend walking in the fullness of the Holy Spirit, taking in God's Word, talking with Him in prayer, hanging out with Spirit-filled, encouraging friends, and developing your spiritual Battlemind, the more rapidly you'll progress in *both* your healing and your spiritual growth.

We won't reiterate the points we made in the previous chapter – but if you need a refresher, go back and re-read Chapter 6. Think of some practical things you can do to incorporate those five elements more centrally in your daily life. We'll be giving you a few ideas along those lines in this section.

2. Connect with God daily

The essence of eternal life is *to know God*. When we stand before Him in heaven, our knowledge and understanding of Him will take a quantum leap (1 Corinthians 13:12). But we can begin to know Him right here, right now. We can learn things about Him that will deepen our relationship with Him and prove to be vital to our spiritual growth. How important is this? Read the Apostle Paul's opinion on the subject:

> **Jesus praying:**
> *This is eternal life, that they may know You, the only true God, and Jesus Christ whom You have sent.*
> **– John 17:3**

> *More than that, I count all things to be loss in view of the surpassing value of knowing Christ Jesus my Lord, for whom I have suffered the loss of all things, and count them but rubbish so that I may gain Christ.*
> **– Philippians 3:8**

? How can you get to know another person and maintain a good relationship with him or her? List three important aspects of how you would normally set about doing that:

1. _____

2. _____

3. _____

The things you wrote above are probably also excellent principles you could use to get to know God. If the person you wanted to become good friends with was real important to you, how often would you try to spend time with him or her? Probably as often as possible, if not every day, right? God qualifies as Someone who is "real important to you!" For this reason, your best plan would be to intentionally set aside some time every day to communicate with Him. Some people like to call this daily meeting with God their "Quiet Time" or their "Daily Devotions." But whatever you choose to call it, this time spent with God can form the cornerstone of your strategy to heal, grow, and get to know your Creator.

Two main objectives in a "Quiet Time"

1. To build a deeper relationship with God, which requires *communication*.
2. To learn about the things of God and His Kingdom, which requires *education*.

As you think about those two objectives, you can probably see that *prayer* would help accomplish the first one, and *Bible study* would help accomplish the second one.

Prayer – talking with God

Set aside part of your Quiet Time for communicating with God. Prayer shouldn't be constricted by a set "formula," but a healthy prayer life should contain at least these four ingredients – easy to remember because they form the acrostic ACTS:

- **Adoration** – Worshipping and praising God for Who He is; expressing our love for Him. For an example of this see 1 Chronicles 29:10-13.
- **Confession** – Admitting sins to God that He brings to your mind; asking forgiveness; seeking His cleansing. For an example see Psalm 51:1-12.
- **Thanksgiving** – Expressing your appreciation to God for things He has done for you. For an example see Psalm 30:1-6.
- **Supplication** – Specific requests you have: could be for yourself or others, for spiritual, material or emotional needs or blessings. For an example see 1 Kings 3:5-10.

Don't forget to spend some time just *listening* to God as well. You have things you want to tell Him, is it possible that He might have some specific things to tell you? Start by addressing God the same way the prophet Samuel did when he was just a boy: *"Speak, Lord, for your servant is listening"* (1 Samuel 3:10).

Bible study – learning about God and His Kingdom.

The other part of your Quiet Time should be spent in God's Word. In Chapter 6 we explored five ways you can approach this:

- **Hearing** – Listening to sermons, tapes or CDs of the Bible
- **Reading** – Covering a section of the Bible for general meaning and content
- **Studying** – Covering a small section slowly, deeply, consulting Bible study aides
- **Memorizing** – Committing verses or portions of Scripture to memory
- **Meditating** – Thinking deeply about Scripture, how it applies to your life

Don't get stuck in a rut – vary what you do in your Quiet Times. For instance: spend a few days or weeks just reading through a book of the Bible, then shift gears and spend a few days or weeks studying just one chapter deeply. Then find a quiet, comfortable spot and listen to a book of the Bible read on a CD. Try different ways!

When?

The rule of thumb is: do it when you know you can be alert. If your household dynamics and your energy patterns allow it, schedule it first thing in the morning. Why? Here are a few good reasons:

- Give God the first and best part of your day as an offering.
- It makes sense to tune the violin *before* the concert.
- Meeting with God first will set the tone of your day.
- If it's first on your schedule, you can be sure other things won't crowd it out.

How Often?

How vital do you think this time is? Most mature Christians would consider it *extremely* vital – on the same level as eating, sleeping, breathing and tooth brushing. We do vital things every day. You may have to skip a day occasionally, and that's okay! You're not breaking a law! But make it a goal to have your Daily Devotions *daily*. Before long, you'll find it undesirable to start a day without them!

Where?

Choose a place that is quiet, comfortable, secluded and free of distraction and interruption. You may have to get creative if you live in a crowded situation – how about your car, garage, furnace room, a closet or storage shed? If the weather is cooperative, consider going to a nearby park or beach. Esther Stoddard Edwards, mother of the great philosopher and theologian Jonathan Edwards – and ten other children – would escape the chaos of her busy household by draping a large towel over herself as she sat in a chair and had her daily Quiet Time. That, plus good earplugs, could work for you!

How long?

Why not start with ten minutes? Most of us could agree to giving the Lord 1/144th of our day – particularly when *we* are the major beneficiaries of that investment! Five minutes in the Bible and five minutes in prayer is an excellent way to start the day. But we must warn you: it won't be long before you'll watch that time extend to twelve minutes. Then fifteen. Then eighteen … twenty … twenty-five …

How will it affect me?

Author Marshéle Waddell writes about how precious her daily time with God became as her Navy SEAL husband was going through some of the worst symptoms of his PTSD:

> I set aside time that I could be alone daily in His presence – more frequently on my face than on my knees. Sometimes I sprinted into His throne room. Other days I could barely crawl to the edge of His courtyards. Either way Jesus met me at my point of need and walked with me into the presence of our Father. I relied on my Savior to intercede for me and on His Holy Spirit to pray for me when I couldn't find the words. While my human tendency in my pain was to pull away from God and from other believers, I made the commitment to guard my one-on-One times with God and to continue to worship and fellowship with His family – come what may.

3. Check your priorities

First on our list should be our relationship with God and our connections to His kingdom. He knows how difficult our lives can become, and how – as Marshéle just stated – we have a tendency to pull away from God when our lives are in crisis. He knows that our world can become all about *us* – our survival, our needs, our wants, our hurts. Those are all legitimate concerns! Yet Jesus put things in proper perspective and gave us a strategy that works every time it's used:

> *But seek first the kingdom of God and His righteousness,*
> *and all these things shall be added to you.*
>
> **– Matthew 6:33**

When Jesus Christ is Lord of our lives, when He's on the throne, when we say to Him, "Not my will, but Your will be done," and when we put our lives under His authority in faith and trust, *that's* when we find that He is more than able to miraculously administrate our survival, needs, wants and hurts in ways we *never* could have devised or even thought about. When He is in the driver's seat of our lives, He is then free to drive us to those green pastures and quiet waters.

With Him as #1, what's next? Here's a good progression that is both biblical and practical:

1. **God**
2. **Self**
3. **Husband**
4. **Kids**
5. **Extended family/Friends**
6. **Ministry/Work**

Spend some time alone with God and ask Him about this list. Is it right for you? Are there some adjustments you need to make in your life to reflect your convictions?

4. Read inspirational books

We are constantly being bombarded with a cacophony of images, words, advertising campaigns, media hype, political rhetoric, new age propaganda and materialistic philosophy. It's a wonder we haven't all turned into giant sponges trying to soak it all up. But there are a number of people on this planet whom God has touched deeply, who have listened intently to Him, experienced Him in profound ways and have been told by Him to tell others what they've learned. And these people have written *books*! No book written by a human will ever sufficiently replace the Book of God (the Bible), but we can still learn important lessons from men and women who have walked with God and written about it.

Ask a trusted friend that you know has a close relationship with God what they've been reading lately, and what they might recommend for you to read. Browse around a Christian book store and pick out a few books that look interesting to you. If your church has a book store or library, ask the person in charge what they would recommend. Look over the "*Additional Resources*" section (Appendix B) at the end of this manual, and see if there are some books that look like they could be helpful to you.

5. Lots of other ideas

Okay, this isn't just *one* principle, it's a *bunch* of them served smorgasbord-style. Without taking the time and space to expand on these suggestions, here is a list of ways you could also think about nurturing your spirit. Read over the list and ask God to speak to you about anything He might want you to pursue further.

- Meditate on and pray through the Scriptures in the "*Promise Pantry*" at the end of this manual (Appendix D).
- Keep forgiveness issues up to date (refer back to Chapter 4). What do you need to forgive others for? Do you need to seek forgiveness from others? If so, for what? Do you need to forgive yourself? If so, for what?
- Meditate on God's attributes.
- Meditate on who you are in Christ – your true identity (refer to Chapter 9).
- Keep a prayer journal. Ask God to give you Scripture promises, write them down, pray and meditate on them. Write down answers to your prayers, no matter how small or insignificant they might seem.
- Ask God to show you His perspective, to see things through His eyes.
- Enlist prayer intercessors. Put your best prayer warriors on active duty. Stay in close contact with them, and regularly let them know your prayer needs.
- Find a trusted spiritual mentor. Don't know where to find one? Ask God to bring one along and to let you know when she shows up!
- Serve others outside your home. But be careful not to do too much too fast. If you are already overwhelmed, don't add to your stress by taking on others' needs too.

❀ ❀ ❀❀ ❀ ❀

My Spirit-Nurture Contract

Starting within the next five days to two weeks (note when, exactly), I will make the following adjustments in my lifestyle, and/or add the following activities:

1. _____
2. _____
3. _____
4. _____

Share this plan with your Battle Buddy! See if she'll join you with a similar contract. Of course, feel free to write down more than four if you'd like to!

❀ ❀ ❀❀ ❀ ❀

Soul-Nurture

As we mentioned earlier, "soul" is the part of you that involves your will, your intellect, your understanding and your emotions. It's the essence of *you*. Everyone has a soul – in fact, you could say that everyone is a soul, created by God:

> *And the LORD God formed man of the dust of the ground, and breathed into his nostrils the breath of life; and man became a living soul.*
>
> **– Genesis 2:7**(KJV)

> *And so it is written, The first man Adam was made a living soul.*
>
> **– 1 Corinthians 15:45** (KJV)

Things you do that mold and stimulate your will, expand and challenge your intellect, deepen your understanding and help you to experience and savor your emotions – these are all things that constitute the nurturing of your soul. Beauty, love, truth, faith, hope, knowledge, wisdom, humility, fun, friendships, challenge, accomplishment, wonder – all these things feed our souls.

In this section, we're going to suggest some activities that will help you feed and nurture your soul. Of course, we encourage you to come up with activities on your own as well, but if you choose to do *nothing*, it would be like deciding to starve yourself to death. Your soul *needs* nourishment just as much as your body does.

1. Remember your strengths

God has endowed you with many strengths, skills, talents, blessings and gifts. You are a work of art! In fact, Ephesians 2:10 refers to us as God's "workmanship." The word used in the original Greek is *poiema* from which we get the English word "poem." In the stress, exhaustion and craziness of your life right now, you may forget that you are God's poem – far more eloquent, deep and full of meaning than anything ever written by Shakespeare! Remembering this should renew your focus and sense of worth. Regularly list strengths and blessings you notice about yourself and review them every night before bed, or in the morning in your Quiet Time with God.

? In fact, take a minute right now and list three things that you would consider strengths, skills, talents or gifts that you possess:

1. _____

2. _____

3. _____

2. Set personal boundaries and margin

Learn how to say "no" to busyness and unnecessary activities that drain your emotional tank. In Chapter 5 you learned how to set boundaries with your husband. You may need to set them with others as well. You may be a chronic "joiner" or the queen of "get-'er-done!" People know this about you and might often take advantage. As soon as there is a need – within your family, neighborhood, church, civic group – you are the first one they call. You are immediately on the scene, with the theme to the "Superman" movie playing in your mind. It's admirable that you are so willing to jump in and help out, but if you're constantly running on fumes, your body's natural boundary will force you to stop.

Here's an important motto to learn, love and live: **"THE NEED IS NOT THE CALL."** You are constantly surrounded by needs, but to see a need doesn't automatically mean that you are called to meet that need. Some probably, but definitely not all! Ask God for discernment to know which needs you are called to meet, and which ones you need to leave for others.

You know what a boundary is, but "margin" is a little different. According to Dr. Richard Swenson who wrote the book *Margin: Restoring Emotional, Physical, Financial, and Time Reserves to Overloaded Lives*, "Margin is the space that once existed between ourselves and our limits. It's something held in reserve for contingencies or unanticipated situations."[4] Today, most of us live right up against our limits, so if anything unplanned crowds in we're immediately *past* our limits and in trouble. As Dr. Swenson wrote:

> Marginless is being thirty minutes late to the doctor's office because you were twenty minutes late getting out of the bank because you were ten minutes late dropping the kids off at school because the car ran out of gas two blocks from the gas station – and you forgot your wallet. Margin, on the other hand, is having breath left at the top of the staircase, money left at the end of the month, and sanity left at the end of adolescence.[5]

3. Schedule personal R & R

Time is one of our most precious personal commodities. We're all given the same amount at the beginning of each day, but we are quickly relieved of it – sometimes willingly, sometimes at gunpoint. Usually, by the end of the day, week, month and year, the time ration for each period is long-gone, and we wish we'd had more. But here's a shocker: ultimately, *you* get to decide how it's used – within reason, of course. You may resent time that is reserved for the mundane (your job, laundry, vacuuming, changing diapers, etc.). And there are those unexpected time thieves (breakdowns, clogged toilets, tornados, meteors). But you are the sovereign queen over what's left! How do you want to spend it?

Pre-designate at least *some* of it for yourself. Feel guilty about that? Don't. Go back and read the second page of this chapter. *It's okay to take care of yourself!* It really is *just fine* to schedule some time to re-charge your soul's batteries. If you do, you'll feel better, act better, react better, and be better able to meet the needs to which you are called. Set aside personal time on a daily basis – you can find fifteen minutes somewhere, can't you? A quarter-hour to spend time reading God's Word or a book of poetry, perhaps pruning your roses, polishing your Harley – whatever! It's time for you to do whatever turns *your* crank.

Set aside an occasional half-day or day to do something you love. Sometimes you should schedule a day to do absolutely *nothing*. Once or twice a year, schedule a personal retreat of three to five days, during which you can totally relax, spend hours with your heavenly Father and get your emotional tanks filled and topped off. Stock up on some "Margin!" We call this "Cave Time" based on when God directed the prophet Elijah to do: spend some time alone in a cave after a stress-filled battle with 450 prophets of Baal and narrowly escaping from the bloodthirsty Jezebel (1 Kings 19:9). Elijah was depressed, discouraged, exhausted and felt like he was completely alone. It was in that place God spoke to him in a *"still, small voice"* (verse 12), re-energized him, and sent him off to his next assignment.

Put it on the calendar – soon! Almost certainly, if your "me time" doesn't get noted on the calendar, it won't happen!

4. Speak truth to yourself

As we mentioned earlier, the world, your flesh and the devil are constantly telling you lies about yourself. All too often we base our opinions of ourselves and our environment on those lies and experience despair and defeat because of it. Instead, we should listen to what our Creator says about us in His Word, and live in *those truths*! As was mentioned earlier, Chapter 9 will go more deeply into God's truths about you, but after you're read it, be sure to constantly remind yourself of those truths. Your soul is listening.

5. Play

No one needed to teach us how to play when we were kids. It came naturally. And we considered it a day ill-spent if we neglected to fulfill our quota of play. But now that we are adults – and the seriousness of life has closed in around us – many of us have forgotten how to play, and forgotten *how* life-giving and rejuvenating it is. Rebecca Radcliffe captures the therapeutic essence of play in her book, *Dance Naked in Your Living Room*:

> A good buddy to play with is a wonderful help when we are feeling bothered by things. The possibilities are many, but we need to get out and do something. It could be a round of golf, a friendly game of croquet, four-square (yes! what we played as kids!), tetherball, a tennis match, shooting hoops, bowling a few lanes, or tossing horseshoes. When we play with friends, we feel nurtured by their affection, their willingness to stand by us and their loyalty. If we feel like talking during our break, these buddies may give us a few words of wisdom. If not, we will return home later to deal with our problems, feeling *much* better from a healthy dose of joyful play.[6]

6. Get counseling

Prayerfully seek godly, professional help. The beneficial insight and feedback of someone who has been trained in what to look for, how to ask the right questions and make biblical suggestions can be invaluable in giving you a healing perspective on your situation. Even if your husband won't go, *you* go. You need to be assured that you aren't losing your mind. He or she can give you tools to help you and your husband to interact at home in healthy, life-giving ways. Here are Marshéle Waddell's observations regarding the counseling she received:

> I didn't want to just put a band-aid on the problem. Given the choice between merely minimizing the impact of PTSD versus trusting God in agreement with other believers for complete healing of my husband's heart and our family, I **chose the miraculous over the minimal**.

> I went to my counselor regularly for more than a year. This step in the process was a healing balm to my wounds. It gave me the motivation and the strength to educate myself about PTSD. I am reading everything I can get my hands on, being careful to look at all of it through the lens of scriptural principles. My own research is giving me the information and perspective I need to better understand my husband's pain, its source, its logic and its potential.

7. Check out something beautiful

God is a creative being and He's put within each of us a profound appreciation of creation and creativity. Much of the Psalms are rhapsodies of reaction to God's handiwork. Beauty feeds our souls. Be sure to schedule some "Beauty Appointments" to places where they keep the beautiful things: art galleries, museums, parks, churches, the oceanside, the mountains. Go alone, or with one of your closest friends – someone who isn't prone to being too "chatty." Don't hurry along, move slowly and deliberately, absorbing the beauty, appreciating the uniqueness of each creation, the genius, the detail. If you have an artsy side to you, think of ways that you could be a creator of beauty. One of your first palettes could be your home. What can you do to make your home a place of beauty?

8. Beware of the traps

When overdone, all forms of self-medicating lead to soul-starving issues. We can justify or rationalize our behavior to a point, but eventually the Holy Spirit will take action and remind us we belong to Him. He loves us too much to just let us go tripping merrily toward the edge of the cliff.

Some efforts to self-medicate affect the body (smoking, drugs, alcohol), while others deeply affect the soul, such as pornography, infidelity and emotional affairs. All of them enslave. If you find yourself being pulled in by any of these traps, if you feel they are starting to control your life, don't try to fight them alone. This is where you've got to call in reinforcements – your Battle Buddy, your parents, close friends, a doctor, counselor, pastor, chaplain. Satan would rather you stay isolated, so he'll play on your sense of shame to keep you quiet. But it'll only get worse. This is why God gave us friends and spiritual allies.

> *Two are better than one, because they have a good return for their work: If one falls down, his friend can help him up. But pity the man who falls and has no one to help him up! Also, if two lie down together, they will keep warm. But how can one keep warm alone? Though one may be overpowered, two can defend themselves. A cord of three strands is not quickly broken.*
> **– Ecclesiastes 4:9-12**

9. Brainstorming

The University of Minnesota on their University Counseling & Consulting Services web site has listed "101 Strategies for Coping with Stress." For the whole list, go to www.uccs.umn.edu/oldsite/lasc/handouts/copingstress.html. Following are just a few – maybe this list will prompt you to think of even more …

- Stop living in the future/past
- Write a journal of your daily activities, thoughts and moods
- List your successes
- Set goals realistically
- Make friends with people who like themselves
- Express yourself
- Take a continuing education course
- Stop collecting people with problems
- Learn to accept what you cannot change
- Develop your personal talents

- Do something exciting
- Focus on one task at a time
- Develop a varied life
- Stop feeling sorry for yourself
- Stop looking for someone to blame
- Stop assuming others can't get along without you
- Start delegating responsibilities
- Sing
- Redefine your priorities

❀ ❀ ❀❀ ❀ ❀

My Soul-Nurture Contract

 Starting within the next five days to two weeks (note when, exactly), I will make the following adjustments in my lifestyle, and/or add the following activities:

1. _____

2. _____

3. _____

4. _____

 Again, share this plan with your Battle Buddy! See if she'll join you with a similar contract. There is no set limit so write down more than four if you'd like!

❀ ❀ ❀❀ ❀ ❀

Body-Nurture

Posttraumatic Stress Disorder and Secondary Traumatic Stress are formally classified as "anxiety disorders," but we gather from their names that they're all about *stress*. As in *too much of it!* Researchers define stress as a physical, mental or emotional response to events that cause bodily or mental tension. Simply put, stress is any outside force or event that has an effect on our body or mind – which can be good or bad. Stress releases powerful neurochemicals and hormones that prepare us for action (to fight or flee). Prolonged, uninterrupted, unexpected and unmanageable stresses are the most damaging.[7] If you're married to a Combat Trauma sufferer, this probably describes your situation to a "T." If not dealt with, emotional stress *will* accumulate and eventually manifest itself physically in ways that are not pleasant. Your immune system will be suppressed, muscle tension and soreness will increase, digestion problems will ensue, fatigue will deepen, you'll desire exercise even *less* and you'll begin spiraling into a depressing, sedentary lifestyle that will rob you of so much of the true *joy* and *life* God wants you to experience.

Going to war or being married to a combat vet are not the only doorways for a stressful experience – there are plenty of stressors in normal 21st century life. Up to 90 percent of doctor visits in the USA may be prompted by stress-related illness, according to the Centers for Disease Control and Prevention.[8] Excess stress is found from sea to shining sea, but add *combat-related stress* to the mix and you've got some *real* stress! Here are four proactive ways you can reduce stress in your body – and since there is such a strong bond between your body and your mind, they will positively affect your mental/emotional state as well.

1. Get some exercise!

Exercise is one of the most effective ways to deal with stress, and yet 75 percent of Americans do not engage in regular physical exercise, and over 30 percent are completely sedentary. And what does this couch-potato existence produce? Of the three most common lifestyle-based killers in America today, number two is poor nutrition and number three is lack of exercise, which add up to overweight and obesity (Centers for Disease Control 2003). So exercise will not only relieve stress, it will also protect you from chronic disease, help you live longer and improve your quality of life.

What happens when I exercise?

Flexing and stretching your muscles, getting your heart and lungs working a little harder, rising to a physical challenge – these trigger beneficial responses all over your body. Your immune and endocrine systems get fired up; helpful antibodies are released; your white blood cell count increases; extra adrenaline and growth hormone is released; serotonin (a depression reducer) uptake is increased; pleasure-inducing hormones like beta-endorphin are released in the brain, creating the euphoria most people feel during and after exercise. Testosterone levels rise in both men and women, and though it's actually a stressor because it calls upon the body to mount a response similar to fight or flee, it does so in a healthy way (don't worry – it's not enough to make you grow a mustache).

Exercise is also a mood-improver, especially for people with major depression. Clinical studies have shown that exercise promotes positive moods, a sense of meaning in life and improves self-esteem. It will actually lower the concentration of stress hormones in your body.[9]

What should I do?

There are two kinds of exercise: *aerobic* ("with oxygen") and *anaerobic* ("without oxygen"). *Both* are good for you in different ways …

Aerobic exercise builds up the cardiopulmonary system (heart, lungs, blood vessels). It includes activities that use large muscle groups, can be maintained for an extended period of time and is rhythmic in nature. Every time you do an aerobic exercise and increase your heart rate appreciably, your body adapts by strengthening your heart and lungs, and creating more capillaries in your muscles and more alveoli in your lungs to distribute oxygen more efficiently throughout your body. Consistent aerobic exercise will reduce body fat and improve weight control, lower resting blood pressure and heart rate, increase your HDL (good) cholesterol, decrease LDL (bad) cholesterol, decrease symptoms of anxiety, tension and depression, enhance your muscles' ability to use oxygen and increase your threshold for muscle fatigue.

Anaerobic exercise builds muscle mass, strength and tone and includes activities of short duration and high intensity which can be sustained up to two minutes. The metabolic processes involved in anaerobic exercise do not require oxygen; they use energy sources that are stored in your muscles. But this process produces lactic acid – the stuff that makes a sprinter's muscles tie up at the end of a race – which is why you can't maintain that intensity for very long (your body quickly filters the lactic acid out, however). Anaerobic exercise strengthens your bones, improves your body's ability to utilize oxygen (improves your max VO2), increases your endurance and ability to fight fatigue, and benefits your heart and lungs. In the long run, increased muscle mass helps a person become leaner and lose weight because muscle uses large amounts of calories – even while you sleep![10]

Choose a variety of exercises – don't get stuck in a rut! Make exercise fun – not a chore. One way to add to the fun and accountability, which we all need, is to find a workout partner (how about your Battle Buddy?). Here is a list of different types of exercises you should consider. Mix them up!

Aerobic Exercises	Anaerobic Exercises
Walking	Weight lifting
Running	Sprinting
Race walking	Interval training/Fartlek
Swimming	Jumping rope
Cycling	Fast or uphill cycling
Aerobics/Dancing	Hill walking/climbing
Racquetball/Tennis	Any rapid burst of hard exercise

Pilates training (elements of both)

Kick-boxing/ Martial arts (elements of both)

As you construct your exercise plan, keep the **FITT** principles in mind:

Frequency: For aerobic exercise: minimum of three days a week with no more than two days off between sessions. Gradually work your way up to 5 or 6 days per week. For anaerobic exercise: every-other day maximum. For weight lifting, you could alternate upper body and lower body on consecutive days. Give yourself at least 1 to 2 days off from all exercise each week.

Intensity: Aerobic exercise should be "moderate" – not too easy, not too hard. About 60 to 85 percent of your "maximum heart rate" would be perfect. To determine what this would be for you based on your resting heart rate and your age, use the calculator at www.sparkpeople. com/resource/calculator_target.asp. Anaerobic exercise will make you sore at first, but after a couple of weeks that will subside. Afterwards, muscle *fatigue* will be normal after a workout, but if you're still getting sore, you may be working too hard. A good "norm" for weight lifting: 4 to 6 exercises each session, 3 or 4 sets of 10 repetitions per exercise. If that's too easy, increase the weight next time. Always do an aerobic warm up and stretching before doing anaerobic exercises.

Time: For aerobic exercise, aim for sustaining your moderate heart rate for a minimum of 20 minutes per session. Gradually work up to 60 minutes over time. For every minute you sustain your exercise over 20, you're putting money in the bank – burning more calories and building more endurance! For anaerobic exercise, start with a 15- to 20-minute session, eventually working up to 45 to 60 minutes.

Type: Much of your plan will depend on how much time you can dedicate to it. Ideally, a target time of up to two hours is appropriate for a combined aerobic and anaerobic workout. This, however, could be beyond what most women can schedule. If you could alternate days – 45 to 60 minutes of aerobic one day, and 45 to 60 minutes of anaerobic the next, for six days and then a day of rest – you would have an excellent program! If you can manage more, all the better!

2. *Get some sleep!*

When a person is deprived of normal sleep, all kinds of difficulties can crop up:

- Aching muscles
- Blurred vision
- Clinical depression
- Accident prone
- Dizziness
- Irritability
- Hypertension

- Slow reaction time
- Daytime drowsiness
- Decreased concentration
- Weakened immune system
- Headache
- Memory lapses
- Slurred speech

- Loss of sexual desire
- Loss of appetite
- Digestion problems
- Suppressed growth hormones
- Obesity

According to the National Highway Traffic Safety Administration, over 100,000 traffic accidents each year in the USA alone are caused by fatigue and drowsiness. During the 20th century, average sleep time per night for Americans dropped by 20 percent from the previous century. We have added 158 hours to our yearly working and commuting time since 1969.[11] Again, sleep deprivation is a big problem for a large percentage of Americans already stressed-out – how much more for the wife of a combat veteran dealing with the additional stress of war on the homefront?

Stages of Sleep

Every night you progress through four to seven "sleep cycles," with each one lasting 90 to 120 minutes and containing five stages:[12]

Stage 1: Transition between wakefulness and sleep. It lasts about 1 to 5 minutes for most people. It may take you a long time to "fall" into this first stage, but you won't stay here long. You'll spend a cumulative total of 2 to 5 percent of your night in Stage 1 sleep.

Stage 2: Baseline sleep, occupying about 45 to 50 percent of your sleep. From this level you'll skip back-and-forth between the other stages of sleep.

Stages 3 & 4: Delta sleep or "slow wave" sleep (because brainwave activity slows down dramatically, almost like you're in a coma). These stages last 15 to 30 minutes and are the deepest and most restorative stage of sleep physically. Your body's immune system goes to work on repairing the day's damage, the endocrine glands secrete growth hormone and blood is sent deep into the muscles to be reconditioned.

Stage 5: REM sleep (for "Rapid Eye Movement"). A very active stage, composing 20 to 25 percent of a normal night's sleep. The sleeper's eyes jerk around quickly as if he's watching a movie behind his eyelids – and he is, in fact, as this is the stage in which vivid dreams occur. This is the most mentally and emotionally restorative stage of sleep during which you process emotions, retain memories and relieve stress.

Planning for better sleep

The quicker and easier you fall asleep, the fewer times your sleep cycles will be interrupted. And the more time you spend in Stages 3, 4 & 5 the better you will feel and the better you will cope with your current stress load. Here are some tips for becoming a better sleeper:[13]

- **TV/Laptop-free zone.** Ideally, the bed is for two things and two things only. (You know what we mean.) If you get involved in other activities when you get into bed, such as watching TV or working, you're not sending your body the message that it's time for sleep.

- **A cool, dark room.** Lower temperature and lack of light is a signal to your pineal gland to kick up melatonin production (a natural relaxant your body makes) and ferry you off to slumber land.

- **White noise.** This refers to sounds that cover a broad range of frequencies and negate or drown out other sounds. The sound of a river, the ocean surf, wind blowing through the trees, an electric fan – these are all white noise producers. There are many companies that sell white noise CDs that can be played all night. When you have white noise playing gently in your bedroom, your sleep will be interrupted less frequently and you'll spend more time in Delta and REM sleep.

- **Shut them out.** If you're still having trouble with too much light or noise in your bedroom, buy some good ear plugs and either a sleep mask or window shades.

- **A good mattress.** You know that you spend a third of your life in bed, right? So why scrimp on the most vital piece of equipment involved in that pursuit? Get the absolute best one you can afford. Good pillows, too.

- **A good rhythm.** Our bodies like rhythms. If you can get yourself into a consistent sleep/wake pattern you will have much more efficient pillow time. Try to turn off the light at the same time each evening, and set your alarm to wake yourself up at the same time each morning – even on weekends. After a while your sleep cycles will adjust and you'll be nicely finishing up your last cycle just before your alarm goes off.

- **Bedtime rituals.** Think of a series of activities you could perform every night to get your body and mind thinking, "Bed … sleep … rest." Reading a chapter in the Bible, praying with your husband, sitting quietly in your living room by the light of a candle, having a cup of tea or glass of warm milk, walking into your back yard and looking at the night sky, writing in your journal …

- **Calming teas.** There are a number of herbal teas that have been clinically proven to contain compounds that will relax your body and mind. Some of the best are: Chamomile, Passion Flower, Valerian, Ashwagandha, Lemon Balm and Lavender.[14]

- **No booze.** Many people think that alcohol helps them sleep – and it does have a tendency to cause drowsiness so that sleep comes more quickly than normal. But before long it wakes you up again and you'll have trouble getting back to sleep. Alcohol is a depressant which can increase nightmares and aggravate an already depressed state. Try to avoid it for a couple of hours before bedtime.

- **No caffeine.** Coffee, some teas, some chocolate (there's only a tiny bit of caffeine in chocolate but some companies add extra) – avoid these at least six hours before bedtime.

3. Eat right!

A man walked into a doctor's office and said, "Doc! I'm sick! Can you help me?"

The doctor looked at him and noticed that he had a french fry sticking out of one nostril, a green bean sticking out of his right ear, a carrot in his left ear and oatmeal in his hair.

"I can see one thing right off," the doctor said. "You're not eating right."

Are you eating right? People who are stressed will often adopt unhealthy lifestyle patterns – sometimes as a defense/coping mechanism, sometimes out of fatigue, sometimes as a quest for comfort. This is nowhere more apparent than in the altered diets of trauma sufferers. The anxiety hormone cortisol makes stressed people crave foods high in fat, sugar and salt. Or they skip meals due to lack of appetite or lack of time. They settle for fast food or easily prepared, highly processed, calorie-loaded foods. They mindlessly munch on junk food snacks, even when they're not really hungry. They forget to drink water – or think that the soda, coffee and wine they drink provide sufficient hydration. Self-medicating with excessive caffeine, sugary foods and drinks, alcohol or drugs might seem like a useful quick fix for some symptoms, but in the long run they only make things worse.

It all adds up to what computer programmers call GIGO: "Garbage In, Garbage Out" and these habits greatly diminish the ability to cope with stress.

Your best bet is a simple one: be intentional about eating regular, healthy meals. Having a good breakfast, a sensible lunch and a small dinner is best – opposite of what most Americans subscribe to, unfortunately. As a traumatic stress sufferer, your appetite may have totally flown the coop, and sitting down to a big meal seems ludicrous. Consider eating 5 or 6 small meals spread throughout the day consisting of tasty but nutritious foods and snacks like fresh fruit and vegetables, salad, cheese, yogurt, kefir, whole-grain breads and crackers, baked or grilled lean meats and fish, whole-grain pasta, fruit and vegetable juices (the *real* stuff, not juice boxes), nuts and seeds. If you can be disciplined about it, there are a lot of good antioxidants in dark chocolate – but limit yourself to one ounce a day!

And don't let yourself get stuck in a rut, eating the same kind of food all the time. Mix it up, in order to get a wider variety of vitamins and nutrients.

Vitamins & minerals

Under normal circumstances, you can absorb most of the vitamins and minerals you need from the foods you eat – *if* you're eating healthy! And since most people living in a crisis situation don't pay much attention to proper nutrition, you'll do yourself a big favor by taking a vitamin and mineral supplement. A simple once-a-day pill should be sufficient, but you might also want to take some additional vitamin C to boost your immune system a bit. Here are some tips from the Mayo Clinic about what to choose:[15]

- **Avoid supplements that provide 'megadoses.'** In general, choose a multivitamin-mineral supplement that provides about 100 percent of the Daily Value (DV) of all the vitamins and minerals, rather than one which has, for example, 500 percent of the DV for one vitamin and only 20 percent of the DV for another. Anything over 100 percent DV your body probably won't utilize anyway. The exception to this is calcium. You may notice that calcium-containing supplements don't provide 100 percent of the DV. If they did, the tablets would be too large to swallow.
- **Look for 'USP' on the label.** This ensures that the supplement meets the standards for strength, purity, disintegration and dissolution established by the testing organization U.S. Pharmacopeia (USP).
- **Look for expiration dates.** Dietary supplements can lose potency over time, especially in hot and humid climates. If a supplement doesn't have an expiration date, don't buy it. If your supplements have expired, discard them. "When in doubt, throw it out!"
- **Store all vitamin and mineral supplements safely.** Store dietary supplements in a dry, cool place. Avoid hot, humid storage locations, such as in the bathroom. Keep them out of the reach of small children – even the "child proof" containers.

Most women need extra calcium as well. When shopping for calcium read the label and find a supplement that tells you how much "elemental calcium" is contained in each pill – not just the total weight of the calcium. You should be getting 1,000 mg (milligrams) of elemental calcium each day (on the label: Percent Daily Value or Percent DV). So if the label says "250 mg elemental calcium" or "25 percent DV calcium," you know you need to take four of those pills per day (at different times of the day, to aid absorption). Avoid calcium supplements that contain unrefined oyster shell, bone meal or dolomite. These products may also contain toxic substances, such as lead, mercury and arsenic.[16]

Binge eating

When a person is depressed, he or she will sometimes seek comfort by "binge eating" – consuming an entire package of cookies, half-gallon of ice cream, jumbo bag of potato chips, etc., at one sitting. The comfort seems real but is very temporary. If it becomes frequent or chronic, it can result in obesity, diabetes, high blood pressure, high cholesterol levels, gallbladder disease, heart disease and certain types of cancer. Besides all this, there are the psychological complications of guilt feelings, self-disgust, a preoccupation with appearance and the tendency to miss work, school or social gatherings to binge – or simply because they feel ashamed of themselves.[17]

All of us will binge-eat occasionally (remember last Thanksgiving?), but if you find yourself doing it more than once a week, it's a problem for which you should get some help. As with all problems, bring it first of all to God and ask for His help, insight and direction as to what to do. There are several therapeutic approaches you could take, including cognitive-behavioral therapy, interpersonal psychotherapy (examining your relationships and making changes in problem areas), self-help groups and treatment with medications such as antidepressants. One thing for you to know about binge eating: *you are not alone.* There are many who struggle with it, and there is a *big* God who wants to help you with it!

4. Go see a doctor!

Many people avoid doctors until they're sick enough to really *need* one. But there are three reasons why you should see your doctor on a regular basis – especially when you are dealing with the load of stress that comes with living with a Combat Trauma sufferer:

Prevention

Your doctor can help you recognize unhealthy aspects of your lifestyle and be a great source of advice on how to make the right choices to keep you healthy. If your doctor is aware of your family history and finds a tendency toward certain diseases, he or she can recommend medication or lifestyle changes that can help you avoid what your genes want to do to you.

Screening

Using tests to find problems at an early stage can help you avoid complications later – especially the biggest of all complications: death. Proper screening can often pick up on developing conditions even before they present symptoms. Early treatment facilitates effectiveness, fewer side effects and a greater chance of a successful outcome. And since you probably don't know what your potential problems are, or what tests might be available, it's vital that you develop a good relationship with your doctor who can figure these things out!

Treatment

When you *know* you're having problems, *go*! Don't try to be Superwoman and – once again – stuff your needs for the sake of your husband or kids. *Do not delay:* if it's something serious, every day you wait could make your problem worse and harder to treat. And when you receive directions about what to do, follow those directions! Take your medicine; do your exercises; go to the therapist! That doctor paid good money to become qualified to give you advice – don't let his or her education go to waste! As we've mentioned before, "You're no good to anybody dead!"

Body-Nurture: Conclusion

It is very common that most caregivers – whether they are professionals in the medical field, counselors, crisis responders, or a spouse taking care of a mate or child – will tend to neglect their own needs so that they can put more of themselves into the care of those who need them. Hopefully, you have seen how this may be helpful and even noble in the short-run, but eventually it will backfire. Remember that you are a human, subject to the same frailties all humans are, and therefore required to take care of yourself. In addition, 1 Corinthians 6:19 proclaims that "*Your body is a temple of the Holy Spirit.*" You don't want God's temple getting all run-down and dilapidated, do you? Each of us needs to work on temple maintenance!

My Body-Nurture Contract

 Starting within the next five days to two weeks (note when, exactly), I will make the following adjustments in my lifestyle, and/or add the following activities:

1. _____

2. _____

3. _____

4. _____

 Same routine: Share this plan with your Battle Buddy! Ask if she'll join you with a similar contract.

Conclusion

There are many things in your life that are beyond your ability to control right now which adds greatly to your stress and anxiety. But there are *some* things you can control. You probably thought about a number of them as you read through this chapter. Stop despairing over what you *can't* do and start getting excited about what you can do! As stress expert Dr. Joan Borysenko has written, "Every day brings a choice: to practice stress or to practice peace."[18] *You* must choose!

Christina's Prayer ...

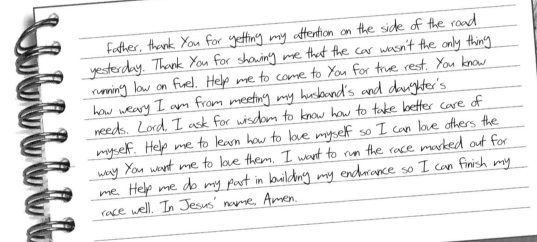

Father, thank You for getting my attention on the side of the road yesterday. Thank You for showing me that the car wasn't the only thing running low on fuel. Help me to come to You for true rest. You know how weary I am from meeting my husband's and daughter's needs. Lord, I ask for wisdom to know how to take better care of myself. Help me to learn how to love myself so I can love others the way You want me to love them. I want to run the race marked out for me. Help me do my part in building my endurance so I can finish my race well. In Jesus' name, Amen.

Promise from God's Word ...

> *Now may the God of peace Himself sanctify you entirely;*
> *and may your spirit and soul and body be preserved complete,*
> *without blame at the coming of our Lord Jesus Christ.*
> *Faithful is He who calls you, and He also will bring it to pass.*
> **– 1 Thessalonians 5:23,24**

8 WHO CARES?
Seeking and Finding Your Support Network

Danielle's Journal ...

I'm not sure how this happened, but I'm pretty positive my hard head had a lot to do with it. I'm flat on my back in the bed, unable to do much of anything without extreme pain. I won't be off to any races any time soon.

Katie and Allison offered to help me rearrange my family room before Michael returns from the field. We had agreed to tackle this project together while our kids were at school. In my stubbornness, I proudly pushed and pulled couches and end tables around by myself until midnight last night. Today I'm paying the man.

When Michael was deployed the first time, I had to step up and take on all his jobs and responsibilities here at the house. When he came back with Combat Trauma, and wasn't quite able to resume his duties around here like before, it became obvious that I would have to cover them a lot longer than I first thought. And for the most part, I'm doing it. But I fight the temptation every day of becoming an overly self-confident, I-don't-need-you-or-anyone-else Jill-of-all-trades. What I think is that my own competence at times surprises even me. I prize my favorite coffee mug inscribed, "Army Wife: The toughest job in the Army." I drink out of it every chance I get. It strokes my inclination to keep believing that I can do it all, independent of anyone else.

I think it's hilarious that Uncle Sam refers to military wives as "dependents." It's ironic that independence is demanded of us dependents! Every time Daddy laces up his desert boots and deploys, Mom must fill two pairs of shoes, his and hers, as his walk away.

My real challenge is not being a dependent or even an independent dependent. When will I learn that I must be an interdependent, one who is willing to accept the help offered to me, or (gasp!) to ask for help when I need it?

My impatient pride has all but paralyzed me. Now that the stress of PTSD has intensified the demands of typical military life for us, I have to admit that my Lone Ranger days have come to an end.

Bridges To Healing

Throughout this manual we have stressed that God is the Healer (Exodus 15:26) – for your husband, your children and for you. But because we live in a fallen world with its various complexities, traps, weaknesses and land mines, no healing is quick and easy. It is a process that moves forward when the environment surrounding a person's woundedness gives God maximum access to his or her soul. We've shared many practical measures you can take to facilitate that, but one of the most effective – and least used – has to do with other people. If you are able to find a few friends who *do* care, and are Spirit-filled, Spirit-directed, unselfish servants of God who want to help, you have found gold! We call these **"Bridge People."** When we get into trouble, God *expects* us to help each other out. There is safety and strength in numbers – even if it's only one or two others. Here's a passage we shared with you in the previous chapter, but in a different translation:

> *Two people are better off than one, for they can help each other succeed. If one person falls, the other can reach out and help. But someone who falls alone is in real trouble. Likewise, two people lying close together can keep each other warm. But how can one be warm alone? A person standing alone can be attacked and defeated, but two can stand back-to-back and conquer. Three are even better, for a triple-braided cord is not easily broken.*

– Ecclesiastes 4:9-12 (NLT)

> When you're weary, feeling small,
> When tears are in your eyes,
> I will dry them all.
> I'm on your side
> When times get rough
> And friends just can't be found –
> Like a bridge over troubled water
> I will lay me down.
>
> – Paul Simon[1]

Battle Buddies. You probably already have at least one Bridge Person in your life – the Battle Buddy you've been sharing some of your assignments with. You could probably consider your Battle Buddy as a "top of the list" Bridge Person – someone you trust implicitly, who has demonstrated uncommon loyalty and commitment to you, and who you know "has your back" at all times. A Battle Buddy would meet all the criteria of a Bridge Person but show an even deeper level of responsiveness to you. But besides this Battle Buddy, you will want to find many more Bridge People.

Friends of faith

When you get the chance, read Mark 2:1-12. This is the story of a paralyzed man and four of his Bridge People. The word had gotten around that Jesus was healing people at a certain house in Capernaum. These four men immediately thought of their paralyzed friend. They knew there was no way he could get there, so they rushed to his house, put him on a stretcher and carried him to Jesus. Unfortunately, they weren't the only ones who had heard about the Healer. The house was crammed full of people and surrounded by hundreds more. The four men cared too much about their incapacitated friend to give up and go home. They hoisted him up on top of the house, tore up the roof and lowered him through the hole down to Jesus! They would not be denied. Then Jesus – *seeing the faith of his friends* – healed the paralyzed man immediately.

There are faith-filled people who want to do that for you – if you'll let them. Some military wives have adopted the macho image of their husbands, trying to be self-sufficient and in need of no one's help. But, if your pride isn't getting in the way, you know that you *do* need some help right now – just like Danielle expressed in her journal. There's no shame in needing and seeking help – every one of us does from time to time. The shame goes to the one who doesn't seek it, preferring to remain proud but forever paralyzed.

> Think where man's glory most begins and ends, and say, "My glory was I had such friends."
>
> – William Yeats

These Bridge People may be old friends, or you may not know who they are at this time. You might not even have met them yet. But they're nearby, motivated by their love for God and their love for you. In this chapter we'll give you some ideas about what to look for and how to get them started.

The four men in the story did not heal their friend – Jesus did. But would the healing have taken place had the men not taken the initiative and altered their friend's environment so that it included Jesus? What does this fact make you think about your current situation and the potential "roof demolishers" you have in your life?

God invented Bridges

There is an obvious principle of Bible interpretation that says, "If it's in God's Word, it's in God's will." As you read the following verses, would you say it is God's will that we should be Bridge People for each other?

Now we who are strong ought to bear the weaknesses of those without strength and not just please ourselves.

– Romans 15:1

Bear one another's burdens, and thereby fulfill the law of Christ.

– Galatians 6:2

Always be humble and gentle. Be patient with each other, making allowance for each other's faults because of your love.

– Ephesians 4:2 (NLT)

Be kind and compassionate to one another, forgiving each other, just as in Christ God forgave you.

– Ephesians 4:32 (NIV)

Confess your sins to one another, and pray for one another so that you may be healed.

– James 5:16

What can we expect from a Bridge Person?

The Bridge People we're talking about in this chapter are people who will help transport us to God, so that He can provide healing. In many ways, they are representatives of His, ambassadors, messengers and liaisons. The following Scriptures will give you some insight as to how a properly-functioning Bridge Person can help you get closer to God. As you read through them, answer the questions asked after each verse.

 A friend loves at all times, and a brother is born for adversity.

– Proverbs 17:17

There are probably a few people to whom you could say, "For better or worse, I'm on your side. Even if you're wrong, I'm still on your side. I've got your back, no matter what." You would consider it an honor to aid them, right? Write down their names:

There are people who feel the same way about you. If you were to list them now, that list would probably be quite similar to the one you just wrote. If any of your friends were in a jam, you'd come to their aid in a heartbeat, wouldn't you? And wouldn't you be upset with them if they concealed from you that they were having trouble, keeping you from putting yourself out for them?

The Point: *Expect* your Bridges to be eager to help you out. They *want to!* Don't hesitate to call on them.

In everything I did, I showed you that by this kind of hard work we must help the weak, remembering the words the Lord Jesus himself said: 'It is more blessed to give than to receive.'

– Acts 20:35 (NIV)

If you're an unselfish person, you would rather give than receive, right? How do you normally act when you have to be the receiver?

So, if you're reluctant to receive, that means you're reluctant to allow your friends to give – which means you are robbing them of a blessing! How can you *live* with yourself?!?

The Point: Don't be a thief! Provide the opportunity for your friends to be blessed by allowing them to give to you.

❀ ❀ ❀❀ ❀ ❀

Understand this, my dear brothers and sisters: You must all be quick to listen, slow to speak, and slow to get angry.

– James 1:19 (NIV)

From this, what would you say a Bridge friend should be good at?

As was mentioned in previous chapters, one of the practices that will help you in your healing is to process your traumatic memories in a safe environment. In other words, you need to *talk* about them. A good Bridge will be a good listener. If they're constantly interrupting you in order to tell *their* story, or if they are freaked out by what you share and keep trying to change the subject, then they probably aren't the one to talk to at the deeper levels.

The Point: Expect a good Bridge Person to be a good listener.

❀ ❀ ❀❀ ❀ ❀

As iron sharpens iron, so a friend sharpens a friend.

– Proverbs 27:17 (NIV)

What does this verse say a Bridge friend will do for you?

What do you think it means for one person to sharpen another?

Sharpening is an intentional process – a knife doesn't sharpen itself. So a good Bridge will take the initiative, reaching out and proactively helping you improve your healing environment. By the way, sharpening is not always pleasant for the knife – sparks fly, it gets real hot, and some of its best cutting-edge material is ground off! In the same way, your Bridge friend may not always stroke your ego just the way you'd like. You may have some nicks and burrs that need to be smoothed out. Be ready for it, and receive it in the same manner in which it's offered: in love.

The Point: Expect a Bridge to be intentional, looking for ways to help you improve your healing environment – some of which might create a few sparks.

❀ ❀ ❀❀ ❀ ❀

An open rebuke is better than hidden love! Wounds from a sincere friend are better than many kisses from an enemy.

– Proverbs 27:5,6 (NLT)

If you had a cancerous tumor, would you prefer that your doctor use a scalpel in the appropriate area, or just say a lot of nice things to you?

Sometimes it hurts to hear the truth, doesn't it? But truth is like medicine – it tastes bad but it's *good* for you! Sometimes we get mad at people when they tell us a distasteful truth. But a true Bridge friend won't care. They are willing to risk their friendship with you, hurting you if necessary, in order to help you in your healing process.

Think back to some of the most influential people in your life. Perhaps it was a parent, a coach, a teacher, a friend, a doctor. Write a couple of their names here:

No doubt you felt the love and respect they held for you. But wasn't there another element in each case? Weren't they also people who were willing to tell you some hard truths? Didn't they get a little tough on you from time to time? When you needed somebody to ruffle your feathers a bit, weren't they willing to volunteer for the honor?

The Point: A good Bridge is willing to risk your friendship in order to open your eyes to a vital truth you may not know.

But encourage one another day after day, as long as it is still called "Today," so that none of you will be hardened by the deceitfulness of sin.

– Hebrews 3:13

Yes, you need to know the hard truths. *But* … you also need that input strongly balanced by a good dose of encouragement. You need to surround yourself with people who are positive and supportive – people who "day after day" catch you doing something right. No one has ever died from receiving too much encouragement, and you won't be the first.

What is something that you need to hear? Write down a piece of encouragement that you have not been receiving lately …

Prayer Assignment: Bring this up with God. Let Him know that you need for Him to bring others around you who will communicate those encouraging words.

Notice something else about that verse. It tells us two things about sin: It *hardens* us and it's *deceitful*. Sin has the same effect on your conscience that a garden trowel has on your hand. The rubbing hurts at first, but after a while a callus forms and it doesn't bother you any more. Sin works the same way. It'll sting your conscience the first few times but, if you keep at it long enough, the discomfort will fade. Then you'll figure it's okay, since you don't feel bad about it anymore. But that's when it's easiest for Satan to slip in his poison daggers – when you can't feel it.

However, if you've got good, positive, salt-and-light-sharing Bridges around you, God's Spirit in them can throw a spotlight on your errors and sins and draw you back to the Father long after you've turned down the Spirit's volume knob in your life.

The Point: Expect massive doses of encouragement from your Bridge friend, but also be open to their kind, corrective influence to keep your heart soft to God's conviction of sin in your life.

The BEST Bridge Person ability: Availability

As you try to identify Bridge People in your life, realize that they don't have to be experts in counseling, psychiatry, medicine or grief management. They don't need Ph.D.s. They just need to be willing to be *there*. Rabbi Harold Kushner, author of *When Bad Things Happen To Good People,* made this observation about some effective Bridge People in his life:

> At some of the darkest moments of my life, some people I thought of as friends deserted me – some because they cared about me and it hurt them to see me in pain; others because I reminded them of their own vulnerability, and that was more than they could handle. But real friends overcame their discomfort and came to sit with me. If they had no words to make me feel better, they sat in silence (much better than saying, "You'll get over it," or "it's not so bad; others have it worse."), and I loved them for it.[2]

❦ ❦ ❦❦ ❦ ❦

A formalized Bridge relationship

It's perfectly alright to carry on a "casual" relationship with people you have identified as Bridge People in your life. You don't *have* to tell them what they are to you. On the other hand, if you've become acquainted with someone who is spiritually mature, compassionate, resourceful and insightful, and they've expressed to you that they *want* to be more intentional about helping you, you may want to pursue a more formal Bridge relationship with her.

If they aren't aware of the "Bridge Person" concept, perhaps you could tell them about it or give them a copy of this manual. They may have been the one who gave *you* this manual, and in that case, they probably know a lot about how to be a Bridge for you (assuming they've read it!).

One of the main things that causes any relationship to self-destruct is "uncommunicated expectations." One person has a set of expectations that the other knows nothing about, and when they aren't met, the pin gets pulled on the friendship grenade. So if you plan to formalize your relationship, it would be a good idea to ask her the following questions:

❑ How much do you understand about Combat Trauma?

❑ Are you willing to learn more about it?

❑ Are you aware of the difficulties my husband and I are having because of his Combat Trauma?

❑ Are you aware of how it is affecting me?

❑ Are you willing to put up with my mood swings, my depression, my anger, my carnality, and not be judgmental toward me?

❑ Would you be willing to pray for me every day?

❑ Would you be willing to do *more* than pray for me?

❑ Would you be willing to balance the encouragement I need from you with the hard truths I may need to hear from you as well, as God leads you to share them?

❑ Can I trust you not to pass on anything I share with you in confidence – that *nothing* goes beyond you, even for the sake of "prayer concerns" shared with others?

❑ Do you really understand what I need from you?

What I Need From You

If she's honest, she'll probably answer that last question in the negative. That's when you can whip out the "*What I Need From You*" piece that you'll have ready to give her. You'll find it in the back of this manual as Appendix C, starting on page 235. This is a set of reproducible pages that you can copy as many times as you need to and give them to anyone who has expressed that they really want to help. It will give a brief explanation of Combat Trauma, help them to better understand the struggles you're experiencing, and give them some specific information about how they can become part of your support network. After your friend has had a chance to read it, get together and discuss it with her. Look over the commitments she is willing to make – and unable to make – and be sure you understand what both of you are committing to. After you've gone over the piece together, let your Bridge keep it, to remind her what you need, and how she agreed to try to help you.

This isn't something that you would want to give to just anybody. It must be someone who you know is "safe" and won't violate confidences – someone who has earned the right to be considered trustworthy and faithful.

Take a few minutes right now and look over the "*What I Need From You*" piece in Appendix C so that you can become familiar with it. You'll notice that after each statement, it gives your potential Bridge Person the opportunity to check a box or two if they agree with it. Point that out as you give it to her. If you come across some of the statements that you *don't* need or want from your Bridge, just cross it out and say, "I don't know *what* they were thinking about when they wrote this one, but it's not on *my* list!"

 Battle Buddy Assignment: Do a little brainstorming with your Battle Buddy and come up with a list of people that you would like to start "formal" Bridge relationships with. Then start praying with your Battle Buddy that God will bring it about.

_____

_____

_____

_____

> Walking with a friend in the dark
> is better than walking alone in the light.
> – Helen Keller

Group Bridges

Those with extensive experience in research and therapy of Traumatic Stress sufferers – whether it's a troop struggling with Combat Trauma or a spouse experiencing Secondary or Primary Traumatic Stress – almost unanimously sing the praises of group settings in helping sufferers work through the difficulties of their past and current experiences. There are many reasons for this:

- In a group, you are actively countering the normal tendency for a Traumatic Stress sufferer to self-isolate.
- You are forging deep friendships with people who truly understand what you are going through, because they are going through it too.
- The depth of your shared experiences opens up communication and support lines that few non-Traumatic Stress sufferers could ever understand or appreciate.
- As group members get to know each other at deeper levels, they take a more active roll in encouraging and supporting each other – "watching each other's back."
- They won't be judgmental, alarmed or abandon you when you're moody, angry or even exhibiting some of the symptoms of PTSD. They'll be far more motivated than most to stick with you through them.
- You have the option of benefiting from the experiences and insights of several people who are in the same boat you are.

- You are multiplying Bridge People in your life – and you are being a Bridge to each of them as well, which enhances your own healing environment.

- During periods when you're taking your "two steps back," you can be encouraged and harvest some hope by hearing of another group member's "three steps forward."

- The give-and-take of a group situation is sometimes less threatening than a one-to-one, eyeball-to-eyeball session with someone you don't know very well.

- You're multiplying your prayer power:

Again I say to you, that if two of you agree on earth about anything that they may ask, it shall be done for them by My Father who is in heaven. For where two or three have gathered together in My name, I am there in their midst.

– Matthew 18:19,20

Some helpful tips

Here are a few principles to keep in mind as you begin to participate in group sessions. Most of these are taken from support group expert Jody Hayes' book, *Smart Love*.[3]

- Once you're in the right group, you may feel safe, but you may also feel shy. This brings us to another paradox of recovery: the more you reveal yourself, the safer you will feel. The more vulnerable you make yourself, the quicker you can recover.

- Share your experiences. Your problems will become clearer when you give words to them. You will discover how much harder it is to fool yourself when you actually hear yourself saying something that you know is either a partial truth or a full lie. At the same time, when you are describing signs of progress or small victories, you will find their effect amplified when you applaud yourself in the presence of others.

- Acknowledge how you feel at the moment, whatever those feelings are. Remember, you are not speaking to please others or to be graded on your recovery. You are speaking to help yourself.

- Embrace your feelings and accept them, even if you feel momentarily miserable. By honestly describing your feelings, you will get a clearer understanding of the experience you are going through. Moreover, there is a significant chance that your painful feelings will diminish. A side benefit is that you will almost always help someone else who is not yet brave enough to speak.

- When speaking, it is important to avoid long, detailed descriptions of your experiences, going into great, gory detail. This will only feed your problem, not release you from it. In addition, it may frustrate and trigger other group members. Keep the focus on how you feel, how events affected you and what you are doing about it.

- When sharing in the group, avoid comparing yourself with others. Each person is at a different place in their healing. Keep your focus on yourself and on how God is working in *your* life.

? Have you considered joining a group of women who are experiencing Traumatic Stress because of their husband's combat experiences? What are your thoughts about it?

_____

_____

_____

When is it time to call in the pros?

You may have done an excellent job of connecting with a number of Bridge People, but still experience struggles that seem more than you can bear. Your level of trauma may be such that you need to see a professional counselor or therapist. Following is a checklist that therapist and writer J. Elizabeth Oppenheim[4] devised to help a person determine if they should seek professional help.

If any of these first 4 warning signs are evident, GET HELP NOW!

- ❑ You are thinking that suicide or death is a plausible, acceptable way to stop your pain.
- ❑ Your concentration is so poor that you are accidentally hurting yourself or others.
- ❑ You are out of control in some way that is endangering your health or the health of others.
- ❑ You have no plans for the future, no hope of your life getting better.

If you don't have a counselor, doctor, pastor or friend you can call, and if you are planning to hurt yourself or someone else right now, call 911, go to an Emergency Room or call a Suicide Prevention Hotline and ask for help. We're serious! *Right now!* Put down the manual and *GO!*

For the next nine signs, if you notice that three or four of them are present, ask friends, your doctor or your pastor for a referral to a counselor or other professional. If you have no other leads, look in the Yellow Pages under Counselors, Therapists or Psychologists and keep looking until you find someone who really helps you.

- ❑ You are unable to work.
- ❑ You cannot keep food down or are eating uncontrollably.
- ❑ You are not sleeping or are sleeping all the time.
- ❑ You have lost interest in everything you used to enjoy; nothing can make you smile.
- ❑ It is too much effort to get dressed, put on make-up, etc.
- ❑ You cannot clean your house to basic sanitation levels or you compulsively clean it late into the night.
- ❑ You are barely functioning but you have other people depending on you to take care of them (children, elders, disabled).
- ❑ You have no one you can talk to honestly about what you're going through – or you've worn out all your friends who would listen.
- ❑ You have a health problem that flares up when you're under stress.

You're not committing to a lifetime of therapy – just hooking up with a well-qualified Bridge Person for a while. This place is only temporary. Get all the support you can as you move through this phase of your life.

Professional therapists can be extremely helpful – or not. Those who come from a strictly clinical/ psychological frame of reference can be helpful with coping mechanisms, talking about your past, dealing with triggers, getting you in touch with your pain and your emotions, among other things. But unless they are aware of the spiritual dimensions of trauma, and understand God as the great Healer, they won't be a true Bridge for you. Their input will be helpful, but you need more.

By the same token, you may encounter a biblical counselor or Christian therapist who really walks closely with God, but isn't well-versed in the physical and psychological aspects of Traumatic Stress. They may be a less-than-optimal Bridge as well.

Following is a list of questions you could ask a potential counselor to get an idea of how effective a Bridge they will be:

1. What is your approach to understanding people's problems and helping them grow, change and become whole again through counseling?

2. What education and experience have you had that has most influenced your approach to counseling individuals struggling with Secondary Traumatic Stress or PTSD?

3. Are you a Christian? How does your faith influence your perspective and practice of counseling?

4. Is it your custom to bring biblical truth into your counseling practice?

5. Do you pray with those you counsel? Do you invite those you counsel to pray as part of their counseling journey?

6. Do you go to a church? If so, where, and how long have you been a member?

7. What are your educational credentials for offering to counsel people with Secondary Traumatic Stress or PTSD? How has your preparation influenced you?

8. Have you experienced severe loss, crisis or trauma in your own life? How has this affected how you counsel Secondary Traumatic Stress and/or PTSD sufferers?

It's important to note that not all counselors or therapists are trained in dealing with combat-related traumatic stress. They may know a lot about victimization issues for women, local critical incident events, assault-related stress, etc. If at all possible, find a counselor who is familiar with Combat Trauma and secondary traumatic stress issues in wives of veterans. War is indeed a stressor of a different color!

Locating a Christian counselor

If you aren't sure where to look for a Christian counselor in your area, here are two places at which you can inquire. They are in contact with two nationwide networks of counselors who could be of help:

- **American Association of Christian Counselors** has constructed a Christian Care Network that you can access online. Go to www.aacc.net. At their home page, you will see several tabs across the top – click on the "Divisions" tab. There will be a drop-down menu – click on "Christian Care Network." Follow the instructions to see if someone in their network has a practice near you.

- **Focus On The Family** also maintains a nationwide network of Christian counselors. You can visit their web site at www.focusonthefamily.com or simply call their headquarters in Colorado Springs at (719) 531-3400 and ask for the Counseling Department.

A few other helpful links

- **Alcoholics Anonymous** – www.alcoholics-anonymous.org (212) 870-3400
- **Al-Anon** – www.al-anon.org 1-888-425-2666
- **Narcotics Anonymous** – www.na.org (818) 773-9999

Danielle's Prayer ...

Lord, I've overexerted myself needlessly. I've tried to shoulder the heavy weight of my trials and responsibilities alone. Lord, You created me and are fully aware of my independent streak. Father, forgive me for any martyr syndrome I've displayed or any pride that deceives me into thinking I can do it all.

You promised in Your Word that where two or three are gathered in Your name, You are there with us. You've said that a cord of three strands is not easily broken. I ask for friends who will speak the truth in love to me, who will go the distance with me, who will listen and be a Bridge to my healing and wholeness. Father, I ask You for friends who truly have my back now that I'm flat on mine.

Promise from God's Word ...

A friend loves at all times, and is born,
as is a brother, for adversity.
- Proverbs 17:17 (AMPLIFIED)

9 WHO AM I REALLY?
Focusing on Your True Identity in Christ

Erin's Journal ...

Military ID cards are good as gold. They are backstage, all-access passes to this crazy life we live. I learned that the hard way when I lost mine last week. I panicked! Without my ID I was paralyzed, unable to get on post or get medical attention or cash a check at the credit union. Everything that's usually simple and quick became impossible. I was turned away from everything I needed to do. End of discussion. All because I didn't have the proper ID.

Just as Scott completed the paperwork hassle for me to apply for a new ID (which he wasn't too pleased about), I found my old one in the pocket of my freshly washed and still warm favorite pair of jeans. It was then that I remembered slipping my ID into my back pocket in my rush to pay for the groceries and get Abigail headed toward the car. The washing machine ate my ID for lunch and the dryer had it for dessert.

Apparently I'm not the only one who's ever lost her ID. So I took a number at the personnel office and got in line. As I waited, I studied my dog-eared card. Its four plastic corners were peeled back like a painful sunburn. My faded photo rendered me unrecognizable, white-washed, crinkled and missing a few facial features. I didn't like that picture anyhow. I'm not the woman in that photo any longer. So much has changed since that day.

When it was finally my turn, I presented my paperwork and actually smiled for the camera. The unimpressed, monotone clerk behind the desk sent the crisp card and glossy photo through a laminator, sealing all the acronyms and numbers she'd sprinkled on my new ID. She handed me the fresh, pristine, all-access pass and hollered, "Next!"

Then it occurred to me that perhaps it's a good thing to lose your ID and let it go through the wash every now and then. Not just military IDs, but our very identities — how we see ourselves and how others see us. The passage of time and painful trials have a way of making us unrecognizable even to ourselves. We use and misuse the codes we're given along the way and the message ends up all scrambled. Our battered edges get peeled back and the critical information fades out of focus.

I realized in that moment that, in my journey through the pain of combat stress, my own identity has come under fire. In my dogged determination to simply survive each day, I've stuffed my own identity inside my back pocket and misplaced my God-given uniqueness and value. I need a new understanding of who I am and how I've changed, but also of what, in my core character, never changes or fades.

Perception and self-perception

We don't often think very deeply about who or what we are, or how our identity can open or shut doors for us. But as Erin's journal entry illustrates, who we are, how we perceive ourselves and how others see us are all extremely important issues. As the saying goes, "Perception *is* reality in the mind of the perceiver." It is crucial that both our perception and self-perception are accurate, and that both line up with what God says is true. As you struggle with the realities of your husband's Combat Trauma and your own traumatic stress, your identity will be assaulted by things far more consequential than washers and dryers. This chapter will help remind you of the *truth* about who you are based on what *God* says about you – not on what the world, Satan, your own despairing meditations or even your husband tells you.

Traumatic stress and identity

When a person experiences traumatic stress, her self-perception is often shaken to the core. While she used to see herself as rational, self-sufficient, adaptive, strong and worthy, she now questions those assessments. They are often replaced by feelings of fear, confusion, powerlessness and helplessness. And that's not all. As trauma and victimization authority Dr. Ronnie Janoff-Bulman writes:

> In addition, victims are apt to experience a sense of deviance. After all, they have been singled out for misfortune and this establishes them as different from other people. This self-perception of deviance no doubt serves to reinforce negative images of oneself as unworthy and weak.[1]

The effects of this negative transformation of your self-image don't remain in the psychological realm. They bleed into your behavior too – your plans, activities, priorities, reactions, values, hopes, dreams, ambition, social interaction … the list goes on and on. Pastor, educator and counselor Dr. Neil Anderson states:

> No person can consistently behave in a manner that is inconsistent with the way he sees himself.[2]

Can't be done. You cannot hold one set of opinions about yourself and try to live according to a different set. You may succeed for a while, but the energy required to keep up that front is enormous. Eventually exhaustion sets in, the mask comes off and meltdown occurs.

While trauma may have started your self-identity ball rolling downhill, there are three other factors that keep it rolling and spin it faster: Satan, the world around you and negative self-talk.

Self-Perception Assessment

Dr. Steven Stosney, an international authority on trauma and victimization, has developed a very useful template that will help you assess your current self-perception – how positively or negatively you view yourself. Dr. Stosney's normal approach goes much deeper than we are able to apply in this manual, but some of the components will be very useful here. There are eight dynamics of self-perception listed below – the positive side and the negative side. Place an "X" somewhere on the line that indicates how you currently see yourself.[3]

Regarded _____	Disregarded
Important _____	Unimportant
Forgiven _____	Accused/Guilty
Valued _____	Devalued
Accepted _____	Rejected
Powerful _____	Powerless
Lovable _____	Unlovable
Connected _____	Separated

Obviously, all the negative voices in your life want to place the "X's" as far to the right side as possible, which keeps you in a vulnerable position. If that's where they are at this point, it's because you have been fed compromised intelligence that has no credible independent verification – in other words, **LIES**! Here's what the Son of God says about Satan:

> *He was a murderer from the beginning, not holding to the truth, for there is no truth in him. When he lies, he speaks his native language, for he is a liar and the father of lies.*
>
> **– John 8:44** (NIV)

At this moment, you are probably not on a physical battlefield, but you are in a war. And as the great Chinese warrior Sun Tzu wrote, "*All warfare is based on deception,*" Satan has been honing his deceptive tactics for thousands of years. He and his network of minions have been observing you since you were a child. They know just what to say and how to say it to deceive you to the max. Their objective is your destruction (1 Peter 5:8), which will diminish the Kingdom of God and grieve the great heart of the King.

Exposing your enemy's deception

In this chapter, we're going to expose as many of Satan's lies as we can. Exposing deception means giving an advantage to those previously deceived. We want you to be able to say with the Apostle Paul, "*We are not ignorant of his schemes*" (2 Corinthians 2:11).

The lies you'll be reading about in this section were spawned by Satan himself. He'll whisper them in your subconscious at your most vulnerable moments. You'll be reminded of incidents in your childhood that validate them. He'll contextualize them in your traumatic events. He'll reinforce them with messages bombarding you from the world system that surrounds you. He'll be sure you're listening when your friends mimic and verify them accidentally or on purpose. And before long, he'll have you telling *yourself* the lies. And we all know how closely we listen to our own opinions.

Following are **eight deceptive traps** Satan and the world have laid for you. Consider whether or not you've heard them before. Each lie will be followed by the countering TRUTH that God wants you to hear.

Deception #1:   – Disregarded –

Lies of the enemy:

- You are a nobody.
- No one cares about you. Why should they?
- No one wants to know you.
- You don't deserve the respect that others get.
- You are such a fraud.
- Who do you think you are, anyway?

Have you heard any of those comments before? Have you ever said them to yourself? Maybe those exact words weren't used, but after their world has been turned upside down, many traumatic stress sufferers hear and swallow those devilish sentiments. "You've proven to be someone who should and must be disregarded." You hear that, you look at your situation, you look at how people respond to you, you consider your own "deviancy" and you resign yourself to the "truth" of those lies.

Spiritual IEDs. To be effective, every lie must have an element of truth. No good deception ever *looks* like a deception. It must appear plausible, rational and believable. The IEDs that your husband had to contend with downrange appeared harmless: a tuft of grass beside the road, a bit of trash, a little rubble. That's why they work. And if we don't have some information to the contrary, we assume that the lies we perceive are the truth.

Well, God wants to give you *true* information that counters Satan's deceptions. Your traumatic stress has changed you – that's the kernel of truth. But to say, "Because I've changed and I'm not functioning as I used to, I am worthy of disregard" is an absolute lie and needs to be opposed by God's truth.

Not only is His Word *true*, it is *living* and *active* according to Hebrews 4:12. That means that it's not just words that some ancient prophet scribbled on paper several centuries ago. It continues to live today. As you read those words, and as the Holy Spirit energizes and breathes life into them, they are the words of God spoken directly to *you*, right here in the 21st century.

The above facts hold true for all eight of the lie-countering truths that we'll be examining below …

Your TRUE Identity: ~ *Regarded* ~

Complete the sentence or answer the question after each verse, highlighting who you really are.

※ ※

[Jesus speaking:] *I no longer call you servants, because a servant does not know his master's business. Instead, I have called you friends, for everything that I learned from My Father I have made known to you.*

– John 15:15 (NIV)

Jesus Christ, the Son of God, calls you His _____

※ ※

So now Jesus and the ones He makes holy have the same Father. That is why Jesus is not ashamed to call them His brothers and sisters.

– Hebrews 2:11 (NLT)

Jesus Christ is not ashamed to call you His _____

※ ※

Even before He made the world, God loved us and chose us in Christ to be holy and without fault in His eyes.

– Ephesians 1:4 (NLT)

You were known, loved and chosen by God how long ago? _____

※ ※

Now you are no longer a slave but God's own child. And since you are His child, God has made you His heir.

– Galatians 4:7 (NLT)

You are God's child and also His _____

※ ※

These Scriptures describe *you* as a friend, sibling, daughter and heir of the King of the Universe! He has had plans for you even before He created Adam and Eve. And you can be sure He's *really* excited that you finally showed up! You are **loved** and **highly regarded**!

※ ※ ※※ ※ ※

Deception #2: — *Unimportant* —

Lies of the enemy:

- Your input is unnecessary.
- You're just a wife – get back in the kitchen.
- Go sit on the sidelines.
- Don't call us, we'll call you.
- What have you ever accomplished?

Your TRUE Identity: ~ *Important* ~

 Answer the question after each verse, highlighting the truth about who you really are.

❀ ❀

But as many as received Him, to them He gave the right to become children of God, even to those who believe in His name.

– John 1:12

Since you have received Christ, you have rightly been named as what?

_____

When you consider all of eternity and all the other animals and angels that God created, how important would you say that was?

_____

❀ ❀

You're here to be salt-seasoning that brings out the God-flavors of this earth.

– Matthew 5:13 (TM)

God has made you to be His _____ on the earth. What do you think that means?

_____

❀ ❀

You're here to be light, bringing out the God-colors in the world.

– Matthew 5:14 (TM)

God has made you to be His _____ in the world. As such, what do you think He meant for you to do?

_____

❀ ❀

For God so loved the world, that He gave His only begotten Son, that whoever believes in Him shall not perish, but have eternal life.

– John 3:16

What kind of life have you been given? _____

How significant do you think it is to be an eternal being?

_____

❀ ❀

Not only do you hold important positions as an eternal child of God; not only has He called you His seasoning and His light on the earth; but you are being trained and qualified for a unique, future leadership in Christ's Kingdom on earth. He was wounded, and all those who follow Him will also receive wounds, as you have. Down through the ages, the men and women who were significantly used by God were wounded in some severe way. You have been through the Refiner's fire – and may still be in the middle of it. There are evil forces doing their best to propel our world into chaos. The Bible predicts that in the end times society will crumble and treacherous times will ensue – and those times may be very close. Who better to lead us through those traumatic times than people like you and your husband? You've been to hell and back. It is hated but familiar territory for you. You're *important* now, but as you are more fully restored to health, you will prove to be *invaluable* in the coming times.

❀ ❀ ❀❀ ❀ ❀

Deception #3:   — Accused/Guilty —

Lies of the enemy:

- You really blew it.
- You're unforgivable.
- You need to be punished.
- You can't be trusted.
- Everyone knows what a hypocrite you are.

Your TRUE Identity: ~ Forgiven ~

? After each verse, write down what it says about who you really are.

❀ ❀

Therefore there is now no condemnation for those who are in Christ Jesus.

– Romans 8:1

Assuming you are a Christian ("in Christ Jesus"), what will you not experience?

_____

❀ ❀

Therefore, having been justified by faith, we have peace with God through our Lord Jesus Christ.

– Romans 5:1

What happened to you by faith? (Hint: the word means "declared not guilty.")

_____

So you are no longer at war with God, now you have _____ with Him. The war is over. You and God are no longer enemies. Your war crimes are no longer being held against you.

❀ ❀

Their sins and lawless acts I will remember no more.

– Hebrews 10:17 (NIV)

What does God think about your sins and lawless acts? (Watch it – trick question!)

_____

❀ ❀ ❀❀ ❀ ❀

Deception #4:   — Devalued —

Lies of the enemy:

- We don't need you.
- You're not good enough.
- You don't have anything useful to say – you're just a woman.
- You are absolutely worthless.
- You really suck!

Your TRUE *Identity:* ~ *Valued* ~

 After each verse, observe why your true designation is "Valued by God":

> *The Lord appeared to us in the past, saying:*
> *"I have loved you with an everlasting love;*
> *I have drawn you with loving-kindness."*

– Jeremiah 31:3 (NIV)

Who loves ya, baby?_____ How long has this been going on?_____

How valuable do you think being loved eternally and wooed into an everlasting love relationship with God makes you?

_____

❁ ❁

> *Don't you realize that your body is the temple of the Holy Spirit, who lives in you and was given to you by God? You do not belong to yourself, for God bought you with a high price. So you must honor God with your body.*

– 1 Corinthians 6:19,20 (NLT)

What has your physical body become?

_____

When Israel was strong and before Christ came, the Temple in Jerusalem was the one place on earth where God was manifested and represented. It was the most magnificent and expensive building on the planet at the time for that reason. Since Christ's resurrection, we have become the Temple of God. Now *we* are where God is manifested and represented. Valuable or not valuable?

_____

Additionally, this verse says we were bought with a high price. What was the price that God the Father paid to buy us?

_____

❁ ❁

> *For God knew His people in advance, and He chose them to become like His Son, so that His Son would be the firstborn among many brothers and sisters. And having chosen them, He called them to come to Him. And having called them, He gave them right standing with Himself. And having given them right standing, He gave them His glory.*

– Romans 8:29,30 (NLT)

So, we were known by God, chosen by Him to become like Jesus Christ, called by God to come to Him, given right standing with Him, and finally given what?

_____

Conquering generals are given glory by their countries. How valuable do you think the glory given by God is?

_____

❁ ❁ ❁❁ ❁ ❁

Deception #5:   — *Rejected* —

Lies of the enemy:

- You're a failure.
- You're such a loser.
- No one wants you.
- You're not qualified.
- Everyone else is better than you.

Your *TRUE Identity:*   ~ *Accepted* ~

? After each verse, observe why your true designation is "Accepted by God":

❀ ❀

To the praise of the glory of His grace,
by which He made us accepted in the Beloved.

– Ephesians 1:6 (NKJV)

God's grace made you *what* in the Beloved (Christ)?

_____

❀ ❀

As you come to Him, the living Stone – rejected by men but chosen by God and
precious to Him – you also, like living stones, are being built into a spiritual house
to be a holy priesthood, offering spiritual sacrifices acceptable to God through
Jesus Christ.

– 1 Peter 2:4,5 (NIV)

The "*living Stone*" is Jesus Christ, who was rejected by mankind (when He was crucified), but always chosen and precious to the Father. In the same way, you were selected by the Master Stonemason to be part of His spiritual construction, and you are therefore shown to be offering *what* kind of spiritual sacrifices to God through Jesus Christ?

_____

So not only are *you* accepted by God, but the sacrifices you're making, your ministry to your husband and kids, everything you are offering up to God He also regards as totally *acceptable*!

❀ ❀

Let us therefore come boldly to the throne of grace, that we may obtain mercy
and find grace to help in time of need.

– Hebrews 4:16 (NKJV)

How are we encouraged to approach God's throne of grace?

_____

Would this indicate that we are *barely* acceptable or *totally* acceptable to God? *(Circle one.)*

❀ ❀ ❀❀ ❀ ❀

Deception #6: — Powerless —

Lies of the enemy:

- You are weak.
- You are damaged goods.
- Can't you do anything right?
- How helpless can one person be?
- Someone's always got to take care of you.

Your TRUE Identity: ~ Powerful ~

 After each verse, answer the questions which indicate your power as a child of the King.

✿ ✿

For God has not given us a spirit of fear,
but of power and of love and of a sound mind.

– 2 Timothy 1:7 (NKJV)

What kind of a spirit has God given us?

_____

✿ ✿

You are from God, little children, and have overcome them;
because greater is He who is in you than he who is in the world.

– 1 John 4:4

"*He who is in the world*" refers to Satan and his allies. Between us and them, which is the more powerful?

_____

✿ ✿

For everyone born of God overcomes the world. This is the victory that has overcome
the world, even our faith. Who is it that overcomes the world? Only he who believes
that Jesus is the Son of God

– 1 John 5:4,5 (NIV)

As a Christian, you are "*born of God.*" "*The world*" referred to is the world system that is ruled over by Satan. When you and the world mix it up, who has the power to win?

_____

If your husband is struggling with Combat Trauma, and if you are experiencing traumatic stress, you probably don't *feel* particularly powerful. You may feel powerless to accomplish basic goals, control your anger, take care of your kids, sleep, conquer your depression – but your weakness is only temporary. When Jesus was taken into custody, flogged, tortured and crucified, He seemed *very* weak – but it was only temporary. In fact, He had massive *latent* power during that entire ordeal. The power was there, just not being used – and for good reasons. You have that same latent power, but the odds are good that it's not being used for *no* good reason!

 Prayer Assignment: Begin asking God to help you release the latent power that He has placed within you. He wants to! Just ask Him!

✿ ✿ ✿✿ ✿ ✿

Deception #7:   — Unlovable —

Lies of the enemy:

- Who would ever love you?
- You're so ugly and boring.
- You are beyond being loved, by God, by your husband or by anyone.
- You really have no redeeming qualities.

Your TRUE Identity: ~ Lovable ~

You are of infinite worth. God sees *Himself* in *you*. You reflect something about God that no one else does. God is so much in love with you that He was willing to sacrifice His Son to redeem you from your sins. Even if you were the only person on earth, He would have done it for you. Obviously, there is *something* about you that is *infinitely* lovable!

> *For I am convinced that neither death, nor life, nor angels, nor principalities, nor things present, nor things to come, nor powers, nor height, nor depth, nor any other created thing, will be able to separate us from the love of God, which is in Christ Jesus our Lord.*
>
> **– Romans 8:38,39**

Make a list from the above verse of the things that God would fight through in order to get to you because of His love for you:

_____

_____

_____

❀ ❀

> *Greater love has no one than this, that one lay down his life for his friends.*
>
> **– John 15:13**

Jesus made this statement shortly before He was crucified. Who do you think were the friends He was referring to, for whom He was about to lay down His life?

_____

❀ ❀

> *But God shows His great love for us in this way: Christ died for us while we were still sinners.*
>
> **– Romans 5:8 (NCV)**

How much love would it take for you to be willing to die for someone else? Would you do it for your mother? For your husband? Your daughter or son? How about for your best friend? You may have heard tales from your husband or on the news about someone putting himself in harm's way so that his comrades could live. *That* was a supremely unselfish, loving act. But have you ever heard of a soldier who gave up his or her life for someone they didn't even know? It happens from time to time and it always amazes us. How could someone be *so* selfless?

But would you be willing to die for someone who had betrayed you, spit in your face, punched you in the stomach and stole your purse, your car and your dog? You would have to be an incredibly loving and forgiving person to die for someone like *that*. And yet, that's who we were – and worse – when Christ died on the cross for us. *That's* how much He loves us!

❀ ❀

For the Lord your God has arrived to live among you. He is a mighty Savior. He will give you victory. He will rejoice over you in great gladness; He will love you and not accuse you. Is that a joyous choir I hear? No, it is the Lord Himself exulting over you in happy song.

– Zephaniah 3:17 (LB)

List at least five loving and supportive things that the above verse says "*the Lord your God*" will do to show how much He loves you (hint: look at the verbs in each clause):

_____

_____

_____

❀ ❀ ❀❀ ❀ ❀

Deception #8: — *Separated* —

Lies of the enemy:

- You are alone and you should stay that way.
- No one wants you around.
- You shouldn't be such a bother to other people.
- People wish you weren't here.
- Can't you go someplace else?

Your TRUE Identity: ~ *Connected* ~

You are connected in two realms …

Connected to God:

? [Jesus speaking:] *I am the vine, you are the branches; he who abides in Me and I in him, he bears much fruit, for apart from Me you can do nothing.*

– John 15:5

What picture of "connectedness" did Jesus use to show how attached we are to Him?

_____

❀ ❀

For you are all children of God through faith in Christ Jesus.

– Galatians 3:26 (NLT)

What are some deep, meaningful ways that children and parents are connected?

_____

_____

❀ ❀

I have been crucified with Christ; and it is no longer I who live, but Christ lives in me.

– Galatians 2:20

This verse indicates that Christ lives *where*?

_____

Connected to the Body of Christ – other Christians:

> *All of you together are Christ's body, and each of you is a part of it.*
>
> **– 1 Corinthians 12:27 (NLT)**

What are all Christians a part of?

_____

What do you know about how the various cells and organs of a body are connected?

_____

❀ ❀

> *You are no longer foreigners and aliens, but fellow citizens with God's people and members of God's household.*
>
> **– Ephesians 2:19 (NIV)**

This verse gives us two pictures of "connectedness" with other people. What are they?

_____

_____

❀ ❀ ❀❀ ❀ ❀

As you work through the difficulties that you and your husband are experiencing due to his Combat Trauma, there will be times when you feel alone, rejected, unlovable, devalued and unimportant. That's when Satan will pile on and do all he can to affirm those thoughts. It's at that time that you need to recognize his tactics. He's using deception to move you closer to despair and defeat. He is lying. How can you tell when Satan is **lying**? Whenever his mouth moves! Counter his lies with the truth.

Make the proclamation on the next page, out loud if possible, based on what you just learned from God's Word.

❀ ❀ ❀❀ ❀ ❀

Suggestion: Make a copy of the "This Is Who I Am" list (or photocopy the whole page) and review it regularly. Meditate on its truths, pray about them, proclaim them! You may want to place the list in your Bible and read it during your Quiet Time. Perhaps you could tape a copy of it on your bathroom mirror and think about its truths as you prepare for the day, or above your kitchen sink to think about as you wash dishes. The more often you consider these truths, the more they will influence your self-perception.

❀ ❀ ❀❀ ❀ ❀

Follow-up

Write today's date here: _____ One month from today, re-take the "Self-Perception Assessment" that you completed at the beginning of this chapter. If you have been regularly thinking about and proclaiming the above truths concerning your true identity, you should notice that your "X's" have traveled a considerable distance to the left!

❀ ❀ ❀❀ ❀ ❀

This is Who I Am

Regarded

I am a friend of the Almighty God of heaven and earth. (John 15:15)

Jesus is not ashamed to call me His sister. (Hebrews 2:11)

I am chosen by God, holy and without fault in His eyes. (Ephesians 1:4)

I am an heir to the riches of the Creator of the universe. (Galatians 4:7)

Important

I have been rightly called a child of God. (John 1:12)

God has made me His salt and light in the world. (Matthew 5:13,14)

I am an eternal being and will never perish. (John 3:16)

Forgiven

I am no longer condemned. (Romans 8:1)

I have been justified before the righteous Judge. (Romans 5:1)

I am at peace with God. (Romans 5:1)

God no longer remembers my sins. (Hebrews 10:17)

Valued

God loves me with an everlasting love. (Jeremiah 31:3)

I am God's temple, bought at a great price. (1 Corinthians 6:19,20)

God knows, chose, called, justified and glorified me. (Romans 8:29,30)

Accepted

I am accepted in Christ. (Ephesians 1:6)

I am a chosen, costly, living stone in God's building. (1 Peter 2:4,5)

I have bold, unrestricted access to God's throne of grace. (Hebrews 4:16)

Powerful

God has given me the spirit of power, love and a sound mind. (2 Timothy 1:7)

God's Spirit in me is greater than any unholy spirits in the world. (1 John 4:4)

I am born of God and believe in Jesus – I'm a world-overcomer. (1 John 5:4,5)

Lovable

I am loved by God and nothing will keep us apart. (Romans 8:38,39)

I am loved supremely – enough for God to die for me. (John 15:13)

I am loved unconditionally, even when I sin. (Romans 5:8)

Connected

I am intimately attached to Christ and bearing fruit. (John 15:5)

I am a member of God's eternal family. (Galatians 3:26)

Christ is as close to me as my heart and lungs. (Galatians 2:20)

I am part of Christ's body with millions of brothers and sisters. (1 Corinthians 12:27)

I am an eternal member of God's Kingdom and household. (Ephesians 2:19)

Erin's Prayer ...

Lord, losing my ID last week taught me so much about who I truly am because of Your love for me. When I see the seal of the USA in the upper left corner of my card, remind me that I am sealed by Your Holy Spirit for all eternity. Thank You that my relationship to You has no expiration date. When I look at my photo, help me to remember that You see past the face I wear for others. You created me and know the real, eternal me. When I'm asked my "sponsor's social," I will thank You that I am not just a number to You. I am not "Property of the U.S. Government," but I belong to You and am a citizen of heaven. Help me to remember that ultimately Jesus is my only active duty sponsor who always makes intercession for me.

Father, as I use my new ID to access my military benefits, help me also to thank you for the privileges that are mine in Christ, Your Son. The blood of Your Son authorizes me to countless blessings and uniquely defines how You see and value me. Thank You that my God-given identity and privileges in Christ will never fade or be taken from me, no matter how many wash cycles and dry spells Your plan for my life includes.

In Jesus' Name, Amen.

Promise from God's Word ...

For God, who said, "Let there be light in the darkness," has made this light shine in our hearts so we could know the glory of God that is seen in the face of Jesus Christ.
We now have this light shining in our hearts, but we ourselves are like fragile clay jars containing this great treasure. This makes it clear that our great power is from God, not from ourselves.
– 2 Corinthians 4:6,7 (NLT)

10 WHO IS THE REAL ENEMY?
Fighting Spiritually For Myself, My Husband and My Kids

Lauren's Journal . . .

I answered the door and was greeted by a gaggle of neighborhood ghouls and goblins. They shouted an eager "Trick or Treat!" and thrust their swinging buckets and bags in my direction. Before I handed out enough treats to ensure that all the local dentists stay in business another year, I tried to guess who each kid was.

"Brandon, is that you?" He giggled behind his Spiderman mask. "Chelsea, is that you?" She shivered with delight inside her glittering Little Mermaid costume. "And who are you two?" I didn't recognize the taller ones towering in the back. They shrugged their shoulders, tilted their heads, then gestured and mimed their way out of the awkward moment. Satisfied with fists full of my Milky Way bars and Malt Balls, they disappeared into the darkness, mission accomplished.

Doorbell after doorbell, the costume parade continued way past curfew. With no candy left, I turned off the front lights and headed for bed. Jason was already there. I crawled between the covers and lay beside my sleeping husband, staring into the thick darkness. Jason's breathing was labored. His body was restless. He had wanted nothing to do with tonight's festivities and had steered clear of it all.

I remembered what Jason told me in an e-mail during his last deployment. He wrote that one of the hardest things about being in a war zone was not being able to recognize the enemy. In past wars, both sides showed their colors and wore their emblems openly and with national pride. Not so in today's Global War on Terror. At checkpoints, black burkas cloak the innocent and the evil alike. Suicide bombers now enlist women and children to do their damage in the marketplaces and mosques. Our enemy has figured out the power of disguise, and he uses it to confuse and defeat us.

Halloween isn't just one day in the year since war came home to live with us. There are many days when I don't even recognize my own husband. He looks like Jason. His voice sounds like Jason's. But too often he behaves nothing like the man I fell in love with and married. In those moments, I want to lean in close and ask, "Jason, is that you?"

I know my husband is not the enemy. I realize that Satan wants more than anything to steal and destroy what God has given to us as lovers, as friends and as life partners. I'm tired of Satan distracting me with the shrug of his shoulders and the tilt of his ugly head. He has disappeared into the darkness with fists full of my marriage and my home for the last time. I'm ready to stand in the gap. I'm ready to fight for my relationship with Jason and for our future together.

Black Hats / White Hats

We realize that your husband is the one who is schooled in the ways of war and you were meant to keep the home fires burning while he fought. So this chapter about warfare might seem more appropriate for *him* than for *you*. But make no mistake – it is for you. You may have had just about all the war-talk you can stomach, and we're sorry to have to dwell on it in this chapter. But there is no way to get around the fact that – as the title of this manual suggests – war has come home with your husband and it will not be ignored.

The war in your home is being fought on three fronts: physical, mental and spiritual. It is absolutely vital to use tactics that meet each threat strategically. Physical difficulties that you or your husband are experiencing need physical solutions; mental/emotional difficulties require psychological approaches; spiritual attacks necessitate spiritual defenses and counter-attacks. Our enemy will often utilize a combination of all three fronts in his efforts to bring us down, but we must be discerning enough to differentiate between them. This chapter will train you in the *spiritual* aspects of fighting your adversary.

And just in case you need some clarification, your adversary is *the devil* – not your husband! Anyone who lives with a reactive, angry, irritable, belligerent and emotionally draining person might feel a natural tendency to become somewhat adversarial. This is especially true when the live-in ogre looks a lot like your spouse, who promised to love, honor and cherish you until death do you part. Feelings of disappointment and betrayal flow easily into the vacuum left by those seemingly abandoned vows. Before you know it, you've got your crosshairs on your husband's back, and your trigger finger is getting itchy. It's at these moments you need to realize that *he is not your enemy!* In every sense of the word he is a *victim* of the enemy's attacks – just as you are. Better that you should stand shoulder-to-shoulder fighting your enemy together.

> *For our struggle is not against flesh and blood, but against the rulers, against the powers, against the world forces of this darkness, against the spiritual forces of wickedness in the heavenly places.*
>
> **– Ephesians 6:12**

One of Satan's favorite tactics is to place enmity between friends and lovers. If he can get them shooting at each other instead of at him, he can just sit back, laugh and watch them take each other out. That is what divorce is all about – and it can happen between the greatest of friends. Even the Apostle Paul and his beloved co-worker and mentor Barnabas once had a falling out which must have been extremely difficult for both men. They disagreed about who would accompany them on a mission trip they were planning …

> *Barnabas wanted to take John, also called Mark, with them, but Paul did not think it wise to take him, because he had deserted them in Pamphylia and had not continued with them in the work. They had such a sharp disagreement that they parted company. Barnabas took Mark and sailed for Cyprus, but Paul chose Silas and … went through Syria and Cilicia, strengthening the churches.*
>
> **– Acts 15:37-41** (NIV)

They eventually reconciled, and John Mark even became one of Paul's most valuable team members. But if Satan can get between these two great men of God, he certainly won't hesitate to try to get you and your husband at each other's throats. If you are aware of his tactics, you'll know when he's at work and can counter them more efficiently. Forewarned – forearmed!

Enemy 101

> Know the enemy and know yourself.
> In a hundred battles you will never be in peril.
>
> – Sun Tzu in *The Art of War*[1]

He may or may not have known God, but this Chinese warrior of the sixth century B.C. knew warfare. After reading Chapter 9, you should have a clearer concept of "yourself." In this chapter, we will follow Sun Tzu's excellent advice and get to know "the enemy." The Apostle Paul expressed the same sentiment regarding our need for preparation in 2 Corinthians 2:11, *"We are not ignorant of his schemes."* (Perhaps he wrote that *after* his blowout with Barnabas!)

You must never lose site of the fact that – despite your husband having been transported away from the physical battlefield – the two of you are locked in a desperate war against a deadly enemy. The spiritual war your souls are engaged in is as real as wars that use bullets and bombs – and just as consequential. As Arthur Matthews, English WWII veteran and missionary wrote, "In Eden, God decreed enmity between the serpent's seed and the seed of the woman. Because of this, the *law of strife* became the *law of life* for the human race."[2] Unfortunately, the Kingdom of God is taking heavy casualties because so many of His soldiers don't know their enemy, and aren't even convinced there *is* a war! Because of this, we've engaged the enemy in many more than Sun Tzu's "hundred battles," but won precious few victories. Peace in our souls is elusive, though we desire it desperately. Our top general during the Revolutionary War tells us how to win it:

> There is nothing so likely to produce peace as
> to be well prepared to meet the enemy.[3]
>
> – George Washington

❀ ❀ ❀❀❀ ❀ ❀

Preparing to meet your enemy

? What do you already know about Satan? Do a little brainstorming and write down anything you can think of regarding his nature, his strategies, his likes, his dislikes, his motives, his destiny, etc.

_____

_____

_____

_____

His origin

Satan started out as Lucifer, one of the most powerful angels in God's command. In Ezekiel 28:11-19, the prophet Ezekiel describes him as having *"the seal of perfection; full of wisdom; perfect in beauty; covered with every precious stone – ruby, topaz, diamond, emerald,"* etc.[4] He must have been an amazing being, because at some point he looked at himself, looked at the all-powerful God of the universe, and thought, *I think I can take Him.* Pride was born in his heart, and Isaiah tells us that he made five pronouncements about the coup he intended to accomplish:

> *I will ascend to heaven;*
> *I will raise my throne above the stars of God;*
> *I will sit on the mount of assembly;*
> *I will ascend above the heights of the clouds;*
> *I will make myself like the Most High.*[5]

Revelation 12 indicates that one-third of the angels believed he could do it, and so they joined his rebellion. Why they made such a foolish choice, we're never told. But this left two-thirds still loyal to God, who triumphed. The rebels – including Satan – were banished from God's heaven, no longer free to roam the universe, confined to one planet: Earth.

❀ ❀ ❀❀❀ ❀ ❀

His objectives

Some time after this, God created man and woman and gave them authority over all the earth. Satan saw this as his grand opportunity to continue his rebellion. Four objectives formed in his mind:

1. Use deceit to steal some or all of their authority and use it against the Kingdom of God
2. Afflict these objects of God's great affection and thereby afflict Him – and if possible, get them to blame their affliction on each other or on God
3. Turn the humans against God – as he did one-third of the angels – and recruit them to his army
4. Use them to stage a second coup attempt – which he feels certain will succeed this time

Most of the book of Revelation contains prophesies about how that second attempt will play out. All the evil we've seen down through history, all the wars, all the pain, all the ungodly ways in which humans treat other humans is all part of Satan's staging of that final push to wrest control of earth from God's hands, and take His place. By the way, he *will not* succeed in this – we've read the last chapter of the book!

❀ ❀ ❀❀ ❀ ❀

His tactics

 Here is a little more detail about how Satan uses deceit to weaken and overcome us. Read each Bible passage below and in the space provided after each selection **record what you observe about Satan's tactics.** The first one is completed for you, so you'll get the idea what we're looking for.

Then Jesus was led up by the Spirit into the wilderness to be tempted by the devil.

– Matthew 4:1

Satan takes the initiative and intentionally tempts people to do wrong – especially when they are isolated. He'll tempt anyone – even the Son of God! So we should all expect it.

But I am not surprised! Even Satan disguises himself as an angel of light. So it is no wonder that his servants also disguise themselves as servants of righteousness.

– 2 Corinthians 11:14,15 (NLT)

_____

_____

The Devil took him [Jesus] to the peak of a huge mountain. He gestured expansively, pointing out all the earth's kingdoms, how glorious they all were. Then he said, "They're Yours – lock, stock, and barrel. Just go down on Your knees and worship me, and they're Yours."

– Matthew 4:8,9 (TM)

_____

_____

This is the meaning of the parable: The seed is God's Word. The seeds that fell on the footpath represent those who hear the message, only to have the devil come and take it away from their hearts and prevent them from believing and being saved.

– Luke 8:11,12 (NLT)

_____

_____

❀ ❀ ❀❀ ❀ ❀

Breaking the code

 Satan's lies and temptations are very subtle – and they haven't changed much in thousands of years. They haven't needed to – they continue to work excellently. Examine the Genesis passage below in which the temptation of Adam and Eve are recorded. **Draw a line from the underlined words of Satan on the left to what he's really saying on the right.** This will help you recognize your enemy's voice …

And the Lord God commanded the man, "You are free to eat from any tree in the garden; but you must not eat from the tree of the knowledge of good and evil, for when you eat of it you will surely die."
— **Genesis 2:16,17** (NIV)

Now the serpent [Satan] *was more crafty than any of the wild animals the Lord God had made. He said to the woman, "Did God really say, 'You must not eat from any tree in the garden'?"*
The woman said to the serpent, "We may eat fruit from the trees in the garden, but God did say, 'You must not eat fruit from the tree that is in the middle of the garden, and you must not touch it, or you will die.'"
"You will not surely die," the serpent said to the woman. "For God knows that when you eat of it your eyes will be opened, and you will be like God, knowing good and evil."
— **Genesis 3:1-5** (NIV)

⊙ "Do you mean that God – that restrictive old meanie – won't let you eat from *any* trees in the garden? I can't believe it!"

⊙ "Don't you see what's going on here? God doesn't want you to experience new, mind-expanding things! He's *limiting* you!"

⊙ "Oh, don't get excited. God tends to misrepresent the facts a lot. Let me straighten you out: you won't *really* die. He was just saying that to keep you under His control."

⊙ "God isn't interested in associating with you – He wants to keep you ignorant and oppressed. He doesn't want you to be as smart as He is!"

Anatomy of a temptation

The framework of most of Satan's temptations contains these five elements. Can you see them implied in the interchange we just looked at?

Major Premise: Restrictions are bad.

Complementary Major Premise: Freedom is good.

Proposition: God's plans are restrictive.

Conclusion: God's restrictive plans are bad and *should not* be followed.

Corollary: My non-restrictive plans are good and *should* be followed.

Notice how logical and true the two Major Premises seem. How can people who appreciate their independence argue with them? No one likes to be restricted, and freedom *is* good. That's the kernel of truth. But we also know that some restrictions are good and some freedoms are bad. If we skate over that fact and accept the Proposition, we find ourselves nodding in agreement with the Conclusion and Corollary.

Name a few restrictions that are good.

_____

_____

Name a few freedoms that are bad.

_____

_____

Satan's primary tactic – Doorways & Footholds

Doorways ...

Genesis 4:1-12 records the birth of Adam and Eve's first two sons, Cain and Abel. Unfortunately, it also records the first murder in history – inspired by The Murderer himself. Cain and Abel had made offerings to God, and for some reason Cain's was not acceptable. We're not sure why – perhaps it had to do with Cain's heart attitude as he presented it. At any rate, Cain became very angry and resentful. God could see what was in Cain's heart and confronted him about it, giving him some very valuable advice – which Cain didn't take.

> *You will be accepted if you do what is right. But if you refuse to do what is right, then watch out! Sin is crouching at the door, eager to control you. But you must subdue it and be its master.*
>
> **– Genesis 4:7 (NLT)**

What? Control? I thought Satan was offering freedom! Anyone who has given in to the "freeing" temptations of Satan knows they eventually lead to bondage. It's interesting that in the last book of the Bible, Jesus also talks about standing at the door: *Here I am! I stand at the door and knock. If anyone hears my voice and opens the door, I will come in and eat with him, and he with Me* (Revelation 3:20). The door spoken of at both ends of the Bible represents our **will**. Whatever we allow to come through that door will influence our choices, our life and our destiny – for good or for evil. And in both verses, *we* have control of the door. We decide what comes in, and what doesn't.

God describes sin (inspired by Satan) as crouching just outside the door of your will, trying to convince you to hold it open for him – because he wants to master you, little by little. You've got two options. You can slam that door shut, sending a loud and clear message to both him and God that you're not interested in his propositions ... or you can leave it open a crack. By doing that, you're saying, "Satan – I'm open to suggestions. How would you meet my needs?" He'll make his proposals. You'll listen. They will sound *very* good. As Eugene Peterson wrote, "Every temptation is disguised as a suggestion for improvement."[6] Improvement is good, right? So after a short period of deliberation, you'll probably swing the door open.

Footholds ...

The principle is presented again in Ephesians 4:26,27 (NIV).

> *In your anger do not sin. Do not let the sun go down while you are still angry, and do not give the devil a **foothold**.*

Anger is not sin, as was mentioned earlier in this manual. But what we do when angry can be sin, or our anger can eventually *lead* us to sin if we don't deal with it in a timely manner. If we let negative attitudes – sinful or not – dwell in us unaddressed, we run the risk of giving the devil a "foothold."

When rock climbing, you need to find a series of footholds to make progress. One foothold will not conquer the pitch – each one enables you to make it to the next. This is a key point to remember about how Satan will try to influence your life. He won't blast in and take over all at once. He can't – such an obvious attempt would alert you. But if he can gain a little foothold – get you to agree to letting him have just a tiny bit of control in a small area, he's gotten just a little closer to conquering you in larger areas. God's advice to you: Don't give him even the first foothold! Once you've given it to him, it will be difficult to get it back!

One other important point: How does Satan get a foothold? **We give it to him.** He cannot seize it by force. He can't overrule our will. But he can deceive us into thinking that we will benefit by agreeing to his suggestions. So we give him that itty-bitty foothold in exchange for something we think will be of more value. We're always wrong.

Exploiting vulnerabilities

> To be certain to take what you attack is
> to attack a place the enemy does not protect.
>
> – Sun Tzu in *The Art of War*[7]

When it comes to targeting our open doors and footholds, Satan has stolen this strategy from Sun Tzu's book – or vice versa. Each of us has areas of weakness, vulnerabilities and undefended places in our lives. Satan is aware of them, and *that's* where he waits. He won't waste time in your areas of strength – he's a skilled strategist patiently scoping out your soft spots and looking for an opportunity to strike.

[?] You will demonstrate *your* skill as a defensive strategist if you will take the time to assess where your vulnerabilities are. Spend a few moments right now and ask the Lord to reveal to you where they might be. Where are your areas of chronic defeat? Which temptations are no match for your resolve? Where have you fallen before?

_____

_____

_____

For a list of *potential* doorways, see Appendix E. You'll notice we emphasize "potential." Encountering one of the events, habits or experiences listed there doesn't necessarily mean you have opened a doorway or given a foothold. But it is possible. If you have had experience with one of the items on the list, spend some time with God asking Him if there is an open door there that needs to be shut.

Closing doorways

"You must subdue it and be its master." (Genesis 4:7) Whenever you become aware of an open door in your life, there are three steps you need to take in order to shut it:

1. **Confess and repent of opening the door.** If it was due to a willful choice on your part, this step is obvious. But some doorways may have started opening when you were in a passive state, and not disobeying God at all: e.g., while under anesthesia, while being traumatized during a physical assault, while in possession of unknown occultic items, dating a demonized person before your met your husband, attending an occult ritual or festival out of ignorance, etc. (see Appendix E for a more complete list). It may be that you later made a willful choice due to something that began at that time. It could be something like becoming psychologically addicted to pain meds after surgery (pain is no longer the problem, but the desire to escape your anxiety through chemical enhancement is). In those cases you should confess the sin, but also intentionally close the original door.

2. **Take action to demonstrate repentance and purify your life.**
   - Release resentment and bitterness
   - Seek forgiveness of anyone you offended or hurt
   - Pay restitution if it's owed
   - Renounce occultic involvement
   - Destroy any offending objects (occultic amulets and games, pornography, books, satanic music, DVDs, drugs, alcohol, etc.)
   - Break off any harmful relationships
   - Put yourself back under God's authority

3. **Reappropriate the filling of the Holy Spirit.** (See Chapter 6.)

Suggested prayer for closing doorways

Father, I confess that I have opened a door to my enemy. I have given him a foothold. I was vulnerable and deceived when I made the decision, but I'm still responsible for it. I confess to You that I [describe what you did to open the door]. I agree with You that it was sin, and I'm sorry for it. Please forgive me. On the basis of Your promise in Your Word, I accept Your forgiveness of my sins. Thank You.

And now, Father, before You and before all the forces of darkness, I renounce my decision and renounce my opening of that door. I shut that door and take back that foothold. Satan, I remove your authority and ability to influence me in that area any longer. I bind you back from it in the name of Jesus Christ, who is my Lord, Savior and King.

Father, please strengthen that area of vulnerability. May it no longer be an undefended place. I commit to taking any further action You tell me to regarding this matter.

I relinquish the throne of my life to You once again. Please fill me, control me and empower me with Your Holy Spirit. Amen.

❀ ❀ ❀❀ ❀ ❀

Our weapons

The weapons of our warfare are not physical weapons of flesh and blood, but they are mighty before God for the overthrow and destruction of strongholds.

– 2 Corinthians 10:4 (AMPLIFIED)

Weapon #1: Our authority

Being one of the most powerful beings God ever created, and honing his warfare skills for centuries, Satan is an adversary more powerful and deadly than anything we can imagine. If we were to go head-to-head with him in our own strength, he'd squash us like bugs.

But the Bible talks about the authority we have been given as servants and soldiers of Jesus Christ. The Greek word for it is:

EXOUSIA: "Right, power, authority, ruling power, a bearer of authority."[8]

It's more than *just* power – it's power *plus authority*. It's like in football. There are 22 men on the field with awesome power. They are strong, fast, and can inflict pain in a multitude of ways, but they aren't in authority. There are five or six other guys down there with striped shirts and whistles who have *exousia*. The players can put people *down*, but the refs can put people *out*.[9]

Ephesians 1:19-23 has a lot to say about Jesus Christ's *exousia*.

That power is like the working of His [the Father's] mighty strength, which He exerted in Christ when He raised Him from the dead and seated Him at His right hand in the heavenly realms, far above all rule and authority [exousia], power and dominion, and every title that can be given, not only in the present age but also in the one to come. And God placed all things under His feet and appointed Him to be head over everything for the church, which is His body, the fullness of Him who fills everything in every way. (NIV)

❀ ❀ ❀❀ ❀ ❀

In this passage (Ephesians 1:19-23), whose (plural) authority does Christ's authority exceed?

_____

_____

 Colossians 2:9,10 states that someone else besides Christ is *also* in possession of this same fullness and *exousia*. Circle who that is in the passage below.

> *For in Christ all the fullness of the Deity lives in bodily form, and you have been given this fullness in Christ, Who is the head over every power and authority* (exousia). (NIV)

❋ ❋ ❋❋❋ ❋ ❋

Your place of warring

There is no authority in the universe higher than Jesus Christ's. No king, no general, no president, no demon, no angel – not even Satan himself can stand before His *exousia*. And since we are now His children, God has equipped us to operate in that same authority as we deal with the forces of

> God raised us up with Christ and seated us with Him in the heavenly realms in Christ Jesus.
> **– Ephesians 2:6 (NIV)**

darkness. As the verse to the right says, we are positioned with Christ in the heavenly realms – a position of immense power and authority over our spiritual adversaries. Christ – and we – have this authority because of Christ's willingness to die on the cross and rise again, thereby defeating Satan, sin and death once and for all.

> It is not for us to fight *for* victory, because *"we are more than conquerors through Him that loved us."* (Romans 8:37) Our fight is *from* victory: and from this vantage point, empowered with Christ's might, and completely enclosed in the whole armor of God, the powers of evil are compelled to back off as we resist them.
>
> – Arthur Matthews in *Born For Battle*[10]

We fight *from* a position of victory and authority, seated with Christ in His heavenly command center. If we try to fight from any other vantage point, we will be defeated. Spiritual warfare expert Mark Bubeck writes in *Overcoming The Adversary*:[11]

> No believer who willfully walks in the sins of the flesh and world can hope to escape Satan's hurt and bondage. Can you imagine what would happen to a soldier who took a little stroll into his enemy's territory during the heat of war? If not killed, he would soon be surrounded and taken captive. Yet, there are believers who think they can carelessly engage in sin without being vulnerable to Satan.

❋ ❋ ❋ ❋

Weapon #2: Our spiritual kevlar

Anyone serious about competitive sports has learned that without a good defense, a good offense is useless. The same holds true in warfare. It doesn't matter how skillful we are with our offensive weapons, if we take one in the chest, we're done. That's why your husband was probably very meticulous about putting on his body armor whenever he was going where bombs and bullets might be. And that's why God invented spiritual armor for our spiritual battles as well.[12] The Apostle Paul writes about it in Ephesians 6:13-17 (NIV):

> *Therefore put on the full armor of God, so that when the day of evil comes, you may be able to stand your ground, and after you have done everything, to stand. Stand firm then, with the **belt of truth** buckled around your waist, with the **breastplate of righteousness** in place, and with your **feet fitted with the readiness that comes from the gospel of peace**. In addition to all this, take up the **shield of faith**, with which you can extinguish all the flaming arrows of the evil one. Take the **helmet of salvation** and the **sword of the Spirit**, which is the Word of God.*

Consider briefly each element of the armor God has given us:[13]

Belt of Truth. Satan's chief tactic is deceit. Our only counter is truth. Any battle strategy is only as good as the intelligence that guides it. Jesus said that He *is* the truth (John 14:6), and He describes the Holy Spirit as "*the Spirit of Truth*" (John 14:17). As we strap on this Belt of Truth, it alerts us to the lies and deceitful tactics of the enemy and helps us fight with efficiency.

Breastplate of Righteousness. The breastplate is like your husband's flak jacket. Its main function is to protect the organs that are vital to life. A person can function without a hand or a leg, but if you lose a heart – no spares. King Solomon urges you to "*Guard your heart above all else, for it determines the course of your life*" (Proverbs 4:23 NLT). Our hearts are guarded by the righteousness of Jesus Christ that was given to us when we were saved. Righteousness is everything that Satan is not, so it repels him like Teflon does scrambled eggs – only better!

Boots of the Gospel of Peace. Boots protect your feet and give you traction and stability. Barefoot, we would move too slowly and fearfully – an easy target in battle. You know that the Gospel brings peace to those who hear it. But don't forget that it also brings peace to *you!* Sometimes, when the world is so difficult to deal with, we become slow, unsteady and unstable. It's easy to lose traction and stumble in that condition. Strap on those Gospel boots of peace, so that you can negotiate the rugged terrain before you. Jesus said in John 16:33, "*These things I have spoken to you, so that in Me you may have peace. In the world you have tribulation, but take courage; I have overcome the world.*" Let His victories bring you peace and stability.

Shield of Faith. The particular shield talked about here is a *thureos* – a very large shield. It could protect a soldier from *anything* that his adversary launched his way. Faith is our shield – or more accurately, the *object of our faith* is our shield. As we believe in and count on His power and authority to protect us, our shield will hold. If we shift our focus to our enemy and his strength, our faith can waiver. The Warrior-King David knew this well, as he wrote in Psalm 3:3, "*But You, O Lord, are a shield about me, my glory, and the One who lifts my head.*"

Helmet of Salvation. As the breastplate protects our torso's vital organs, the helmet protects our other vital organ and the command center of our lives: our brain. If the head is injured, the rest of the body will malfunction. Satan's *main* attacks won't target our feet or our houses or our jobs – though he may hit them as a diversion. His ultimate objective is to influence and control our *minds*. If he can turn our will to do his bidding, he's turned us completely. This is why, at the moment of salvation, God gave us this helmet to protect our minds from Satan's influence.

Sword of the Spirit. This is a unique implement, because it can be both a defensive *and* an offensive weapon. The sword of the Spirit is the Word of God. When Jesus was attacked by Satan in the wilderness (Matthew 4:1-11), He parried every thrust of His adversary with a verse of Scripture, and eventually sent him on a hasty retreat. As the Apostle Paul affirms, "*For the Word of God is living and active and sharper than any two edged sword*" (Hebrews 4:12). More about this in the next section.

When your husband was in a war zone, he probably never went anywhere outside the wire without first putting on all his body armor. In our international war on *Satan's* terror, there is no Green Zone. Every step we take is behind enemy lines. So it would be wise to *intentionally* put on our *spiritual* armor each day before we venture out into the world. If you do, you will notice a much higher degree of effectiveness in your ability to cope and even to minister as you continue to recover from your traumatic stress. And you'll take fewer hits as you maneuver through enemy fire.

Following is a suggested prayer you could pray each morning. This is not a magical prayer – the words aren't important. God looks at the heart, so to the degree these words reflect what your heart wants to express, God will hear them. Visualize each piece of armor as you put it on.

Dear Father, I stand before You this morning in order to receive the armor You have for me today. I receive from Your hand and wrap around my waist your belt of truth. May I receive, believe and speak only Your truth. I receive from Your hand and strap to my torso the breastplate of righteousness – the righteousness of Jesus Christ given to me the day I was saved. Guard my heart with it. I receive from Your hand and put on my feet the boots of the gospel of peace. May these boots give me stability and speed in my warring. And may Your peace fill my being and flow out to those around me.

I receive from Your hand and take in my [left/right] hand the shield of faith, with which I will deflect the missiles of my enemy, except for the ones You want to use for my purification and Your glory. I receive from Your hand the helmet of salvation, bought for me almost two thousand years ago when Jesus Christ died on the cross for me, and rose again. Guard my mind with it. Finally, I receive from Your hand and take in my [right/left] hand the sword of the Spirit, which is Your Word. Give me skill to use it to defend myself and attack my enemy. So clothed in this armor, equipped with this sword and backed by Your authority, may I this day push back the kingdom of darkness and expand the Kingdom of Light. I pray this in the name of Jesus Christ, my Savior, Redeemer, God and King, Amen.

❁ ❁ ❁ ❁

Weapon #3: The Word of God

How things get done in the Kingdom of God

In each of the following passages, something is being accomplished by God or by representatives of God. Read each passage, looking for what it is that is "making it happen."

Then God said, "Let there be light"; and there was light. **– Genesis 1:3**

Then Jesus said to him, "Go, Satan! For it is written, 'You shall worship the Lord your God and serve Him only.'" **– Matthew 4:10**

Jesus said to the paralytic, "Get up, pick up your bed and go home." And he got up and went home. **– Matthew 9:6**

Jesus said to the man, "Stretch out your hand!" He stretched it out, and it was restored to normal. **– Matthew 12:13**

Jesus rebuked him, saying, "Be quiet, and come out of him!" The unclean spirit cried out with a loud voice and came out. **– Mark 1:25,26**

Jesus rebuked the wind and said to the sea, "Hush, be still." And the wind died down and it became perfectly calm. **– Mark 4:39**

Jesus cried out with a loud voice, "Lazarus, come forth!" The man who had died came forth, bound with wrappings. **– John 11:43,44**

Peter said, "I do not possess silver and gold, but what I do have I give to you: In the name of Jesus Christ the Nazarene – walk!" With a leap he stood upright and began to walk. **– Acts 3:6-8**

Paul said to Elymas the magician, "You who are full of deceit and fraud ... now, behold, the hand of the Lord is upon you, and you will be blind and not see the sun for a time." And immediately a mist and a darkness fell upon him. **– Acts 13:8-11**

Paul turned and said to the spirit, "I command you in the name of Jesus Christ to come out of her!" And it came out at that very moment. **– Acts 16:18**

What does each passage have in common, in terms of what was done just before the supernatural event occurred?

_____

_____

Hopefully you were able to see that the way things are accomplished in the spiritual realm is not through muscle-power, electricity, computers, bulldozers or bombs. It gets done by *the spoken word*.

In the listing of your spiritual armor, the Sword of the Spirit is clearly equated with God's Word. When God wanted to create, He commanded matter into existence. When Jesus wanted to neutralize Satan, heal, calm a storm, raise the dead, control a demon, He spoke a word of commandment. When Jesus' disciples needed to heal or engage in spiritual warfare, they followed His example and spoke commands as representatives of their Master.

This is also how Jesus wants *you* to fight your enemy. You occupy the high ground, you have superior fire power, righteous authority and allies that are not of this world. You accomplish your offensives by *speaking* your commands to your enemy, just as Jesus did when He fought Satan in the wilderness in Matthew 4.

Spiritual ammo

Each time Jesus was attacked, He came back at His enemy with Scripture. Follow His example! Suppose your enemy is coming at you with a temptation to go to bed with someone other than your husband. He is available and willing – what are you going to do? Grab some spiritual ammo! Recall what God's Word says on this subject and use it against your tempter (Satan, not the one you're lusting after!), just as Jesus Christ showed you. Here's a suggested confrontational pattern:

> *Father, Satan is tempting me to sin against You. He wants me to commit adultery. But I desire to master him. Please fill me with Your Holy Spirit. I take my position seated with Christ at Your right hand in the heavenly realms above all forces of darkness. With Your blessing and protection, and in Your authority, I ask You to help me resist my enemy, and thereby defeat him.*

> *Satan, I address you in the name and authority of the Lord Jesus Christ, King of kings and Lord of lords – who has bought me with His blood and made me a child of the Most High God. I am aware of your attempts to cause me to sin. In doing so, you have transgressed the commandment of God, for He has said in His Word, "You shall not commit adultery." You are trying to get me to commit this sin, so you are in the wrong. Therefore, in the authority given to me by God Himself, I command you to cease your activities directed at me, remove yourself from my area and go where Jesus Christ tells you to go.*

> *Thank you, Father, for this victory. Just as your angels ministered to Jesus after His fight with Satan, I ask that You would minister to me as well, and strengthen that vulnerable area in my life. Amen!*

 In doing this, you are following a very clear pattern that God has set up in His Word. You see it in James 4:7,8. Compare each component of the verse with each of the three paragraphs above.

First paragraph = **Submit to God.**
Second paragraph = **Resist the devil and he will flee from you.**
Third paragraph = **Draw near to God and He will draw near to you.**

Advance or retreat?

Here's an important distinction that all God's spiritual warriors need to be aware of. You may have heard it said, "Resist temptation" and "Flee the devil." This is a good example of how Satan twists the truth in order to engineer our defeat, because God tells us to do the *exact opposite*.

When it comes to temptation, we are to *flee*! As Proverbs 4:14,15 says:

> Do not enter the path of the wicked and do not proceed in the way of
> evil men. Avoid it, do not pass by it; turn away from it and pass on.

When it comes to direct confrontation with the devil, we are to *resist*! Don't back down, don't run, *fight*. If we do, *he'll* run, as we just read in James 4:7, *Resist the devil and he will flee from you.*

Here's the fun part. It doesn't say we have to engage him and beat him to a pulp or try to pull off some overwhelming victory in order to make him retreat. All we have to do is resist. That's it! He'll see our *exousia*, recognize our training, and run for the hills!

Need some ammo? Check out your very own *Spiritual Warfare Ammo Bunker* found in Appendix F of this manual. There's plenty there! But if you come up against an attack of the enemy and don't see the exact bullet, bomb or missile you need in the bunker, do some searching of the Scriptures on your own and add it to your supplies.

! Wouldn't you like to try out your new weaponry? Ask God to show you an area in which Satan has been attacking you lately. Select your "ammo" verse, and then engage the enemy! Use the prayer pattern suggested on the previous page. Then, sometime tomorrow come back to this manual and write down what happened.

_____

_____

_____

_____

_____

_____

Warfare praying

As mentioned earlier, the words of our prayers are not nearly as important as the attitude of our heart. If we have an adversary as ruthless as Satan and his kingdom of darkness, and if our main weapon in fighting him is through prayer, then we should become experts in prayer. How do we get there? One of the best ways to learn how to pray is to pray! But even though it's our heart and not our words that are crucial, most of us still need help with how to form the words to express our hearts. This can be overcome by praying "prepared prayers" of those who are accomplished and experienced in this holy discipline. To the extent that their words express what we desire, we make their prayers ours, and learn to follow their helpful examples.

Warfare praying can be a very emotional, even scary undertaking. Warfare prayer expert Dr. Mark Bubeck writes about how important it is that our prayers be based on the firm foundation of scriptural truth and not on anything else:

> The believer's emphasis in spiritual warfare must be upon a biblical, doctrinal approach
> to the subject. Subjective feelings, emotional desires and fervent sincerity are not
> sufficient weaponry against Satan. He yields no ground to emotion or sincerity. He
> retreats only from before the authority the believer has through his union with the
> Lord Jesus Christ and the absolute truth of the Word of God.[14]

Dr. Bubeck advocates that when it comes to warfare praying, we should pray "doctrinal prayers" as we resist our enemy. They draw their power from the absolutes of truth available to believers through the finished work of Christ and provide a pattern of using doctrinal truth as you pray for others. Following are a few examples of doctrinal prayers that you could pray for yourself, your husband and your kids.

Prayer for spiritual victory

Dear Heavenly Father, I praise You that I am united with the Lord Jesus Christ in all of His life and work. By faith I desire to enter into the victory of the incarnation of my Lord today. I invite Him to live His victory in me. Thank You, Lord Jesus Christ, that You experienced all temptations that I experience and yet never sinned.

I enter by faith into the mighty work of the crucifixion of my Lord. Thank You, dear Father, that through Jesus' blood there is moment-by-moment cleansing from sin, permitting me to fellowship with You. Thank You that the work of the Cross brings Satan's work to nothing.

I enter by faith into the full power and authority of my Lord's resurrection. I desire to walk in the newness of life that is mine through my Lord's resurrection. Lead me into a deeper understanding of the power of the Resurrection.

By faith I enter into my union with the Lord Jesus Christ in His ascension. I rejoice that my Lord displayed openly His victory over all powers as He ascended into glory through the very realm of the prince of the power of the air.

I enter into my victory aggressively and claim my place as more than a conqueror through Him who loves me. I offer up this prayer in the name of the Lord Jesus with thanksgiving. Amen.

– Mark Bubeck[15]

Prayer for your marriage

Loving heavenly Father, I thank You for Your perfect plan for our marriage. I know that a marriage functioning in Your will is fulfilling and beautiful. I bring our marriage before You that You might make it all You desire it to be.

Please forgive me for my sins of failure in our marriage. [One may specify and enlarge confession.] *In the name of the Lord Jesus Christ, I tear down all of Satan's strongholds designed to destroy our marriage. In His name, I break all negative relationships between us that have been established by Satan and his wicked spirits. I will accept only the relationships established by You and the blessed Holy Spirit. I invite the Holy Spirit to enable me to relate to ____ (spouse's name) in a manner that will meet his/her needs.*

I submit our conversations to You, that they may please You. I submit our physical relationship to You, that it may enjoy Your blessing. I submit our love to You, that You may cause it to grow and mature.

Open my eyes to see all areas where I am deceived. Open ____'s eyes to see any of Satan's deceptions upon him/her. Make our union to be the Christ-centered relationship you have designed in Your perfect will. I ask this in Jesus' name with thanksgiving. Amen.

– Mark Bubeck[16]

Prayer for your husband and the trials he's facing

Lord, You alone know the depth of the burden my husband carries. I may understand the specifics, but You have measured the weight of it on his shoulders. I've not come to minimize what You are doing in his life, for I know You work great things in the midst of trials. Nor am I trying to protect him from what he must face. I only want to support him so that he will get through this battle as the winner.

God, You are our refuge and strength, a very present help in trouble (Psalm 46:1). You have invited us to "come boldly to the throne of grace, that we may obtain mercy and find grace to help in time of need" (Hebrews 4:16). I come before Your throne and ask for grace for my husband. Strengthen his heart for this battle and give him patience to wait on You (Psalm 27:1-4). Build him up so that no matter what happens he will be able to stand strong through it. Help him to be always "rejoicing in hope, patient in tribulation, continuing steadfastly in prayer" (Romans 12:12). Give him endurance to run the race and not give up, for You have said that "a righteous man may fall seven times and rise again" (Proverbs 24:16). Help him to remember that "the steps of a good man are ordered by the LORD, and He delights in his way. Though he fall, he shall not be utterly cast down; for the LORD upholds him with His hand." (Psalm 37:23,24)

I pray he will look to You to be his "refuge until these calamities have passed by" (Psalm 57:1). May he learn to wait on You because "those who wait on the LORD shall renew their strength; they shall mount up with wings like eagles, they shall run and not be weary, they shall walk and not faint" (Isaiah 40:31). I pray that he will find his strength in You and as he cries out to You, You will hear him and save him out of all his troubles (Psalm 34:6). In the name of Jesus Christ, I pray, Amen.

– Stormie Omartian[17]

Prayer for your children

Father, I come to You in the name of Jesus, on behalf of my son/daughter ____. I thank You, Lord, that You have given him/her to me as a heritage to love and raise to Your glory. I ask You to forgive me for my failures to lead and guide him/her in the way he/she ought to go. I thank You that You are the God who restores and who brings good out of evil.

Take even my past failures, Lord, and use them to Your glory as You faithfully draw ____ to Yourself. I thank You that through You I am mighty and can pull down the strongholds of the enemy. I exercise that authority now in the mighty name of Jesus.

And in Jesus' name I bind the powers of darkness that would blind ____ to Your truth and I command them to loose him/her now. And Father, in Jesus' name, I ask that You would draw ____ to Yourself, convicting him/her of sin by Your Holy Spirit. I plead the protection and deliverance of the blood of Jesus over ____ and by faith claim ____ for the kingdom of God. In Jesus' name, Amen.

– Ray Beeson & Kathi Mills[18]

For additional examples of doctrinal prayers, please check out some of the excellent books in our *Additional Resources* section in Appendix B that pertain to this chapter. You will also find a number of prayers like these on the "From the Inside Out" web site, found at http://home.mchsi.com/~ftio/warfare-prayers.htm.

❀ ❀ ❀❀ ❀ ❀

Lauren's Prayer ...

Heavenly Father, I realize now that my husband is not the only soldier in this family. I, too, am enlisted in the ranks. My battles, however, belong not to this nation, but to You, Lord. While my husband invades enemy territory by sea, air or land, I must engage the invisible enemy on my knees. Thank You, Lord, that You know how brutal the battlefield can be. Thank You that You have issued me combat gear designed for my spiritual, physical and emotional protection. Thank You that the weapons I fight with have Your divine power to demolish the enemy's strongholds. Thank You that with these God-given weapons I can demolish arguments and every pretension that sets itself up against Your plans for my husband, our family and for me.

Lord Jesus, You tell me in Your Word that You are the Gate. You tell me that all others are thieves and robbers. The thief offers me so many other ways out of this war zone where I am fighting for my marriage, my family, my sanity. You are the Gate! I realize now that You are the only way out of this pain. You are the only safe exit out of this battle.

Thank You that, although sin crouches at the door, You stand at the door. Lord, teach me to stand, too. In Jesus' Name, Amen.

Promise from God's Word ...

Children, you belong to God, and you have defeated these enemies.
God's Spirit is in you and is more powerful than the one that is in the world.
– 1 John 4:4 (CEV)

11 HOW CAN I HELP MY HUSBAND?
Contributing To Your Husband's Healing Environment

Danielle's Journal ...

Spring is finally here. When I looked outside this morning, white flower petals swirled around in a happy dance on my driveway. My grandmother always said that when the dogwoods drop their blossoms, it's safe to plant your garden. So I pulled out the plans for my flower beds, the ones I sketched during the darker, dreary months of winter. I made a beeline for the nursery before another minute of spring had sprung. I filled the back of my car with flats brimming with red petunias and yellow marigolds for the sunny areas of my yard and rosy impatiens and white alyssum for the shade.

I tied my hair back with a bright bandana and slipped on my stiff gardening gloves. I turned fresh peat and fertilizer into the sleepy soil with a shiny new shovel. I knelt in the shade beside the front beds where the fresh dirt cushioned my knees. The new plants trusted me with their fragile flowers and delicate stems as I took them out of their first home and transplanted them in front of mine. They depended on me to make their new home a safe place where they could grow and reach their full potential. Defenseless, they had no choice but to consider me faithful to provide the best environment in which they could get re-established and flourish for a season.

I stood back and admired my efforts. My dull house was now a charming cottage, the dead grays and browns of winter replaced by splashes of color and the promise of life. The front door stood open. Through the screen I could see Michael in the family room, slumped in his recliner, staring into the back yard. I watched him for a long moment. My warrior, my strong husband, looked fragile. Defenseless. Vulnerable. Part of me wanted to burst through the screen door and scoop him up in my arms and hold him close. Part of me wanted to shelter him and to shout at anyone who got too near.

Whether he realizes it or not, Michael needs me desperately now. I have been his closest friend and biggest fan for so long. I know I must take care of myself as we journey through combat trauma, but I must also take steps to make our home a place where Michael feels safe and can heal. I see signs of new growth, but they are tender and fragile. I need to be willing to get my hands dirty to make his surroundings sunny, shaded or sheltered as his soul is restored, and as safe as I can from the storms of life.

I know very well by now that I am not Michael's cure-all. I cannot fix his problems or erase his struggles. But I can apply what I learned during the darker, dreary months of wondering what was happening to my man. The dogwoods have dropped their blossoms. It's time to plant my garden. The war has come home. It's time to roll up my sleeves and use my energies to create and manage a colorful and quiet setting that invites growth, beauty and life.

Broadening your vision

The main thrust of this manual up to this point has been to help you gain a better understanding of your current stressful situation and how to do a better job of taking care of you. It is a prevalent and honorable characteristic of most wives and mothers to place the welfare of their husband and children ahead of their own – often to their own detriment. But as we've noted before, if you go down, who will take care of your charges then? Who will take care of you?

We hope we've given you some helpful perspectives on how to survive and prosper in the traumatic stress you have been experiencing. But we know you also have a heart to care for your man and, if you have any, your children. This chapter and the next will help you identify some of their crucial areas of concern, and give you some practical ways to be a "bridge of healing" for them.

Thank you for your support

It's a very good thing that you *do* still have a continuing desire to minister to and support your husband. Why? Because you are in a better position to do it than anyone else on the planet. According to the Center for Deployment Psychology of the American Psychiatric Association:

> One of the strongest predictors of recovery following trauma is social support. In general, families provide the primary source of social support. Spouses and intimate partners are typically identified as the chief source of social support.[1]

Your support of your Combat Traumatized husband is the most powerful avenue of aid that he could possibly find – whether he knows it or not. Bridget Cantrell and Chuck Dean in their course workbook for returning veterans entitled *Turning Your Heart Toward Home* make this observation:

> For the partner or family member living with a person with PTSD it is important for them to be supportive. You can actually be a "second set of eyes" by heightening your awareness and increasing your empathy, so that you can understand how your loved one is being affected by the symptoms of PTSD … The chances of this happening are better if the partner or family member understands, and is involved with them on their journey towards healing."[2]

But as you continue in your role as your husband's Number One Caregiver, it's very important that you don't see yourself as the all-powerful superheroine who is supposed to burst on the scene, rescue your husband and fix all his problems. Dr. Aphrodite Matsakis, internationally recognized trauma expert and former clinical coordinator for the Vietnam Veteran's Outreach Center in Silver Springs, Md., gives us a very important warning:

> Although you may want to be as supportive as you can, you cannot be all things to your trauma survivor. No matter how much you love him or her, your love cannot "fix" the past or "make right" all the injustices he/she experienced. If you exhaust yourself trying to nurture your loved one, you may end up full of resentment when he/she does not heal as rapidly or as thoroughly as you would have hoped.
>
> The Al-Anon acronym "C-C-C" applies here. C-C-C stands for Cause, Control and Cure. *You did not **cause** the trauma survivor's problems. You cannot **control** him or her and you cannot **cure** him or her.* While you definitely can be supportive, you can't undo the past, no matter how much he or she might like you to and how much you might wish to do so.[3]

Why bother?

Despite your heroic and unselfish efforts, have you ever found yourself asking, "Why do I stick with this guy? Do I really need this? Why don't I just leave?" If you have wondered that, you're not alone. According to Defense Department officials, the divorce rate among active-duty Army officers and enlisted personnel almost doubled between 2001 and 2004 – and there are no divorce statistics available about what happens *after* married couples leave the military. But so far you, and many other courageous wives, have elected to stay with their husbands for admirable reasons. Dr. Charles Figley, Founding Editor of the Journal of Traumatic Stress, cites a study of wives of Israeli veterans with PTSD which examined why and how they were able to stay in their troubled marriages. Most of the women had considered divorce, but decided not to go through with it for five main reasons:[4]

- Feeling a strong sense of moral commitment toward their husband
- Fearing for their husband's lives if they weren't there to help
- Drawing from a reservoir of good feelings they had from before their husband's deployment when their marriages were happy
- Appreciating their husband's courage and determinations as they observed them struggling with PTSD, which encouraged them to struggle on as well
- Observing an increased sensitivity on the part of their husbands toward her emotional difficulties and those of their children

? If you'll spend a few moments examining your heart, one or more of these reasons may describe why *you* are toughing it out – or perhaps you have other reasons. Write down why you are staying in your marriage. It doesn't matter if you would consider it a noble reason or not (e.g., "I can't afford to move out"). Why are you sticking with him?

How can I help?

If we wanted to, we could probably make this chapter 100 pages long. But in a great show of mercy and conciseness, we'd like to pass on to you some insights dealing with seven crucial areas in which you can be a tremendous help to your husband. When we cover issues that seem like an area of great need in your relationship, please consider the books we've recommended relative to this chapter in Appendix B (*Additional Resources*) for deeper insight. There is only so much that can be stuffed into one chapter!

We do want to mention, however, that some of the suggestions we make here may not seem practical to all readers. Every relationship is different. Levels, modes, experience and depth of communication vary from couple to couple. Add to that the extreme relationship stressor of Combat Trauma, and you could have some *real* challenges. You might find it very difficult to imagine you and your husband sitting down together and quietly discussing your household roles, communication issues or sexual intimacy. That's okay! You simply might not be there yet – but that doesn't mean you won't be six months or a year from now. If you come across a suggestion that just seems impossible, don't put pressure on yourself and try to push for it right away. Make it a matter of prayer, and see how God might change the landscape over time. What may be impossible today may be perfectly plausible in the future!

1. Redefine and clarify roles and responsibilities

When your husband was deployed, you adopted multiple roles – roles that used to be divided between "his" and "hers." Your role designations may have been flawed even *before* deployment, but they are surely jumbled now since he's come back with Combat Trauma. Not only are you possibly working a full- or part-time job, you may also be a mother, responsible for every detail in your children's lives. But now that your husband is back and trying to cope with his combat experiences, it may sometimes feel like you have inherited *another* child. As Melanie, a mother of three and wife of a combat vet wrote in Aphrodite Matsakis' book *Vietnam Wives*,

> I am also responsible for most of the details of my husband's life – arranging his medical appointments, explaining and protecting him from his parents, my parents, the social workers and the neighbors. I take care of all his paperwork too, and since he's one of those vets who hates the IRS, I take care of all the family finances as well.[5]

There are two reasons why you should take the time to redefine, clarify and delegate some of your roles and responsibilities: (1) to avoid your early demise and (2) as a positive way of involving your husband in his own healing. He is going to feel a little "out of it" for a while as he tries to reintegrate into family life. While he was gone, you shifted gears into a highly efficient "do everything" mode out of necessity, and either consciously or unconsciously you may be thinking that to alter anything will destroy the efficiency of your smooth-running machine. "If it ain't broke, don't fix it!" Besides that, his Combat Trauma may be compromising his competencies, so you could be reluctant to jeopardize your machine by putting him in charge of any parts of it. For both of your sakes, you *must* make the effort to do so. As Dr. Kathleen Gilbert, Associate Professor of Applied Health Science at Indiana University, writes:

> By overfunctioning, the woman not only increases her own stress but also adds to the disenfranchisement of her husband from the family. Her efforts to fulfill roles traditionally held by the husband may be seen by him as evidence that she believes him to be incapable of carrying out his role. Alternatively, he may also contribute to his own disenfranchisement by abandoning those roles when he sees her as willing to take them on.[6]

❀ ❀ ❀ ❀

Chore inventory

On a separate sheet of paper – preferably *with* your husband – write a list of all household chores and responsibilities. List everything, no matter how small or insignificant you might think it could be. Include things like taking out the trash, getting the car fixed, doing the grocery shopping, paying the bills, reading the kids a bedtime story, mowing the lawn, taking the dog to the vet, washing the dishes, etc. To the left of the list, make two narrow columns side-by-side. At the top of the left column write "Now" and write either your initial or your husband's initial next to each chore designating who is currently in charge of it. In the right column, head it with the word "Ideal" and put the initial of the person who should ideally be taking care of each chore. In some cases you might have to write a "B" for both, designating something that would need to be done by whomever is available when it's needed (like taking the dog to the vet). But try to limit those as much as possible.

If your husband is fully-employed and you aren't, there will probably be more items marked with your initial than his, and that's to be expected. But that doesn't mean that *all* of them should be yours! Nowhere is it written in stone that the typical gender-based roles of 20th century America are inviolable. As Dr. Matsakis writes, "'Mothering' does not have to include laundering; 'fathering' does not have to exclude it."[7] Discuss each role and responsibility together and try to achieve some sort of equity.

If his Combat Trauma is particularly severe, and he has symptoms that prohibit him from taking on a normal load of responsibilities, it's still important for his healing that he be given *something* he can do every day. A huge component of the devastation of Combat Trauma is the loss of control. If you can help him to gain a sense of control in even a little bit of his world, it can make a significant difference. Dr. Robert Hicks, an Air Force Reserve specialist, counselor and expert on PTSD, highlights how strategic this is, and describes it as "slaying the mental and psycho-dragons that convince us that there is nothing we can do":

> As human beings made in the image of God, we have been given a certain stewardship of our environment (see Genesis 1:26). We have the deep-seated need to rule the environment of our lives … Trauma makes the best people dysfunctional for a while. But when we begin to come out of our shells through supportive care, we need to regain some of the lost control. We must take up the sword and do some dragon killing.

In psycho-jargon, this principle is called *re-establishing the locus of control*. For our own mental maintenance we need a place or sphere that we can control. We can't control everything, but we need to regain the control of something. In regaining the smallest areas of control, we can begin to rebuild our shattered identity and world.[8]

It's important to keep in mind, however, that the contrasts between his heart-pumping assignments in the war zone and his mundane chores at home is huge. He may have a difficult time swapping the adrenaline rush of walking through a hostile neighborhood in Fallujah with taking the dog for a walk. This will take some "re-learning," which will take some time. Be understanding and patient with him in this transition period.

A variety of roles. Depending on how your husband is doing, and what "season" of recovery he is in, your role will vary. Below are a number of possible roles you could be taking on as the wife of a Combat Trauma sufferer. None of them are inherently "wrong." Some are simply practical while others are decidedly heroic and noble. Put a check-mark next to roles you are currently fulfilling in your husband's life, or add additional ones you don't see on the list:

❑ Wife	❑ Listener	❑ Social Chairman
❑ Mother	❑ Good Samaritan	❑ Entertainment Director
❑ Chauffeur	❑ Lover	❑ Best Friend
❑ Medical Administrator	❑ Healing Environment	
❑ Pharmacist	Administrator	
❑ Encourager	❑ Secretary	
❑ Calming Influence	❑ Bookkeeper	

Battle Buddy Assignment: Share the above list with your Battle Buddy and talk about any of the items that caused you any difficulty – either because you checked them or because you couldn't check them.

❦ ❦ ❦ ❦

A non-role

Don't take the role of his "fixer." You must constantly remind yourself that *God is his healer and you are not!* If you try to assume a role that you are not equipped for, you'll only frustrate yourself and annoy your husband – or worse, slow down his recovery. Patience Mason is married to Robert, a Vietnam War veteran, who came back from combat with PTSD. Since little was known about the disorder until 1980, Patience dedicated her life trying to help her husband through whatever it was he was experiencing. She'll admit to you today that she did many things wrong, but learned from her mistakes.

> I used to do this all the time, trying to fix Bob. I didn't know he had PTSD, but I knew he had problems (not me) so I kept coming up with solutions: read this book, see a shrink, move, new job, read this book. None of them ever worked, partly because I did not know what the problem was but mainly because I didn't know *whose* problem it was. I thought it was *my* problem. I thought *he* was my problem. I saw no egoism in this. I saw myself as a very loving, giving person who would do anything to help her husband. I didn't see that I also couldn't tolerate his very natural emotions because I thought trying to cheer him up and keep him from expressing anger was nice. I could not allow him to express anger, sadness, despair – so he was unable to heal.[9]

❦ ❦ ❦❦ ❦ ❦

2. Learn how to have a good fight

All relationships encounter conflict from time to time. But when one of the combatants is afflicted with Combat Trauma, it will probably happen more frequently than normal. For this reason you and your husband need to agree to certain "rules of engagement." Usually, when a couple is in the heat of an argument, there is no interest in rules – it's "every man (or woman) for himself!" And when a couple is *not* arguing, they aren't interested in contemplating the rules – why think about negative things when things are going so positively? But if both of you have a clear understanding and agreement about how to *resolve* conflict ahead of time – instead of simply how to win it – your fights will be shorter, less hostile and less damaging. And over time, there will be fewer of them!

First, think about what's going on during an argument, and how the basic mechanics of conflict communication could be improved. If you and your husband can agree to and internalize the following eight parameters, your confrontations will be much more productive:[10]

Focus on:	**Rather than:**
One issue at a time	Many issues
The problem	The person
Behavior	Character
Specifics	Generalities
Expression of feelings	Judgment of character
"I" statements	"You" statements
Observation of facts	Judgment of motives
Mutual understanding	Who's winning or losing

Next, reconsider who you are arguing with, and how he should be treated. John Gottman, in his book *The Seven Principles for Making Marriage Work*, writes:

> To a certain degree, [solving problems] comes down to having good manners. It means treating your spouse with the same respect you offer to company. If a guest leaves an umbrella, we say, "Here. You forgot your umbrella." We would never think of saying, "What's wrong with you? You are constantly forgetting things. Be a little more thoughtful! What am I, your slave to go picking up after you?" We are sensitive to the guest's feelings, even if things don't go well … What's really being asked of you is no more than would be asked if you were dealing with an acquaintance, much less the person who has vowed to share his or her life with you.[11]

> *Do not repay evil with evil or insult with insult, but with blessing, because to this you were called so that you may inherit a blessing.*
> **– 1 Peter 3:9** (NIV)

Why is it easy to be pleasant to a guest who forgets his umbrella, yet so hard to cut our mate some slack? Two reasons: we have low expectations of a stranger, and we have little history with them. On the other hand, we have built high expectations with our spouse – which have been dashed time and time again, establishing a history of disappointments. Each one triggers our memories of all the ones which preceded it. As Tim and Joy Downs, marriage and family instructors and authors of *The Seven Conflicts,* advise:

> The first step, then, is to be less of a historian and more of an ambassador – an ambassador of *goodwill*. Goodwill is the simple willingness to approach your mate with the same respect, kindness and consideration that you would a stranger. It sounds so basic – and it is. It is as basic to conflict resolution as oxygen is to life. Without it, a disagreement will go nowhere – because we *want* it to go nowhere. There is no rule or principle or "tip from the experts" that can overcome a heart attitude committed to hurt rather than heal.[12]

❀ ❀ ❀ ❀

What's really going on here?

Though we often don't realize it, most of our conflicts take place on two levels: the *flashpoint issue* (which the argument erroneously focuses on), and the *real issue*. If you and your husband seem to argue frequently over the same subjects, it might be helpful to try and assess what could be the underlying, *real* subject you are at odds about. In their book *The Seven Conflicts*, Tim and Joy Downs – who have been instructors for Campus Crusade for Christ's FamilyLife Marriage & Parenting Conferences since 1985 – do an excellent job of identifying seven common disagreements in a marriage, and help us sort out the root causes. Here is a brief summary, but we recommend you read the entire book to gain a firmer grasp on the principles:[13]

What the arguments are about (flashpoint):	The real underlying issue:	Chief components:
Disagreements about money, responsibility, overprotecting or underprotecting the kids	**Security** – the need to be safe, knowing you and yours are protected from harm and want	**Protection** – survival, safety, stability, comfort, limit risk **Provision** – make sure we have enough; save, stockpile, supply
Role of the in-laws, priority of children, a husband's wandering eyes, amount of time spent at work or with other friends	**Loyalty** – the need to feel unreserved commitment to you and the relationship	**Faithfulness** – being able to count on someone no matter what **Priority** – moving the other person to first place in your life
Upkeep of the house, obeying traffic laws, social, family or household obligations and roles	**Responsibility** – the need to be sure we're doing what we "ought" to do	**Obligation** – an internal sense of what is owed **Expectation** – your idea of how other people anticipate you will perform
Feeling unappreciated, not noticing your mate's appearance, not taking the initiative with the kids, unwilling to deal with the messiness of your mate's emotions	**Caring** – the need to experience concern, empathy and encouragement	**Awareness** – mental and emotional alertness to your mate's feelings and concerns **Initiative** – willingness to do something about an observed need
Household organization, personal records, punctuality, the way you spend your leisure time	**Order** – the need to have things organized, orderly and predictable	**Structure** – everything in its place; things work better with a plan **Control** – keep a grip on the steering wheel of life through forethought & discipline
Time spent at social functions, time with each other versus time alone, the priority of friendships, use of leisure time	**Openness** – the need for privacy versus the need to be with people	**Sociability** – the desire to connect with others or not; extrovert/introvert behavior **Energy** – what drains you; what recharges you: being with people or being alone?
About any topic, but it shifts from the content of the discussion to its style, not what you say but how you're saying it	**Connection** – the need to hear and be heard, to understand and to be understood	**Communication Style** – the way you seek to interact with your spouse **Decision-Making Style** – the way you choose between options

Here's how it works:[14]

He: Look what I found in the trash can. Our toaster!

She: It's our *old* toaster.

He: You weren't going to throw it away were you?

She: Of course. We just bought a brand-new one.

He: But it still works. Look, I'll plug it in … See?

She: Why would we save the old toaster when we have a brand-new one? We don't need two.

He: What if the new one breaks? It's good to have a backup.

She: Jack, our attic is *filled* with "backups."

He: Why would you throw away a perfectly good toaster?

She: If it were "perfectly good," why in the world did we buy a *new* one?

He: I just don't like to waste things. I guess *my* family didn't have money to burn like *yours* did.

The husband in this story didn't really want a toaster that badly. He wanted *Security*. That's his natural bent. If the new toaster breaks, they have another. They're *Protected*. They can continue to *Provide* (toast – wow!). But as he tries to give a logical rationale for his desire, he chooses to counter-attack by pointing out his wife's problem of "wastefulness" – and really ramps it up by laying the ultimate blame on her family! So now they're going to spend the rest of the evening arguing about everything *but* Security.

If, on the other hand, this couple had been aware of those seven hidden, foundational issues that seem to give birth to most arguments, they could have gotten to the heart of the matter and resolved it with much less bloodshed and tears.

"Fighting the good fight" takes skill and training. When your husband is your opponent, the objective is that you *both* win. Invest the time – with your husband – to learn more about how to resolve conflicts in a productive, godly manner. Tim and Joy Downs have another very entertaining, humorous and practical book on this subject that you might consider: *Fight Fair! Winning at Conflict Without Losing at Love*.

❀ ❀ ❀❀ ❀ ❀

3. Pray for your husband

Since you are not the Healer, and since your main job has to do with helping to construct an environment favorable for your husband's healing, and since God is the one who *can* accomplish healing and restoration, it makes sense that you would want to spend a great deal of time talking to God about your husband.

But how should you pray? What should you pray about? As we've mentioned earlier in this manual, prayer is simply talking with God. You don't have to use flowery words or speak in King James-ese. Your sentences don't have to be grammatically correct. God is supremely interested in your heart, and simply wants you to pour it out to Him. So you can pray for or about *anything*!

> *Be anxious for nothing, but in everything by prayer and supplication with thanksgiving let your requests be made known to God. And the peace of God, which surpasses all comprehension, will guard your hearts and your minds in Christ Jesus.*
>
> **– Philippians 4:6,7**

What do *you* want to see accomplished in your husband's life? What needs have you observed that you know are beyond your ability to "fix"? In what areas is he struggling, getting frustrated with, becoming fearful about? A good way to keep track of these prayer concerns is to start a notebook and begin writing them down as you think about them. The process of writing will tend to crystallize your thoughts and help you to be aware of all aspects of the issue. It will also help you not forget about them, so that you can "keep on asking, keep on seeking, keep on knocking" as Jesus instructed us to do (Luke 11:9). Leave room to write in the answers, too!

In Luke 11 Jesus shares a story that is designed to illustrate how important it is to be *persistent* in our prayers and not give up (verses 5-10). Then, in Luke 18:1-8, He makes the point again using a different story. Now, it may seem strange to you that we should have to keep bringing the same prayer requests to God repeatedly. Does He forget them? Shouldn't we be able to pray them just once, and leave it up to God to answer however He sees fit? Wouldn't that show more faith? These objections may seem logical, but what should we do when the Son of God – who probably knows a lot about such things – instructs us to *pray persistently*? We should probably listen to Him! God says, *"As the heavens are higher than the earth, so are My ways higher than your ways and My thoughts than your thoughts"* (Isaiah 55:9). God's actions may sometimes not make sense to us, but they make perfect sense to Him! So as illogical as it may seem, we need to make use of this genuine "secret" of prayer that Jesus Himself affirms.

Praying Scripture

The Bible gives us good criteria for getting "yes" answers to our prayers:

> *This is the confidence which we have before Him, that, if we ask anything according to His will, He hears us. And if we know that He hears us in whatever we ask, we know that we have the requests which we have asked from Him.*
>
> **– 1 John 5:14,15**

But how can we know if we're "*asking according to His will*"? Ordinarily, the only way we will know for sure is when we see our request actually come to pass. But there is one way we can know ahead of time that we're praying within God's will: when we pray Scripture! Since the Spirit of God wrote the Bible, we can have confidence that when we pray His words back to Him – not taking them out of context – we are praying some powerful prayers according to His will. Following are a few prayers from Scripture which we have adapted for your use.

From Ephesians 1:17-21:

> *God of our Lord Jesus Christ, the Father of glory, please give my husband, ____, a spirit of wisdom and of revelation in the knowledge of You. I pray that the eyes of his heart may be enlightened, so that he will know what is the hope of Your calling, what are the riches of the glory of Your inheritance in the saints, and what is the surpassing greatness of Your power toward us who believe. I know that these are in accordance with the working of the strength of Your might which You brought about in Christ, when You raised Him from the dead and seated Him at Your right hand in the heavenly places, far above all rule and authority and power and dominion, and every name that is named, not only in this age but also in the one to come.*

From Ephesians 3:14-19:

> *I bow my knees before You, Father, from whom every family in heaven and on earth derives its name, that You would grant my husband, ____, according to the riches of Your glory, to be strengthened with power through Your Spirit in the inner man, so that Christ may dwell in his heart through faith; and that, being rooted and grounded in love, ____ may be able to comprehend with all the saints what is the breadth and length and height and depth, and would know the love of Christ which surpasses knowledge, and that he may be filled up with all of Your fullness.*

From Colossians 1:9-12:

> *Mighty Father, I ask that my husband, ____, may be filled with the knowledge of Your will in all spiritual wisdom and understanding, so that he will walk in a manner worthy of You, to please You in all respects, bearing fruit in every good work and increasing in the knowledge of You; strengthened with all power, according to Your glorious might, for the attaining of all steadfastness and patience; joyously giving thanks to You, Father, Who has qualified us to share in the inheritance of the saints in Light.*

From 1 Chronicles 4:10:

> *Oh gracious Lord, I ask that You would bless my husband, ____, indeed and enlarge his border, and that Your hand might be with him, and that You would keep him from harm that it may not pain him.*[15]

❀ ❀ ❀ ❀

Doctrinal Prayers

As we mentioned in Chapter 10, another powerful way to pray is through "doctrinal prayers" – prayers that have firm biblical doctrine at their core. Following is a great example of a doctrinal prayer by Dr. Mark Bubeck on the subject of our spiritual armor from Ephesians 6:13-18 – adapted a bit for your use. You and your husband should put on your spiritual armor every day – but if he can't or won't, as his wife you have the authority to put it on *for* him based on the oneness you have in Christ through your marriage. As you pray this prayer, visualize yourself putting each piece of the armor on your husband.[16]

Heavenly Father, I receive from Your hand and put on my husband, ____, the armor of God with gratitude and praise. You have provided all that my husband needs to stand in victory against Satan and his kingdom.

I confidently take the belt of truth and wrap it around ____'s waist. Thank you that Satan cannot stand against the bold use of truth. May my husband walk in truth, believe only the truth, and speak only the truth.

Thank you for the breastplate of righteousness which I strap to my husband's torso. My husband embraces the righteousness which is his by faith in Jesus Christ. I know that Satan must retreat before the righteousness of God.

You have provided the solid rock of peace. I claim the peace with You that is ____'s through justification as I place on his feet the sandals of the preparation of the Gospel of peace. I desire Your peace to touch my husband's emotions and feelings through prayer and sanctification.

Eagerly, Lord, I lift up the shield of faith and fasten it to my husband's (left/right) arm. May it protect him against all the blazing missiles that Satan fires at him. I know that You are his shield.

I recognize that ____'s mind is a particular target of Satan's deceiving ways. I take from Your hand and place on my husband's head your powerful helmet of salvation, purchased by Jesus Christ's death on the cross of Calvary.

With joy I lift the sword of the Spirit, which is your Word, and I place it in my husband's (right/left) hand. Help him to choose to live in its truth and power. Enable him to use Your Word to defend himself against Satan, and also to wield the sword well, to push Satan back, and to defeat him.

Thank You, dear Lord, for prayer. Help me to keep my husband's armor well-oiled by my prayers. All these petitions I offer You through the mighty name of our Lord Jesus Christ.

 Do it yourself. It isn't hard for you to construct your own doctrinal prayers. Simply take a passage of Scripture that is especially meaningful to you, alter a few words and turn it into your prayer. Here's an example of how that is done:

Psalm 23:1-3

The LORD is my shepherd,
*   I shall not want.*
He makes me lie down in green pastures;
*   He leads me beside quiet waters.*
He restores my soul;
*   He guides me in the paths of righteousness*
*   For His name's sake.*

Doctrinal Prayer

Dear Lord, help my husband to see You as his shepherd. Help him to see that as he stays close to You, he will never lack anything. ____ needs rest in his body and in his soul so badly. Please make him lie down in Your green pastures. Lead him beside Your quiet waters where he may drink deeply, undisturbed. You know how war has ravaged his soul; please heal and restore his soul. Guide ____ in the paths of righteousness for Your name's sake.

Now write one yourself using this passage:

Psalm 18:16-19

He sent from on high, He took me;
He drew me out of many waters.
He delivered me from my strong enemy,
And from those who hated me,
for they were too mighty for me.
They confronted me in the day of my
calamity, but the LORD was my stay.

❀ ❀ ❀❀❀ ❀ ❀

4. Explore issues of sexual intimacy

A recent study by Kansas State University's School of Family Studies and Human Services of male Army soldiers, who recently returned from Iraq or Afghanistan, and their spouses found that the two issues that had the greatest negative impact on their relationship were sexual and sleep problems.[17]

When a troop returns from combat after many months of sexual deprivation, it's quite normal for passions to be running high upon his return. But if he is struggling with Combat Trauma at some level, he may quickly begin to experience "performance" problems as a common symptom of his disorder. Anti-depressants can also cause impotence as a side effect. For most men, this is a very embarrassing development, and it may cause them to avoid having sex for fear that they would continue to "fail." Or he may shun personal contact with his wife as a manifestation of "avoidance" symptoms. If these issues are not addressed early on, the reaction of many military wives becomes, "Sex? What's that?"

Many wives mistakenly interpret this loss of sexual interest by their husbands as a personal rejection and as a sign that she is no longer attractive to him. She may experience a level of depression because of her husband's coldness, or she may respond to her husband's withdrawal by withdrawing herself. For the sake of her marriage, she may try to reconnect sexually only to be rejected again and be driven deeper into a fog of depression and self-doubt.

If this is your experience, we want to assure you that there are many more factors involved in your husband's sexual problems than your attractiveness or unattractiveness. If you ask him to explain his actions, he won't have a clue what to tell you. He's just as confused about it as you are. As "Jim," a Vietnam veteran, writes in Aphrodite Matsakis' book *Vietnam Wives*:

> I've been thinking about 'Nam lately. The thoughts just interfere with everything. My depression takes over and I'm an utter flop in bed. My wife never minds when I can't perform. She always says she loves me just the way I am. Yet I can't stand to even talk to her and I despise her for loving me, maybe because I despise myself somehow. I turn my back on her too, because I don't want her to see my face. I want to hide what's going on inside of me – the fear, the anger, the hate. I want her to go away, but I also need her. Without her, I have nobody … When I get like this, I feel crazy – here I am, pushing away one of the few people in the world who really cares about me.[18]

Your husband's reluctance to be intimate with you may have its roots in fear – fear of being attacked or losing control. Dr. Matsakis observes:

> Certain aspects of the sexual relationship may serve to trigger such fears in the vet. Simply taking off his clothes or lying down may make him feel vulnerable and defenseless. He may also be threatened by shutting the bedroom door or by having the lights off … More fundamentally, however, sex can be threatening to a vet, or to any man, because it requires "giving in" to a woman and surrendering to his sexual desire. While a man might very much desire sexual pleasure and release, he may fear the loss of control which such surrender implies.[19]

Too much!

For some wives of combat vets, the problem is the opposite: their husband insists on having sex a number of times a week or day. Sex becomes an imperative, and when their wives refuse them, they feel desperately unloved and rejected. For these men, it's not a matter of seeking sexual release in the sex act, but of finding security, self-esteem and "victory." It can be due to the intense loneliness often felt by a Combat Trauma sufferer. If they are isolating themselves, they are missing the normal smiles, hugs, compliments or any of the visual, verbal or physical "strokes" that come through normal relationships with supportive friends. So sex becomes a substitute for in-depth emotional communication or even for casual socialization. For other vets who are given more to the "arousal" symptoms of PTSD, the sex act becomes a way of cooling his emotions, feeling like he's in control, and asserting his masculinity. His wife becomes a human tranquilizer, which most women come to resent.

Solutions?

Sexual problems between married couples are very complex. It would be impossible to deal with such complexity in one book, much less in one portion of one chapter, as you have here. Obviously, we recommend you both make it a matter of prayer and communication if you're having problems in this area, but in such delicate and multi-faceted matters God will often work through the wise counsel of a trained therapist or counselor. Time, space and the insight of an intermediary will be useful. As you work though many of the other issues addressed in this manual, many of your sexual issues could be resolved as well.

In the meantime, you and your husband should not retreat from each other, but be intentional about reconnecting at every level. Rekindle the friendship and romantic aspects of your relationship. As Armstrong, Best and Domenici say in *Courage After Fire*:

> If the experience of deployment and war has changed you or your veteran in significant ways, you may now feel that you're living with a stranger. Get to know each other again, with the understanding that neither of you may be exactly the same person you were when you first met. Set aside a date night to get reacquainted. You may need to review your basic values and priorities if they've changed for one or both of you since your veteran's deployment.[20]

❀ ❀ ❀❀ ❀ ❀

5. Become intentional about communication

Any marriage where communication isn't happening will soon be in trouble. If a couple is intent on healing a hurting relationship, they must be willing to undertake the sometimes difficult work of talking things out.

Good conversations often start out with a question: "How have you been?" "What have you been up to?" But to get to where the deep treasures are, more insightful questions need to be asked. You may not be particularly talented in the area of asking questions, so we'd like to provide you with a tool you could use to get communication rolling.

We call it "The Dialog Coach," and it's meant to coach you into a time of productive dialog by providing a few good opening questions. Don't try to go through *all* the questions in one sitting! You may want to set up a series of special date nights where you could go out to dinner and take just a few of these questions during the chocolate mousse and cappuccino. Or you might like to do it at home (after taking the interruptions, uh, *children* to a babysitter) or while on a drive. You don't have to take the questions in order.

Flip a coin (or something) to decide who will ask the first question. After answering, Spouse #2 asks the same question of Spouse #1. Alternate the asking and the responding. Don't interrupt your husband while he's sharing, and don't argue! You may want to repeat what you hear from time to time to make sure you understand, and ask questions if you want some clarification or need to know more.

Dialog Coach

1. What was the hardest thing for you during the time we were apart?
2. Could I have supported you better in that area?
3. What did you look forward to most as deployment drew to a close?
4. Who was the greatest support to you during the deployment period? What did he/she/they do that helped you so much?
5. What's one of your favorite memories of "us" before deployment?
6. In what ways were your expectations of the deployment time shattered? Fulfilled?
7. What expectations did you have concerning me that aren't being fulfilled?
8. What do you need the most from me right now?
9. Tell me something good and right that I've been doing for you since deployment ended.
10. Tell me something I've been doing that's making it hard on you.
11. What's one of your big dreams for the future?
12. What's one thing God taught you while we were apart?
13. Was your faith in God challenged while we were apart? How? How's it doing now?
14. Describe an awesome half-day date you'd like to take me on.
15. Tell me about something you're struggling with currently that you'd like to see changed. Can you think of any way I can help you in that area?
16. How do you think we should handle it when we have a disagreement with each other?
17. When you have a hard time sleeping, what do you think about?
18. What's your favorite way to relax?
19. What do you like to do for fun? What did you do for fun when you were a teenager?
20. Whom do you wish we could be spending more time with?

❀ ❀ ❀❀ ❀ ❀

Don't force him to talk about the details of his upsetting memories if he isn't comfortable doing so. The mindset of most combat veterans is to "protect." They may feel that, to disclose too much graphic detail to you would violate that conviction. They may not want to expose you to their nightmarish memories because they are concerned they could harm you too. If you feel you are strong enough to hear about his horrific experiences, communicate that to him – and then brace yourself. Dr. Charles Figley offers some practical ideas on how to prepare yourself for these potentially upsetting disclosures:

> Familiarize yourself with the combat events the warrior's unit might have experienced. Asking others who served in that unit would likely risk resentments and is generally not recommended. However, written information is available … A Web search for "Iraq blog" (or "Afghanistan blog," etc.) will pull up additional/updated sites to peruse. Be prepared for crude language and explicit descriptions or pictures.[21]

What he shares could be more than you bargained for. As Patience Mason advises, "Remember, it is okay to say you are overwhelmed and can't listen any more. It is okay to ask your survivor for help. They aren't helpless."[22]

Also, don't insist that he talk with you about what he's working on with his counselor or therapist. Respect his need not to disclose certain aspects about his past or his current treatment. Some wives can become jealous or resentful that the warrior shares more with his counselor than with her. What they don't realize is that it is precisely because he *does* care for his wife – and cares less for the counselor – that he shields her from hearing about his traumatizing experiences.

For some more in-depth "coaching" about how to respond when your husband talks about his combat experiences, see *Courage After Fire* by Keith Armstrong, Suzanne Best and Paula Domenici, Chapter 7, page 181.

Back off!

If your husband indicates that, "I just can't deal with this now!" it's okay to drop the subject. You may be getting too close to triggering deeper depression, rage reactions or even a dissociative state. Leave it alone for now and perhaps bring it up at some later date.

Combat Trauma sufferers swing between an emotionally shut down state and one that is hyperalert. Either way, he's sometimes in a "no-think" zone, and unable to focus on issues that you want him to. He may be preoccupied with managing his symptoms and trying to keep from going deeper into his confusing malaise. His inability to respond to you the way both of you would like him to is frustrating for him, and it can make him feel like a failure. Give him the grace and freedom *not* to respond if the subject upsets him too much.

Suicide talk

Take any comments your husband might make about suicide seriously. If he mentions that he's been thinking about "checking out," or if he talks about how it would probably be easier on you (and the kids) if he wasn't around any more, or if you notice any of the signs listed below, urge him to seek professional help immediately. If he won't, you should share your concerns with a therapist, counselor, chaplain or pastor. Here is a list from Aphrodite Matsakis' book *Trust After Trauma* that will give you some indicators that suicide is a distinct possibility for your husband:[23]

1. Announcements of suicidal thoughts or intentions, such as, "I'm going to kill myself," "I won't be here for the holidays," "You won't have to worry about me anymore," "This might be the last time you see me," or "This is my last day."
2. Suicidal writings, drawings or notes written as if already dead
3. Termination behaviors (giving away prized possessions, writing a will, cleaning up unfinished business, saying good-bye to friends and relatives, purchasing a burial plot, writing his own eulogy, designing his own tombstone, purchasing a one-way ticket to a potential suicide location)
4. Noticeable withdrawal from family or friends or previously-attended therapy
5. Any dramatic changes in mood or emotional state
6. Changes in eating habits that result in significant weight gain or loss
7. Changes in sleeping habits (increased sleeping, fitful sleep, insomnia)
8. Loss of interest in friends and formerly pleasurable activities such as sex, music, sports
9. Difficulties with concentration
10. Recent interpersonal loss (death in the family, rejection by a significant person)
11. Increased alcohol, drug or food usage
12. Decreased functioning at work or in school
13. Preoccupation with fanatical or cult material
14. Outbursts of violent or rebellious behavior (especially if out of character)
15. Psychomotor retardation – slumped posture, slow movements, repetitive behavior and statements
16. Any evidence of loss of touch with reality
17. Excessive or inappropriate guilt

If your husband is already in some kind of treatment, encourage him to share his suicidal thoughts with his therapist. Left unaired, such negative thoughts can quickly grow and develop into a full-blown suicide crisis.

What not to say

Following are a few common conversational hand grenades that you want to avoid using at all costs. They show a lack of understanding of Combat Trauma, shallow empathy, simplistic theology and in many cases, self-centeredness.

- *Get over it.*
- *Forget about the past; the past is past.*
- *Put it behind you and move on.*
- *Just let go and let God.*
- *If you'd just do what I tell you, you'd be fine.*
- *Get a life.*
- *Snap out of it!*

- *I can't have any fun with you because you freak out all the time.*
- *I've had it with you! I can't take it any more!*
- Name-calling, such as: *psycho, cry-baby, sicko, whiner, emotional cripple.*
- Mocking his symptoms, such as: *Big, brave soldier can't even drive to the store.*

Humor him

That is, inject humor into your interactions whenever you can. Laughter can be a healing influence, give a broader perspective on life's challenges and provide a sense of closeness and camaraderie. *A cheerful heart is good medicine*, it says in Proverbs 17:22.

Remind him

Remind him of his awesome survival skills and strengths. Those whom the military has trained to stay alive in the midst of combat are some of the most supremely adaptable and capable people on the planet. Help him to focus not only on the things that are wrong, but also on his many skills, gifts and talents. Communicate your confidence in him: Since he survived a *war*, he can surely triumph in this battle with Combat Trauma.

Include him

Include him in household decision-making processes. He may be having a hard time making decisions, but it will contribute to his feelings of uselessness if you make all the decisions alone and just inform him after-the-fact what they were.

Indulge him

As Cantrell and Dean advise, "Plan for ways to be sensitive to your loved one's idiosyncrasies. For example, it is considerate to ask them where *they* would like to sit in a restaurant. Refrain from demanding that they go shopping at crowded malls. Do what you can to keep the kids from crawling on him too much. Do not take it personally if your loved one does not hug as much as you would like. If you give them space by understanding and respecting [their personal boundaries], hopefully they will draw closer in time."[24] Most of those altered behavior patterns and strange, new preferences are directly related to their Combat Trauma symptoms. If he knows that you're doing you best to be sensitive to them, his trust and openness toward you will increase.

❀ ❀ ❀❀ ❀ ❀

6. *Be proactive about his healing environment*

As you've read several times in this manual, the most beneficial activity the wife of a Combat Trauma sufferer can engage in on behalf of her husband is to help construct the healing environment in which God has optimal access to his body, soul and spirit. There will be components from all three realms that play an important role in his healing – the physical, the mental/emotional and the spiritual. If you remain passively sitting on the sidelines and expect him to take the initiative completely, his healing environment will not be optimal. Here are a few suggestions as to how you can be actively supportive of him and his healing environment:

Counseling

The fresh perspective and corrective feedback of a wise and experienced counselor can really streamline the healing process. If your husband (or you) are hanging on to various "thinking errors" regarding reality, cause-and-effect behavior, and how to move away from self-limiting or even self-destructive mindsets and activities, your journey toward "new normal" will take many unnecessary detours. The best situation would be to find a counselor, therapist, chaplain or pastor who would be willing to counsel both of you together and individually. If your husband refuses to go, go alone. You'll be able to receive a number of helpful coping perspectives and techniques that will enhance your relationship with your husband, and he may eventually see the wisdom of joining you.

Also encourage your husband to become involved in a group therapy program if a good one is available to you. The Department of Veterans Affairs says in their "Support and Family Education" publication:[25]

> In general, groups counter the profound sense of isolation, social withdrawal, mistrust and loss of control. The acknowledgement by victims that they are not alone, can support others, and can safely share their traumatic experiences within a responsive social context provides an opportunity of healing.

Medication

If your husband's doctors or therapists have prescribed medications, become an authority on what each of them is and does, what his proper dosage is, when he is supposed to take them and what the side effects are. In his traumatized state, he may often forget about them. Sometimes he may refuse to take them because of how they make him feel. If that's the case, speak with his health professional about it and see if they can adjust the dosages.

Spirituality

Be sure to keep your relationship with Christ a daily top priority, but don't flaunt your spirituality and self-discipline in front of your husband. If he's struggling in his faith, this may make him resentful of your "religiosity" and push him even farther from God. If he's trying to deepen his walk with God, you don't want him to compare his sometimes halting gait with your less-hindered one and become discouraged. Your best strategy: Matthew 5:16 – simply let your light shine. Or another way to put it:

> In the same way, you wives should yield to your husbands. Then, if some husbands do not obey God's teaching, they will be persuaded to believe without anyone's saying a word to them. They will be persuaded by the way their wives live. Your husbands will see the pure lives you live with your respect for God. It is not fancy hair, gold jewelry, or fine clothes that should make you beautiful. No, your beauty should come from within you – the beauty of a gentle and quiet spirit that will never be destroyed and is very precious to God.
>
> **– 1 Peter 3:1-4 (NCV)**

Ask God to give you gentle, creative ways to encourage him to deepen his relationship with his Healer, and to assume his role as the spiritual head of the family. Don't be critical if he doesn't live up to your expectations, or if he struggles with various sins that you don't have problems with. You – and all Christians – have not been called to judge, but to love.

Combat Trauma Healing Manual

You may want to provide him with a copy of the companion manual to the one you have in your hands. Many of the issues and ideas we've shared with you in this manual have also been covered in the other, but from a troop's perspective. In many ways, the two complement each other. If you are both familiar with the concepts that are presented in your respective manuals, it could be a good aid to communication and a way of encouraging each other as you walk through the Combat Trauma valley together. Consider joining up with a few other couples and going through the *Combat Trauma Healing Manual* together in a small group setting. It's written for veterans suffering the trauma of war, but wives will benefit from its content as well.

Exercise

You both need to work out. Why not become training partners? This way, you can encourage each other, help each other roll out of the sack each morning even when you don't feel like it and give each other kudos as you see improvements.

Fun

As you sail the ocean of your pain and difficulty, provide some "islands of refreshment" along the way. Think through ways the two of you could engage in satisfying hobbies together, vacations, leisure time with family and friends, recreational activities, ways of relaxing. Give each other things to look forward to.

Substance Abuse

If your husband is abusing drugs or alcohol, it's imperative that you help him get into a program that will give him freedom in this area. Your husband needs to learn that it is possible to cope with his strong emotions and despair without numbing himself with chemicals. Be especially proactive on this one – even to the point of intervention.

7. Don't neglect your own needs

In Chapter 7 we emphasized the importance of nurturing your body, soul and spirit and shared a number of practical ways to go about doing that. But this chapter is about helping *your husband*, and we want to help you realize more fully that when you take care of yourself properly, you *are* actually helping your husband as well.

Patience Mason, whose husband struggled with PTSD for many years after the Vietnam War, learned a great deal about this point and shares it with other wives:

> Everyone focuses on the survivor's problem. Feeling good about ourselves depends on how well the survivor is doing. We're brought up to believe that if we are a good enough wife, mother, father, husband, child, our family members will have no problems … To recover, family members need to take the focus off the survivor. By focusing on ourselves we take the burden of "making us happy" off the survivor. That makes it easier for them to deal with their problems if they choose to. It also makes it less easy for them to blame their problems on us … Furthermore, when we start to take care of ourselves, we show (not tell) our survivors that it is okay to take care of themselves. Playing the Lone Ranger, doing for others and never asking for help, does not fit with what we're telling the survivor to do – get help! Why should they if we don't?[26]

Don't let yourself get isolated

If you are struggling with secondary traumatic stress or PTSD, you know by now that one of the symptoms you may have to contend with is the tendency to self-isolate. On top of that, if you are focusing on your husband and his needs, you may tend to jettison anything in your life that doesn't revolve around your husband's care – further isolating yourself. If you lose all of the vital avenues of support that you need to keep yourself physically, mentally, emotionally and spiritually healthy, you will soon be of no use to your husband. We are herd animals. We are a cell within a body of cells. We are redwood trees in a stand. We need each other.

Set some goals

In the final chapter of this manual we'll share some ideas about setting goals. All of us need to feel productive. The drive to accomplish *something* is a healthy drive – unless it gets out of balance. People dealing with anxiety disorders often lose that drive, and they drift aimlessly for months or years. If you were a normal young woman before your husband was deployed, you probably had many goals and dreams that you wanted to accomplish – some with him, some on your own. Don't lose those! If you allow your husband's difficulties to keep you from setting and achieving worthy goals, it could lead to bitterness on your part and a severe strain in your relationship with your husband.

Don't wait until reading the last chapter before setting some goals. Ask God to give you a goal that you could start pursuing today. He knows your gifts, talents and abilities. He knows what will give you a sense of accomplishment. Ask Him to give you a dream and then get ready to be inspired!

Pray for endurance

Obviously, there are many things that you should be praying for yourself. But endurance is a key characteristic, and one that is very appropriate for a woman married to a Combat Trauma sufferer to desire. It's not the drama and intensity of your husband's condition that would normally lead to the end of your marriage. It's the *duration* of the condition. Ask the Lord to help you understand what He means when He encourages us to "wait" on Him:

> *But those who wait on the LORD*
> *Shall renew their strength;*
> *They shall mount up with wings like eagles,*
> *They shall run and not be weary,*
> *They shall walk and not faint.*

– Isaiah 40:31

When you look closely at the order of the above verse, you might think it seems a bit anticlimactic. A Creative Writing teacher might suggest that the "*walk and not faint*" part should be first, ending up with the exciting crescendo of "*mounting up with wings like eagles.*" But the Spirit of God knows the proper order. The "eagle wing mounting" describes the early stages of our difficulties. They can be exciting, dramatic, heroic times for us as caregivers to a needy, beloved person. But after a while the excitement drains off, and it becomes a wearying run, a faint-prone walk – if we're not making the trip in the power of the Spirit of God. Those who are walking and not fainting are the ones who have discovered the vital secret of abiding in Christ over the long-haul in their trials. Ask God to give you endurance, so that you can be there as long as it takes for your husband, your children, and yourself to experience His healing.

❀ ❀ ❀❀ ❀ ❀

Conclusion: It will be worth it!

Dr. Aphrodite Matsakis makes a point that should motivate any woman to "hang in there" through the long months or years of caring for a husband who is struggling with Combat Trauma:

> It is a truism that spiritual love is born of sorrow. In going through difficult times together and in facing the sorrows inherent in having been traumatized, you and your survivor can know a closeness that transcends relationships based on superficialities. Your commitment to each other will be real and substantial. Not only in your relationship with your survivor, but in all the parts of your life you will have acquired an invaluable ability: You will have learned how to make positive use of your frustration, fear, anger and pain. In this and in many other ways, you and your survivor will be able to consider yourselves truly victorious.[27]

❀ ❀ ❀❀ ❀ ❀

Danielle's Prayer ...

Lord Jesus, thank You that You were willing to roll up Your sleeves and do the dirty work of coming into the world to save us. Thank You that You handle us with deep love and tender care as You transplant us from one season of life to the next. Lord, You took off Your outer garment and wrapped a towel around Your waist to wash Your disciples' feet. You were glad to take off the outer layers that You wore in the public eye so that You could serve the ones You loved most.

Lord, make me more like You. Help me to be willing to do the tedious, tiring things that will serve my husband, the one I love here the most. I ask You for the wisdom to know how to create and how to manage a quiet and healing place for him and for our fragile relationship. I know I will need to be patient. Gardens take time and several seasons to bloom and be fruitful. Help me to remember Your word, "I planted the seed, Apollos watered it, but God made it grow. So neither he who plants nor he who waters is anything, but only God, who makes things grow" (1 Corinthians 3:6,7). Thank You, Lord, that I am Your fellow worker in bringing about the healing my husband needs. In Jesus' name, Amen.

Promise from God's Word ...

> *Give away your life; you'll find life given back, but not merely given back – given back with bonus and blessing. Giving, not getting, is the way. Generosity begets generosity.*
>
> **– Luke 6:38 (TM)**

HOW CAN I HELP MY CHILDREN?
Making a Safe, Healthy Environment For Your Kids

Christina's Journal ...

Maria knows something isn't right at home. She senses the tension between Angelo and me. She suspects her home is shaken. Even at her tender age, she already recognizes that our ship is off-course and taking on water. She doesn't understand why we are stressed to the seams. Because I have tried to cover for Angelo at every turn, she doesn't know the half of it. But after today's heartbreak, I simply cannot shelter her from the truth of her father's wounded heart and soul any longer.

We were packing the car for a road trip to visit cousins one state away. Angelo and Maria were coming in and going out the back door, loading our luggage, drinks and snacks for the 12-hour drive. I was in the kitchen cleaning up breakfast. Maria wasn't in the best of moods, but nothing really out of the ordinary for an eight-year-old. I just figured she was fussy due to having to wake up early and that she would soon be asleep again once we got underway.

When Maria came through the back door again, the wind sucked it shut with a loud bang. It startled all three of us. Angelo started yelling at her about her "attitude" and swung his arm into the small of her back as she walked past him. The impact sent her reeling forward. Stunned, she turned around with large questioning eyes. I just stood there in shock at the sink, staring, my mouth hanging open.

Totally out of character, Angelo moved in close to her face and started yelling at her, nose-to-nose. I don't even remember what he was angry about now. She spun around and high-tailed it to her bedroom. He stayed right on her heels, yelling, scaring her to death and scarring her for life with words he can never take back. She ran into her room. He stood tall and wide in the door frame, still screaming at her, the veins in his forehead bulging and turning blue.

I trailed after them down the hall, horrified. Then he said it. Something so outrageous and unrelated and crazy. Red-faced and out of control, he yelled, "I'd rather have a dead child than a disobedient one!!!" That's when I discovered the grizzly bear inside of me. She rose up, growling and showing her sharp teeth. I jumped between the two people I love the most in this world and glared at Angelo, my eyes warning him to back off. He steamed in the doorway for a few scary seconds, then turned and walked away. I reached for Maria. She crumpled in my arms, shaking and trying to catch her breath. We held each other, both of us crying. Where do I start? How do I begin to explain to her why Daddy is so different since he returned from the war? How do I put big people problems into little people language? How do I undo the damage already done? How do I reassure her that she is dearly loved, especially after today? How will she ever trust her father or feel safe in his presence again?

Little people dealing with big people problems

The journey from infancy through childhood and adolescence to adulthood is already difficult and confusing enough for both parents and children. Add the volatility of a father struggling with the ravages of Combat Trauma, and you've got a truly mystifying voyage. How *can* Maria comprehend what her father is struggling with? All she knows is that the daddy who used to love and take care of her has now – for reasons unknown – become her tormentor and enemy. How can Christina help her daughter to understand that her daddy still truly loves her, but that he just isn't able to show it right now?

The primary instinct of every parent – *especially* of mothers – is to protect their children. But within your heart this instinct is competing with several others as well: to be supportive, honoring and protective of your husband, to preserve your marriage, to keep yourself safe, to maintain a harmonious and loving household, to pursue your relationship with God … the list could go on. No wonder you feel confused and even paralyzed from time to time! *All* of these instincts cannot *always* be your top priority. So one of your most difficult jobs as the wife of a Combat Trauma sufferer is to try to pick the right priority at the right moment. This – perhaps more than any other issue – requires a strong connection between you and God, and a heart that is continually seeking Him and asking what your response or next step should be. It's more than you can figure out on your own, but not too much for God – and He wants to help you with it:

> *But if any of you needs wisdom, you should ask God for it. He is generous to everyone and will give you wisdom without criticizing you.*
>
> **– James 1:5** (CEV)

How combat trauma can affect kids

One of the main reasons your husband went to war may have been so that his children could live in peace and safety. But when a troop brings the war home because of his Combat Trauma, the home itself can become a war zone. Obviously, it's the *last* thing any husband or father would want. But sometimes a trauma sufferer doesn't have the ability to keep it from happening.

Nobody has as much influence on a child as a parent – especially during the pre-teen years. For this reason, we want to assist you in helping your husband minimize the negative influences that his Combat Trauma-altered persona could be having on your children, and accentuate the positive influence he could have.

Depending on the symptoms your husband is exhibiting and depending on how old your children are, he could be having any of the following effects on them according to Dr. Jennifer Price, writing for the V.A.'s National Center for PTSD:[1]

Parent's Symptoms	Effects on Children
Re-experiencing: vivid daytime memories or nightmares involving intense emotions such as anger, grief, fear, guilt; dissociative episodes.	Frightening; may not understand what is happening or why; may worry about parent's well-being; may worry their parent cannot properly care for them.
Avoidance/Numbing: avoiding places, people or events that remind them of their trauma; don't want to do things or go places; isolating; emotionally distant; tired; depressed; substance abuse to numb.	May feel the parent isn't interested in them or doesn't love them; tries harder to get the parent's attention which the parent finds annoying and results in further distancing.
Arousal: Hypervigilant; jumpy; exaggerated startle response; sleeping problems; irritable; angry; short fuse; fits of rage; poor concentration; adrenaline junkie; substance abuse to stay "hyped up."	Frightened of the parent; may feel their parent is always mad at him/her; may question their parent's love; may worry that their parent cannot properly care for them; avoids the parent.

In her research on children of combat veterans, Dr. Kate L. Harkness, professor of psychology at Queen's University, Toronto, Canada, found that children often respond to a combat-traumatized parent by assuming one of three main roles:[2]

- The "over-identified child" who experiences secondary traumatization and presents many of the symptoms the parent with PTSD is having.
- The "rescuer child" who takes on parental roles and responsibilities to compensate for the parent's difficulties.
- The "emotionally uninvolved" child who receives little emotional support, which results in problems at school, depression, anxiety and relational problems later in life.

Dr. Harkness points out that these don't represent every possible reaction, but they offer some useful ways of understanding how symptoms might develop for these children.

? As you consider each of your children, can you recognize any of the above roles emerging in them? If so, list them here for each child:

_____

_____

Can children get PTSD?

Yes. Even though they are still young and their brain's reactive pathways are still developing, children have the same responses to danger that adults do. According to the National Child Traumatic Stress Network:[3]

> Age, developmental maturity, and experience can influence posttraumatic stress reactions. More than twenty years of studies have confirmed that school-age children and adolescents can experience the full range of posttraumatic stress reactions that are seen in adults. We might wish to believe that children under five years of age are too young to know what was happening and whatever impression was left would be forgotten soon. However, recent studies show that traumatic experiences affect the brains, minds, and behavior of even very young children, causing similar types of reactions as seen in older children and adults.

This is all the more reason for mothers who are married to Combat Trauma sufferers to be pro-active about protecting their children from the unintended damage that could be done to them.

Common problems faced by children of Combat Trauma sufferers[4]

In the box next to each problem listed below, rank on a scale of 1 to 5 how each child seems to be exhibiting the problem that is talked about, where:

1 = "I don't see this problem at all in my child."

5 = "I see this *very* strongly in my child."

Put the child's initial next to the box that pertains to him or her. For more than three children, just add more boxes in the margin.

☐
☐
☐
☐
Social and behavioral problems. Children of veterans with PTSD are at higher risk for behavioral, academic and interpersonal problems. Their parents report that they are more depressed, anxious, aggressive, hyperactive and delinquent compared to children of combat veterans who don't have PTSD. Chaotic family experiences can make it difficult to establish positive attachments to parents, which then make it difficult for them to create healthy relationships outside the family as well. If the parent veteran participated in abusive violence (i.e., atrocities) while in combat, the children may experience even more acute behavioral disturbances.[5]

☐
☐
☐

Emotional problems and secondary traumatization. Children of PTSD sufferers are also at a higher risk of being depressed or anxious than children of non-sufferers. They may start to experience some of their parent's symptoms (e.g., nightmares about their parent's trauma, difficulty concentrating in school, etc.). Some researchers describe the symptoms as *secondary traumatization*, much like what *you*, the wife of a Combat Trauma sufferer, can experience.[6] But just as you can develop *primary* traumatic stress due to violence occurring in your home, the same can happen to your children. Their symptoms can even progress into PTSD, just as yours can.

☐
☐
☐

Identification and re-enactment.[7] Children who live with a war-traumatized father may start to identify with him emotionally. In an effort to connect with him (either consciously or unconsciously), they might begin to present their own set of PTSD symptoms. They may also begin to re-enact some aspects of their father's traumatic experiences because the parent has difficulty separating past experiences from present – so the child does, too.

☐
☐
☐

I can fix it. Many children feel that they have somehow caused their father's difficulties, observing that when they disobey or make a mistake, their father throws a fit. If there are no rule infractions or slip-ups, peace reigns in the household. So they put enormous pressure on themselves to be perfect children. Patience Mason, wife of a Vietnam veteran, describes this mindset from the child's point of view:[8]

> I used to think that if Mom and I were nice enough, Daddy wouldn't be so unhappy;
> if I were neat enough and never made a mess;
> if I were polite enough and never got smart with Dad or Mom;
> if I worked hard and got good grades;
> if I hit a lot of home runs at Little League;
> then Daddy would be nice too.
> When I would try real hard and Daddy was still upset, I would get real depressed.

Of course, no matter how "perfect" they are, Daddy doesn't get fixed, and this adds to the child's frustration and sadness. In addition, the energy required to exhibit such perfect, un-kidlike behavior is immense and few kids can sustain it for long without causing themselves emotional damage.

☐
☐
☐

Traumatic expectations. As children grow up, they learn from their experiences and form a picture of how things work in the world. The confusing scenarios that unfold in a home where a parent is an abuser rather than a protector can result in "traumatic expectations." The National Child Traumatic Stress Network describes it like this:[9]

> Children and adolescents are forming a world view that is constantly changing. Trauma experiences can create the sense that things can go horribly wrong at a moment's notice, that no one can really provide protection, and that laws don't really work. Adolescents can then think it is not worth working toward a better future or that it is better not to get close to others just to lose them in a tragic way.

As they grow into their adolescent and adult years, people with traumatic expectations are typically cynical, depressed, unmotivated, isolated and hopeless about the future.

☐
☐
☐

Unrecognized symptoms. Children don't always react to stress and trauma the way adults do, nor do they possess the same level or range of coping behaviors as adults. This can be a real problem for a parent who is looking for certain stress cues from her children. Not seeing what she's looking for (especially in preschool children), the mother may conclude that her child is just fine. As Dr. Don Catherall, cofounder and director of the Phoenix Institute in Chicago, which specializes in treating trauma survivors of all ages points out:

Indeed, many children manifest their psychological distress so differently from adults that it can easily go unnoticed. For example, they often develop sleep-related problems: they can't go to sleep, they wake up frequently, they become especially fearful at night, or they have bad dreams. Most children also regress in their physical and emotional development. They may have greater difficulty controlling their bladder or bowels, often redeveloping a problem (such as bed-wetting or thumb-sucking) that they'd previously outgrown. They frequently develop separation anxiety and find it very difficult to tolerate being away from their parents. Often, they start wanting to sleep with their parents again. And they may develop entirely new symptoms, particularly phobias in which they become highly fearful about some specific situation.[10]

If you put a lot of 4s and 5s in the boxes for one or more of your children, and these behaviors have persisted for more than a couple of months, it would be a good idea to talk with your pastor, chaplain or a counselor about it. If nothing else, have a chat with your Battle Buddy and see what advice she might give you. It *could* be that the symptoms will resolve on their own, but why risk it? The earlier in the process your child gets help, the better.

Family dynamics

The following section on Family Dynamics was written specifically for this manual by the wife of a career military man who wishes to remain anonymous. We'll call her "Rachel" in this chapter. Her husband has been deployed to combat locations multiple times all over the world and as a result developed chronic PTSD. "Rachel's" observations are gathered from years of experience, and should give you some insights into your own situation ...

There are several dynamics going on in the household of a combat veteran with children. The more children, the more dynamics.

Father-Child: When my husband sees kids (his own or others), he remembers the barefoot, hungry, scared kids of various war-torn countries he's fought in, scurrying for cover, begging for his MREs or Power Bars, homeless or orphaned – or even dead. He sees images of kids dying in makeshift hospitals or lying dead on the roadsides. It angers him (disproportionately) when his own kids or *any* kids he comes in contact with are whiney, ungrateful, spoiled, disrespectful or oblivious of the blessings and freedoms they are handed every day. Some of our family's most painful memories are rooted in my husband's memories of Iraqi children, vented on his own children.

Child-Father: From the time they are itty-bitty, military kids understand (according to their age and maturity) that Daddy is a soldier, sailor, pilot, etc., and they are accustomed to Daddy leaving for training or deployments. However, kids today comprise the first generation whose parents went to war since Vietnam. Most of us parents cannot truly identify with what they are feeling or experiencing, because we have not been where they are (unless you have a parent who is a Vietnam War veteran). There is a strange mix of pride and shame in the child-father dynamic. The child is very proud of their warrior dad and appreciates his hard work and valor. However, at the same time the child is embarrassed by his/her father who now exhibits anti-social or inappropriate behavior in the home and in public. The embarrassment is closely followed by frustration and anger.

A veteran's child hungers intensely for his or her father's affection, affirmation and attention. Because Dad is dealing with his own issues, he is not interacting with his child as before. Avoidance. Irritability. Intolerance. Aggression. They all play into the child-father relationship. When the child doesn't get affection, etc., he or she will look for it and find it other places, which can be especially consequential for pre-teen and teenage daughters.

If their dad has become a yeller or has become aggressive or violent since he returned, the children do not feel safe any longer. They also want to protect their mother from their dad.

Mother-Child: I became the mediator and filter between the outside world and my husband and my children. When it was time to go to war, my husband and I were very frank with our kids. We didn't sugarcoat anything. They knew the odds and the dangers. At the same time, we did not exaggerate these deployments over any of the previous deployments or separations. The biggest difference in these most recent conflicts was the imbedded media and media coverage. We allowed our children to watch the invasion and the bombing of Baghdad for only three days. Then I turned the TV off. This was a predetermined plan my husband and I had agreed upon. It was wise to limit their intake of media coverage of the conflict, the fallen, the political issues, the protestors, etc. I think this helped rein in fear and confusion to a degree.

When my husband starting showing signs of PTSD after returning from Iraq, I made the mistake for several years of covering for him when the children experienced or witnessed something inappropriate from him. This was a huge mistake. If I had known then what I know now, I would have been as frank and open as possible with them about their father's actions, words and PTSD from Day 1. But I didn't understand what was happening, so I tried desperately to make and keep peace, hoping this would give my kids a semi-normal, happy environment in which to grow up. In some ways, my shielding them accomplished that, but in other ways, by patching and keeping peace, I caused what my counselor refers to as "life traps" – inappropriate and ineffective patterns of dealing with difficulties that will hinder them as adults. Now I'm having to backstroke and open up discussions and wounds in order to explain a lot of memories (and current developments) to them in the context of PTSD.

Mother-Father: When my husband responds way out of line to a normal parenting challenge, I experience an intense protective instinct. In the past, due to my conservative Christian upbringing, I've "submitted" to the head of the household even when I didn't agree with his verdict/ punishment. However, in the past couple of years when he's been unfair or mean or frighteningly loud or aggressive, I step in. This doesn't help the situation at all in the immediate, but I cannot just stand there passively and watch as the children are emotionally or physically abused. When this situation is repeated day in and day out in a family, kids start to distance themselves from Dad and start taking cover "behind" Mom, regardless of their ages. Dad interprets this as Mom coddling the kids – which escalates his anger – and gives him the sense that "everyone is turning against me!" It's a downward spiral, but it's necessary to take action to shield the kids during these episodes to protect them and to help my husband understand that there are boundaries he needs to observe in how he relates to the children.

Sibling-sibling: This same protective response rises up in my children when Dad explodes all over one child and not the others. Not that the non-targeted children can actually *do* anything to rise up and stop the attack, but they *feel* it. And so they stuff their emotions as best they can – way down. If one child seems to be the target of Dad's anger more often, there's a palpable resentment in that child's heart not only toward his father but also toward his other siblings as well. He or she knows the other kids are messing up too, but they never seem to get Dad's wrath. The sense of injustice is vented more easily on that child's siblings than on Dad.

? As you consider the five Family Dynamics described above, which ones do you feel are operating within your family in a healthy, supportive manner? Why?

Which ones are *not* operating in a healthy, supportive manner? Why?

Approaches to avoid

Following are three actions that parents sometimes take toward their children with the intention of helping them, but they actually end up making the situation worse.

- ⊘ **Silence.** When a child is told not to discuss the distressing behaviors they observe at home, his or her anxiety tends to increase. Children worry about the struggling parent's symptoms and have difficulty understanding why he is acting so differently than he did before going to war. If they aren't given some kind of explanation, they may create their own ideas about what the parent experienced, which can be even more horrifying than what actually happened.[11]

- ⊘ **Overdisclosure.** Saying too much can be a problem as well. If a child is exposed to too much graphic detail about his Daddy's traumatic war experiences or even what he is currently struggling with when the child isn't there, he could experience secondary trauma – and even PTSD – in response to the horrific images generated in his mind.

- ⊘ **Covering up or making excuses for Dad.** By finding ways to excuse your husband's hurtful behavior, you teach your children that his way of resolving problems is acceptable. As "Rachel" pointed out earlier, this can lead to "life traps" later on. Rachel writes, "If he acts like a jerk, so be it. Eventually the children will begin to ask Dad why he talks and acts the way he does, and it will register with him. You'd be surprised how bold a hurt or confused child can be."

❀ ❀ ❀❀ ❀ ❀

Approaches to embrace

1. Explain without providing graphic details

Your husband – their Daddy – is different from how he was before he went off to war. Not trying to explain this to your children is like trying to ignore an elephant in your family room. Look for "teachable moments" when your kids are particularly open to input about Dad. These could come after your husband has had a blow-up of some sort, won't come to dinner because he'd rather stay isolated in the basement, has punished a child out of proportion to the offense, etc. How much you share will depend upon the child's age and maturity level. Whenever they have questions, answer them with honesty and at a level that is appropriate to their age. With every answer, assure them of two things:

- It's not their fault
- Things are going to work out okay eventually

In any case, there is no need to go into the specific traumatic details of what your husband experienced. You can speak in generalities so they can understand the load your husband is carrying, but you don't want their minds to come up with images that are too troubling or graphic. What you share will depend on their age. For younger, elementary-age children, you could say something like, "All wars are very difficult because the men and women who fight in them sometimes have to do things they hate to do. When bad people threaten our country, we try to work it out by talking. But if they won't listen, we have to send our military – many people just like your Daddy – to try to make them stop. This sometimes means a soldier might even have to kill another person, which was very, very hard for your father to do, even though he was very brave. Or it might mean that one of the enemy soldiers hurt or almost killed your Daddy – which was very scary for him, as it would be for anyone. These experiences have made him very sad – and even angry at the enemy soldiers – and that's why he's acting the way he is right now. He's having a hard time forgetting about some of the things that happened to him while he was fighting in the war."

Dr. Annette M. La Greca, professor of Psychology and Pediatrics at the University of Miami, offers a few additional tips to help you as you discuss war with your child:[12]

- Use words and language appropriate for your child. For example, when speaking to young children, use words such as "hurt" instead of "injured' or "car" instead of "vehicle."

- Be neutral. Do not judge or criticize your child. Make comments like these:

  "That's interesting." *"Tell me more about it."* *"What do you mean?"*

- Be truthful with your child. Provide honest answers and information. It's okay to let your child know how you feel about what is happening, but be careful not to scare or alarm your child.

- Explain that what is happening in the war is real – unlike violent movies, cartoons, video games or television programs. Help your child to understand that during war, real people are involved and some may die or get hurt.

- Be reassuring, but don't make unrealistic promises. For instance, if it comes up, you can tell your child that our government is doing everything it can to protect us, but do not promise that there will not be any more terrorist attacks in the United States.

❧ ❧ ❧ ❧

2. Assure them it's not their fault

Children are just learning how to live, and as such are constantly receiving "correction" from their parents. When something goes wrong in the house, it's frequently their fault – at least that is often their perception – and the correction is sometimes administered with emotion and anger. When a father's PTSD-generated anger comes down on them, it's natural for them to conclude that once again they have done something wrong. They need to be assured and reassured that this is *not* their fault! The child may have done something wrong, but they are not to blame for their Daddy's inappropriate reaction.

❧ ❧ ❧ ❧

3. Understand the family dynamics and keep communication very open

Make it clear to your kids that you want them to share with you what's going on inside them and what they are feeling about how their father is acting or how it's affecting their relationships with their siblings. And then *listen* to them without judging them or becoming defensive about your husband. You might think, "This child is reaching completely off-the-wall conclusions about his Dad. He's exaggerating, misinterpreting what his father says and does, and making him out to be a monster. Well, I won't stand for it!" Remember that they are children, and don't have the discernment, insight and years of experience you have. Let them talk – voicing their frustrations will provide a measure of therapy all by itself. As positively and gently as you can, correct their misconceptions and distorted views of the events they share with you. "I can understand how you might feel that way. I certainly would have at your age. But let me give you another way to think about it …"

Don't minimize their concerns, but respond with warmth, love, empathy and reassurance. Help them to know that you're on their team, and be appreciative and affirming whenever they open up to you.

What should I tell them?

That will all depend on how mature each child is. A teenager could understand most of what is presented in Chapter 1 of this manual, if you walk him or her through it and stop from time to time to ask and answer questions. Younger children might need you to approach the subject on a more basic level.

Patience Mason – mentioned several times in this manual – has written a small book that a mother can use to help explain her husband's PTSD to a school-aged child. It's entitled *Why Is Daddy Like He Is?* and is available through Patience Press (www.patiencepress.com). Here are some of the issues in the book she recommends communicating to your child:

- Breaking down the term PTSD into PT meaning "after danger," Stress, because it's very stressful to be in danger, and Disorder meaning your life gets out of order – not like it would have been if you'd never been in danger.

- Helping the child to understand that this is a common reaction to really bad experiences. It happens to many other men besides their daddy.

- Comparing how Dad feels with how the child felt when they experienced an awful experience in the past. In the book, the mother reminds the child of the time his kitty was run over by a car. It helps the child identify with how the father is feeling.

- Talking about some of Dad's symptoms, and what a "symptom" is, speaking about it like the symptoms of a cold: runny nose and cough. In this she shows the usefulness of explaining something new by comparing it with something familiar. If the child understands that these symptoms are common among soldiers who have experienced trauma, it takes some of the edge off the scariness.

- Explaining that it was important sometimes for Daddy to get angry so he could fight hard and stay alive. Many things about the war made Dad angry – it would make anyone angry. But he's having a hard time getting rid of that anger and, unfortunately, "it ends up getting splattered all over us."

- That the family is not responsible for his anger, and they can't fix it. Dad is going to have to work through this himself.

- Knowing these things makes it easier for the family to love him while he goes through it. In the meantime, the kid's job is to keep on being a kid.

It's a simple, practical little book, and we highly recommend you get it and use it with your elementary school-age children. Patience Mason has also written "*Why Is Mommy Like She Is?*" for the children of women veterans struggling with Combat Trauma.

Talk about feelings

Any kind of conflict – war or family arguments – will draw emotions to the surface. If they are not acknowledged and dealt with, they'll get suppressed and will show up later, incubated and much worse than they started out. Dr. Bridget Cantrell and Chuck Dean, authors of *Down Range: To Iraq and Back,* give us some practical ideas on this:

> Try to recognize the feelings underlying children's actions and put them into words. Say something like, "I can see you have feelings about this. Tell me more about them." Be careful not to tell your children how *they* are feeling, instead let them tell you. A very good technique to express emotion is through art, music and acting. Invite the child to use these methods to physically demonstrate their feelings. (Younger children may find that using these alternative modes of communication are easier ways to express themselves.)[13]

Dr. Ilona Pivar of the National Center for PTSD, gives these recommendations about talking with your kids about feelings:

> Encourage your children to freely express their concerns and feelings. All children want to be included in family matters, and they want to be listened to and understood. They have ideas and feelings but may not know how to express them, or how to resolve them. "If war is bad, why is Mommy going to war?" "If war is bad, why are we doing it?" "Is killing other people okay?"
>
> Don't be afraid to talk about your feelings, even if you are conflicted or confused. If children know adults are being honest and respectful to them, they will feel safer. Do the best you can, even when you don't know all the answers.[14]

You should never *force* your child to talk about his or her feelings. If they get upset when you try to get them to open up, let it drop for now, and look for a more opportune time later. But there are ways of helping them open up. Make some casual reference to your own worries or frustrations about what's happening in your home – but not in a way that is critical of your husband. This will help your child to realize you share similar feelings and you *just might* understand what he's going through. It also helps him realize that you are a real person who can cry as well as laugh, and it models an appropriate way to release feelings – talk about them.

Physical contact

Look for opportunities to comfort and reassure your children through physical touch. Younger children should be hugged, cradled and kissed as often as practical to communicate your love and affirmation. They need it and will almost always respond positively to it when they feel stressed about things. But older children and teens also need physical contact – whether they'll admit it or not! However, timing is everything with teens (i.e., "Mom! Not in front of my friends!!"). But look for ways to touch them that lets them know that you love them and are looking for ways to "stay in contact" with them.

❀ ❀ ❀ ❀

4. Pray specific, applicable Scripture over your children daily

You're working hard to create a healing environment for yourself and for your husband. Obviously, you will have the same objective for your children. More than any other force, your heavenly Father can help your children deal with the issues created by their earthly father. Daily, Scripture-inspired prayer will make a *huge* difference in your children's outlook, confidence, resilience and spiritual health. Following are a number of prayers – covering a wide variety of topics – which you could either pray directly for your children, or use as patterns for prayers you compose on your own.

Praying for a healthy and correct view of the Heavenly Father

LORD God, my child's understanding of what a father should be conflicts with her painful experiences with her own father lately. It's my deepest concern that she come to know You as her true and eternal Father. I ask You to prevent her pain from defining who You are and blinding her from how much You truly love her. I pray that through her personal struggles with her earthly father she would learn that no man can protect her, provide for her or comfort her the way You, her Heavenly Father, can. Help me to pray according to Your Word. Help me to believe that whatever I ask according to Your will and in Your Son's name, I will receive.

*I pray that ____ will know and rely on the **love** You have for her. You **are** love. You have drawn ____ with an everlasting love and have drawn her with loving-kindness. (1 John 4:16; Jeremiah 31:3)*

*I pray that ____ will come to understand and believe that You are the **faithful** God and that You keep Your covenant of love with him and to a thousand generations of those who love You and keep Your commandments. (Deuteronomy 7:9)*

*I pray that ____ will know that You are a **gracious and merciful** God and that she will turn to You for the grace and mercy her heart needs during these difficult days. (Nehemiah 9:31)*

*Father, I pray that my child will know that You are **aware** of his pain. You are the only One Who daily **bears his burdens**. You are a **shield** around ____ and You bestow glory on him and lift up his head. You are **his mighty rock and his refuge**. I pray that ____ will trust in You at all times and will pour out his heart to You, for You are **his refuge**. (Psalms 68:19; 3:3; 62:7,8)*

*You are the **One Who sees** ____. You know my daughter's limits and You see her challenges. Lord, You know fully the temptations that lure her and that sound comforting and liberating to her. Jesus, You Yourself suffered when You were tempted and You alone are **able to help** ____ when she is being tempted. Lord, You've said that no temptation has seized ____ except what is common to man. You've promised to be **faithful** and not to let ____ be tempted beyond what she can bear. When ____ is tempted, I ask You to make her aware of the **way out** so that she can stand up under it. (Hebrews 2:18; 1 Corinthians 10:13)*

*Father, reveal Yourself to _____ as the **God who performs miracles**. Help him to believe that nothing is too difficult for You. I pray that before he even calls, You will answer. While he is still speaking, You will hear him. Display Your power on his darkest days. I pray he will know from personal experience that You are **the LORD who heals him** as well as the One Who heals his dad. (Psalm 77:14; Luke 1:37; Isaiah 65:24; Exodus 15:26)*

Praying for Christ-like character in my child

Boldness – *Thank You, Lord Jesus, that You sympathize with _____'s weakness, for You have been tempted in every way, just as she is; yet, You were without sin. Help _____ learn to approach Your throne of grace with confidence so that she may receive mercy and find grace to help her in her time of need. (Hebrews 4:15,16)*

Compassionate – *Lord, clothe _____ with the compassion of Jesus and enable him to be empathetic towards his father's pain and to bear with him. (Colossians 3:12)*

Forgiving – *Father, I pray that You will give _____ a forgiving heart, for You forgive us when we forgive those who sin against us. If we do not forgive men their sins, You will not forgive ours. Help _____ to forgive others as You have forgiven her. Soften her heart towards her father and enable her to truly forgive his sins against her. (Matthew 6:14,15; Colossians 3:13)*

Joyful – *I pray that in spite of the suffering, _____ will experience the joy that Your Holy Spirit gives to those who welcome Your message. (1 Thessalonians 1:6)*

Obedient – *Lord Jesus, as a son You learned obedience from what You suffered. I ask You to strengthen _____ so he will obey his parents in everything, for this pleases You. I ask that his father will not embitter him and that he will not become discouraged. Help _____ to show proper respect to him in every situation. (Hebrews 5:8; Colossians 3:20,21; 1 Peter 2:17)*

Peace-loving – *Father, I ask that You will help _____ make every effort to do what leads to peace and to mutual edification in our home. I pray that she will speak only what is beneficial and encouraging when she's around her dad. Keep her from growing weary in doing good so that at the proper time she will reap a harvest if she doesn't give up. (Romans 14:19; Ephesians 4:29; Galatians 6:9)*

Perseverance – *I pray that _____ will keep his eyes fixed on You, Lord, through all that still lies ahead for us. Help my son to consider Jesus who endured such opposition from sinful men, so that he will not grow weary and lose heart. I pray _____ will not throw away his confidence. Richly reward his confidence in You. Strengthen him to persevere so that when he has done the will of God, he will receive what you have promised. I thank You that _____ is not of those who shrink back and are destroyed, but of those who believe and are saved. (Hebrews 12:2,3; 10:35,39)*

Prayerfulness and Peace – *Father, cultivate in _____ a lifestyle of prayer as she learns to pray in the Spirit on all occasions with all kinds of prayers and requests. I pray that _____ will come to know You as her generous and faithful Provider in every need. Father, I pray that _____ will be anxious for nothing, but in everything by prayer and petition, with thanksgiving, she will learn to present her requests to You. Guard her heart and her mind in Christ Jesus with the peace of God that transcends all our understanding. (Ephesians 6:18; Philippians 4:6,7)*

Self-control – *Father, help _____ not to be like others who are asleep, but let him be alert and self-controlled. Lord, since my son belongs to the day and not to the night, let him be self-controlled. (1 Thessalonians 5:6)*

Servant's Heart – *Lord, I pray that You will encourage _____ to serve her dad wholeheartedly, as if she were serving You. Reward her, Lord, for whatever good she does. I pray that her father will be won over without words by the purity and reverence of her life. (Ephesians 6:7; 1 Peter 3:1,2)*

❀ ❀ ❀ ❀

Here are two powerful "doctrinal prayers" for the spiritual protection of your children, from Dr. Neil Anderson and Steve Russo, who wrote *The Seduction of Our Children*:[15]

Dear Heavenly Father, I bring my child _____ to you. I declare myself and my family to be under Your authority. I acknowledge my dependency on You, for apart from Christ I can do nothing. I ask for Your protection during this time of prayer. Since I am in Christ and seated with Him in the heavenlies, I take authority over all that You have entrusted to me. I declare my child to be eternally signed over to the Lord Jesus Christ. I renounce any and all claims Satan has on my child. I accept only the will of God for myself and my family. I now command Satan and all his demons to leave my child alone. I ask for a hedge of protection around my child and my home. I submit myself to You and ask You to fill me with Your Holy Spirit. I dedicate myself and my child as temples of the living God. I ask this in the precious name of Jesus, my Lord and Savior. Amen.

Dear Heavenly Father, I ask for Your divine protection for _____. I pray that You will put a hedge of protection around him so that no harmful influences can affect him. I commit him to You for Your care, and I assume all my responsibilities for training him in the Lord. I also assume the responsibility for the attitudes and actions in him that are the result of my training. I ask for Your Holy Spirit to guard his heart and bring to his mind all that he has learned from your Word. I thank You that, when he is tempted, You will provide him with a way of escape, and he will not be tempted beyond his ability in You to endure. I ask that the way he lives may be a witness to Your presence in his life. May whatever he does be done to the glory of God. I ask this in the precious name of my Lord and Savior Jesus Christ. Amen.

As you invest time praying daily over your children, many of your tension and fears will be lifted. As "Rachel" points out, "God pours out His grace and will meet the child's needs in ways you cannot. God promises to work ALL things for the good for those who love Him and are called according to His purposes – even the ugliness of PTSD in a child's environment."

❀ ❀ ❀ ❀

5. Help your children respect your husband's triggers

Your children need to know that some of the common characteristics of someone with Combat Trauma include hypervigilance, exaggerated startle response, fight or flight reactions, flashbacks, etc. Depending on the age of your children, you probably won't use those exact words, but you should at least communicate the concepts. Help them to understand that, "when Daddy was in the war, he had to be very alert and ready for action at all times – just to be sure that he could stay alive in case the enemy attacked him. It was so important for him to be ready for anything that he thought about it all the time he was over there. Now he's having a hard time *not* thinking about it. In a way, his brain is "stuck" like that. So when certain things happen here at home that remind him of the time he spent in the war, his mind and body react automatically as if an enemy is attacking him."

Then, with a pencil and paper in front of you, think through with your children the various things that trigger your husband. Turn it into a brain-storming session. Try to get *them* to suggest what sets him off by recalling what happened just before previous times when Dad got angry or abusive or sad. If they aren't able to come up with triggers that you know about, add them to the list after their observations are exhausted.

With the list you've come up with, you can now help each other remember to avoid actions that will trigger your husband's symptoms. And when they forget and trigger him accidentally, they'll see his reaction more as a symptom of his disorder, rather than as a personal attack on them.

"Rachel" makes a good point:

> By recognizing how and why children can trigger a PTSD sufferer (noise, commotion, disturbing memories), she can steer away lots of situations that could ruin everyone's day. For a season, she needs to expect little from her husband in the way of fathering or in the tolerance department. His nerves are raw and his memories are fresh. In time, he will probably re-engage as a dad and begin to enjoy his role again. But for now, keep your expectations low.

❈ ❈ ❈ ❈

6. If physical safety is an issue, take them out of the home

As we mentioned in Chapter 5, "I Don't Feel Safe – What Should I Do?" there may come a time when you feel that you or your children are in danger. If your husband is becoming increasingly threatening either in word or action, if you sense that he's about to cross the line into any sort of abuse and he is not willing to talk with you about your concerns, it's time to execute your emergency escape plan we presented in that chapter.

You need to take this action not only for the sake of safety, but also because of how it can affect your children over time as they observe their daddy in this condition and see him becoming abusive. According to *The Domestic Violence Sourcebook* by Dr. Dawn Bradley Berry:

> Adolescents from abusive homes run a much higher risk of substance abuse, suicide or running away. The trauma continues through adulthood. Many men in prison – some estimates place the figure as high as 90 percent – were abused or witnessed abuse in the home while growing up. Even children who break the pattern and don't grow up to be violent themselves suffer terribly. According to a Johns Hopkins Children's Center study, teenagers exposed to violence, especially in the home, are more likely than others to become depressed or hopeless.[16]

❈ ❈ ❈ ❈

7. Make time for each child

As "Rachel" writes, "A mother is wise to create or look for opportunities to have one-to-one time with each individual child every few days. A bedtime story, a walk, a dinner together – these provide a chance for the child to ask a difficult question or to vent some painful emotions in the safety of your togetherness. For now, it's best not to share with hubby what the child has said or expressed – not until some measure of healing has come."

As we mentioned earlier, don't confront your children or force them to talk about their feelings if they don't want to. A parent needs to understand and respect a child's timing and ability to cope with the stress that exists in the house.

As you have the opportunity to get "up close and personal" with your child, the intimate atmosphere may bring your emotions closer to the surface – which is great if you don't allow it to go too far. It's important to communicate your heart in an honest and open fashion, but it's also important to balance that with conveying your own emotional stability to your child by remaining calm. Phoenix Institute of Chicago director Dr. Don Catherall advocates this balance:

This doesn't mean that you're never upset or unsure. Nor does it mean that you should present an artificial "happy face" around your child that parodies your real feelings. Rather, it simply means that you should make an effort to be steady for your child when you're together. You can discuss his fears and your own assessment of the dangers that may exist, but the central issue is that you must not burden him with your own fears. For your own emotional support, you must go elsewhere. You can be close to your child, but above all else, he shouldn't be made to feel he must reassure you. If you need to "fall apart," do so at a time and place to which your child won't have access.[17]

❀ ❀ ❀ ❀

8. Enlist the help of your extended family

Your siblings, your parents, grandparents, aunts and uncles – regardless of how far they live from you – can be a terrific source of help for your kids. They may be able to provide direct aid if they live nearby, but even the long-distance relatives can contribute to your kids' well-being. "Rachel" shares some good advice on that subject:

> I think it's critical to communicate (versus covering up) what is truly happening in your home and family to your adult extended family members, especially grandparents and closer aunts and uncles. They can minister to your children alongside you and fill in some gaps during the healing process. A phone call or encouraging note from Grandma. A fishing trip with Uncle Joe. They can also provide a peaceful home to visit at times – especially if they, too, are adult children of vets.

❀ ❀ ❀ ❀

9. Try to maintain family routines, such as dinner together, church or sports outings

We're not talking about trying to ignore the elephant in the living room. If the man of the house has PTSD, most of the normal household routines are going to be disrupted. But whenever possible, try to keep them intact. Since Dad is so unpredictable, familiar rituals and routines provide children with a sense of continuity, comfort and security. This may also give your child a deeper sense of control over their lives as they are able to predict "what's coming next." Routines can also be a good, home-based distraction from their worries about Dad.

By working to maintain normal family routines, you will be reminding your child in vivid ways what has *not* changed, and more importantly, that you still have each other.

What about TV, videos, etc.?

One common family routine in many households centers around home entertainment media. Older children understand that violence shown in most movies, TV shows and video games is staged and fake. And – for better or for worse – a steady diet of violent images seems to be tolerated and even expected by most young people today. But actual news footage of war and terrorism violence is another thing. And younger children may have trouble distinguishing between the fantasy of Hollywood and what is real. In addition, young children don't have much of a sense of distance, and may believe that the violence they see on TV is very close to them. Dr. Annette La Greca advises that these forms of entertainment should be restricted for the child's sake:

> Limiting your child's exposure to upsetting images of war, terrorism and violence will be particularly helpful for your child. This is especially important for children who have a parent or relative in the military or who have experienced recent trauma. Upsetting images may lead to fears, bad dreams and trouble sleeping. Limit television shows that include war-related programming, particularly the news and special programs about war. It will also help to limit television shows, movies, magazines, Internet sites and video games that have a lot of violence.[18]

10. Empower your kids

As we've mentioned earlier in this manual, one of the most troubling aspects of experiencing any sort of trauma is the loss of control. When your husband's Combat Trauma symptoms are dominating the home, everyone else is giving up some of their territory to accommodate him. The unfairness of this isn't lost on the children. Think of ways that will put *some* power back in their hands.

- Let them make decisions about clothes they wear, meals, desserts, family outings, chores, bedtimes (within reason).
- Give them greater responsibilities around the house. Ask them to help prepare dinner, help with yard work or even home repair. Help them see that by doing more they're helping you, helping their father and helping each other. Add the incentive of an increased allowance commensurate with their increased responsibilities.
- Encourage them to get involved in service projects in their community or with their church. As they are able to give their time and energies to others, they'll feel better about themselves, and it will take their focus off of their difficulties.

❀ ❀ ❀ ❀

11. Seek professional help

There are multiple treatment options open to affected families. Of course, if your husband is getting help and improving, this will benefit everyone in the family. But you can also involve your children in family therapy – individually, all together or both. If your husband is getting some coaching on how to be more supportive of the children during family therapy sessions, the times will be more productive. Young children can be involved in art or play therapy. Older children and teens can engage in supportive talk therapy. The main objective: provide a place where each child can have a voice in expressing what he or she needs.

Because so much is being learned about how strongly PTSD can affect families, Veterans Affairs PTSD programs (www.va.gov) and Vet Centers (www.va.gov/rcs/) across the country are beginning to offer group, couples and individual counseling programs for the families of veterans. Check the *Endnotes* for more information on the Vet Centers.[19]

❀ ❀ ❀❀ ❀ ❀

? Review the eleven "Approaches To Embrace" above. Based on what you read, what are three things you plan to do immediately (or in the very near future) that will help your children?

1. _____
_____
_____

2. _____
_____
_____

3. _____
_____
_____

❀ ❀ ❀❀ ❀ ❀

Christina's Prayer ...

Father, I forgive my husband for what he said and did today. Please help my precious daughter to do the same. Fill her heart with compassion for her father. Help her to show him the love he so desperately needs. Give her the courage to reach out to him again.

Lord, help me to understand how children may be triggering my husband. They are so full of life and questions and energy. It's taxing even for us who aren't directly touched by trauma. Father, help me to remember that when he sees and hears children, he remembers the faces of the ones he saw near the front lines. He remembers how his heart broke for them as he saw their despair and panic. Perhaps, more importantly, they remind him of the scared child inside himself that's running from all he's experienced. I can't imagine the pain of such memories, Lord. Father, I know with all my heart how deeply he loves his own child. Help him to distinguish between the past and the present.

I pray for my child, Lord. You promised in Your word that You cause all things to work together for good for those who love You and are called according to Your purposes. You say "all things." That includes the tragedy of PTSD spilling over into the life of my child. I pray, as we walk this path toward healing, that my daughter will draw near to You and come to know You as her loving and faithful Father. Thank You that You can meet her needs in ways I never could. Teach me to pray for my child, claiming Your promises on her behalf. Give me the courage to protect her when necessary.

In Jesus' Name, Amen.

Promise from God's Word ...

May our sons flourish in their youth like well-nurtured plants.
May our daughters be like graceful pillars, carved to beautify a palace.

– Psalm 144:12 (NLT)

13 HOW DO I GET BACK TO "NORMAL"?
The Journey To Peace and Stability

Erin's Journal ...

Our trip to New York City was a whirlwind. Our weekend getaway came and went in a New York minute. We still managed to hit all the biggies: the Statue of Liberty, Ellis Island, Broadway. And, of course, we couldn't leave without paying our respects at Ground Zero.

We tumbled out of the taxi and quickly realized we were walking around something sacred and sobering. There's surprisingly little to see there — a few markers and temporary memorials. But the memories of what took place on 9/11 still cast long, sad shadows across every visitor's heart. We milled around, peering through the perimeter of scaffolding and fences. Construction trucks still crawl around in the hole that hatred dug that day. One can't help but look up and remember the height, the beauty and the strength of the World Trade Center buildings that once stood head and shoulders above the city's skyline and the thousands of irreplaceable, precious lives that were stolen and silenced that day.

Back at the hotel, I read more about the WTC, its clean-up and reconstruction as Scott slept. I learned that a new amphibious ship is being built with tons of steel salvaged from the demolished towers. The USS New York will be a vessel for fighting terrorism around the world. She will be commissioned soon and based in Norfolk, Virginia.

For a moment I couldn't breathe. Like the Twin Towers, my husband and I were blind-sided by a destructive force. We will never be the same individuals or the same couple we were before. Our marriage will never be as it was before the war. And I grieve what was stolen and silenced. Yet, from the rubble, we are gathering what is still useful, what is still strong. From our own Ground Zero, we are salvaging what endured: our common faith in Christ, our commitment to our vows, our love for one another and our hope in God's promises to heal us. We are learning to rebuild our relationship and our individual lives from the foundation upward.

The USS New York ... the same steel with a different configuration and a new purpose ... to defend lives, to confront the enemy, and to remind us that strength and beauty can rise from the ashes ... to remind us that the spirit of freedom is indestructible.

My marriage ... my own life ... the same faith, same hope, same love with a different configuration and a new purpose ... to be walking, breathing reminders to others as well as to ourselves that the Spirit of Life, Light and Freedom Who lives inside us is indestructible, no matter what the enemy does and to inspire others to trust in God's power to give a crown of beauty for ashes, the oil of gladness instead of mourning, and a garment of praise instead of despair (Isaiah 61:3).

What we've lost ... what we've gained

For almost any American who meditates on what happened to our country on September 11, 2001, our hearts are struck by at least two emotions: **dismay** over the unjustified devastation and loss, and **determination** as we face our future courageously with a new, realistic and strengthened hope. We don't have any illusions about a return to the "Happy Days" of the 1950s – or even the relative peace and prosperity of the 80s. We know the world has changed forever. But we are not going to curl up and die because of what terrorists did to us on that devilish day. New York City, Washington, D.C., and Somerset County, Pennsylvania, have cleaned up the mess, mourned their dead, and are rebuilding – with a view to becoming stronger, more savvy and *better than ever*. The *USS New York* is a symbol of that determination. Strength gathered from the rubble!

For almost any wife whose husband came back from war with Combat Trauma, those same two emotions and sentiments abide as well. There is **dismay** over what was lost in the war zone, things that no longer seem to exist in the relationship, and the unfairness of it all. But where God is, there is also hope. And the hope breeds **determination**. And this determination can build a marriage that is also stronger, smarter and *better than ever*. Your continued love and commitment to your husband is a symbol of your determination. Strength will be gathered from the rubble that war has produced in your lives.

Both you and your husband are intimately acquainted with personal devastation, loss and grief. You've gained this familiarity not because you sought it out or expected it, but because you were taken there forcibly by the trauma resulting from your husband's unselfish commitment to protect the freedoms of our country and *your* unselfish commitment to support *him*.

But as Ralph Waldo Emerson wrote, "He has seen but half the universe who has never been shown the house of Pain."[1] It's an education you probably would have rather done without, but you have gained much knowledge and wisdom having seen the inside of that dark house.

And it won't be for nothing. As the Apostle Peter wrote under the inspiration of the Holy Spirit, "*May the God of all grace, who called us to His eternal glory by Christ Jesus, after you have suffered awhile, perfect, establish, strengthen, and settle you*" (1 Peter 5:10). The Bible doesn't sugar-coat what you're going through: it calls it *suffering*! But afterwards comes a perfecting, an establishing, a strengthening and a settling which the rest of the world knows nothing about. You and your husband have been placed in an environment that has the potential of bringing both of you to heights of satisfaction, strength, influence and leadership that were out of reach prior to your husband's soul-wounding. You have gained precious credentials which uniquely qualify you to hold positions only few can occupy. And whether it feels like it or not right now, God is *well-pleased* with you.

> *I will bring that group through the fire and make them pure.*
> *I will refine them like silver and purify them like gold.*
> *They will call on My name, and I will answer them.*
> *I will say, "These are My people,"*
> *and they will say, "The Lord is our God."*
>
> – **Zechariah 13:9** (NLT)

Neither your journey nor your final destination will be *normal*, as the title to this chapter implies. At least, not the normal you remember. When you hear the word "normal" your mind probably snaps back to how things were prior to your husband's deployment. How desperately you would love to return to *that* normal! But if we were to sell you the illusion that you *could* go back there, it would be a cruel and heartless deception. Just as the world changed forever on 9/11, your world has been changed by your husband's trauma. The pre-deployment "normal" no longer exists.

What God now has in mind for you is a **"New Normal."** And it's going to be *better* than the old normal in many, many ways. When you think about it, though, this has happened to you before. There was a time when you were single, and everything about that life seemed normal. But when you got married, you had to redefine normal. You took on a new role in life and a new way of thinking (encompassing *we* instead of only *I*, for instance). You'll never be that single girl again (even if – God forbid – you should get divorced). You've become *one flesh* with another human being, 'til death do you part. If you have kids, when the first baby came along you were launched into *another* new life, and what was normal for a young married woman was gone. Time to redefine normal *again*! Everything that grows, changes. "Normal" is constantly shifting and in need of redefinition.

We're not saying that your next New Normal will involve champagne toasts and bouquet tosses. But we *are* saying that you are on your way to a level of existence that will be better than ever. Just as Jesus' normal was burned away by the trauma of his crucifixion so that He could inherit the New Normal of the resurrection, so your old normal is being transformed into a glorious *New* Normal. As Elisabeth Elliot wrote, "There is a necessary link between suffering and glory."[2] Jesus said:

> *I tell you the truth, unless a kernel of wheat is planted in the soil and dies, it remains*
> *alone. But its death will produce many new kernels – a plentiful harvest of new lives.*

> **– John 12:24** (NLT)

❀ ❀ ❀❀ ❀ ❀

? Would it be too shocking to say your husband died over there on the battlefield? In many respects he did. Spend a few moments thinking about that concept. In what ways did your husband die while he was deployed? Feel free to use extra paper if you need more room …

_____

_____

_____

_____

Jesus' promise in the above Scripture (John 12:24) is that, because of those deaths, abundant new life is going to be produced – in both you and your husband. You both have suffered many losses, as did Jesus. And just as Jesus' biggest loss became the doorway to His greatest gain, so your pain will crack open the door of your husband's Combat Trauma and give you entrance to a world of light and life that you never could have experienced otherwise.

? Name one outrageous, over-the-top thing that you hope you will find in that New Normal world:

_____

_____

❀ ❀ ❀❀ ❀ ❀

After you have suffered awhile …

This metamorphosis we've been speaking of doesn't happen quickly or all at once. We don't get to experience "microwave maturity." God apparently prefers crock pots – He likes what the *process* produces. He likes quality, and quality can't be rushed. He takes a thousand years to make a decent redwood tree; a squash He can do in a month.

And it doesn't happen if we sit passively and wait for Him to "zap" us. God has required that we partner with Him intentionally through the process. He's expecting us to be proactive about creating an environment that gives Him maximum access to our hearts and souls. Our transformation will occur as we respond positively to His overtures and obey His instructions. There is no easy way – but "easy" is seldom worthwhile in the long run. The only way to resurrection is through the cross and the tomb. As you look around, it's easy to see you're on the right road, isn't it?

❀ ❀ ❀❀ ❀ ❀

Becoming intentional about the New Normal

It takes two

The journey to the land of New Normal isn't one you can make by yourself. It's going to be a team effort involving both you and that person who is now bone of your bone and flesh of your flesh (Genesis 2:23). Throughout this manual we have shared many suggestions that will help you complete that trip to New Normal. In this chapter, we want to help the two of you make a plan, or in military jargon: "define your mission." This chapter is meant to complement Step 10 of the *Combat Trauma Healing Manual* which we wrote for your husband. If he has a copy of that publication, it would be helpful; but if he doesn't, you can both work through the various issues together from this manual. Some of the steps outlined in this chapter you can work through alone, but it's best if you and your husband do them together.

Just as every mission in a war is comprised of many interrelated and coordinated movements, so your mission to New Normal will also have several components that need to be thought through:

- **What Needs To Change?** – Vocation? Location? Companions?
- **Facing Triggers Together** – Helping each other with traumatic responses
- **Setting Personal Goals** – Regarding your family, exercise, finances, etc.

If you don't set about actually making objective plans in these three areas, you will continue to "float" at your current level of confusion and stagnation. As Benjamin Franklin once said, "The Constitution only gives people the right to *pursue* happiness. You have to catch it yourself." So let's go catch some!

Don't make me laugh!

We realize that not every suggestion we offer in this manual or in this chapter will be possible for every couple. Everyone is in a different place on the road to New Normal. For some, the idea of sitting down with your husband and discussing finances or chores is utterly laughable. For others whose husbands' Combat Trauma isn't too severe, such reasonable give-and-take may be no problem at all. But the hard truth is that to do nothing will maintain the status quo indefinitely. It will take intentional, active *work* to make any progress toward New Normal. And it will only happen as you and your husband move in tandem toward the worthy goals you craft for yourselves.

Maybe you can't imagine applying some of the ideas in this chapter right now, but perhaps you will in a month, six months or a year. If nothing else, we hope that this chapter will plant some seeds in your heart and mind, and give you some faith goals to begin praying toward. As you pray about them, you begin to walk by faith, which gives God something He can partner with and bless. You'd be amazed what a solid year of prayer can do for *any* area of concern! But if you have no vision for your future, it's hard to have faith, and even harder to pray about it. So anything in this chapter that you are not able to immediately take action on, allow it to become a prayer goal for your future.

❀ ❀ ❀❀ ❀ ❀

What needs to change?

Vocation?

If your husband is still on active duty, he may feel that he is already in the right vocation for the long term. God may have given him a warrior's heart and a commitment to serve as part of our country's "exoderm." The military provides families with unique opportunities to travel the country and the world, and they offer job security and avenues for advancement that are seldom found in the civilian workforce. If these points are appealing to your husband, a career in the military is a good fit for him and – hopefully – for you. But if you have some real reservations about him continuing on in the military, it is very important that the two of you discuss it. If just talking about it doesn't resolve the issue, you may need to visit a clergyman or a counselor to help you work through the issue together.

On the other hand, it may be that after your husband's significant contribution to our nation's defense, he visualizes himself contributing to society in other ways, such as through education, business, police/fire, Christian ministry, etc.

 Whatever the case, he needs to ask himself a simple question and the two of you should discuss it: ***How much do I like my job?*** What would he give it on a scale of 1 to 10, with 10 being perfect? Put his answer in the upper box next to this paragraph. For comparison, how much do *you* like his current vocation? Put your number in the lower box. If there's a difference, why do you think that is? Do you feel you ought to discuss this with your husband? With your Battle Buddy?

If your husband answered anything less than a 7, then he should probably begin thinking and praying about God *eventually* leading the two of you in a different direction.

However, we want to emphasize "eventually" very strongly. If he is still dealing with severe symptoms of PTSD he does *not* need the extra stress of trying to learn a new job right now. He shouldn't make *any* major changes to his present routines until he feels good-and-ready – even eager – to do so, with confirmation from you and other Bridge People in your lives. A good rule of thumb: for every month he spent downrange, he should give himself at least that many months before making any major decisions - *minimum*. He needs to give his decision-making skills a chance to sharpen up and become a bit more objective and less emotional after his traumatic experiences.

This may not be the time for a major change – but it is a *great* time for dreams. It's a period where you and he can be asking God what *He* would suggest for your future. He has something in mind for which you as a couple would be perfectly suited. He created you and wired you in a certain way and brought you together as husband and wife. He wants to communicate to you what would fulfill you – if you'll be willing to listen and take action.

> *"For I know the plans that I have for you," declares the LORD, "plans for welfare and not for calamity to give you a future and a hope."*
>
> **– Jeremiah 29:11**

Remind your husband of the fact that there's a big difference between a "job" and a "career." When he got his first job, it's likely that his only criterion was: "Will they actually pay me *money*?" He landed the job at the burger joint, and quickly realized it wasn't something he wanted to do for the rest of his life. But he didn't quit because he needed the money. Based on that experience, though, he began to ponder what kinds of jobs he would *prefer*. Once he started to gravitate toward one general vocation, he took steps to break into it. That may even be the reason he joined the military.

The "happily-ever-after" story ends with him finding his ideal vocation which becomes a lifelong *career*, and is more like a "calling" because of how satisfying it is. Unfortunately, expectations are sometimes torpedoed along the way to perfection. When that happens, people are often so far down the road they can't figure out how to make a U-turn, so they choose to continue on, abandoning their dreams and considering their disenchantment to be acceptable.

❀ ❀ ❀ ❀

What about you?

All that was written in the previous two paragraphs is applicable to *you*, too! There are many close, successful marriages in which the husband and the wife pursue different careers. They have to be more intentional about maintaining their heart-ties with each other, but with God's help, a clear calling and lots of selfless and understanding communication between you and your husband, it can be done! Spend time talking with your husband about *your* dreams. In what ways has God gifted you? What kind of work refreshes and energizes you? How could your family's priorities and schedule be adjusted so that you and your husband could successfully pursue two careers? Would your husband consider staying in the military, while you began to learn or sharpen new skills for a new career? Dr. Aphrodite Matsakis in her book *Vietnam Wives* shares a very motivating observation regarding a two-career household:

> Many a marriage has been saved by the wife forging ahead toward her goal, even in some small manner. In several cases, had the woman not pursued one of her vocational ambitions, she would have been strongly tempted to abandon her marriage. The sense of achievement, self-regard and self-respect these women acquired by pursuing even one of their own goals gave them the strength to cope with husbands who had little to offer emotionally because of their PTSD.[3]

This is a time for new beginnings for you – a time to define your New Normal. And if your current job or your husband's job doesn't fit your dreams, it's time to imagine what would.

 Prayer Assignment: Start making it a part of your daily prayer time to ask God to give you a vision for what you and your husband should do with the rest of your lives. And while you're at it, ask Him to show you how to bring that vision into the realm of reality. As scientist and writer Douglas H. Everett wrote: "There are some people who live in a dream world, and there are some who face reality; and then there are those who turn one into the other."[4] God can help you turn your dreams into reality if you'll look to Him for direction. He wants you in the right spot just as intensely as you do!

※ ※ ※ ※

Dream career

? Do you already have a dream? If you could do *anything* career-wise, what would it be? What would you like to see yourself doing ten years from now?

_____

_____

_____

WWII veteran, minister and writer Frederick Buechner counsels us:

> The voice we should listen to most as we choose a vocation is the voice that we might think we should listen to least, and that is the voice of our own gladness. What can we do that makes us gladdest; what can we do that leaves us with the strongest sense of sailing true north and of peace, which is much of what gladness is? … I believe that if it is a thing that makes us truly glad, then it is a good thing and it is our thing and it is the calling voice that we were made to answer with our lives.[5]

Check the *Additional Resources* in Appendix B pertaining to this chapter for some good books that will help you think through what would be fulfilling career choices for your husband and for you.

※ ※ ※※ ※ ※

Location?

Obviously, if your husband is still on active duty, you don't have a lot of control over your location. "Military readiness" never takes a time out. We know how rough it can be on a family when your husband returns from a difficult deployment and has to saddle up again after a short period of down time. The intense preparation, integration of new members assigned to his unit, getting equipment back in shape, late hours and probable training deployments require yet more time away from home – and all of that takes its toll on *you*. The post-deployment tempo has both good and bad aspects to it, but it's a reality of military life – as you well know.

On the other hand, the military lifestyle offers unprecedented opportunities for travel and adventure, a unique sense of community and camaraderie and valuable equipping of family members for future life experiences. For some of you, "home" truly is where the military sends you.

But if you are now separated from the military (or soon will be) and have control of where you live, there are some important things to consider. As we tried to demonstrate in Chapter 8, "Bridge People" are among the most vital elements of your healing environment. If your husband is struggling with Combat Trauma, and if you are experiencing secondary or even primary trauma because of it, you both need a good contingent of Bridge People around you. In most cases, Bridge People are probably right there where you currently live – those people who supported and encouraged you while your husband was deployed. These relationships are already established and strong, and no additional energy is needed to find and build new ones. Moving to a new location would mean trying to get established in a place where you don't know anybody, and would therefore be without that key "bridge" element. You might think, "Well, we'll just make new friends," but don't forget that if you and your husband are dealing with trauma, you are probably in a strong self-isolating mode right now. With so many other stresses wearing you down, it's likely you'll be hiding in the back room when the Welcome Wagon® shows up.

A move is stressful for anyone, any time. And as mentioned before, you don't need additional stress in your world right now. Again – if at all possible – we recommend that you delay any decision regarding a major move using the same criteria we mentioned for a major vocational change: a minimum of one month of contemplation for each month he was downrange.

If your husband is still on active duty and gets assigned to a new location, it is imperative that you begin looking for new Bridge People immediately. Asking God to help you assemble a new support network needs to become a part of your daily prayer time.

You may be perfectly content to stay right where you are the rest of your life. Great! If you can match your dream vocation with your current location, that's a good recipe for contentment. But if you're not happy with your location, or if your dream vocation might mean that you need to live elsewhere, there will come a time when you and your husband will feel strong and stable enough to make the move.

But let your vocations dictate your location as much as possible. You may find this very difficult to believe, but there are people living in *Hawaii* who have grown tired of it and are thinking about a move to Los Angeles! True! Your location can provide a wonderful context for life, but it's *only a context*. What you exchange your time for day-in and day-out forms a much larger portion of your life, and if that isn't satisfying, even Hawaii will seem like a prison. But if your career and calling make you wake up every morning saying, "I can't wait to get to work!" it doesn't really matter where you live. Writer Tad Williams provides a great perspective:

> Never make your home in a *place*. Make a home for yourself inside your own head. You'll find what you need to furnish it – memory, friends you can trust, love of learning, and other such things. That way it will go with you wherever you journey.[6]

And as the Apostle Paul put it:

> *I have learned in whatever state I am, to be content.*
>
> **– Philippians 4:11** (NKJV)

❀ ❀ ❀❀ ❀ ❀

Vocation + Location = Really Nice!

The ideal, of course, would be to combine your dream vocations with your dream location. Do you feel called to be a dolphin trainer? Then you probably also love warm, sunny locales. Professional snowboarder? You'd better love places that get snowbound from time to time. Does your husband enjoy launching manned rockets? Then hopefully Houston or Cape Kennedy is okay with you.

Then again, you and/or your husband's dream vocations may involve frequent shifts of location. Some people start to feel stagnant after they've been in the same spot for more than a few months. Some specifically joined the military to "see the world," and that mobile lifestyle suits them just fine. If your husband is still on active duty, you are definitely in the right place. His vocation will certainly dictate your location! If you're not on active duty any more, you can still pursue a career that will keep you flitting around the world to your heart's content. Take your home with you, as Tad Williams recommended above. But don't forget to weigh the effect frequent moves will have on your children – both positive and negative.

You may not be able to name a particular city, state or country, but you can probably identify certain characteristics of your ideal location – as can your husband. Sit down with your husband and ask him, "If they could match up with your vocation, what would be five characteristics of your ideal location?" Put his responses in the left column. Then think through your top choices and enter them in the right column. Are they mainly similar or dissimilar? If they are very dissimilar, this would be a good topic to discuss to find out which characteristics are dearly held, and which ones aren't that important.

Characteristics of Husband's Ideal Location	Characteristics of Wife's Ideal Location
1.	1.
2.	2.
3.	3.
4.	4.
5.	5.

 Prayer Assignment: In your prayer times, begin asking God if He would combine both of your dream vocations with your ideal location. It may seem like too much to ask, but our God *loves* to delight His children – especially those who have had to endure the hardships you have. Jesus said so Himself:

> *Until now you have asked nothing in My name. Ask, and you will receive,*
> *that your joy may be full.*
> — **John 16:24** (NKJV)

As amazing and extravagant as it may seem, sometimes the main criterion God has for answering your prayer with a "*Yes!*" is simply, "Will it bring My child joy?"

❀ ❀ ❀❀ ❀ ❀

Companions?

Battle-blasted or not, *everyone* needs good friends – but *especially* the battle-blasted. So many people don't appreciate the wealth represented by a loyal, compassionate friend until they are in desperate need of one. Do you have at least a couple of friends like this:

"A friend is someone who sees through you and still enjoys the view."   – Wilma Askinas

"A real friend is one who walks in when the rest of the world walks out."   – Walter Winchell

"A friend knows the song of my heart and sings it to me when my memory fails."   – Unknown

"A friend is a person with whom you dare to be yourself."   – C. Raymond Beran

"A friend is a single soul living in two bodies."   – Aristotle

So if you *do* have some friends like this, it is *not* time to swap them out! If, in addition, they have husbands who have been deployed and come back with Combat Trauma, you are wealthy indeed. They can understand and relate to you at levels that no one else can. Cultivate those friendships like you were growing money trees!

But not all of your companions are necessarily *good* friends – even among the sisterhood of combat veteran's wives. Your shared experiences have connected you at deep levels, and friendships forged on the anvil of crisis are strong indeed. But you may need to do some hard thinking about whether or not some of these companions are a liability to your healing. Think about each "marginal" companion of yours and assess their effect on you. Consider each of the following statements:

- ❑ When you're with them, do they make you feel "up" or do they drag you down emotionally?
- ❑ Will they let you talk about your difficult experiences with your husband, or do they avoid or change the subject?
- ❑ Do they dominate conversations, preferring to recite all their problems rather than give you a chance to share what you're dealing with?
- ❑ Do you tend to drink too much alcohol when you're with them?
- ❑ Are they encouraging you – either directly or indirectly – to use illegal drugs?
- ❑ Do they influence you to re-take the throne of your life and engage in behavior that you know grieves the Holy Spirit?
- ❑ Are they frequently finding reasons for you to skip church and other faith-building functions?
- ❑ Are they antagonistic or critical about your relationship with God?
- ❑ Are they trying to pull you away from other friends that are a positive influence on you?
- ❑ Do they engage in a lot of negative, critical talk, seldom having anything good to say about their husbands, their husbands' job or the military?
- ❑ Do they stifle your creativity, enthusiasm, hope and faith, or show disdain for your dreams in the name of "Be realistic!"?

If more than two or three of the negative statements above apply to your friend, this person may not be the best companion for you. This doesn't mean you can't be available to support her as needed, but for the sake of your own recovery, you should limit your "hang time" with her. You may be thinking unselfishly, "But I can be a good influence on her." And you might be. But if you are still struggling with secondary or primary traumatic stress, the reverse is more likely. As the Apostle Paul warns us:

> *Do not be misled: "Bad company corrupts good character."*
>
> **– 1 Corinthians 15:33 (NIV)**

So choose your company carefully – but do choose! We all need those Bridge People from time to time. Trying to make it through your current battle without them will prove very difficult. As anthropologist and writer Zora Neale Hurston observed:

> It seems to me that trying to live without friends is like milking a bear to get cream for your morning coffee. It is a whole lot of trouble, and then not worth much after you get it.[7]

Taking stock

? In Chapter 8 (page 127) you were encouraged to make a short list of people to pray for with whom you could begin a formal "bridge relationship." Continue praying for and cultivating those good friendships! But are there some other people that might fall into the category of "bad company" with whom – at least for the present – you need to spend less time? Ask God who they might be, and if anyone comes to your mind, write their names down here (if you worry about confidentiality, you could skip writing them down here if you'd prefer):

_____

_____

_____

❀ ❀ ❀❀ ❀ ❀

Facing triggers together

In Chapter 1, we discussed the physiological and psychological basis of Combat Trauma and PTSD. The specific traumatic experiences your husband had while downrange were so profound that his brain took special note of them. Anytime he approaches a person, place, thing or experience that is similar to his original trauma, his right brain whips out its "photo album" and puts on an intense presentation (sights, sounds, smells, tastes), attempting to alert him of the mortal danger that could be waiting there. His logical left brain gets muted. The calming influence of his hippocampus gets pinched off. He's on a "re-experiencing" detour which, if his right brain would only *listen*, his left brain could explain why he didn't need to take that journey today.

In Chapter 2, we explained how and why you may have developed secondary and/or primary traumatic stress, and that *you* may have specific triggers as well. Certain people, places, objects or experiences can cause your symptoms to spike just like your husband's.

By now you are probably well aware of what your husband's triggers are as well as what triggers you. In the space provided below, write down any people, places, things or experiences that trigger those re-experiencing episodes, and what the typical effect is (use additional paper if needed):

Mine ✓	His ✓	Trigger	Effect

Your husband has many options in his arsenal with which to counter these troubling episodes. With you as his Number One asset, along with the influences of the Holy Spirit, God's Word, prayer, the Christian community and the positive mindset of his Spiritual Battlemind (all of which are examined in Step 3 of *The Combat Trauma Healing Manual*), together you and he have created an environment where the Holy Spirit can transform and heal his wounded soul. Hopefully, he has Bridge People in his life who will walk with him through the dark forests. He has the assurances from God that he has nothing to fear. And he has the testimony of reality that he's being told the truth – there will probably *not* be a sniper on the highway overpass today and no IEDs hidden in rubbish by the side of the road.

But what about you? What about the triggers and fears you listed in the exercise above? If the two of you can be Battle Buddies regarding this sensitive area of your lives – if you can be aware of each other's triggers and commit to bearing each other's burdens – these episodes will eventually lose their power.

Not every husband who is struggling with PTSD is willing or able to bear his wife's burdens or listen to her share about her triggers – especially if one of her major triggers is *him*. But some husbands *do* want to know about the triggers so that they can be supportive when they are able. You'll have to be the judge of which category your husband is in presently. Ask the Lord for discernment on this issue. If you sense that your husband is just not ready to deal with a conversation about your triggers, put it off until a better time in the future. A few months from now, he may have experienced enough healing and growth to be receptive and supportive.

What to do when your husband is triggered

When he's in a dissociative state

Maybe it's the unanticipated smell of a dead animal by the side of the road, an ambulance siren, a slamming door, or a painful anniversary. Maybe it's a series of circumstances or events mixed with poor sleep, inadequate diet and financial anxieties. Whatever the case, sometimes the trigger can cause a PTSD sufferer's body and mind to part company for a while. He thinks he's back in the war zone; he's shouting to his friends; he's barking orders; he crouching behind chairs; he's running for his life. What do you do?

As mentioned in Chapter 5, if your husband has shown any tendencies toward violent behavior in the past – if he's shoved or hit you or your kids, put his fist or boot through a wall, been aggressive or threatening or if he has a criminal record that includes violence, ***it's important that you leave the area immediately***. You really have no idea what he might do in that state, so it's best to not risk harm to yourself or to your children.

If he hasn't exhibited any violent tendencies in the past and you feel safe enough, you could stay with him – but keep your distance. Speak to him in a calm, gentle voice and help him sort out where he is at that moment. Apply any of the suggestions written below that you can. He may not seem to be aware of you, but there is a good chance that you're getting through to him at some level, and before long your presence and soothing voice could have a very positive effect.

When he's "present" and able to interact

If after a triggering incident your husband is still aware of reality and his surroundings and is responsive to your voice, here are some suggestions of how you can help "bring him down" from his agitated state:

- **Pray.** Ask God to give you wisdom and insight about what to do. Ask the Holy Spirit to calm your husband's heart, soul and mind, and to shield him from any evil forces which might be trying to take advantage of your husband's confused state to make things worse. If you sense the enemy's presence, apply some of the principles you learned in Chapter 10 on spiritual warfare.
- **Be there.** If there seems to be no threat of violence, your simple presence will be very comforting to him. Marshéle's husband Mark has told her after some of his PTSD episodes, "Just knowing you're there and not going anywhere means so much to me."
- **Be calm**. It will not help the situation in the least if you start freaking out, become overly talkative, demand that he respond to you, nag him to stop his behavior, cry or become overtly emotional. Speak in quiet, reassuring tones. Assure him of your love over and over.

- **Touch.** If he seems receptive (not agitated or combative), make some sort of physical contact with him. Hold his hand, put your hand on his shoulder, back or thigh. Put your arm around him or embrace him. In some cases it may be a good idea to let him know ahead of time what you are going to do. "Can I hold your hand?" "I'm going to put my hand on your back." This can be a *huge* calming influence for most men in this situation.

- **Slow breathing.** If he's hyperventilating, gently urge him to focus on his breathing, and ask him to try to slow it down. "Take some deep, slow breaths, Honey. Try to slow down your breathing." If he starts to get dizzy, have him breathe into a paper sack for a minute or so. If he's holding his breath or taking very shallow breaths, remind him, "Take a breath, Hon. Don't forget to breathe."

- **Help him get reoriented.** He may be having trouble grasping the context of where he is or what he's doing. Reassure him that he's nowhere near a battle zone. Help him to recognize his surroundings by saying things like, "It's okay, Babe. You're home. You're in Virginia. You're safe. You know that, don't you? I'm here with you. You're in your own home and there are no enemy fighters anywhere near here. They're thousands of miles away, and you're here with me. God's right here with us too. Don't worry. He's keeping us safe." This will help bring him back from the *memory* to the *present moment*.

- **Get him to verbalize.** If you can get him to respond to questions you ask or requests you make, it can help bring him back to the present quickly. By interacting with you, it forces the right and left sides of his brain to make connections which counters what's going on in a psychotic episode. Ask questions related to the here-and-now or get him to describe what he sees around him. Any kind of *facts* about his surroundings that you can get him to acknowledge will be helpful. Here are a few examples of how you could get him to talk:
  - ➢ Do you remember what day of the week it is?
  - ➢ Can you tell me what time it is?
  - ➢ What color socks (underwear, shirt, shoes) are you wearing?
  - ➢ What are you planning to do later today?
  - ➢ Let's go over here and sit down for a minute.
  - ➢ Look over your left shoulder and tell me what you see there. Now look over your right shoulder. Do you see any danger?
  - ➢ Tell me what you're feeling right now.

- **Offer to leave**. If you're in a public place or visiting friends, ask your husband if he'd like you to take him out of there. If he indicates that he does, then do it immediately. Say, "Okay, we're going *right now*." Offer your quick apologies to your hosts if necessary, and then head for open spaces or back home – whichever he prefers.

- **If he's shut down.** Sometimes triggered veterans will just close their eyes, duck their heads, possibly curl up on a couch or the floor and try to escape in their minds. They won't talk or acknowledge anyone's presence. Stay with them, touch them, and in a quiet, gentle voice, assure them that you're there and will wait with them. You could say something like, "I'm right here with you. When you're ready, I want you to come back to me and talk with me. I love you. Take your time, I'm here." Then, be patient and wait.

- **Afterwards.** After an intense fight-or-flight response, the veteran will be exhausted. Be very willing to adjust your plans for the rest of the day or evening. He may need to go home and sleep for a few hours, or all night.

- **If kids are around.** If your husband is becoming aggressive or violent it's important to get your children to a safe place. Tell them to go to their room, close and lock their door, or tell them to go next door. Yes, this will probably make him even more angry, but your courage here is necessary for the sake of your kids. First, distract his attention away from the *kids* (so they can leave) and then distract his attention away from his *anger*. You could ask questions like:

➢ What has happened? What has gotten you so upset?

➢ What can we do to make this better? How can I help you?

➢ We don't want to involve the kids in this, do we? Let's work this out, just you and me.

➢ Can we sit down (or go take a walk together) and talk about this?

The bottom line in helping your husband through his triggered time: know your man. Be aware of the things that trigger him and find ways to avoid them. It can be exhausting, but with the Lord's help you need to be constantly assessing his mood – is it a good day or a bad day? Modify your tone, plans and expectations based on that barometer. Learn from your mistakes. Marshéle prays at the beginning of every day, "Help me to say and do only the things that will help my husband."

What about me?

As mentioned earlier, how much you can depend on your husband to help you with *your* triggers is going to depend on how far he's traveled down the road toward his own healing. Some wives will be able to share their list of triggers with their husband, and they can work out a strategy concerning what to do when one of them is triggered. Others must keep their expectations quite low. Your best bet for now is to share your trigger list with your Battle Buddy (and Bridge People if you feel comfortable about it) and discuss how they can help you if they're around when you're triggered. If you're with your husband when you feel you're approaching a triggering event (or if he's triggering you), a good strategy is to leave the room and deal with it alone with the Lord's help.

Setting personal goals

> Planning is bringing the future into the present so that you can do something about it now.[8]
>
> – Alan Lakein, time management expert

This section could have begun with the old and absolutely true adage: "If you fail to plan, plan to fail." But Lakein's observation should help us to recognize the positive side of planning: it is *future oriented*. If your husband is suffering with Combat Trauma, his present is *stuck* and so is yours. And continuing to focus on his past isn't going to get him unstuck. Like a Humvee sunk past its axles in a mud bog, a cable needs to be stretched out and secured to something *solid* and stable and the winch turned on. In Christ, your future is secure. Spirit-directed planning is your cable-and-winch that will pull you out of your current quagmire.

Besides, as baseball legend and Yankee philosopher Yogi Berra warns us: "If you don't know where you're going, you'll probably end up somewhere else." Your future awaits – and you *do* want to get there!

Setting goals: How to

Setting goals involves getting a clear idea of what you want to ultimately accomplish (like "graduate from college") and then writing out the steps that will help you attain it. How to actually *write* those goals in a way that will make them achievable takes a little work, but it will be worth it.

A good criterion for writing any goal uses the acronym **SMART**. Here's what each letter stands for:

SPECIFIC – There must be some detail and precision to it, and some sense of time. To say, "I would like to learn how to decorate cakes" is not very specific. But to say, "I want to complete the Wilson Cake Decorating course so I can make a cake for my daughter's wedding" is very specific.

MEASURABLE – Your goal statement must contain some objective element that will let you know when you've achieved it or are achieving it. To say, "I would like to be a better mother" is a worthy goal, but how would you know when you *became* a better mother? Instead, link your desire to measurable action. "I will read my son a bedtime story every night I'm home for the next month," or "I will read three books about parenting within the next year and discuss them with my husband," would both be measurable. Can you put it on a checklist? Then it's probably measurable.

ATTAINABLE – It must be a goal for which you can devise a plan to attain it. If you can't work out the steps that would be involved in getting you to your destination, it's not attainable. Enthusiasm, faith and courage are advantages when setting out on any journey, but if you leave with no road map, they won't help much.

REALISTIC – Given your present resources, is it reasonable to believe the goal could be achieved? For instance, if you've never held any kind of public office, it's not very likely you'll be successful running for the governor of your state. At least not the *first* time you try. This is not to say you shouldn't build a "faith factor" into your goals. But if you do, be sure your faith is strong enough to see it through to the end.

TANGIBLE – It must have substance and objectivity rather than be merely a vague desire. "I would like to be happy" is a nice sentiment, but not tangible. What specifically would *make* you happy? That would more likely be a *goal*. Can you put it on your calendar? That's a good test of tangibility.

❀ ❀ ❀❀ ❀ ❀

Setting goals: Layering them according to priorities

As you begin to write out goals, remember that there are only so many hours in a day, and that you probably won't have unlimited time to pursue all your goals at all times. So it will be necessary for you to layer and prioritize them.

A very simple way of doing this – relative to each major desire that God brings into your mind – is to set them according to three time frames:

- **Long-range** – Major pursuits that may take five to twenty years to achieve.
- **Medium-range** – Specific goals that can be achieved in one to five years.
- **Short-range** – Specific goals that can be achieved within a day to a year.

A collection of short-range goals will add up to one medium-range goal. The achieving of a series of medium-range goals will bring about the accomplishment of a long-range goal.

Next, prioritize them according to how passionately you desire each long-range goal. Decide which goals belong on your "A" list, which on your "B" list, and which go on your "C" list. Based on this prioritizing, it will be much easier for you to decide which specific activities relative to each goal need to be transferred to your "To do list" and your calendar. If you're like most of us, if it doesn't get on the calendar, *it does not exist!* So "calendarize" your goals whenever possible!

Setting goals: Dreaming in the important areas

> I have had dreams and I have had nightmares,
> but I have conquered my nightmares because of my dreams.[9]
>
> – Dr. Jonas Salk (developer of the Polio vaccine)

How thoroughly have your nightmares – or your husband's nightmares – eradicated your dreams? Nightmares happen when you're asleep and passive, but the dreams we're talking about here spring into being when we are awake and intentional. *Those* dreams, fed by God's Spirit, are what have the power to conquer our nightmares. "Major on the majors" is a popular credo. If we aren't succeeding in the major areas of our lives, no amount of success in the minor areas will gratify us. And minor dreams won't displace major nightmares.

 For this reason, we'd like you to spend a little time thinking about those major areas. We're supplying you with a list of eight areas here, but it is not necessarily complete. There may be other issues unique to your life that need to be addressed. Please write them out on additional sheets of paper. In each of the following areas, ask God to give you some vision regarding where you need to be headed. What do you think would be *good* for you? What would be good for your family? What are some of your long-range desires in each area? At this point, you don't need to work out layering or prioritizing them. Just write down whatever the Lord brings to your mind.

1. Goals regarding my relationship with my husband:

2. Goals regarding my relationship with my kids (if you have any):

3. Goals regarding my vocation:

4. Goals regarding my location:

5. Goals regarding my finances:

6. Goals regarding diet and exercise:

7. Goals regarding my medical issues:

8. Goals regarding my excesses (alcohol, drugs, food, sex, etc.):

Now, if you're serious about this, here's what we want you to do. In a separate notebook, or on separate sheets of paper, write out each of the goals you wrote at the top of a page – one goal per page. Those constitute your "Long-range goals." Break each down into two to five "Medium-range goals" that would combine to help you reach the long-range goal at the top of the page. Then, beneath each medium-range goal, write out two to five "Short-range goals" that would help you accomplish each medium-range goal. If those goals are "SMART" enough, transfer them to your calendar.

By doing this, you are indeed "bringing the future into the present" so that you can truly bring about a New Normal for yourself and your husband. Nothing can be done about what happened in the past, but *everything* can be done about what happens in the future!

> *Delight yourself in the Lord; and He will give you the desires of your heart.*
> *Commit your way to the Lord, trust also in Him, and He will do it.*
>
> **– Psalm 37:4,5**

In Step 10 of *The Combat Trauma Healing Manual*, your husband was also given an exercise designed to help him create some practical goals. If he has completed that section in his manual, ask him if he'd like to compare goals. How similar are they to yours? Do you feel his are SMART? What does he think about your goals? How can you work together to help each other achieve the goals you have written down?

❈ ❈ ❈❈ ❈ ❈

The beauty of brokenness

You are probably well aware of the fact that your journey to New Normal will not be easy. As you and your husband work to salvage usable things from the rubble that the war left behind, it is important to be realistic in your expectations. But it's also important to see the process through the eternity-filled eyes of God. It can be a painful, sometimes shattering process, but the end result is *absolutely beautiful!*

In a certain region of northern Italy, artisans in many of the villages produce beautiful vases, each piece fetching a very good price due to the skill that has been passed down from generation to generation.

But there is one particular village that produces vases that command ten times the price of any of their neighbor's goods. The vases are so valuable because of the crafting technique the artisans of this village use. They make the vases just as all the other villages in the region do, but then they smash them, shattering them into dozens of pieces.

Then, with the greatest care and skill, the artisans laboriously reassemble the vase, using glue that has been mixed with gold. When finished, every golden vein contributes a magnificent element to the vase, adding immensely to its beauty and value.

This process is very similar to what you are experiencing currently. Your husband's Combat Trauma has shattered your life in many ways, but the eternal Artisan is in the process of rebuilding both him and you. And every re-glued crack, every scarred-over wound will contribute to your beauty and value in ways you cannot yet fathom.

This is probably why the resurrected Christ retained His scars, even in His glorified body. For all of eternity, they symbolize something *beautiful* to each of us who were saved by them, to all the angels who observed His ultimate sacrifice of love and to the Father Who observed the obedience of His only Son.

So will your scars – seen and unseen – be gloriously beautiful.

You and your husband have been in some dark places since his traumatic experiences downrange. You are both probably still fighting your way out of that darkness toward your New Normal. God's desire is to *help* you. The sentiment of what God said to His servant Cyrus can be a promise to you as well:

> *I will go before you and will level the mountains;*
> *I will break down gates of bronze and cut through bars of iron.*
> *I will give you the treasures of darkness,*
> > *riches stored in secret places,*
> > > *so that you may know that I am the Lord,*
> > > > *the God of Israel, who summons you by name.*
>
> **– Isaiah 45:2,3 (NIV)**

He knows your name. He knows your husband's name. He has called both of you. He'll see to it that neither mountains, gates of bronze, bars of iron or the blackest darkness will keep you from where He wants you to go. And there are treasures hidden in that darkness He wants to give you. As you receive them, you'll know for sure the God of Israel is the One who has been with you in that dark cave of trauma. Those who have never entered the darkness will never touch those treasures. But He's holding them out to you.

May God give you the sight to see the treasures meant for you, accept them and use them for your healing and for the glory of the Kingdom of God.

And may the golden veins of your restored soul be evident to everyone for all eternity.

❀ ❀ ❀❀ ❀ ❀

Erin's Prayer ...

Lord Jesus, in the dark days that followed the cross, Your disciples must have felt that all was destroyed. Their plans and dreams of a bright future with You came crashing down around them in a matter of hours. Their hearts were crushed beneath the weight of Your death. They certainly could not see the way ahead.

You told them in advance that everything would soon be different for them. The familiar would not exist ever again. You told Your friends that the difficulties ahead would demand that they believe Your words, act on Your words, persevere and overcome. Thank You, Lord, that in their most frightened, isolated times, You showed up. You gave them glimpses and brief conversations with You that renewed their hope and faith.

At times I see glimpses of the man I married, the one with whom I saw a bright future before the war came home with him. The occasional, pleasant conversation or the gentle touch of his hand or even that infrequent shared laugh fuels my faith and keeps me believing that You still raise the dead! Father, I ask that You will allow me to see more of my husband — the one my heart misses and loves — from time to time in the months and years of healing still on our horizon. These reminders of what remains enable me to do the work of reconstruction and of finding our "new normal."

In Jesus' Name, Amen.

Promise from God's Word ...

So keep a firm grip on the faith. The suffering won't last forever. It won't be long before this generous God who has great plans for us in Christ – eternal and glorious plans they are! – will have you put together and on your feet for good. He gets the last word; yes, He does!

– 1 Peter 5:10 (TM)

APPENDIX A
Would You Like to Know God Personally?

Yes, you can know God personally, as presumptuous as that may sound. God is so eager to establish a personal, loving relationship with you that He has already made all the arrangements. He is patiently waiting for you to respond to His invitation. You can receive forgiveness of your sin and assurance of eternal life through faith in His only Son, Jesus Christ.

The major barrier that prevents us from knowing God personally is ignorance of who God is and what He has done for us. Read on and discover for yourself how you can begin a life-changing relationship with God.

❀ ❀ ❀❀ ❀ ❀

The following four principles will help you discover how to know God and experience the abundant life He promised.

1 God *loves* you and created you to know Him personally.

God's love

God so loved the world, that He gave His only begotten Son, that whoever believes in Him should not perish, but have eternal life.

– John 3:16

God's plan

Now this is eternal life: that they may know You, the only true God, and Jesus Christ, whom You have sent.

– John 17:3 (NIV)

❀ ❀❀ ❀

What prevents us from knowing God personally?

Man is sinful and separated from God, so we cannot know Him personally or experience His love.

Man is sinful

All have sinned and fall short of the glory of God.

– Romans 3:23

Man was created to have fellowship with God; but, because of his own stubborn self-will, he chose to go his own independent way and fellowship with God was broken. This self-will, characterized by an attitude of active rebellion or passive indifference, is an evidence of what the Bible calls sin.

Man is separated

But your iniquities have made a separation between you and your God, and your sins have hidden His face from you so that He does not hear.

– Isaiah 59:2

The wages of sin is death. [spiritual separation from God]

– Romans 6:23a

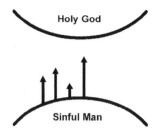

This diagram illustrates that God is holy and man is sinful. A great gulf separates the two. The arrows illustrate that man is continually trying to reach God and establish a personal relationship with Him through his own efforts, such as living a good life, philosophy, or religion – but he inevitably fails.

❀ ❀❀ ❀

The third principle explains the only way to bridge this gulf ...

3 *Jesus Christ is God's only provision for man's sin. Through Him alone we can know God personally and experience God's love.*

He died in our place

God demonstrates His own love toward us, in that while we were yet sinners, Christ died for us.

– Romans 5:8

He rose from the dead

Christ died for our sins ... He was buried ... He was raised on the third day according to the Scriptures ... He appeared to Peter, then to the twelve. After that He appeared to more than five hundred ...

– 1 Corinthians 15:3-6

He is the only way to God

Jesus said to him, "I am the way, and the truth, and the life; no one comes to the Father, but through Me."

– John 14:6

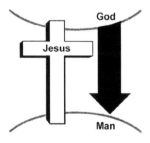

This diagram illustrates that God has bridged the gulf that separates us from Him by sending His Son, Jesus Christ, to die on the cross in our place to pay the penalty for our sins.

❀ ❀❀ ❀

It is not enough just to know these three truths …

4 We must individually receive Jesus Christ as Savior and Lord; then we can know God personally and experience His love.

We must receive Christ

As many as received Him, to them He gave the right to become children of God, even to those who believe in His name.

– John 1:12

We receive Christ through faith

By grace you have been saved through faith; and that not of yourselves, it is the gift of God; not as a result of works, that no one should boast.

– Ephesians 2:8,9

When we receive Christ, we experience a new birth

Read **John 3:1-8** in your Bible.

We receive Christ by personal invitation

[Christ speaking] *Behold, I stand at the door and knock; if anyone hears My voice and opens the door, I will come in to him.*

– Revelation 3:20

Receiving Christ involves turning to God from self (repentance) and trusting Christ to come into our lives to forgive us of our sins and to make us what He wants us to be. Just to agree intellectually that Jesus Christ is the Son of God and that He died on the cross for our sins is not enough – nor is it enough to have an emotional experience. We receive Jesus Christ by faith, as an act of our will.

❀ ❀❀ ❀

These two circles represent two kinds of lives:

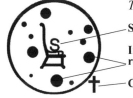

The Self-Directed Life

Self is on the throne

Interests are directed by self, resulting in discord, frustration

Christ is outside the life.

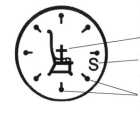

The Christ-Directed Life

CHRIST is on the throne

Self is yielding to Christ

Interests are directed by Christ, resulting in harmony with God's plan

Which circle best represents your life?

Which circle would you like to have represent your life?

❀ ❀❀ ❀

The following explains how you can receive Christ:

You can receive Christ right now by faith through prayer

(Prayer is simply talking with God)

God knows your heart and is not so concerned with your words as He is with the attitude of your heart. The following is a suggested prayer:

"Lord Jesus, I want to know You personally. Thank you for dying on the cross for my sins. I open the door of my life and receive You as my Savior and Lord. Thank You for forgiving me of my sins and giving me eternal life. Take control of the throne of my life. Make me the kind of person You want me to be."

Does this prayer express the desire of your heart?

If it does, pray this prayer right now, and Christ will come into your life, as He promised.

❧ ❧❧ ❧

How to know that Christ is in your life

Did you receive Christ into your life? According to His promise in Revelation 3:20, where is Christ right now in relation to you? Christ said that He would come into your life and be your friend so that you can know Him personally. Would He mislead you? On what authority do you know that God has answered your prayer? (The trustworthiness of God Himself and His Word.)

The Bible promises eternal life to all who receive Christ

The witness is this, that God has given us eternal life, and this life is in His Son. He who has the Son has the life; he who does not have the Son of God does not have the life. These things I have written to you who believe in the name of the Son of God, in order that you may know that you have eternal life.

– 1 John 5:11-13

Thank God often that Christ is in your life and that He will never leave you (Hebrews 13:5). You can know on the basis of His promise that Christ lives in you and that you have eternal life from the very moment you invite Him into your life. He will not deceive you.

❧ ❧❧ ❧

An important reminder …

Do not depend on feelings

The promise of God's Word, the Bible – not our feelings – is our authority. The Christian lives by faith (trust) in the trustworthiness of God Himself and His Word. This train diagram illustrates the relationship among **fact** (God and His Word), **faith** (our trust in God and His Word), and **feeling** (the result of our faith and obedience) (John 14:21).

The train will run with or without the caboose. However, it would be useless to attempt to pull the train by the caboose. In the same way, we as Christians do not depend on feelings or emotions, but we place our faith (trust) in the trustworthiness of God and the promises of His Word.

Now that you have entered into a personal relationship with Christ ...

The moment you received Christ by faith, as an act of your will, many things happened, including the following:

1. Christ came into your life (Revelation 3:20 and Colossians 1:27).
2. Your sins were forgiven (Colossians 1:14).
3. You became a child of God (John 1:12).
4. You received eternal life (John 5:24).
5. You began the great adventure for which God created you (John 10:10; 2 Corinthians 5:17 and 1 Thessalonians 5:18).

Suggestions for Christian growth

Spiritual growth results from trusting Jesus Christ. A life of faith will enable you to trust God increasingly with every detail of your life, and to practice the following:

G – Go to God in prayer daily (John 15:7).

R – Read God's Word daily (Acts 17:11). Begin with the Gospel of John.

O – Obey God moment by moment (John 14:21).

W – Witness for Christ by your life and words (Matthew 4:19; John 15:8).

T – Trust God for every detail of your life (1 Peter 5:7).

H – Holy Spirit – Allow Him to control and empower your daily life and witness (Galatians 5:16,17; Acts 1:8).

> *The righteous man shall live by faith.*
> **– Galatians 3:11**

If you would like to learn more about your new relationship with God, contact Military Ministry at 1-800-444-6006 and ask for the "Rapid Response Center," or go online to www.looktojesus.com.

Fellowship in a good church

God's Word admonishes us not to forsake "the assembling of ourselves together ..." (Hebrews 10:25). Several logs burn brightly together; but put one aside on the cold hearth and the fire goes out. So it is with your relationship with other Christians. If you do not belong to church, do not wait to be invited. Take the initiative; call the pastor of a nearby church where Christ is honored and His Word is preached. Start this week, and make plans to attend regularly.[1]

❀ ❀ ❀❀ ❀ ❀

---

[1] This is a version of the Four Spiritual Laws, written by Bill Bright. Copyright 1965, 1988, Campus Crusade for Christ, Inc.

B Appendix B
Additional Resources

1: What Happened to My Husband?
Understanding Combat Trauma

Down Range: To Iraq and Back by Bridget C. Cantrell, Ph.D. and Chuck Dean [WordSmith Publishing, 2005]. Cantrell is an expert in traumatic stress and specializes in counseling war veterans. Dean is a Vietnam war veteran and has served as the National Chaplain for the Society of the 173rd Airborne Brigade. This book provides a great resource on PTSD in general and dedicates a lot of space to reintegration issues. It's written not only for the veteran, but for his or her family as well.

Failure To Scream by Robert Hicks [Thomas Nelson, 1993]. Hicks is an Air Force Reserve specialist on traumatic stress issues, military chaplain, counselor and instructor at military schools and conferences. The book examines the hazards of internalizing posttraumatic pain and gives sound, encouraging insight into how to gain freedom from your past hurts and experience lasting healing. Strong biblical basis for his approach and the points he makes.

I Can't Get Over It – A Handbook for Trauma Survivors by Aphrodite Matsakis, Ph.D. [New Harbinger Publications, 1996]. Matsakis is a private psychotherapist and the clinical coordinator for the Vietnam Veterans' Outreach Center in Silver Springs, MD. This is a very practical, extensive resource which explains the nature of PTSD and describes the healing process with a number of practical concepts, approaches and suggestions. Great section on identifying triggers that set off flashbacks, anxiety attacks, etc. Also a great section that will help a person determine whether he or she could have PTSD through the extensive use of assessment questionnaires.

The New Guide To Crisis & Trauma Counseling – A Practical Guide for Ministers, Counselors and Lay Counselors by Dr. H. Norman Wright [Regal, 2003]. Wright is a certified trauma specialist who has had a very successful counseling and teaching ministry for decades. Author of over 70 books on counseling and other Christian subjects. This book is a must-read treasure-trove of practical, biblically-based concepts for any counselor; covering subjects of loss, grief, trauma, crisis intervention, PTSD, death, suicide, family and children's issues, etc.

PAIN: The Gift Nobody Wants by Dr. Paul Brand and Philip Yancey [HarperCollins, 1993]. This is a personal saga of Paul Brand, a world-renowned hand surgeon and leprosy specialist whose pioneering work amongst leprosy patients has earned him numerous awards. He comes to the conclusion that pain is a necessary part of life. Dr. Brand provocatively questions our societal inability to accept or deal with pain, and provides strategies to treat, live with, and heal pain.

Searching For Memory: The Brain, The Mind and The Past by Dr. Daniel L. Schacter [Basic Books, 1996]. Schacter, a Harvard psychology professor, has produced a full, rich picture of how human memory works; an elegant, captivating tour de force that interweaves the latest research in cognitive psychology and neuroscience with case materials and examples from everyday life.

Unspeakable: Facing Up to the Challenge of Evil by Os Guinness [HarperSanFrancisco, 2005]. A Christian perspective of why there is evil and suffering in a world ruled by an omnipotent, benevolent God. Historically, an examination of man's inhumanity to man and how eastern religions, secular humanists and Bible-followers attempt to account for it.

War and the Soul by Edward Tick, Ph.D., [Quest Books, 2005]. Tick is a clinical psychotherapist and the Director of Sanctuary: A Center for Mentoring the Soul. This book focuses on PTSD as a disorder of the identity. Tick feels that war's violence can cause our very soul to flee and be lost for life. It's a book that's sometimes mystical, sometimes very practical and always insightful.

When God Doesn't Make Sense by Dr. James C. Dobson [Living Books, 2001]. Examines the question of why God allows terrorist attacks, sickness, sorrow, death, etc. Very encouraging to someone who has been left disillusioned by life's afflictions and trauma. Sensitive answers to the "why" questions.

Winning Life's Toughest Battles: Roots of Human Resilience by Dr. Julius Segal [Ivy Books, 1987]. Using his studies of people in adverse situations (including P.O.W.'s, concentration camp survivors, and hostages) as well as personal experiences, Segal has created a short but powerful guide for anyone facing the crises of everyday life. Five strategies: communication, taking control, finding a purpose, shedding guilt, and showing compassion are each given separate chapters and then combined in an epilogue that neatly summarizes the essence of the work.

2: What's Happening to Me?
Understanding Secondary Traumatic Stress

As Silver Refined: Learning to Embrace Life's Disappointments by Kay Arthur [Waterbrook Press, 1997]. Tackles the questions that arise when life doesn't turn out as planned. Arthur demonstrates that Christ uses our disappointments, failures and despair as tools to burn away the dross to refine us like silver to be reflections of His goodness.

Healing the Wounds of Trauma: How the Church Can Help, by Margaret Hill, Harriet Hill, Richard Bagge, Pat Miersma [Paulines Publications of Africa, 2004, 2007]. Written by four members of Wycliffe International who have conducted extensive workshops on trauma counseling for church leaders in African countries experiencing war and genocide. Excellent chapters on how to help people communicate and process their grief.

The Hiding Place by Corrie Ten Boom [Chosen Books, Baker, 1970]. The story of a young woman whose family was sent to a Nazi concentration camp. They all died, but she survived due to a clerical error. It's gripping tale of how faith triumphs over evil.

In Harm's Way - Help for the Wives of Military Men, Police, EMTs & Firefighters by Aphrodite Matsakis, Ph.D. [New Harbinger Publications, 2005]. Matsakis is a licensed psychologist with more than 25 years' experience in the field of trauma recovery. She has also written many books on the subject. This book will lead you through a step-by-step process where you will learn to: Examine and cope with fear, loneliness & emotional stress; discover strategies for handling time, money & sexual intimacy; address children's needs & build a strong, healthy family life; manage the readjustment issues that can occur during homecoming; learn to communicate more effectively about the issues that matter to you.

PAIN: The Gift Nobody Wants by Dr. Paul Brand and Philip Yancey [HarperCollins, 1993]. This is a personal saga of Paul Brand, a world-renowned hand surgeon and leprosy specialist whose pioneering work amongst leprosy patients has earned him numerous awards. He comes to the conclusion that pain is a necessary part of life. Dr. Brand provocatively questions our societal inability to accept or deal with pain, and provides strategies to treat, live with, and heal pain.

The Problem of Pain by C. S. Lewis [HarperCollins, 1940]. Makes the point that we always consider pain to be a "problem" because our finite, human minds selfishly believe that pain-free lives would prove that God loves us. By asking for this, we actually want God to love us less, not more than he does. "Love, in its own nature, demands the perfecting of the beloved; the mere 'kindness' which tolerates anything except suffering in its object is in that respect at the opposite pole from Love."

Veterans and Families' Guide to Recovering from PTSD by Stephanie Laite Lanham [Purple Heart Service Foundation, 2007, www.purpleheartfoundation.org or e-mail phsf@purpleheartfoundation.org]. Lanham is a Psychiatric Nurse Practitioner at The Acadia Hospital in Bangor, Maine, and is affiliated with the Bangor Vet Center. Lanham's booklet provides clear definitions of the symptoms of PTSD & STSD in order for you to recognize and understand what your husband and you are dealing with.

Where is God When it Hurts? by Philip Yancey [HarperCollins, 1977]. Deals realistically with the challenging and painful questions that come after crises of pain and suffering. Drawing from powerful scriptural examples as well as the life experiences of others, Yancey tackles the tough questions of the faith like, "Why is there so much pain in the world?" and "Is there a message behind the suffering?"

3: Why Am I So Sad?
Dealing with Loss and Grief Issues

100 Ways to Defeat Depression by Frank B. Minirth; States V. Skipper; and Paul D. Meier [Baker Book House, 1979]. This short read takes Scriptures from the Bible, and uses the wisdom of three excellent Christian counselors to offer pertinent tips to a person suffering with depression. Organized well, this book allows you to focus quickly on specific problems and symptoms of depression.

Affliction by Edith Schaeffer [Fleming H. Revell, 1978]. Attempts to answer the age-old question that comes with affliction – why? This books helps to identity the sources of affliction – "our own failures; the sins of others; the nature of physical existence; the wiles of Satan" – and helps you to discover the source of your affliction which may be important when dealing with it. This book doesn't attempt to give an easy answer to suffering; rather, she recognizes that affliction does not come from God – but He uses it to help us grow in our faith and to teach us how to comfort others.

Crisis Counseling: What To Do and Say During the First 72 hours by H. Norman Wright [Regal Books, 1993]. Wright is one of America's best known Christian marriage and family counselors. This is a classic written for the professional counselor, teacher, pastor, youth worker, or concerned friend who seek the tools "to provide honest, practical and biblically-based assistance to anyone who is in crisis." Wright combines biblical advice with his practical experience gleaned from years of counseling, teaching, and writing counseling materials.

Experiencing Grief by H. Norman Wright [Broadman and Holman, 2004]. Filled with numerous constructive suggestions for those experiencing the loss of a loved one.

God Works The Night Shift: Acts of Love Your Father Performs Even While You're Asleep by Pastor Ron Mehl [Multnomah, 1994]. Gold Medallion Winner. Pastor Ron died in 2003 after a 23-year-long battle with leukemia – so he is well-acquainted with the night shift. In this book he demonstrates that, despite the way things sometimes appear, God is continually at work in our lives. He reminds us that God often does His best work in the darkness.

A Grief Observed by C. S. Lewis [HarperSanFrancisco, 1961, 2001]. This is a journal that C. S. Lewis kept in the months following his beloved wife Joy's death from cancer. Though Lewis is one of the most learned, influential and inspirational Christians of the past hundred years, even he could not escape the dark agony of trauma. In his stepson's words, "It is a stark recounting of one man's studied attempts to come to grips with and in the end defeat the emotional paralysis of the most shattering grief of his life."

The Grief Recovery Workbook: Helping You Weather the Storms of Death, Divorce, and Overwhelming Disappointments by Chaplain Ray and Cathy Giunta [Integrity Publishers, 2002]. This is an excellent self-guided workbook, useful for the hurting individual, small group leader, or any person caring for wounded souls. Chaplain Ray uses his experience in professional crisis care to explore the recovery process which involves: "learning to live without the fear of abandonment; enjoying fond memories without painful feelings of loss, guilt, and remorse; acknowledging and talking about your feelings to others," and many more.

If You Want to Walk on Water, You've Got to Get Out of the Boat by John Ortberg [Zondervan, 2001]. This is an inspiring book which reflects on the biblical story in Matthew 14, where Peter walks on water. Challenging you to face your fears of failure, to discover the unique calling that God has on your life, and to experience the exhilaration of living life through the power of God. This books helps you to recognize the obstacles in your life which are preventing you from experiencing the power of God that allows the believer to do the unimaginable.

On Death and Dying by Elisabeth Kübler-Ross [Simon and Schuster, 1997]. Kübler-Ross was a Swiss physician who was outraged at how other physicians of her day would shun those who had received a diagnosis of terminal illness. She spent the next several decades staying close to the dying and studying how they reacted and coped with end-of-life crisis. This book is a landmark classic on the stages of grief.

A Path Through Suffering: Discovering the Relationship Between God's Mercy and Our Pain by Elisabeth Elliot [Servant Publications, 1990]. In this book, Elliot shows through Scripture that "there is a necessary link between suffering and glory." Through a journey that is sometimes filled with pain, suffering, loss and grief, Elliot tenderly asks challenging questions to explore the sovereign nature of a God who cares for us, even in our finite understanding of life's challenging circumstances.

Shattered Dreams: God's Unexpected Pathway to Joy by Larry Crabb [WaterBrook, 2001]. Graphically retelling the biblical story of Naomi and Ruth, Crabb shows us how God sometimes strips us of our dreams and happiness, in order to bestow dreams that are even more wonderful for His children.

Tear Soup: A Recipe for Healing After Loss by Pat Schwiebert & Chuck DeKlyen [Grief Watch, Portland, OR, www.griefwatch.com]. This is a DVD version of a classic book, suitable for all age groups. It's a story of a woman who has suffered a great loss in her life, and so she must cook up her own unique batch of "tear soup" to help her process her grief, find comfort and ultimately fill the void in her life created by her loss. Not combat-related, but the principles here will be useful to anyone. Affirms the bereaved, educates the unbereaved. Great for grieving kids, too.

Turn My Mourning Into Dancing: Finding Hope in Hard Times by Henri Nouwen [Word Publishing/ Thomas Nelson, 2001]. Gathers Nouwen's deep experiences as a pastor, a teacher and a thinker to gently point the way towards a grounded way of life – even during the darkest trials.

The Way of the Wound: A Spirituality of Trauma and Transformation by Dr. Robert Grant [self-published, 1999]. Grant conducts workshops in the U.S. and internationally for professionals who encounter trauma. He addresses not only the psychological side of their crisis, but also the spiritual needs of trauma victims. The book takes the reader through four phases of experience and recovery, with a strong spiritual message throughout. Contact him at 1121 Juanita Ave., Burlingame, CA 94010.

4: Forgiveness: Is It Possible?
The Empowering Nature of Forgiveness

Exploring Forgiveness by Robert Enright and Joanna North [University of Wisconsin Press, 1998]. World-renowned authorities in the study of forgiveness, Enright and North have compiled a collection of twelve essays ranging from a first-person account of the mother of a murdered child to an assessment of the United States' post-war reconciliations with Germany and Vietnam. This book explores forgiveness in interpersonal relationships, family relationships, the individual and society relationship, and international relations through the eyes of philosophers and educators as well as a psychologist, police chief-turned-minister, law professor, sociologist, psychiatrist, social worker, and theologian.

Forgive and Forget by Lewis Smeeds [HarperOne, 1996]. Dr. Smeeds is one of the pioneers in the area of forgiveness research. For anyone who has been wounded by another and struggled to understand and move beyond feelings of hurt and anger, this classic book on forgiveness shows how to heal our pain and find room in our hearts to forgive. Included in the book: the four stages of forgiving; forgiving people who are hard to forgive; how people forgive; why forgive? Dr. Smeeds comes from a Christian perspective, but the principles are universally applicable.

Forgiveness By Charles Stanley [Thomas Nelson, 1987]. Charles Stanley's book clearly explains what forgiveness is, why you need it, and what happens when we will not forgive. Stanley's direct approach to the topic makes it easy to read and evaluate on a personal level.

The New Freedom of Forgiveness by David Augsburger [Moody Press, 2000]. In this provocative book, Augsburger uses the example of Jesus in the Bible as the only model of forgiveness. Augsburger writes that forgiveness should not be motivated by a self-centered desire for personal peace, rather, we ought to forgive and strive for reconstructing the broken relationship with the offender as a normal course of action.

When You Can't Say "I Forgive You" by Grace Ketterman & David Hazard [NavPress, 2000]. Ketterman has authored close to twenty books and has her own private psychiatry practice at the Center for Behavioral Development in Kansas City, Missouri, and is an adjunct professor at the Nazarene Theological Seminary. Hazard is an author and the founder of the New Nature Institute. This book takes you step by step along the path of complete forgiveness – a forgiveness that admits pain, attempts to understand the other person, and finally, lets go.

5: I Don't Feel Safe – What Should I Do?
Physical and Emotional Security for You and Your Kids

Boundaries in Marriage by Dr. Henry Cloud and Dr. John Townsend [Zondervan, 1999]. Cloud and Townsend are popular speakers, psychologists, cohosts of New Life Live! radio program and are authors of many books. This particular book helps to clarify what boundaries are, how to build boundaries in your marriage, and resolve conflicts in marriage using this information.

The Domestic Violence Sourcebook by Dawn Bradley Berry, J. D. [Lowell House, 2000]. Berry is a writer and lawyer who has worked extensively in the area of civil rights law. This book is packed with resources, legal and psychological advice, and specifics to help any one who may find themselves fearing for their safety.

Domestic Violence – What Every Pastor Needs to Know by Rev. Al Miles [Fortress Press, 2000]. Miles works for Pacific Health Ministry as coordinator of the Hospital Ministry Department at The Queen's Medical center, Honolulu, Hawaii. An excellent resource for a pastor and other religious leaders, that offers a strategic, biblically-based and compassionate handling in helping to minister to those who suffer from domestic violence.

The Lord Hears Your Cries – Hope and Strength from the Scriptures in the Midst of Domestic Violence by PASCH – Peace and Safety in the Christian Home (order from www.peaceandsafety.com). Great little promise book to keep with your Bible to help you through the hard times.

No Place for Abuse – Biblical & Practical Resources to Counteract Domestic Violence by Catherine Clark Kroeger & Nancy Nason-Clark [InterVarsity Press, 2001]. Kroeger is an adjunct associate professor of classical and ministry studies at Gordon-Conwell Theological Seminary. Nason-Clark is professor of sociology at the University of New Brunswick and author of *The Battered Wife: How Christians Confront Family Violence*. They provide a scriptural basis and practical ways for the church and individuals to respond to domestic violence so that no home will be a place of abuse.

Verbal Abuse by Dr. Grace Ketterman, M.D. [Servant Publications, 1992]. Ketterman is a writer and former Medical Director of the Crittenton Center in Kansas City, Missouri. This is a recovery guide for victims and abusers, and shatters the myth that verbal abuse 'isn't so bad.'

***When Love Hurt*s** by Jill Cory & Karen McAndless-Davis [WomenKind Press, 2003]. Cory & McAndless-Davis are counselors with years of experience working with women who have experienced abuse. This is a marvelous, practical book that not only supplies information but explains how to personally process it in your own life.

Women, Abuse, and the Bible – How Scripture Can Be Used to Hurt or Heal contains a collection of papers, written by counselors, biblical scholars, an abuser and survivors, edited by Catherine Clark Kroeger, Ph.D., & James R. Beck, Ph.D. [Baker Books, 1996]. Kroeger is adjunct associate professor of classical and ministry studies at Gordon-Conwell Theological Seminary. Beck is professor of counseling, Denver Seminary. Kroeger and Beck address the issue of abuse and offer practical and creative ways to healing.

Women Battering by Carol J. Adams [Fortress Press, 1994]. Adams is a graduate from Yale Divinity School and is a nationally recognized author regarding the needs of abused women. This book is theologically grounded and practically applied, and would be an excellent resource for your pastor and church support team.

6: Where Is My Healing Place?
Constructing Your Healing Environment

Connecting With God by Chris Adsit [Disciplemakers International, 2001]. Associate National Director of Discipleship with Campus Crusade for Christ's Military Ministry, Adsit has been making disciples and training disciplemakers since the early 1970s, and he is the author of the manual you now hold in your hands. *CWG* examines twelve foundational areas in which every Christian needs to be functional. It goes into much more depth on most of the subjects in this chapter. As the title suggests, the study's goal is to help the growing Christian deepen his or her various connections with God.

Enjoying the Presence of God: Discovering Intimacy with God in the Daily Rhythms of Life, by Jan Johnson [NavPress, 1996]. This book "offers simple, tangible insights into practicing God's presence and makes them relevant to ordinary people as they play sports, dig in the garden or rock a baby … *Enjoying the Presence of God* will give you the opportunity to surrender to His presence and enjoy just being with Him." During this time in your life, where better can you find healing but in the presence of God?

Loving God with All Your Mind by Elizabeth George [Harvest House Publishers, 1994]. The pressures of daily living – exacerbated by the stress you are experiencing – can drain us with fear, worry, depression. Elizabeth looks into Philippians 4:8, and shares how you can know the inner joy that comes from focusing your mind completely on what is true, pure, lovely and good. Elizabeth writes from experience, not theory.

Loving Your Military Man by Beatrice Fishback [FamilyLife Publishing, 2007]. An excellent in-depth, interactive study on the eight mindsets in Philippians 4:8.

A Mind Renewed by God: Forever Changing the Way You Think and Live by Kimball Hodge [Harvest House, 1998]. This book is a study on Romans 12:1,2 and explains why studying, meditating on and obeying the Word is important for renewing your mind. This relates to Element #5: Mindset – Spiritual "Battlemind" for divine healing.

7: How Do I Take Care of Me?
Nurturing Your Spirit, Soul and Body

31 Days of Praise by Ruth Myers [Multnomah Books, 1994]. From the foreword by Pamela Reeve: "If you don't know how to praise, it will open up the path for you. If you have trouble verbalizing your feelings, it will help you put into words what is on your heart. As you use it day by day you'll learn fresh and exciting ways to bring glory and pleasure to God. You'll discover anew your Father's understanding, His deep and abiding compassion for you … the strength of His Word to meet your deepest longs and needs."

Between Walden and the Whirlwind by Jean Fleming [NavPress, 1985]. In this little book, part of "The Christian Character Library" by NavPress, Jean describes a life 'increasingly characterized by a whirlwind of disciplines and demands.' In her search for 'simple' she discovers that *focusing* life, not simplifying it, is the key to truly Christ-centered living. Jean's honesty is refreshing and approachable. She helps us find hope in the chaos of life.

Calm My Anxious Heart by Linda Dillow [NavPress, 1998]. Linda and her husband lived in Europe and Asia, and she learned that there is a lot to be anxious about. This book (including a 12-week Bible study) describes her journey to contentment … and trusting God with the *What Ifs*, *If Onlys* and *Whys*.

Come Away My Beloved by Frances J. Roberts [Kings Press, 1970]. This classic devotional reads like love letters from God. Each 'letter' is biblically-based and draws the reader closer to the heart of God. This is a wonderful book to read in your quiet place.

God's Garden of Grace by Elizabeth George [Harvest House Publishers, 1996]. Elizabeth explains growing in God's garden of grace and enjoying a spiritual harvest of the fruit of the Spirit (Galatians 5:22,23) as only being possible "when we yield to God and allow His Spirit to work in us." This book contains a study guide which will help us apply the lessons learned as she delves into the various attributes of the fruit of the Spirit. It is very encouraging to see what the Grace of God has provided for us.

Hinds' Feet on High Places by Hannah Hurnard [Tyndale House Publishers, 1975]. From a review by Bob Kellemen, Ph.D.: "Hurnard writes with elegance and interest, telling a parable or allegory of Christ shepherding a terrified child on the journey of faith. Her encounter with her two guides, '[Sorrow and Suffering]' and Christ's explanation of their purpose in her life, teaching a life lesson every person, regardless of age, must learn."

Who Calls Me Beautiful? Finding Our True Image in the Mirror of God by Regina Franklin [Discovery House Publishers, 2004]. Franklin helps to identify the factors that influence your own understanding of beauty. She helps you to see yourself as God sees you, giving you the freedom to be the unique and beautiful woman He has created you to be.

8: Who Cares?
Seeking and Finding Your Support Network

Hope for the Home Front by Marshéle Carter Waddell [One Hope Ministry, 2003]. The most important "bridge" a wounded warrior must have is his or her spouse. Marshéle is the wife of Navy SEAL Mark Waddell, who served his country through nine deployments in every hot spot in the world over the past two decades. The price he paid was PTSD, and the price Marshéle paid is secondary trauma. This book honestly describes the struggles associated with being married to a PTSD sufferer and the triumphs God brings to their relationship. The book "ministers to those who are entrenched at home in the battle for their marriage, their children, their faith, and their sanity, which are all caught in the crossfire."

Hope for the Home Front Bible Study: God's Timeless Encouragement for Today's Military Wife by Marshéle Carter Waddell [One Hope Ministry, 2004]. Practical, 10-week, in-depth, interactive Bible study for individual or small group application. Goes deeper into many of the same subjects as her book, and facilitates a great deal of biblical input along the way. It is a call to arms for every woman who wants not only to survive, but to live in victory on life's battlegrounds. www.hopeforthehomefront.com.

Learning How to Trust … Again by Dr. Ed Delph and Alan & Pauly Heller [Destiny Image, 2007]. Written to the PTSD sufferer to provide a very practical roadmap for re-establishing trust with you when it has been broken, this book is useful for you to understand that journey as well.

Smart Love by Jody Hayes [Jeremy P. Tarcher/Putnam, 1989]. Though the book is written as a codependency recovery workbook for women in addictive over-dependant relationships, the principles enumerated in the book regarding group therapy are classic, practical and helpful in a wide variety of applications.

To Love Mercy: Becoming a Person of Compassion, Acceptance, & Forgiveness by C. Samuel Storms [NavPress, 1991]. This book may be intended more for your Battle Buddy than for you. Although it could help you as you seek to love your husband. This book contains the tools we can use "to care for the brokenhearted, encourage the downcast and advise the ill-informed." As Christians, we are often ill-equipped to be true Battle Buddies. Dr. Storms' book is encouraging for the encourager, challenging for those tempted to be judgmental, and refreshing as we see the compassionate heart of God.

Two Hearts Praying as One by Dennis & Barbara Rainey, [Multnomah Publishers, 2002]. The toughest part of your healing journey may come as you invite your spouse into the journey with you. Joining your hearts before God is the single most transforming, intimate experience in your marriage following your life downrange. This ten-minute-a-day, 30-day adventure provides a bridge in your marriage to understand each other, reduce conflict, and knit your hearts back together again.

9: Who Am I Really?
Focusing On Your True Identity In Christ

Abba's Child: The Cry of the Heart for Intimate Belonging by Brennan Manning [NavPress, 1994, 2002]. You are a child of the Father, Abba, beloved and accepted. But we have bought into the lie that we are worthy of God's love only when our lives are going well. Brennan Manning encourages us to take off the masks and claim our true identity as God's child, to freely accept our belovedness as a child of the heavenly Father.

Christlife: Identifying Your True and Deepest Identity by Ruth Myers [Multnomah, 2005]. Written very personally, and is especially engaging to women. Draws from her years of experiences as a Christian leader with the Navigators, and her own journey through life. The focus is on understanding who you really are in Christ and discarding false impressions, leading to self acceptance and joy.

Discovering Your Identity in Christ by Charles Stanley [Thomas Nelson, 1999]. Part of the "In Touch Bible Study Series." It gives a very biblically-based treatment of what God's Word says about you. Shows how God uses life's challenges and experiences to unlock your potential and confirm that you truly are a "masterpiece in the making."

Free At Last: Experiencing True Freedom Through Your Identity in Christ by Dr. Tony Evans [Moody Publishers, 2001]. A very engaging, conversational, yet deep work by one of the best Christian communicators in the United States. It covers topics such as clarifying your identity, recognizing the "battle within," and "reprogramming your mind." The main objective of this book is to break the bondages in your life by knowing the truth about who you are in Christ.

Manual of the Core Value Workshop by Dr. Steven Stosny [Copyright © 1995, 2003, Steven Stosny]. Stosny is the founder of Compassion*Power* and author of *Treating Attachment Abuse: A Compassionate Approach*. His techniques for emotional regulation are practiced all over the world. Check his web site at www.compassionpower.com.

Roll Away Your Stone by Dutch Sheets [Bethany, 2007]. A very inspirational and motivational book by one of the most effective Christian leaders of our day. Full of insights about how we can recognize the bondages our enemy has introduced in our lives, and who we truly are in Christ. "An action plan for conquering the lies that keep you defeated."

Victory Over the Darkness: Realizing the Power of Your Identity in Christ by Neil T. Anderson [Regal Books, 1990]. Teaches how realizing who you are in Christ can help free you from the burdens of your past, and how to become the spiritual man or woman you want to be. This book teaches the necessities to knowing how to help yourself grow deeper in your relationship with the Lord.

10: Who Is The Real Enemy?
Fighting Spiritually For Myself, My Husband and My Kids

The Adversary: The Christian Versus Demon Activity by Mark I. Bubeck [Moody Press, 1975]. In this book, Bubeck seeks "to alert Christians to the battle they are engaged in and to give them specific, effective guidelines in dealing with the devil and demonic powers." This book addresses the key elements of spiritual warfare the Christian must be aware of with topics like: warfare with the flesh and with the world, fear, aggressive prayers, tools for warfare, and many others.

The Bondage Breaker by Neil T. Anderson [Harvest House, 1990]. Daring to face the tough issues of bondage, Anderson explains how and why the believer needs to be aware of the traps of the enemy, while providing Scripture to help you to find the freedom and victory that God has for every one of His children. The book confronts sin head-on, but does so in a way that inspires and facilitates change.

Breaking Strongholds: How Spiritual Warfare Sets Captives Free by Tom White [Servant Publications, 1993]. This book will open your eyes to the realities of spiritual strongholds which may be affecting you, your family or church. White will help you to understand spiritual warfare, and help arm you with the weapons to defend yourself against the attacks of the enemy.

Holding on to Heaven With Hell on Your Back by Sheila Walsh [Thomas Nelson, 1990]. "Satan seems to be winning." Sheila was overwhelmed with the barrage of human tragedy as she worked on the 700 Club. She took a look at Job's life to learn ten principles for 'holding on to heaven when hell is on our backs.' Jesus is worth it. Jesus is enough.

Overcoming The Adversary: Warfare Against Demon Activity by Mark I. Bubeck [Moody Press, 1984]. The focus of this powerful book is to help prepare the believer for battle. Bubeck spends a great deal of time digging into the Scriptures teaching you how to wear the full armor of God in warfare. Very grounded in Scripture, this book teaches and examines the strategies and weapons that God provides for victory in the life of the believer.

The Spiritual Warrior's Prayer Guide by Quin Sherrer and Ruthanne Garlock [Servant Publications, 1992]. Sherrer and Garlock advocate that using the Word of God is the strongest spiritual weapon that God has given each believer. In this book, they teach how to declare God's promises over your life to gain spiritual victory. Organized topically, this book allows for easy access to a myriad of Scriptures to claim and apply to your life.

The Weapons of Your Warfare: Equipping Yourself to Defeat the Enemy by Larry Lea [Creation House, 1989]. Lea boldly writes that spiritual warfare is not an option for the believer, but a requirement. He challenges you to become aware of the tactics of the enemy so you can exercise your God-given authority to overcome the dark influences that the enemy uses against us. This book will provoke you to become an unyielding warrior against the influence of the enemy in your life.

A Woman's Guide To Spiritual Warfare by Quin Sherrer and Ruthanne Garlock [Servant Publications, 1991]. This book will open every women's eyes to the spiritual battles and attacks that the enemy uses to threaten and overwhelm women in particular. It will help you to recognize and break the effects of generational curses, show how to incorporate and strengthen spiritual disciplines and how to use the strength of the Lord to fight for your marriage and children.

11: How Can I Help My Husband?
Contributing to Your Husband's Healing Environment

Fight Fair! Winning at Conflict Without Losing at Love by Tim and Joy Downs (Moody Publishers, 2003). Mentioned in this chapter as an entertaining, humorous and practical book on resolving conflicts in a productive, godly manner.

Intercessory Prayer by Dutch Sheets [Regal Books, 1996]. As you pray for your husband and your children … and yourself, this book will encourage and inspire you as it instructs you about prayer. As Bill Bright said, "*Intercessory Prayer* is illuminating and motivating. Dutch Sheets sheds fascinating light on this sometimes mysterious subject. Readers will want to pray more, and they will see more results."

Loving Your Military Man by Beatrice Fishback [FamilyLife Publishing, 2007]. Bea and her husband Jim are the European directors for Military Ministry. When Jim was an army officer, he and Bea had to learn how to maintain a strong Christian marriage in the midst of the pressure, loneliness and separations of military life. This ten-part Bible study, based on Philippians 4:8, does an excellent job of encouraging military wives in how to triumph over these difficulties, support their husbands and become the women God intends them to be.

Prayers for Our Military and Their Families by Cheri Fuller. A 8 ½" x 3 ½" prayer card which leads you through prayers for protection, mercy, strength, etc., for your loved one and others serving in our military.

The Power of a Praying Wife by Stormie Omartian [Harvest House Publishers, 1997]. A great book to guide you through praying for your husband concerning key areas in his life including his spiritual walk, his emotions, his health and physical protection, his faith and his future.

Prayers That Avail Much by Germaine Copeland [Harrison House, 1997]. A great book to learn how to pray using Scripture.

Scriptural Prayers for the Praying Woman – Transform Your life Through Powerful Prayer [White Stone Books, 2003].

Trust After Trauma: A Guide to Relationships for Survivors and Those Who Love Them by Dr. Aphrodite Matsakis [New Harbinger Publications, 1998]. Dr. Matsakis is a private psychotherapist and the clinical coordinator for the Vietnam Veterans' Outreach Center in Silver Springs, Md., specializing in PTSD. This book provides a great deal of practical information so that trauma survivors understand their emotions and behavior. It also offers insight for loved ones and partners of trauma survivors. Great sections on dealing with feelings of guilt, and on stabilizing relationships with non-traumatized partners.

Wild at Heart: Discovering the Secret of a Man's Soul by John Eldredge [Thomas Nelson, 2001]. This book is written for men, but can help us as women to understand them better. What is their essential masculinity? Why do they perceive things the way they do?

12: How Can I Help My Children?
Making a Safe, Healthy Environment for Your Kids

Brats: Our Journey Home, [Brats Without Borders, 2005]. This 90-minute documentary (DVD) by Bridget Musil and narrated by Kris Kristofferson, a military brat himself, presents "what it is like growing up as a military brat constantly moving, changing schools, making new friends, losing track of old friends and how this affects us as adults." Recommended by a 'brat' on our team, this film can help you see life from your children's point of view. It can also help adult 'brats' to begin to dialog on the impacts – good and bad – of having grown up military. Available through www.militarybrat.com.

Down Range: To Iraq and Back by Bridget C. Cantrell, Ph.D., and Chuck Dean [WordSmith Publishing, 2005]. This book was mentioned earlier in connection with Chapter 1. But in back is a section on "Preparing Families for the Homecoming." The portion on pages 144-150, "Section Four: How Can I Prepare My Children," has very good descriptions of the emotional responses of children. It can be hard to put ourselves in the shoes of children. This will help in seeing through their eyes.

Every Day I Pray for My Teenager – A Handbook of Scriptural Prayers for the Mothers of Teenagers by Eastman Curtis [Creation House, 1996].

Finding My Way – A Teen's Guide to Living with a Parent Who Has Experienced Trauma by Michelle D. Sherman, Ph.D., & DeAnne M. Sherman [Seeds of Hope Books, 2005]. Dr. Michelle Sherman is a clinical psychologist and the Director of the family Mental Health Program at the Oklahoma City Veterans Affairs Medical Center. DeAnne Sherman, Michelle's mother, is a teacher with over 40 years of experience educating, mentoring and empowering teenagers. This book is an invaluable tool for teenagers who are confused and frightened by what is happening to their parent. This book helps teens to understand common reactions to trauma, sort through complex feelings, learn coping skills, deal with their friends, identity helpful resources and find hope.

How to Pray for Your Children by Quin Sherrer [Regal Books, 1998]. This book is very practical, addressing the guidelines for and hindrances to prayer and also addressing specific areas for prayer: friends and those in authority, wayward children, stepchildren and adopted children, adult and in-law children, special needs children. A very useful tool in your arsenal for helping your children.

My Book About The War and Terrorism – A Guided Activity Workbook for Children, Families and Teachers to encourage healthy expression, learning and coping by Gilbert Kliman, M.D., Harriet Wolfe, M.D., Edward Oklan, M.D., M.P.H. [The Children's Psychological Health Center, Inc., 2003 – order online: www.cphc-sf.org]. A great book to help children process through their thoughts and feelings regarding the war.

The Seduction of Our Children by Neil T. Anderson & Steve Russo [Harvest House Publishers, 1991]. Dr. Neil Anderson is the founder of Freedom in Christ ministries and has served as the chairman of the Practical Theology Department at Talbot School of Theology. He has been recognized for many years as a real pioneer in the area of spiritual warfare and prayer. This book exposes how Satan is trying to subtly seduce our children away from Christ and what you as a parent can do to defend them from our ruthless enemy.

Why Is Daddy Like He Is? by Patience Mason [Patience Press, 1992]. This booklet is written for you to go through with your children to help them voice the questions and express the feelings they have about their daddy.

13: How Do I Get Back to "Normal"?
The Journey to Peace and Stability

Courage After Fire by Keith Armstrong, L.C.S.W., Suzanne Best, Ph.D., Paula Domenici, Ph.D. [Ulysses Press, 2006]. This book is specifically for the returning veteran and his or her family. It gives them a clear idea of the challenges that lie ahead for them, and provides a toolbox of useful insights and coping exercises that can assist in saving a marriage or put a veteran's life back on track.

Defending The Military Marriage by Lt. Col. Jim and Beatrice Fishback [FamilyLife Publishing, 2004]. In this excellent small group Bible study, the Fishbacks (European Directors of Military Ministry) discuss how to maintain a strong, Christ-centered, supportive marriage while one or both spouses are in the military. This *HomeBuilders Couples Series*® study covers items such as communicating, basic training, sexual accountability and love.

Defending The Military Family by Lt. Col. Jim and Beatrice Fishback [FamilyLife Publishing, 2005]. A small group Bible study by the Fishbacks (mentioned above) that focuses on how to build a strong, Christ-centered family in the midst of the stresses, moves and separation generated by a military career.

How To Get Control of Your Time and Your Life by Alan Lakein [Signet, 1974, 1989]. Lakein is one of the most sought-after experts on time management. This book is a classic containing practical suggestions for setting goals, achieving them and organizing your life. It has sold over 3 million copies since it first came out, and continues to be inspirational to anyone wanting to live life more efficiently.

The Homesick Heart: Longing for Spiritual Intimacy by Jean Fleming [NavPress, 1995]. We are all homesick for a place we've never been. You are homesick for what you had before. Jean reminds us that God is also longing … longing to be close to you. Jean shares her thoughts as she learns to rediscover that "home" is in Him.

I Don't Know What I Want, But I Know It's Not This: A Step-by-Step Guide to Finding Gratifying Work by Julie Jansen [Penguin, 2003]. Jansen is a strong proponent of "one size does NOT fit all." Contains many creative exercises to help you get in touch with what you really love to do, and why you find certain jobs unsatisfying. A very practical and inspirational guide.

Marriage Makeover: Minor Touchups to Major Renovations by George Kenworthy [FamilyLife Publishing, 2005]. Think back to chapter one: PTSD is a common reaction to uncommon events. Your marriage has been exposed to those uncommon events, too. Whether your husband's time downrange has dinged your marriage or has pressed you to your limits, there is hope. This book provides numerous "makeover" principles that will provide health and healing to your marriage.

What Color Is Your Parachute 2008: A Practical Manual for Job-Hunters and Career-Changers by Richard Nelson Boles [Ten Speed Press, 2007]. This has been the best-selling job hunting book in the world for the past 20+ years (it's obviously been revised from time to time). The book offers up-to-date, practical techniques to help job seekers find meaningful work and mission.

Military Resources

Army Reserve Family Programs Online – "The Army Reserve Family Programs are committed to offering education, training, awareness, outreach, information, referral, and follow-up." – www.arfp.org

Military OneSource – "Military OneSource is a 24/7 toll-free information, referral and counseling service – 1-800-464-8107. Designed to help you deal with life-issues – 24 hours a day, 7 days a week, 365 days a year. You can call in and speak to a master's level consultant or you can go online to access information or e-mail a consultant. Resources are available at no cost to you." – www.militaryonesource

- Care for you and your family
- Manage your everyday life
- Available anytime, anywhere
- Your privacy is assured

National Center for PTSD (NCPTSD) – "The National Center for PTSD (NCPTSD) aims to advance the clinical care and social welfare of U.S. Veterans through research, education and training on PTSD and stress-related disorders. The PTSD Information Center has Fact Sheets and Videos to answer your questions on trauma, PTSD and related issues." – www.ncptsd.va.gov

APPENDIX C
What I Need From You – How to be a "Bridge to Healing" for me

BRIDGES TO HEALING

1. I need you to know about the Combat Trauma my husband is experiencing.

Whenever a person is deployed to an area where combat is taking place, it's very likely they will return with "Combat Trauma" (also known as "Deployment Related Stress"). This is a spectrum of reactions to the abnormal stressors of war that can encompass the physical, mental, emotional and spiritual components of a person's life. It could include relatively mild reactions that are very common and expected, such as deployment and reintegration stresses, or very severe reactions such as Posttraumatic Stress Disorder (PTSD). The mild reactions will usually sort themselves out after a few weeks, but the severe reactions require proactive intervention, and may last for months, years or for a lifetime. A person who experiences acute (intense, constant) PTSD will probably never be the same again – but they can establish what we call a "new normal" where they can cope with the symptoms of their disorder and lead positive, productive lives despite it.

The two most severe forms of Combat Trauma – Acute Stress Disorder and PTSD – develop when a person is exposed to a traumatic event (or multiple events) which involve actual or threatened death or serious injury, witnessing such an event, or even hearing about it happening to a family member or close friend. The person's response is one of intense fear, helplessness or horror.

When a person experiences this kind of event, their body reacts in a strong, involuntary "fight or flight" mode in order to protect itself against the deadly threat. It becomes a disorder when the person gets "stuck" in that mode. They might continue to "**re-experience**" the traumatic event through recurrent nightmares, violent daydreams, flashbacks and dissociative episodes (where they think they are actually back in battle, fighting for their lives). They might also experience "**avoidance**" symptoms where they go to great effort to avoid any thoughts, feelings, activities, places or people that remind them of their traumatic experiences. They will self-isolate, stop doing many of the things they used to enjoy, avoid crowded places, and have difficulty making social connections or having loving feelings. They may misuse drugs or alcohol to help them "forget" and dull their senses or to hype themselves up. They might also experience "**arousal**" symptoms where they have difficulty falling or staying asleep, are frequently very irritable and angry, have difficulty concentrating, are hypervigilant (expecting and preparing for an attack at any time), easily startled, and desire to be involved in high-risk, edgy activities such as speeding, fighting, skydiving, etc. They may also get into self-mutilation through cutting or excessive tattooing and piercing.

Bottom line: my husband is not weak, crazy or cowardly. He has been *wounded*. Some people call it a *wound of the soul* or a *wound of the mind*. Some call it a *wound of the identity*, since so much of what he used to think was true about himself has been destroyed. But he's just as wounded as any amputee, and in dire need of *healing*.

❏ *I have a basic understanding of what your husband is experiencing.*

❏ *I still have more questions.*

❀ ❀ ❀ ❀

2. I need you to know about the Spousal Combat Trauma I'm experiencing.

When a person is married to someone with Combat Trauma, they can experience a variety of distressing symptoms as they react to his/her symptoms. As a result of having to adjust her lifestyle (and her kids' lifestyle) to accommodate the stressful behavior of the veteran, a wife can exhibit many of the same symptoms her husband is experiencing. This is called "Secondary

When War Comes Home

Traumatic Stress." She can actually end up experiencing all of the symptoms that someone with PTSD experiences even though she wasn't exposed to the trauma of combat.

In some cases, if a person's Combat Trauma symptoms cause him to become emotionally or physically abusive, a wife can develop *Primary* Traumatic Stress (like the Combat Trauma symptoms mentioned above, which can also produce PTSD). But whatever the case, I need you to understand that I – just like my husband – am wounded.

Here are some of the symptoms I'm experiencing that concern me the most:
(Note to wife: Choose from the Symptom Inventory on page 26.
You might also want to share your PTSD Self-Test on page 29.)

_____

_____

_____

_____

❑ *I have a basic understanding of what you're experiencing.*

❑ *I still have more questions.*

❀ ❀ ❀ ❀

3. I need you to know that I realize you are not my healer. God is.

The Bible says in Exodus 15:26 – *"For I, the Lord, am your Healer."* I believe that Combat Trauma is a very complex condition, and that it won't respond to any "quick fix" approach. God is my Creator, and He knows how to care for me and for my husband. But I also know that *my* responsibility is to work at constructing an environment that will give God maximum access to my soul. This environment contains many elements, but one of the most important ones is *you*! I don't want you to take on the burdensome responsibility to try to "fix" me – you couldn't accomplish that anyway. But what I need you to do is to help me keep close to God. Let me know when I'm allowing that healing environment to deteriorate. Keep lifting my eyes and thoughts and faith to God. Give me your input and feedback when you see ways that I can improve on that environment.

❑ *I won't try to be your healer – I'll let God take that job.*

❑ *I'll help you with your healing environment.*

❀ ❀ ❀ ❀

4. I need you to know that I love my husband, and I want to do everything I can to save our marriage and live a good life together for the rest of our days.

I may lose my patience with him, may become critical of him and may become very angry with him. From time to time I may even say that I want to leave him. But as long as he is not posing a danger to me or our children, I will move past my frustrations with God's help (and yours) and continue to pursue oneness in our marriage.

❑ *I know you love your husband. I'll take your frustrated responses to him with a grain of salt.*

❀ ❀ ❀ ❀

5. I need your confidentiality.

Can I trust that nothing I share with you in confidence does NOT go any further than you? You may be tempted to share something I confided with you as a "prayer request" with some of your friends, and you may even have pure motives in doing that. But who knows where it will go after that? It will hurt me terribly if you gossip to others about me. I don't even want you to share my

236

confidences with your husband, my husband or even your pastor – unless you genuinely feel I'm becoming a danger to myself or to others, or that I am *in* danger.

❑ *Anything you share with me stays with me. I will not pass it on to anybody else.*

❑ *I will come to you first if I feel you are in danger.*

❀ ❀ ❀ ❀

6. I need your listening heart.

Not that I want to do all the talking, but it seems as if no one at home really listens to me. It would be *so* wonderful to have someone ask me how I'm doing and then really, really listen. Listen to me with your ears, your eyes and your heart. Try to grasp what I'm saying even when I'm not doing a very good job of communicating. You don't have to try to analyze or solve my problems. I'm grateful for your desire to do so, but often I just want someone like you to listen.

There will be times when all I need is a comforting presence – without words. I don't want you to think that you have to validate our friendship by sharing some pithy words of wisdom. When those come (at the appropriate times) they will be welcomed! But don't feel that your silent presence doesn't communicate anything. It does. I'm blessed by your nearness, your gentleness, your quietness.

❑ *You can count on me to be a good listener.*

❑ *You can count on me to be a "silent" presence with you.*

❀ ❀ ❀ ❀

7. I need you to read my mind.

Well, not exactly. What I mean is I'm hoping that you can pick up on various cues I might be giving you (either consciously or unconsciously) and figure out ways to lighten my load without having to ask you, or without you having to ask me. I may be reluctant to ask – feeling like I'm being a burden.

❑ *I'll do my best at reading your mind. I'll ask God for His discernment.*

❀ ❀ ❀ ❀

8. I need you to grant me grace, not judge me.

There may be times that I won't be responding to the stresses in my life with a great deal of godliness. My speech may become profane. I may say things that exhibit a lack of trust in God. I may be at the end of my rope and talk about giving up. I may even say things that hurt you and may make you want to abandon our friendship. During those times, I need you to understand that it's my pain talking. If I'm acting this way around you, it's because I feel comfortable and accepted by you. I feel I can be "real" with you, and I'm confident that you won't judge or reject me during those moments of distress.

❑ *I won't judge you when your pain is talking. I'll stick with you.*

❀ ❀ ❀ ❀

9. I need you to give me space.

Sometimes I just want and need to be alone. This may require more mind-reading on your part, but sometimes not. If we're getting into a difficult area of conversation, and I say I don't want to talk about it right now, just drop it. Don't get offended. There's a good chance I'll want to come back to it later, but not right now. You may call me and want to get together, and I'll come up with some lame excuse. Pretend you don't notice how lame it is and try me again in a day or two. Your availability and attentiveness is precious to me – but we all need alone time every now and then.

❑ *I'll try to be aware when you need some space. Feel free to just tell me directly when you do.*

10. I need you to pray for me and for my family.

You will know more about me than the vast majority of my acquaintances. God will be strengthening our connection as we go through this process together. You'll know what I need; you'll know my requests both spoken and unspoken. I'm trusting God to be the primary change-agent in my life, so I need you on my team lifting me up before His throne day-by-day.

Here are a few things you could start praying about right away (and please, keep these matters between you and God unless I tell you it's okay to share):

_____

_____

_____

❏ *I'll pray for you and your family every day.*

✿ ✿ ✿ ✿

11. I need your genuine touch and eye contact.

I'm not getting a lot of genuine affection or attention at home. A new widow will tell you that being touched (a real hug, a hand on the shoulder, taking her hand) is one of the things she misses and craves most. As a combat veteran's wife I sometimes feel much like a widow. Hug me like you mean it. Look me in the eye as you speak, and listen – it means a *lot*. I get enough of the 1000-yard stare at home – from you I need the 24-inch stare.

❏ *You'll get plenty of eye contact, touches and hugs from me!*

✿ ✿ ✿ ✿

12. I need you to tell me the truth.

It will take courage and discernment on your part, but I would be grateful if you were willing to lovingly speak the truth to me. Don't dump the truck on me and don't hit me with a 2-by-4. But tell me what I need to hear. Hold me accountable to the faith standards you know I own. God's Word tells me that the wounds of a friend are faithful. Tell me the truth straight up, but reassure me of your love when you do.

And don't take my side automatically when I rail against my husband. When I'm angry with him (or anyone else), don't call down fire from heaven on him. Pray for God's perspective and truth about our unique situation and pray for us *both* unconditionally. Gently let me know what you see.

> Here's *Judgmental*: "How can you call yourself a Christian and say such things about your husband!?!"
>
> Here's *Supportive*: "It must drive you crazy when he does that. Let's try to figure out a response that would be more productive and make a way for God to work in the situation."

❏ *I'll try my best to speak the truth to you in love. I'll be supportive and non-judgmental.*

✿ ✿ ✿ ✿

13. I need you to remind me.

Remind me of fun times in the past or even something that happened yesterday. Remind me of joyful times. Remind me of my strengths, my talents and my blessings and stir me up from time to time. Encourage me to use my gifts and talents. I need to be reminded that I matter.

❏ *I'll remind you of your blessed past. I'll keep you aware of your blessed present and future, too.*

14. I need you to make me laugh.

I need that "internal massage." Help me lighten up. Call me up and ask me out for dinner or a cup of coffee. Take me to a "chick flick" that guarantees a smile. Tell me the great jokes you receive in your e-mail. Take my pain seriously, but help me keep it in perspective. If I don't laugh, I'll cry.

❑ *I'll find some ways to make you laugh. We'll laugh together!*

❀ ❀ ❀ ❀

15. I need you to help me sleep, relax and renew.

Could you take my kids for a night or a weekend sometime, so I could really sleep in for once? Would you help me set up a personal retreat where I can get away to sleep, take long walks and to think and pray? I need you to keep hounding me about sleep needs.

❑ *I'll look at my calendar and get back to you with a plan of how I can help you out with that extra sleep you need.*

❀ ❀ ❀ ❀

16. I need you to *not* tell me that things aren't so bad.

I know that others are worse off than I am – and I'm grateful for God's grace towards me. I know Romans 8:28, and I truly believe that God *is* going to work all of this together for my good. But doggone it, there are still times when I'm really struggling and hurting and in despair, and my life *is* difficult. I know people mean well, but sometimes it feels like they are minimizing or discounting what I'm going through. When I'm hurting, let me cry. Hold me and don't say anything. You could cry with me.

❑ *I won't discount your pain. I'll be a shoulder to cry on when you need me to be.*

❀ ❀ ❀ ❀

17. I need you to be my workout partner.

I know I need to exercise, but it's hard to push myself in that direction when I already feel so tired, stressed and sore. Would you consider being my workout partner? If you can't do that, would you hound me about starting a regular exercise program, and hold me accountable to it?

❑ *Let's talk about how I can help you with your exercising.*

❀ ❀ ❀ ❀

18. I need you to help me in some practical ways.

Combat Trauma sufferers usually don't operate anywhere near the capacities they enjoyed before deployment. Consequently, I have to cover for a lot of the things my husband used to do and assumed he would re-claim when he returned home – but I'm struggling to complete these tasks and sometimes I can barely make it through a day. From time-to-time, I could really use some help in the following ways: (Suggestions: lawn care, babysitting, house cleaning, home repair, transportation, grocery shopping, etc.)

_____

_____

_____

I really appreciate your being available to help me – but I don't expect you to drop everything for me when I have a need. I don't want you to become resentful of me when you can't take care of your own responsibilities.

❑ *I'll circle anything I think I can help you with.*

19. I need your husband.

What I mean is, I need your husband to call my husband from time to time and invite him to do something dude-ish. My husband needs to know that he's still needed, wanted and important. Ask for his help in doing something he's good at. He really needs male affirmation right now.

❏ *I'll talk with my husband about how he might be able to reach out to your husband.*

❀ ❀ ❀ ❀

20. I need you to let me help you.

If I'm always on the receiving end, I'll lose my sense of worth and dignity. Help me remember that I have things to offer, that I'm still needed, that I can still be a giver. I may not always have the time or energy to do what you ask, but I want you to ask. Jesus said that the greatest in God's kingdom was the servant of all. You have served me so faithfully, let me return the favor.

❏ *I promise to let you know of some things you can do for me.*

❀ ❀ ❀ ❀

21. I need your strength and endurance.

This is a marathon. I don't need a flash-in-the-pan friend. Nor do I need an enthusiastic-but-empty offer of help or friendship. I need kindred spirits who will go the distance with me. Those women are incredibly hard to find. Don't give up on me. If I know you're there running with me, it gives me hope.

❏ *I won't give up on you! Unless I get knocked out of the race, I'm in it with you all the way!*

❀ ❀ ❀ ❀ ❀ ❀

The owner of this copy of *When War Comes Home* has the publisher's permission to make as many copies of this "What I need From You" piece as is needed for personal use.

MILITARY MINISTRY

Faith in the Foxhole...
Hope on the Home Front...
To the Ends of the Earth.

A Division of Campus Crusade for Christ International

P.O. Box 120124, Newport News, VA 23612-0124
Phone: (757) 928-7200 or (toll-free) 1-800-444-6006
e-mail: info@militaryministry.org
www.militaryministry.org

APPENDIX D
The Promise Pantry –
Comfort Food for the Soul
(Fat-Free Zone!!)

When I am afraid ...

Psalm 28:7 (NIV) – *The LORD is my strength and my shield; my heart trusts in Him, and I am helped. My heart leaps for joy and I will give thanks to Him in song.*

Psalm 62:3a,5-7 (CEV) – *I feel like a shaky fence or a sagging wall ... Only God gives inward peace, and I depend on Him. God alone is the mighty rock that keeps me safe, and He is the fortress where I feel secure. God saves me and honors me. He is that mighty rock where I find safety.*

Isaiah 41:10 (RSV) – *Fear not, for I am with you, be not dismayed, for I am your God; I will strengthen you, I will help you, I will uphold you with My victorious right hand.*

John 14:27 (CEV) – *I give you peace, the kind of peace that only I can give. It isn't like the peace that this world can give. So don't be worried or afraid.*

1 Peter 5:7 (NIV) – *Cast all your anxiety on Him because He cares for you.*

When I feel all alone ...

Psalm 9:10 (NIV) – *Those who know Your name will trust in You, for You, LORD, have never forsaken those who seek You.*

Psalm 34:18 – *The LORD is near to the brokenhearted and saves those who are crushed in spirit.*

When I have no hope ...

Psalm 42:5,6a (CEV) – *Why am I discouraged? Why am I restless? I trust You! And I will praise You again because You help me, and You are my God.*

Psalm 143:4-8 (CEV) – *I have given up all hope, and I feel numb all over. I remember to think about the many things You did in years gone by. Then I lift my hands in prayer, because my soul is a desert, thirsty for water from You. Please hurry, LORD, and answer my prayer. I feel hopeless. Don't turn away and leave me here to die. Each morning let me learn more about Your love because I trust You. I come to You in prayer, asking for Your guidance.*

Lamentations 3:22,23 (NIV) – *Because of the LORD's great love we are not consumed, for His compassions never fail. They are new every morning; great is Your faithfulness.*

Lamentations 3:25,26 (LB) – *The Lord is wonderfully good to those who wait for Him, to those who seek for Him. It is good both to hope and wait quietly for the salvation of the Lord.*

When the worries of the day keep me awake at night ...

Psalm 4:8 (ESV) – *In peace I will both lie down and sleep; for You alone, O LORD, make me dwell in safety.*

Psalm 63:6,7 (LB) – *I lie awake at night thinking of You – of how much You have helped me – and how I rejoice through the night beneath the protecting shadow of Your wings.*

Proverbs 3:24 (NIV) – *When you lie down, you will not be afraid; when you lie down, your sleep will be sweet.*

When I'm at the end of my rope ...

Psalm 61:2,3 (NIV) – *From the ends of the earth I call to You, I call as my heart grows faint; lead me to the rock that is higher than I. For You have been my refuge, a strong tower against the foe.*

Psalm 84:5 (NIV) – *Blessed are those whose strength is in You, who have set their hearts on pilgrimage.*

Matthew 11:28-30 (LB) – *Come to me and I will give you rest – all of you who work so hard beneath a heavy yoke. Wear My yoke – for it fits perfectly – and let Me teach you; for I am gentle and humble, and you shall find rest for your souls; for I give you only light burdens.*

2 Corinthians 12:9 (NIV) – *...My grace is sufficient for you, for My power is made perfect in weakness ...*

James 1:2-4 (LB) – *... is your life full of difficulties and temptations? Then be happy, for when the way is rough, your patience has a chance to grow. So let it grow, and don't try to squirm out of your problems. For when your patience is finally in full bloom, then you will be ready for anything, strong in character, full and complete.*

When I can't seem to stop crying, inside and out ...

Psalm 56:8 (LB) – *You have seen me tossing and turning through the night. You have collected all my tears and preserved them in Your bottle! You have recorded every one in Your book.*

Psalm 126:5,6 (NIV) – *Those who sow in tears will reap with songs of joy. He who goes out weeping, carrying seed to sow, will return with songs of joy, carrying sheaves with him.*

Revelation 21:4 (NIV) – *He will wipe every tear from their eyes. There will be no more death or mourning or crying or pain, for the old order of things has passed away.*

When my husband can't be there for me ...

Isaiah 54:4-6,10 (NIV) – *Do not be afraid; you will not suffer shame. Do not fear disgrace; you will not be humiliated. You will forget the shame of your youth and remember no more the reproach of your widowhood* [the word for widowhood means forsaken or discarded]. *For your Maker is your husband – the LORD Almighty is His name – the Holy One of Israel is your Redeemer; He is called the God of all the earth. The LORD will call you back as if you were a wife deserted and distressed in spirit – a wife who married young, only to be rejected, says your God ... Though the mountains be shaken and the hills be removed, yet My unfailing love for you will not be shaken nor My covenant of peace be removed, says the LORD, who has compassion on you.*

When I want to react and strike back at my husband ...

1 Chronicles 4:10 (NKJV) – *And Jabez called on the God of Israel saying, "Oh, that You would bless me indeed, and enlarge my territory, that Your hand would be with me, and that You would keep me from evil, that I may not cause pain!" So God granted him what he requested.*

Proverbs 10:12 (NIV) – *Hatred stirs up dissension, but love covers over all wrongs.*

Proverbs 31:11 (NKJV) – *The heart of her husband safely trusts in her ...*

1 Corinthians 13:7,8 – *[Love] ... bears all things, believes all things, hopes all things, endures all things ... Love never fails.*

When my husband becomes abusive ...

2 Samuel 22:3 (NKJV) – *The God of my strength, in whom I will trust; my shield and the horn of my salvation, my stronghold and my refuge; my Savior, You save me from violence.*

Psalm 17:4-6 (NIV) – *As for the deeds of men – by the word of Your lips I have kept myself from the ways of the violent. My steps have held to Your paths; my feet have not slipped. I call on You, O God, for You will answer me; give ear to me and hear my prayer.*

Psalm 25:1-5 (CEV) – *I offer You my heart, LORD God, and I trust You. Don't make me ashamed or let enemies defeat me. Don't disappoint any of Your worshippers, but disappoint all deceitful liars. Show me Your paths and teach me to follow; guide me by Your truth and instruct me. You keep me safe, and I always trust You.*

Psalm 72:14 – *He will rescue their life from oppression and violence; and their blood will be precious in His sight.*

Psalm 140:1 (NIV) – *Rescue me, O LORD, from evil men; protect me from men of violence.*

Isaiah 40:27-31 (CEV) – *You people of Israel, say, "God pays no attention to us! He doesn't care if we are treated unjustly." But how can you say that? Don't you know? Haven't you heard? The LORD is the eternal God, Creator of the earth. He never gets weary or tired; His wisdom cannot be measured. The LORD gives strength to those who are weary. Even young people get tired, then stumble and fall. But those who trust the LORD will find new strength. They will be strong like eagles soaring upward on wings; they will walk and run without getting tired.*

When I don't know what to do ...

Psalm 16:7 (LB) – *I will bless the Lord who counsels me; He gives me wisdom in the night. He tells me what to do.*

Psalm 32:8 – *I will instruct you and teach you in the way which you should go; I will counsel you with My eye upon you.*

Proverbs 3:5-8 (AMPLIFIED) – *Lean on, trust in, and be confident in the Lord with all your heart and mind and do not rely on your own insight or understanding. In all your ways know, recognize, and acknowledge Him, and He will direct and make straight and plain your paths.*

Jeremiah 33:3 (RSV) – *Call to me and I will answer you, and will tell you great and hidden things which you have not known.*

John 10:27 (NIV) – *My sheep listen to My voice; I know them, and they follow Me.*

James 1:5 (LB) – *If you want to know what God wants you to do, ask Him, and He will gladly tell you, for He is always ready to give a bountiful supply of wisdom to all who ask Him; He will not resent it.*

When I don't feel protected ...

Psalm 18:30-32 (NKJV) – *As for God, His way is perfect; the word of the LORD is proven; He is a shield to all who trust in Him. For who is God, except the LORD? And who* is a rock, except our God? It is God who arms me with strength, and makes my way perfect.

Psalm 62:7,8 (NIV) – *My salvation and my honor depend on God; He is my mighty rock, my refuge. Trust in Him at all times, O people; pour out your hearts to Him, for God is our refuge.*

When I am exhausted and don't think I can make it one more day, hour or even a minute ...

Nehemiah 4:14 (LB) – *Don't be afraid! Remember the Lord who is great and glorious; fight for your friends, your families, and your homes!*

Psalm 13 (CEV) – *How much longer, LORD, will You forget about me? Will it be forever? How long will You hide? How long must I be confused and miserable all day? How long will my enemies keep beating me down? Please listen, LORD God, and answer my prayers. Make my eyes sparkle again, or else I will fall into the sleep of death. My enemies will say "Now we've won!" They will be greatly pleased when I am defeated. I trust Your love, and I feel like celebrating because You rescued me. You have been good to me, LORD, and I will sing about You.*

When I get tired of always trying to do the right thing ...

2 Corinthians 12:9,10 – *And He has said to me, "My grace is sufficient for you, for power is perfected in weakness." Most gladly, therefore, I will rather boast about my weaknesses, so that the power of Christ may dwell in me. Therefore I am well content with weaknesses, with insults, with distresses, with persecutions, with difficulties, for Christ's sake; for when I am weak, then I am strong.*

Galatians 6:9 (LB) – *And let us not get tired of doing what is right, for after a while we will reap a harvest of blessing if we don't get discouraged and give up.*

When I keep blowing it ...

Proverbs 28:13 (NKJV) – *He who covers his sins will not prosper, but whoever confesses and forsakes them will have mercy.*

1 John 1:9 (RSV) – *If we confess our sins, He is faithful and just, and will forgive our sins and cleanse us from all unrighteousness.*

When I feel unloved ...

Song of Solomon 2:4 – *He has brought me to His banquet hall, and His banner over me is love.*

Song of Solomon 7:10 – *I am my beloved's and His desire is for me.*

Zephaniah 3:17,18 (RSV) – *The LORD, your God, is in your midst, a warrior who gives victory; He will rejoice over you with gladness, He will renew you in His love; He will exult over you with loud singing.*

When I feel like I'm sucked dry and I have nothing more to give ...

Luke 6:38 (NIV) – *Give, and it will be given to you. A good measure, pressed down, shaken together and running over, will be poured into your lap. For with the measure you use, it will be measured to you.*

1 Corinthians 2:9 (NKJV) – *But as it is written: "Eye has not seen, nor ear heard, nor have entered into the heart of man the things which God has prepared for those who love Him."*

When God seems far away ...

Isaiah 49:15,16 – *Can a woman forget her nursing child and have no compassion on the son of her womb? Even these may forget, but I will not forget you. Behold, I have inscribed you on the palms of My hands; your walls are continually before me.*

Romans 8:38,39 – *For I am convinced that neither death, nor life, nor angels, nor principalities, nor things present, nor things to come, nor powers, nor height, nor depth, nor any other created thing, shall be able to separate us from the love of God, which is in Christ Jesus our Lord.*

When I feel like the hordes of hell are fighting against us ...

2 Kings 6:15-17 – *When the attendant of the man of God had risen early and gone out, behold, an army with horses and chariots was circling the city. And his servant said to him, "Alas, my master! What shall we do?" So he answered, "Do not fear, for those who are with us are more than those who are with them." Then Elisha prayed and said, "O LORD, I pray, open his eyes that he may see." And the LORD opened the servant's eyes, and he saw; and behold, the mountain was full of horses and chariots of fire all around Elisha.*

2 Chronicles 20:15b – *...Do not fear or be dismayed because of this great multitude, for the battle is not yours but God's.*

2 Thessalonians 3:3 (LB) – *But the Lord is faithful; He will make you strong and guard you from satanic attacks of every kind.*

When darkness overwhelms me ...

Psalm 16:7-9,11 (CEV) – *I praise You, Lord, for being my guide. Even in the darkest night, Your teachings fill my mind. I will always look to You, as You stand beside me and protect me from fear. With all my heart, I will celebrate, and I can safely rest ... You have shown me the path to life, and You make me glad by being near to me. Sitting at Your right side, I will always be joyful.*

Isaiah 42:16 (NIV) – *I will lead the blind by ways they have not known, along unfamiliar paths I will guide them; I will turn the darkness into light before them and make the rough places smooth. These are the things I will do; I will not forsake them.*

Isaiah 45:3 – *And I will give you the treasures of darkness, and hidden wealth of secret places, in order that you may know that it is I, the LORD, the God of Israel, who calls you by your name.*

When I feel like I've fallen into a deep pit of despair ...

Romans 8:14-18 (RSV) – *For all who are led by the Spirit of God are sons of God. For you did not receive the spirit of slavery to fall back into fear, but you have received the spirit of sonship. When we cry, "Abba! Father!" it is the Spirit Himself bearing witness with our spirit that we are children of God, and if children, then heirs, heirs of God and fellow heirs with Christ, provided we suffer with Him in order that we may also be glorified with Him. I consider that the sufferings of this present time are not worth comparing with the glory that is to be revealed to us.*

1 Peter 1:6,7 (LB) – *So be truly glad! There is wonderful joy ahead, even though the going is rough for a while down here. These trials are only to test your faith, to see whether or not it is strong and pure. It is being tested as fire tests gold and purifies it – and your faith is far more precious to God than mere gold; so if your faith remains strong after being tried in the test tube of fiery trials, it will bring you much praise and glory and honor on the day of His return.*

When I'm worried about my kids ...

Psalm 127:3 (LB) – *Children are a gift from God; they are His reward.*

Proverbs 22:6 (RSV) – *Train up a child in the way he should go, and when he is old he will not depart from it.*

Philippians 2:13 (RSV) – *For God is at work in you* [and your children], *both to will and to work for His good pleasure.*

When I'm worried about how we are going to pay our bills ...

Matthew 6:25-34 (RSV) – *Therefore I tell you, do not be anxious for your life, what you shall eat, or what you shall drink; nor about your body, what you shall put on. Is not life more than food, and the body than clothing? Look at the birds of the air: they neither sow nor reap nor gather into barns, and yet your heavenly Father feeds them. Are you not of more value than they? And which of you by being anxious can add one cubit to his span of life? And why are you anxious about clothing? Consider the lilies of the field, how they grow; they neither toil nor spin; yet I tell you, even Solomon in all his glory was not arrayed like one of these. But if God so clothes the grass of the field, which today is alive and tomorrow is thrown into the oven, will He not much more clothe you, O men of little faith? Therefore do not be anxious, saying, 'What shall we eat?' or 'What shall we drink?' or 'What shall we wear?' For the Gentiles seek all these things; and your heavenly Father knows that you need them all. But seek first His kingdom and His righteousness; and all these things shall be yours as well. Therefore do not be anxious about tomorrow; for tomorrow will be anxious for itself. Let the day's own trouble be sufficient for the day.*

Philippians 4:6,7 (LB) – *Don't worry about anything; instead, pray about everything; tell God your needs, and don't forget to thank Him for His answers. If you do this, you will experience God's peace, which is far more wonderful than the human mind can understand. His peace will keep your thoughts and your hearts quiet and at rest as you trust in Christ Jesus.*

Before we shut the pantry door,
a blessing for you ...

We *"pray that the Lord
will bless and protect you,
and that He will show you mercy
and kindness.
May the Lord be good to you
and give you peace."*

Numbers 6:24-26 (CEV)

E APPENDIX E
Doorways and Footholds

This is the list mentioned in Chapter 10, on page 153. Please keep in mind that this list represents *possible* doorways. Just because you have experienced one of the occurrences listed below, it doesn't mean that you have opened a doorway or provided a foothold for the enemy – but you may have. That's something you and the Lord will have to discern together.

> *But if any of you lacks wisdom, let him ask of God, who gives to all generously and without reproach, and it will be given to him.*
>
> **– James 1:5**

1. Indulgence in occultic music, literature, art, dancing, etc.
2. Possession of (known or unknown) and/or use of occultic records, tapes, books, pictures, charms, books, souvenirs, tools, games (Ouija Board™, Dungeons & Dragons®, etc.)
3. Holding on to grudges or bitterness against God and others
4. Destructively negative self-image
5. Anorexia, bulimia
6. Attempted suicide, thoughts of suicide
7. Rebellion against authority
8. Dating relationships or close friendships with demonized people
9. Sexual immorality with demonized people
10. Habitually participating in sexual immorality with anyone
11. Sexual involvement with a prostitute – even once
12. Parents, relatives or other close authority figures who have accepted satanic influence; i.e., witch, warlock or satanist
13. Ancestors or dead relatives who accepted satanic influence
14. Seeking or giving consent to occultic power or revelation (spirit guides, going to a psychic, medium or fortune teller, having an astrological chart made, etc.)
15. Fascination with occultic power, occultic revelation, or psychic phenomena in general (taking e.s.p. tests or psychic aptitude tests)
16. Involvement in psychic phenomenon, such as astral projection, levitation, spells, magic, fortunetelling, séances, channeling, or being present when these phenomena occurred
17. Involvement in or attending occultic rituals, festivals, masses, sacrifices, etc.
18. Involvement in martial arts rituals (no problem with martial arts, it's a matter of how deeply you may have participated in their rituals)
19. Involvement with "New Age" medicine, such as biofeedback, hypnosis, self-hypnosis, subliminal tapes, acupuncture, etc. (some of these procedures are harmless and even beneficial, but there is the potential for satanic involvement – so ask God for discernment)
20. Deliberate rejection of what is known and understood to be true
21. Participation in false religions or cults
22. Abuse of drugs and/or alcohol
23. Abuse of herbs
24. Escapism through thrill-seeking, science fiction, soap operas, or some other addicting hobby or activity (again, these activities can be harmless, but if they have led to an addiction, it's a vulnerability)

25. Hedonism, an absorbing pursuit of entertainment and/or body pleasure
26. Fascination with violence, especially violence devoid of justice, such as sadism or masochism
27. Torture - either as a victim or a perpetrator
28. Prolonged or persistent jealousy
29. Pornography
30. Fascination with UFO phenomena, attempts to contact extraterrestrial beings
31. Prolonged sleeplessness (this could simply be a symptom of PTSD, but still you should ask the Lord if there is possibly a doorway here)
32. Chanting or other cultic/occultic forms of worship
33. Blaspheming the Holy Spirit; i.e., repeatedly and consistently rejecting the work of the Holy Spirit as He reveals truth and convicts of sin
34. Vivid, recurrent, disturbing dreams as a child
35. Victim or perpetrator of rape or incest
36. Victim or perpetrator of violent sexual, physical or emotional assault
37. Victim or perpetrator of child abuse
38. Institutionalization (jail, psych ward, etc.)
39. Shock or trauma (Yes, your combat experiences could have created open doors, but not necessarily. Ask God about it.)
40. General anesthesia (In this totally passive state, open doors are possible, but not probable. Ask God.)
41. Very prolonged, unshakable grief
42. Involvement at high levels with Masons, Eastern Star, Rainbow, etc.
43. Obsession with occultic novels (such as Harry Potter and Goose Bumps)

For direction regarding how to close open doorways, see Chapter 10, page 153.

❋ ❋ ❋❋ ❋ ❋

APPENDIX F
Spiritual Warfare Ammo Bunker

Use these Scriptures when involved in spiritual warfare. They are your "*sword of the Spirit, which is the Word of God*" (Ephesians 6:17). Remember how Jesus used these weapons against Satan when He was tempted in the wilderness (Matthew 4:1-11): "*It is written ...*"

Anger

Proverbs 16:32 – *He who is slow to anger is better than the mighty, and he who rules his spirit, than he who captures a city.*

James 1:20 – *For man's anger does not bring about the righteous life that God desires.*

Deceit/lying

Leviticus 19:11,12 – *Do not steal. Do not lie. Do not deceive one another. Do not swear falsely by my name and so profane the name of your God. I am the Lord.*

Proverbs 12:22 – *The Lord detests lying lips, but he delights in men who are truthful.*

Disobedience to God

John 14:21 – *Whoever has My commands and obeys them, he is the one who loves Me; and he who loves Me will be loved by My Father, and I too will love him and show Myself to him.*

1 Samuel 15:22b – *To obey is better than sacrifice, and to heed is better than the fat of rams.*

Disrespect for authority

Ephesians 5:21 – *Submit to one another out of reverence for Christ.*

1 Peter 2:13 – *Submit yourselves for the Lord's sake to every authority instituted among men; whether to the king, as the supreme authority, or to governors, who are sent by him to punish those who do wrong and to commend those who do right.*

Drugs and alcohol

Proverbs 20:21 – *Wine is a mocker and beer a brawler; whoever is led astray by them is not wise.*

Ephesians 5:18 – *Do not get drunk on wine, which leads to debauchery. Instead, be filled with the Spirit.*

Envy

Galatians 5:26 – *Let us not become conceited, provoking and envying each other.*

Proverbs 14:30 – *A heart at peace gives life to the body, but envy rots the bones.*

Fearfulness

Isaiah 41:10 – *Do not fear, for I am with you; do not be dismayed, for I am your God. I will strengthen you and help you; I will uphold you with my righteous right hand.*

2 Timothy 1:7 – *For God did not give us a spirit of timidity, but a spirit of power, of love and of self-discipline.*

Greed/coveting

Exodus 20:17 – *You shall not covet ...*

Matthew 16:26 – *What good will it be for a man if he gains the whole world, yet forfeits his soul?*

Hatred

Leviticus 19:17 – *Do not hate your brother in your heart ...*

1 John 4:20 – *If anyone says, "I love God," yet hates his brother, he is a liar. For anyone who does not love his brother, whom he has seen, cannot love God, whom he has not seen.*

Idolatry

Exodus 20:4 – *You shall not make for yourself an idol in the form of anything in heaven above or on the earth beneath or in the waters below.*

1 John 5:21 – *Dear children, keep yourselves from idols.*

Jealousy

Proverbs 27:4 – *Anger is cruel and fury overwhelming, but who can stand before jealousy?*

Romans 13:13 – *Let us behave decently, as in the daytime ... not in dissension and jealousy.*

Lack of faith

Romans 1:17 – *... the righteous will live by faith.*

Hebrews 11:6 – *And without faith it is impossible to please God, because anyone who comes to Him must believe that He exists and that He rewards those who earnestly seek Him.*

Laziness

Proverbs 6:9-11 – *How long will you lie there, you sluggard? When will you get up from your sleep? A little sleep, a little slumber, a little folding of the hands to rest – and poverty will come on you like a bandit and scarcity like an armed man.*

Colossians 3:23 – *Whatever you do, work at it with all your heart, as working for the Lord, not for men.*

Lust

2 Timothy 2:22 – *Flee the evil desires of youth, and pursue righteousness, faith, love and peace, along with those who call on the Lord out of a pure heart.*

1 Peter 2:11 – *Dear friends, I urge you, as aliens and strangers in the world, to abstain from sinful desires, which war against your soul.*

Malice

1 Peter 2:1 – *Therefore, rid yourselves of all malice and all deceit ...*

1 Peter 2:16 – *... not using your liberty for a cloak of maliciousness, but as the servants of God.*

Materialism

Hebrews 13:5 – *Keep your lives free from the love of money and be content with what you have, because God has said, "Never will I leave you; never will I forsake you."*

Luke 12:15 – *Then He said to them, "Watch out! Be on your guard against all kinds of greed; a man's life does not consist in the abundance of his possessions."*

Pride

1 Peter 5:5,6 – *...Clothe yourselves with humility toward one another, because, "God opposes the proud but gives grace to the humble." Humble yourselves, therefore, under God's mighty hand, that He may lift you up in due time.*

Proverbs 29:23 – *A man's pride brings him low, but a man of lowly spirit gains honor.*

Profanity

Ephesians 4:29 – *Do not let any unwholesome talk come out of your mouths, but only what is helpful for building others up according to their needs, that it may benefit those who listen.*

Ephesians 5:3,4 – *But among you there must not be even a hint of ... obscenity, foolish talk or coarse joking, which are out of place, but rather thanksgiving.*

Rebellion

Proverbs 17:11 – *An evil man is bent only on rebellion ...*

Romans 13:2 – *He who rebels against the authority is rebelling against what God has instituted, and those who do so will bring judgment on themselves.*

Revenge

Leviticus 19:18 – *Do not seek revenge or bear a grudge against one of your people, but love your neighbor as yourself. I am the Lord.*

Proverbs 25:21,22 – *If your enemy is hungry, give him food to eat; if he is thirsty, give him water to drink. In doing this, you will heap burning coals on his head, and the Lord will reward you.*

Matthew 6:14,15 – *For if you forgive men when they sin against you, your heavenly Father will also forgive you. But if you do not forgive men their sins, your Father will not forgive your sins.*

Self-centered

Proverbs 12:15 – *The way of a fool seems right to him, but a wise man listens to advice.*

Philippians 2:3,4 – *Do nothing out of selfish ambition or vain conceit, but in humility consider others better than yourselves. Each of you should look not only to your own interests, but also to the interests of others.*

Slander/gossiping

Proverbs 10:18 – *He who conceals his hatred has lying lips, and whoever spreads slander is a fool.*

Ephesians 4:29 – *Do not let any unwholesome talk come out of your mouths, but only what is helpful for building others up according to their needs, that it may benefit those who listen.*

Sullenness

Psalm 118:24 – *This is the day the Lord has made; let us rejoice and be glad in it!*

Philippians 4:4 – *Rejoice in the Lord always. I will say it again: Rejoice!*

Theft

Exodus 20:15 – *You shall not steal.*

1 Peter 4:15 – *If you suffer, it should not be as a murderer or thief or any other kind of criminal …*

Unforgiving spirit

Matthew 18:21,22 – *"… Lord, how many times shall I forgive my brother?" … Jesus answered, "I tell you, not seven times, but seventy times seven."*

Matthew 6:14,15 – *For if you forgive men when they sin against you, your heavenly Father will also forgive you. But if you do not forgive men their sins, your Father will not forgive your sins.*

Wrath/rage

Psalm 37:8 – *Refrain from anger and turn from wrath; do not fret – it leads only to evil.*

Proverbs 12:16 – *A fool's wrath is quickly and openly known, but a prudent man ignores an insult.*

G APPENDIX G
Glossary: Explanations and Acronyms

Explanations

Acute Distress Disorder – The development of characteristic anxiety, dissociative and other symptoms that are experienced during or immediately after a traumatic event (and begin within a maximum of four weeks of the traumatic event), last for at least two days, and either resolve within four weeks after the conclusion of the traumatic event or the diagnosis is changed. When symptoms persist beyond one month, a diagnosis of Posttraumatic Stress Disorder (PTSD) may be appropriate if the full criteria for PTSD are met. The symptoms cause clinically significant distress or impairment in social, occupational, or other important areas of functioning or impair the individual's ability to pursue some necessary task. The stressors involved are the same as described for PTSD.

> **Source:** (DSM-IV-TR) American Psychiatric Association: *Diagnostic and Statistical Manual of Mental Disorders*, Fourth Edition, Text Revision (Washington, D.C., APA, 2000), pp. 469-472.

Acute PTSD – *See Posttraumatic Stress Disorder*.

Adjustment Disorders – The development of emotional or behavioral symptoms in response to an identifiable stressor(s) occurring within three months of the onset of the stressor(s) and resolving within an additional six months. These symptoms or behaviors are clinically significant as evidenced by *either* of the following: marked distress that is in excess of what would be expected from exposure to the stressor and/or significant impairment in social or occupational (academic) functioning.

> The general categories of Adjustment Disorder symptoms include depression, anxiety and disturbance of conduct (violation of the rights of others) or a combination of those three.

> Once a stressor (or its consequences) has terminated, the symptoms do not persist for more than an additional six months. However if the symptoms occur in response to a chronic stressor (e.g., a disabling medical condition) or to a stressor that has enduring consequences (e.g., financial and emotional difficulties associated with a divorce), they may persist beyond six months and it is termed **Chronic Adjustment Disorder**.

> Adjustment Disorder can be triggered by a stressor of any severity and may be a single event or multiple events. They may be recurrent or continuous events. They may affect a single individual, an entire family, or a larger group or community. Bereavement due to the death of a loved one is not considered a stressor unless the reaction is in excess of, or more prolonged than, what would be expected.

> **Source:** (DSM-IV-TR) American Psychiatric Association: *Diagnostic and Statistical Manual of Mental Disorders*, Fourth Edition, Text Revision (Washington, D.C., APA, 2000), pp. 679-683.

Battle Buddy – In our context: Someone who has some idea of what you're going through, and with whom you could feel comfortable and safe sharing your frustrations, joys, concerns and prayer requests without fear of judgment or gossip (page 27).

> Military use: Fellow troops who have gained your trust and whom you know you could count on to watch your back when you were in dangerous situations together.

Battlemind – "Armor for your Mind," a training program developed by the Army to prepare soldiers for deployment, and then for their transition back home. "A Warrior's inner strength to face adversity, fear and hardship during combat with confidence and resolution. It is the will to persevere and win." Battlemind includes ***combat skills*** and the battle mindset that sustains survival in the ***combat-zone***. The BATTLEMIND acronym stands for: **B**uddies, **A**ccountability, **T**argeted Aggression, **T**actical Awareness, **L**ethally Armed, **E**motional Control, **M**ission Operation Security, **I**ndividual Responsibility, **N**on-defensive (combat) driving, **D**iscipline and Ordering. There is further training for soldiers transitioning back home to not let combat behaviors and reactions determine how they will respond at home. For more information: www.battlemind.army.mil.

Campus Crusade for Christ International – From the web site, www.ccci.org: "Campus Crusade for Christ exists to help fulfill the Great Commission by winning, building and sending in the power of the Holy Spirit. We also help the body of Christ do evangelism and discipleship."

Chronic Adjustment Disorder – *See Adjustment Disorder*

Chronic PTSD – *See Posttraumatic Stress Disorder.*

Code Blue – a medical emergency in which paramedics are dispatched to aid a person undergoing cardiac arrest.

Compassion Fatigue – "Compassion fatigue is defined as a state of exhaustion and dysfunction – biologically, psychologically and socially – as a result of prolonged exposure to compassion stress and all that it evokes. Prolonged exposure means an ongoing sense of responsibility for the care of the sufferer and the suffering, over a protracted period of time. The sense of prolonged exposure is associated with a lack of relief from the burdens of responsibility, the inability to reduce the compassion stress. Moreover, traumatic recollections are provoked by compassion stress and prolonged exposure. These recollections are of traumatic memories that stimulate the symptoms of PTSD [see page 26] and associated reaction, such as depression and generalized anxiety. Compassion Fatigue is inevitable if, added to these three factors, the helper experiences an inordinate amount of life disruption as a function of illness or a change in lifestyle, social status, or professional or personal responsibilities."

Source: Dr. Charles R. Figley (Ed.), *Compassion Fatigue – Coping With Secondary Traumatic Stress Disorder in Those Who Treat the Traumatized* (New York: Brunner-Routledge, 1995). p. 253.]

Compassion Stress – *See Secondary Traumatic Stress.* Secondary Traumatic Stress is also called "Compassion Stress" [Source: Charles R. Figley (Ed.), *Compassion Fatigue – Coping With Secondary Traumatic Stress Disorder in Those Who Treat the Traumatized* (New York: Brunner-Routledge, 1995). p. xv, 2,3,14,15.]

Combat/Operational Stress Reaction – Normal reactions to abnormally stressful events – such as combat or other dangerous operations. COSRs are **not** a medical illness and people who experience COSRs are **not** sick or weak. COSRs are our bodies' way of protesting or slowing us down when we have pushed ourselves past the regular limits of endurance. The 'symptoms' of COSRs can look a lot like the symptoms of PTSD, ASD or Adjustment Disorders. The difference though is that the typical COSR has only a few symptoms and they tend to occur *immediately* after stressful action and get better quickly without significant 'treatment.'

Source: U.S. Army Center for Health Promotion & Preventive Medicine brochure: "Redeployment Health Guide: A Service Member's Guide to Deployment-Related Stress Problems," January 2006.

Combat Trauma – A general term we apply to the spectrum of distressing reactions a troop may have to the trauma of combat. It would include all conditions from the mild end of the spectrum (Reintegration Issues) to the severe end of the spectrum (PTSD). It describes the same spectrum of conditions that the U.S. Army Center for Health Promotion & Preventive Medicine calls "Deployment-Related Stress."

We recognize that all levels of Combat Trauma can be experienced by troops who were deployed in roles that were not directly combat-related. Long periods of sleep-deprived duty, monotony and stressful assignments while far from home and family can produce various levels of stress and anxiety in deployed troops. When these conditions are combined with living under the imminent threat of mortar and RPG attacks, IEDs and carbombs, the symptomology can rise to the level of Acute Stress Disorder and PTSD. We reason that combat operations (or the threat of combat) dictate *all* deployments and so even "non-trigger-pullers" are still involved in combat to some degree and could therefore be considered "Combat Trauma sufferers" as well, when they exhibit the same symptoms.

Deployment Stress – Being on life-or-death alert almost all of the time; taking part in traumatic, horrific events; physical woundings; near-death experiences; wounding and death of comrades; concern for family's welfare while downrange; anxiety over kids' development; missing out on important family occasions, births, deaths; fears regarding the spouse's loyalty and fidelity while separated; poor communication infrastructure; feeling of helplessness regarding family emergencies; loneliness; boredom; fatigue; sleep deprivation; discomfort; fear; sadness; exhaustion.

Fartlek – An athletic training technique, used especially in running, in which periods of intense effort alternate with periods of less strenuous effort in a continuous workout. A workout using this technique.

Source: *The American Heritage® Dictionary of the English Language, Fourth Edition.* Houghton Mifflin Company, 2004.

In the toilet – in a bad condition. **Source:** *Cambridge Dictionary of American Idioms©*, Cambridge University Press, 2003

Lachrymatory – "Also called lachrymal. A small, narrow-necked vase found in ancient Roman tombs, formerly thought to have been used to catch and keep the tears of bereaved friends." See www.tearbottle.com or www.timelesstraditionsgifts.com.

Source: Dictionary.com Unabridged (v 1.1). Random House, Inc.

Military Ministry – From the web site, www.militaryministry.org: "At Campus Crusade Military Ministry, our privilege and responsibility is to assist chaplains and commanders with caring for the spiritual well-being of troops and their families. We do this in many ways, but all focus on the gospel because 'faith comes by hearing, and hearing comes by the Word of God.' We seek to help every troop, every leader, every family member hear and receive the life saving message about Jesus. Identifying with Paul in the book of Romans, our 'heart's desire and earnest prayer to God is that they (military men, women, and families) might be saved.' Only in this way will they be truly ready, spiritually ready, to face the challenges which will certainly come their way." Military Ministry is a division of Campus Crusade for Christ International.

National Domestic Abuse Hotline: 1-800-799-SAFE (7233), 1-800-787-3224 (TTY)

The Navigators – From the web site, www.navigators.org: "Navigators have invested our lives in people for 75 years, coming alongside them one to one to study the Bible, develop a deepening prayer life, and memorize and apply Scripture. An interdenominational, nonprofit organization, The Navigators is dedicated to helping people navigate spiritually, to know Christ and to make Him known as they look to Him and His Word to chart their lives. Our ultimate goal is to equip them to fulfill 2 Timothy 2:2 – to teach what they have learned to others."

Pilates – A system of exercises that promotes the strengthening of the body, often using specialized equipment. [After Joseph Pilates (1880-1967), German-born American physical fitness instructor who developed the system.]

Source: *The American Heritage® Dictionary of the English Language, Fourth Edition.* Houghton Mifflin Company, 2004.

Reintegration Issues – Tension that increases in a returning troop (and his/her spouse and children, if married) as they encounter various difficulties during the transition from deployment back to home and family life.

Sources: "Spouse Battlemind Training," brochure produced by Walter Reed Army Institute of Research, January 2007; "Courage to Care: Becoming a Couple Again" handout by the Uniformed Services University of the Health Sciences (www.usuhs.mil), Summer, 2004; "Roadmap to Reintegration" by U.S. Army Europe found at www.per.hqusareur.army.mil. reintegration, June 2008.

Posttraumatic Stress Disorder – The development of characteristic symptoms following exposure to an extreme traumatic stressor involving direct personal experience of an event that involves actual or threatened death or serious injury, or other threat to one's physical integrity; or witnessing an event that involves death, injury, or threat of death or injury experienced by a family member or other close associate. The person's response to the event must involve intense fear, helplessness or horror. The symptoms (see the list of symptoms on page 18) must last more than one month and cause clinically significant distress or impairment in social, occupational, or other important areas of functioning. If the duration of symptoms is less than three months, it is termed **Acute PTSD**. If the duration of symptoms is three months or more, it is termed **Chronic PTSD**. If the onset of symptoms is at least six months after the stressor, it is termed **PTSD With Delayed Onset**.

Source: (DSM-IV-TR) American Psychiatric Association: *Diagnostic and Statistical Manual of Mental Disorders*, Fourth Edition, Text Revision (Washington, D.C., APA, 2000), pp. 463-468.

Pre-deployment Stress – Immediate anxiety when notified of an impending deployment; wide range of emotions; financial, emotional and logistical stresses involved with preparing the family for the troop's absence; increase in training tempo in preparation for the mission; traumatic outbursts for couples who don't know how to cope with the looming reality of long-term separation.

PTSD With Delayed Onset – *See Posttraumatic Stress Disorder*.

Running on fumes – continuing to do something when you have almost no energy left. **Source:** *Cambridge Dictionary of American Idioms©*, Cambridge University Press, 2003

Secondary Traumatic Stress – "One of several terms, including "compassion stress," "compassion fatigue," and "secondary victimization" (Figley, 1983), "co-victimization" (Hartsough & Myers, 1985), "traumatic countertransference" (Herman, 1992), and "vicarious traumatization" (McCann & Pearlman, 1989) that have been used to label the manifestations and processes of distress reported by persons in close proximity to victims of traumatic events that they themselves did not actually experience. The term is used … in both its narrow and broad sense. In the narrow sense, it refers to the transmission of nightmares, intrusive thoughts, flashbacks, and other symptoms typically experienced by traumatized individuals, to persons close to them. In the broad sense, it refers to any transmission of distress from someone who experienced a trauma to those around him or her and includes a wide range of manifestations of distress in addition to those that mimic post-traumatic stress disorder (PTSD) (Galovski & Lyons, 2004)."

Source: Dr. Rachel Dekel & Dr. Zahara Solomon, "Secondary Traumatization Among Wives of War Veterans with PTSD." Article in Dr. Charles R. Figley and Dr. William P. Nash, *Combat Stress Injury* (New York: Routledge, 2007). p. 138.

Secondary Traumatic Stress Disorder – *See Compassion Fatigue.* Dr. Charles R. Figley, one of the world's foremost authorities in Secondary Trauma, uses the term "Secondary Traumatic Stress *Disorder*" however, it has not yet been formally defined by the professional mental health community at large.

Triage – (1) A process for sorting injured people into groups based on their need for or likely benefit from immediate medical treatment. Triage is used in hospital emergency rooms, on battlefields, and at disaster sites when limited medical resources must be allocated … (3) A process in which things are ranked in terms of importance or priority. (From *American Heritage Dictionary*)

Vet Centers – There are over 200 Vet Centers in the United States, the US Virgin Islands, Puerto Rico and Guam. The Vet Center was designed to assist and provide counseling for veterans who have served in a combat zone. The services offered include: individual and group counseling for PTSD, reintegration issues, military sexual trauma (MST); marriage and family counseling, addiction information and assessment, assistance with VA benefits and claims, bereavement counseling for families, and much more.

To find a Vet Center near your community and how your husband can initiate services, go to www.vetcenter.va.gov or call 1-800-905-4675 (EST) or 1-866-496-8838 (PST).

Vietnam – The Vietnam War, also known as the Vietnam Conflict, occurred from March 1959 - April 30, 1975. Escalation of the war officially started January 31, 1965.

VO2 max – (also *maximal oxygen consumption*, *maximal oxygen uptake* or *aerobic capacity*) is the maximum capacity of an individual's body to transport and utilize oxygen during incremental exercise, which reflects the physical fitness of the individual. The name is derived from V - volume per time, O2 - oxygen, max - maximum.

Source: Wikipedia

Acronyms

ASD – Acute Stress Disorder

AWOL – Absent Without Leave

COSR – Combat/Operational Stress Reaction

DSM-IV, APA, 1994 – American Psychiatric Association: *Diagnostic and Statistical Manual of Mental Disorders*, **Fourth** Edition, **1994**

FAP – Family Advocacy Program

IED – Improvised Explosive Device, an explosive device often used in unconventional warfare

MPH – Master of Public Health

OEF – Operation Enduring Freedom, Afghanistan, October 7, 2001-

OIF – Operation Iraqi Freedom, Iraq, March 19, 2003-

PTSD – Posttraumatic Stress Disorder

RPG – Rocket-Propelled Grenade

STS – Secondary Traumatic Stress

STSD – Secondary Traumatic Stress Disorder

Bible translations

(AMPLIFIED) – The Amplified Bible

(NIV) – New International Version®

(CEV) – Contemporary English Version

(NKJV) – New King James Version

(ESV) – English Standard Version

(NLT) – New Living Translation

(LB) – the Living Bible

(RSV) – Revised Standard Version

(NCV) – New Century Version

(TM) – The Message

ND NOTES

1: What Happened to My Husband?
Understanding Combat Trauma

1. Quote from Will Durant found at www.brainyquotes.com.
2. Adapted from American Psychiatric Association: *Diagnostic and Statistical Manual of Mental Disorders*, Fourth Edition, Text Revision (Washington, D.C., American Psychiatric Association, 2000), p. 463.
3. Combat Trauma Spectrum adapted from U.S. Army Center for Health Promotion & Preventive Medicine, *Redeployment Health Guide: A Service Member's Guide to Deployment-Related Stress Problems*, January 2006.
4. Veterans Health Administration, Office of Public Health and Environmental Hazards, "Analysis of VA Health Care Utilization Among US Southwest Asian War Veterans: *Operation Iraqi Freedom Operation Enduring Freedom*," PowerPoint presentation, October 2007.
5. C. W. Hoge, et al. "Combat Duty in Iraq and Afghanistan, Mental Health Problems and Barriers to Care," *The New England Journal of Medicine*. Vol. 351, No. 1, July 1, 2004.
6. Donald Meichenbaum, *A Clinical Handbook/Practice: Therapist Manual for Assessing and Treating Adults with Posttraumatic Stress Disorder* [Institute Press, 1994], p. 23
7. Observations from Dr. H. Norman Wright, *Crisis & Trauma Counseling*, p.198-205, and Patience H. G. Mason (www.patiencepress.com), Post Traumatic Gazette, Issue 1, May/June 1995.
8. Quote from Patience H. G. Mason (www.patiencepress.com), Post Traumatic Gazette, Issue 1 May/June 1995.
9. Description of symptom categories from The Australian Centre for Posttraumatic Mental Health – www.acpmh.unimelb.edu.au
10. Definition from Mayo Clinic: www.mayoclinic.com/health/traumatic-brain-injury/DS00
11. Brain Injury Association of America (www.biausa.org), "Traumatic Brain Injury in the United States: A Call for Public/Private Cooperation" Article: http://www.biausa.org/elements/2007_tbi_in_us_revised.pdf
12. TBI symptoms from Brain Injury Association (www.biausa.org), Centers for Disease Control and Prevention (www.cdc.gov/ncipc/tbi), Dr. Daniel Amen, M.D. (www.amenclinics.com)
13. Dr. Julius Segal, *Winning Life's Toughest Battles*, p. xii, quoted in Robert Hicks, *Failure To Scream*, p. 79.

2: What's Happening to Me?
Understanding Secondary Traumatic Stress

1. Quote from article by Charles R. Figley, "Strangers at Home: Comment on Dirkzwager, Bramsen, Adèr, and van der Ploeg, (2005)" in *The Journal of Family Psychology,* 19:2 (June 2005).
2. Charles R. Figley (Ed.) *Treating Compassion Fatigue* (New York, London: Routledge, 2002), pp. 2,3.
3. Charles R. Figley "Compassion Fatigue: Toward a New Understanding of the Costs of Caring" in B. H. Stamm (Ed.) *Secondary Traumatic Stress: Self-care Issues for Clinicians, Researchers, and Educators (2nd ed.)* (Lutherville, Md.: Sidran, 1999), p. 10. Figley equates "Secondary Traumatic Stress" with "Compassion Stress" in other articles.
4. American Psychiatric Association: Diagnostic and Statistical Manual of Mental Disorders, Fourth Edition, Text Revision. Washington, D.C. 2000), p. 463, 464. Figley made the same observation in *Compassion Fatigue – Coping With Secondary Traumatic Stress Disorder in Those Who Treat the Traumatized* (New York, London: Brunner-Routledge, 1995), p. 4.
5. Mary S. Cerney, Ph. D., "Treating the 'Heroic Treaters,'" Chapter 7 in Charles R. Figley: *Compassion Fatigue* (1995) referenced above, p. 137.
6. Most of these symptoms were gleaned from Dr. Charles Figley's *Compassion Fatigue* (1995) referenced above, especially Chapter 4: "Working With People With PTSD: Research Implications" by Mary Ann Dutton and Francine L. Rubinstein, pp. 85-87.
7. Adapted from C. R. Figley, A. B. Baranowsky & J. E. Gentry, "Compassion Fatigue Scale – Revised" in C. R. Figley (Ed.), *Compassion Fatigue: Volume II* (New York: Brunner/Mazel, 1999) and also found in Figley's *Treating Compassion Fatigue* (2002), pp. 134,135.
8. Eric Scalise, Ph.D,, Ed.S, LPC, LMFT, VP of Professional Development for AACC. Nine points from an online seminar, Regent University School of Divinity: "Compassion Fatigue: How to Avoid Burnout In Ministry" – www.regent.edu/acad/schdiv/resources/online_seminars.shtml#foltz_23

3: Why Am I So Sad?
Dealing with Loss and Grief Issues

1. Rabbi Dr. Earl A. Grollman – quote found in www.DailyCelebrations.com.
2. Frank O'Conner – quote found in www.gaia.com.
3. Rev. Barrie E. Henke, *Coping With Compassion Fatigue* (St. Louis, Mo.: Concordia Publishing, 1994), pp.7,8.
4. "Chaplain Ray" Giunta, *Grief Recovery Workbook* (Integrity Publishers, 2002), p. 63.
5. More examples of Jesus' grief: Matthew 26:37,38; Mark 3:5; Luke 19:41.

6. Dr. H. Norman Wright, *The New Guide to Crisis & Trauma Counseling* (Ventura, Calif.: Regal, 2003), p. 64.
7. Quote from Dr. May found in ibid, p. 87.
8. Quote from Margaret Hill, Harriet Hill, Richard Baggé, Pat Miersma, *Healing The Wounds of Trauma* (Paulines Publications of Africa, 2007, 2004), p. 37.
9. For more insight or to purchase one of these lachrymatories, go to www.tearbottle.com or www.timelesstraditionsgifts.com.
10. This point and the one before it are from Dr. Aphrodite Matsakis, Ph.D., *I Can't Get Over It* (New Harbinger Publications, 1996), p. 202.
11. C. S. Lewis, *A Grief Observed* (HarperSanFrancisco, 2001, 1961), p. 33.
12. Dr. Larry Crabb, *Shattered Dreams* (WaterBrook, 2001), p. 109.
13. C. S. Lewis, *A Grief Observed*, pp. 5,6.
14. C. S. Lewis, *A Grief Observed*, pp. 61,62.
15. Dr. Larry Crabb in *Shattered Dreams*, pp. 157,158
16. Hebrews 12:2 (NIV) – *Let us fix our eyes on Jesus, the author and perfecter of our faith, who **for the joy set before Him** endured the cross, scorning its shame, and sat down at the right hand of the throne of God.*
17. Written by the late Pastor Ron Mehl, who died in 2003 after a 23-year-long battle with leukemia. He was well-acquainted with the night shift. Quoted in Dr. H. Norman Wright, *Experiencing Grief* (Nashville: Broadman & Holman, 2004) p. 22.
18. C. S. Lewis, *A Grief Observed*, p. 11.
19. Matthew 7:7,8 (NLT) – *Keep on asking, and you will receive what you ask for. Keep on seeking, and you will find. Keep on knocking, and the door will be opened to you. For everyone who asks, receives. Everyone who seeks, finds. And to everyone who knocks, the door will be opened.*
20. This partial list of coping mechanisms was taken from www.changingminds.org under their "Explanations/Behaviors/Coping" tab.
21. Quote by Lilias Trotter, missionary to Africa from 1888 to 1928. Found in Elisabeth Elliot, *A Path Through Suffering* (Servant Publications, 1990).
22. Ibid, p. 41.
23. Quote by David Shepherd in Dr. Larry Crabb, *Shattered Dreams*, p. 161.
24. Quote by Thomas Merton in a letter to Jim Forest, director of the Fellowship of Reconciliation, quoted by Henri Nouwen in *Turn My Mourning Into Dancing* (W Publishing/Thomas Nelson, 2001), p. 60.
25. Dr. Harold Ivan Smith in *When Your People Are Grieving* (Beacon Hill Press, 2001), p. 38. Dr. Smith speaks widely on the subjects of grief and death, and conducts "grief gatherings" around the U.S.
26. "Chaplain Ray" Giunta, *Grief Recovery Workbook*, p. 15.
27. Robert Hicks, *Failure To Scream* (Nashville: Thomas Nelson, 1993), p. 187.
28. Idea from Dr. Benjamin Keyes, Ph.D., Ed. D., Coordinator for Regent University's D.C. Campus Counseling Program.
29. Matthew 19:29; Joel 2:21-27.

4: Forgiveness: Is It Possible?
The Empowering Nature of Forgiveness

1. *Merriam-Webster's Deluxe Dictionary, Tenth Collegiate Edition* (Pleasantville, NY: Reader's Digest, 1998), p. 720.
2. International Forgiveness Institute headed up by Dr. Robert D. Enright, a Christian and the unquestioned pioneer in the scientific study of forgiveness. Web site: www.forgiveness-institute.org. His book *Exploring Forgiveness* (Univ. of Wisconsin Press, 1998) is a seminal work on the subject.
3. Rev. Al Miles, *Domestic Violence: What Every Pastor Should Know* (Minneapolis: Augsburg Fortress Press, 2000), p. 133.
4. Lewis B. Smedes, *The Art of Forgiving: When You Need To Forgive And Don't Know How* (New York: Random House, 1996), p. 21.
5. From class on Interpersonal Communication conducted by Wanda Fisher, who was at the time the Director of Counseling at Eugene Faith Center, Eugene, OR.
6. James MacKnight, M.A., D.D., *A New Literal Translation from the Original Greek of All the Apostolical Epistles with a Commentary, Vol. 1* (Grand Rapids: Baker Book House, no date), pp. 440, 441.
7. Dr. Albert Barnes, *Notes on the New Testament: Romans* (Grand Rapids: Baker Book House, 1949), p. 289.
8. Dr. Adam Clarke, *A Commentary and Critical Notes: Vol. 6* (Grand Rapids: Baker Book House, no date), p. 142.
9. Beverly Flanigan, *Forgiving The Unforgivable: Overcoming the Legacy of Intimate Wounds* (New York: Wiley Publishing, 1992), p. 46.
10. Lewis B. Smedes, "Forgiveness: The Power To Change The Past" – article in *Christianity Today*, January 7, 1982, quoted at www.iloveulove.com.
11. Idea from Dr. Grace Ketterman, *Verbal Abuse: Healing the Hidden Wound* (Ann Arbor, Mich.: Servant Publications, 1992), p. 222.
12. Malachy McCourt quote from www.thinkexist.com.
13. Shared during an informal talk by Dr. Gothard at Campus Crusade for Christ headquarters in Orlando, Florida, at a "Prayer and Fasting Summit" in 1995. Dr. Bill Gothard is the President of the Institute of Basic Life Principles in Oak Brook, Ill. (www.iblp.org).
14. Lewis B. Smedes, *The Art of Forgiving: When You Need To Forgive And Don't Know How* (New York: Random House, 1996), p. 26.
15. Dr. Grace Ketterman and David Hazard, *When You Can't Say I Forgive You* (Colorado Springs: NavPress, 2000), p. 176.

5: I Don't Feel Safe – What Should I Do?
Physical and Emotional Security for You and Your Kids

1. Dawn Bradley Berry, J.D. *The Domestic Violence Sourcebook* (Los Angeles: Lowell House, 2000), pp. 1-4.
2. C. J. Newton, M.A., "Domestic Violence: An Overview," *Mental Health Journal*, www.FindCounseling.com, Feb. 2001.

3. Definitions adapted from Berry, *The Domestic Violence Sourcebook*, p. 3, and through conversations with Jackie Hudson, MS, MFT, LPC, co-founder of Peace and Safety in the Christian Home (PASCH), Eugene, Ore., (www.peaceandsafety.com). Input also from the "Power and Control Wheel" in Jill Cory and Karen McAndless-Davis' *When Love Hurts* (New Westminster, B.C.:WomanKind Press, 2003), p. 31.

4. T. F. Baily and W. H. Baily *Operational Definitions of Child Emotional Maltreatment*. Final Report of a Federal Project. Augusta, Maine, 1986. Quoted in Ketterman, *Verbal Abuse*, p. 13. (see endnote #6 below)

5. Verbal Abuse categories from Patricia Evans *The Verbally Abusive Relationship* (Avon, Mass., Adams Media Corp, 1992, 1996).

6. Dr. Grace Ketterman *Verbal Abuse: Healing the Hidden Wound* (Ann Arbor, Mich.: Servant Pub, 1992), p. 13.

7. Additional physical abuse list from chapter review and revision by Dr. Benjamin Keyes, Ph.D., Ed. D., Professor and Program Director for the Masters in Counseling Programs at Regent University, Virginia Beach, Va.

8. Dr. Lenore E. Walker *The Battered Woman* (New York: Harper & Row, 1979), pp. 55ff.

9. For an excellent treatment of the "Cycle of Abuse" (and other battered women issues) see Jill Cory and Karen McAndless-Davis' *When Love Hurts* (New Westminster, B.C.:WomanKind Press, 2003), pp. 8-28.

10. Ibid, p. 15.

11. Most of this list appears in Berry, *The Domestic Violence Sourcebook*, p. 244-246. Some of the points were originally published by the National Coalition Against Domestic Violence – www.ncadv.org, the Duluth Domestic Abuse Intervention Project – www.duluth-model.org, the National Technical Assistance Center on Family Violence (now Office of Technical Assistance) – www.nasmhpd.org/ntac.cfm, personal security expert Gavin de Becker & Associates – www.gavindebecker.com, and PTSD and domestic abuse expert Dr. Benjamin Keyes (see vitals at endnote # 7 above).

12. Ibid, p. 7,8

13. Catherine Clark Kroeger and Nancy Nason-Clark, *No Place For Abuse* (Downers Grove, Ill.: InterVarsity Press, 2001), p. 37.

14. This point and the one before it in ibid, p. 83. Statistics from the Massachusetts Department of Youth Services.

15. Berry, *The Domestic Violence Sourcebook*, p. 9.

16. From recorded phone conversation with Dr. Benjamin Keyes – see endnote #7 above for vitals.

17. Catherine Clark Kroeger "The Abused Bride of Christ" article on PASCH web site: www.peaceandsafety.com.

18. Dr. Henry Cloud and Dr. John Townsend, *Boundaries In Marriage* (Grand Rapids: Zondervan, 1999), pp. 11, 43.

19. For some very practical suggestions on how to establish appropriate consequences for your spouse, see Cloud & Townsend, *Boundaries In Marriage,* cited above, pp. 225-228.

20. Ibid, p. 221.

21. Most of these measures are suggested by Christians Addressing Family Abuse (CAFA) headquartered in Eugene, Oregon. You can contact them at (541) 686-6000.

22. This information is a very short summary and leaves out all the ifs, ands and buts. The news release that describes the Restricted Reporting policy can be found at www.defenselink.mil/releases/release.aspx?releaseid=8320. The official policy can be found at www.defenselink.mil/news/Mar2005/d20050318dsd.pdf .

23. Information about the Family Advocacy Program is available online at www.defenselink.mil/fapmip. The Resources page on this web site provides links to the FAP for each branch of the service.

6: Where Is My Healing Place?
Constructing Your Healing Environment

1. William R. Bright, *Have You Made The Wonderful Discovery of the Spirit-Filled Life?* (Orlando, Fla.: Campus Crusade for Christ, 1966,1995). Illustrations used by permission.

2. WORD HAND ILLUSTRATION. Copyright © 1976, The Navigators. Used by permission of NavPress, Colorado Springs, Colo. All rights reserved.

3. Rosalind Rinker, *Prayer: Conversing With God* (Grand Rapids: Zondervan, 1959), p. 23.

4. From *Evangelism Explosion* by Dr. James Kennedy (Tyndale, 1977) appendix A.

5. Additional Scriptures which describe the gifts of the Holy Spirit: Romans 12:6-8, Ephesians 4:11.

6. Kenneth S. Wuest, *Wuest's Word Studies From the Greek New Testament, Volume 1* (Grand Rapids: Eerdmans, 1955), p. 130.

7. For an excellent in-depth, interactive study on the eight mindsets of this verse (Philippians 4:8), see *Loving Your Military Man* by Beatrice Fishback. Available through Military Ministry at www.militaryministry.org/products/loving-your-military-man.

7: How Do I Take Care of Me?
Nurturing Your Spirit, Soul and Body

1. Quote from www.thinkexist.com, or see www.barbaradeangelis.com.

2. Katherine L. Karr, *Taking Time for Me* (Buffalo, NY: Prometheus Books, 1992), p. 57.

3. Quote from www.brainyquotes.com.

4. Dr. Richard Swenson, M.D., *Margin: Restoring Emotional, Physical, Financial, and Time Reserves to Overloaded Lives* (Colorado Springs: NavPress, 2004), back cover.

5. Ibid, p. 13.

6. Rebecca Radcliffe, *Dance Naked In Your Living Room* (Minneapolis: EASE Publication, 1999-2004), p. 54.

7. From MedicineNet.com – www.medterms.com.

8. From Mercola.com – Dr. Joseph Mercola quoting a USA Today article from March 22, 2005.

9. Medical information in this and the previous two paragraphs are from Claire Michaels Wheeler, MD, Ph.D., *10 Simple Solutions to Stress* (Oakland: New Harbinger Publications, 2007), pp. 113-116.

10. Information on aerobic and anaerobic exercise from "Physical Activity and Health: A Report of the Surgeon General," CDC, 1999 – found at SparkPeople.com: www.sparkpeople.com/resource/reference_aerobic.asp or _anaerobic.asp.

11. Statistics from Jeff Davidson, MBA, CMC, *The Complete Idiot's Guide to Managing Stress* (USA:Penguin Group, 1999), pp. 157,158.

12. Information at http://library.thinkquest.org/C005545/english/sleep/stage.htm.

13. Tips came from www.realage.com/stayingyoung/youtoolstips.aspx?tip=1 and Davidson, *The Complete Idiot's Guide to Managing Stress*, pp. 160-167.

14. See http://herbal-properties.suite101.com/article.cfm/soothing_teas.

15. Nutritional tips found at www.mayoclinic.com/health/supplements/NU00198.

16. Calcium facts found at www.mayoclinic.com/health/calcium-supplements/AN00964.

17. See www.athealth.com/Consumer/disorders/Bingeeating.html.

18. Joan Z. Borysenko, Ph.D., *Inner Peace for Busy People* (Carlsbad, Calif.: Hays House, 2001).

8: Who Cares?
Seeking and Finding Your Support Network

1. From *Bridge Over Troubled Water* by Paul Simon, 1969. Sung by Paul Simon and Art Garfunkle on the album "Bridge Over Troubled Water."

2. Rabbi Harold Kushner, *Living A Life That Matters*, pp. 123-124; Quoted in Harold Ivan Smith, *When You Don't Know What to Say* (Kansas City, Mo.: Beacon Hill Press, 2002), p. 11.

3. Jody Hayes, *Smart Love* (New York: Penguin Book, 1989). p. 22,23.

4. From a currently unpublished manual by therapist and writer J. Elizabeth Oppenheim, M.A.: *A Crash Course In Crisis Management: Useful Life Skills for People Who Don't Want Them*. Also available from her: *Survival Rations: Encouragement for Troops at the Crossroads* (devotional). You can contact her at elizabeth@oppenheimgroup.com.

9: Who Am I Really?
Focusing On Your True Identity In Christ

1. Quote by Dr. Ronnie Janoff-Bulman in "The Aftermath of Victimization: Rebuilding Shattered Assumptions," found in Dr. Robert Hicks, *Failure To Scream* (Nashville: Thomas Nelson, 1993), p. 28,29.

2. Dr. Neil T. Anderson, *Victory Over the Darkness: Realizing the Power of Your Identity in Christ* (Ventura, Calif.: Regal Books, 1990), p. 43.

3. Opposed pairs of core values/core hurts are found in Dr. Steven Stosney's *Manual of the Core Value Workshop* [Copyright © 1995, 2003 Steven Stosney] and in other publications of his. For a fuller explanation, consult his web site: www.compassionpower.com.

10: Who Is The Real Enemy?
Fighting Spiritually For Myself, My Husband and My Kids

1. From *The Art of War* by Sun Tzu, translated by Samuel B. Griffith (Oxford University Press, 1963), p. 84.

2. R. Arthur Matthews. *Born For Battle* (New York:OMF Books, 1978), p. 11.

3. George Washington quote from Wisdom Quotes: www.wisdomquotes.com.

4. Ezekiel 28:12-19. In this passage, the Spirit of God is speaking through the prophet Ezekiel against the King of Tyre – a very devilish king. In this pronouncement He was in essence saying, "King of Tyre, your characteristics are just like Satan's. Now let me tell you his history – and his destiny."

5. Isaiah 14:12-17. Same idea here as in endnote #4. Isaiah is directing God's words of judgment to the King of Babylon, but content clearly applies in a broader sense to Satan.

6. Eugene Peterson (translator of *The Message*) in *A Long Obedience In The Same Direction* (InterVarsity Press, 1980, 2000), p. 127.

7. From *The Art of War*, p. 96.

8. Colin Brown (Ed.), *The New Int'l Dictionary of New Testament Theology* (Regency, 1967, 1971), Vol. 2, p. 606.

9. Analogy from Dr. Tony Evans, Pastor of Oak Cliff Bible Fellowship in Dallas, Texas, former professor at Dallas Theological Seminary and Chaplain of the Dallas Cowboys and Dallas Mavericks.

10. R. Arthur Matthews in *Born For Battle*, p. 27, 28.

11. Dr. Mark I. Bubeck, *Overcoming The Adversary* (Chicago: Moody Press,, 1984), p.17.

12. Lauren, in the illustration on page 147, is wearing her spiritual armor as she prays with her child.

13. For an in-depth, inspiring, practical six-chapter treatment of our spiritual armor, see Dr. Mark I. Bubeck's *Overcoming The Adversary*, pp. 64-120.

14. Dr. Mark I. Bubeck, *The Adversary: The Christian Versus Demon Activity* (Chicago: Moody Press, 1975), p. 21.

15. Dr. Mark I. Bubeck, *Spiritual Warfare Prayers* (pamphlet) (Chicago: Moody Press, 1997).

16. Ibid.

17. Stormie Omartian, *The Power of a Praying Wife* (Eugene, Ore.: Harvest House, 1997), pp. 114,115.

18. Ray Beeson & Kathi Mills, *Spiritual Warfare and Your Children* (Nashville: Thomas Nelson, 1993), p. 79.

11: How Can I Help My Husband?
Contributing to Your Husband's Healing Environment

1. See "Families in the Wake of Trauma PowerPoint presentation at http://deploymentpsych.org/CDPpresDaveFamiliesandPTSD.ppt.
2. Bridget C. Cantrell, Ph.D., and Chuck Dean, *Hearts on the Homefront: Phase #1 of "Turning Your Heart Toward Home" Workbook Course* (Bellingham, Wash.: Hearts Toward Home Int'l, 2005), p. 7. www.heartstowardhome.com.
3. Aphrodite Matsakis, Ph.D., *Trust After Trauma* (Oakland: New Harbinger, 1998), p. 316.
4. Charles R. Figley, Ph.D., and William P. Nash, M.D., *Combat Stress Injury* (New York: Routledge, 2007), pp. 141,142.
5. Aphrodite Matsakis, Ph. D., *Vietnam Wives* (Baltimore: Sidran Press, 1996), p. 123.
6. Charles R. Figley, Ph.D., Editor, *Burnout in Families: The Systemic Costs of Caring* (Boca Raton, Fla.: CRC Press, 1998), pp. 65,66.
7. Matsakis, *Vietnam Wives*, p. 379.
8. Robert Hicks, Ph.D., *Failure To Scream* (Nashville: Thomas Nelson Publishers, 1993), pp. 86,87.
9. Patience Mason, "How Does PTSD Affect Families?" Issue #2 of the *Post Traumatic Gazette* (internet web site found at www.patiencepress.com/samples/2ndIssue.html. - "Everyone focuses on the survivor's problem."
10. "Secrets of Loving Confrontation" from Campus Crusade for Christ's FamilyLife *Weekend to Remember* Conference manual (2007), p. 92.
11. John Gottman and Nan Silver, *The Seven Principles for Making Marriage Work* (New York: Three Rivers Press, 1999), pp.158,159.
12. Tim and Joy Downs, *The Seven Conflicts: Resolving the Most Common Disagreements in Marriage* (Chicago: Moody publishers, 2003), p.175.
13. Ibid, summary on pp. 148-153.
14. Ibid, p. 51.
15. For an excellent, faith-building study on this prayer, see Bruce H. Wilkerson's book, *The Prayer of Jabez: Breaking Through to the Blessed Life* (Sisters, Ore.: Multnomah Publishers, 2000).
16. Dr. Mark I. Bubeck, *Spiritual Warfare Prayers* (pamphlet), (Chicago: Moody Press, 1997).
17. Goff, Crow, Reisbig & Hamilton, Kansas State University School of Family Studies and Human Services: "The Impact of Individual Trauma Symptoms of Deployed Soldiers on Relationship Satisfaction," appearing in the *Journal of Family Psychology*, Sept. 2007, Vol. 21, No. 3, pp. 344-353.
18. Matsakis, *Vietnam Wives*, p. 93,94.
19. Matsakis, *Vietnam Wives*, p. 98,99.
20. Keith Armstrong, L.C.S.W., Suzanne Best, Ph.D., Paula Domenici, Ph.D., *Courage After Fire* (Berkeley: Ulysses Press, 2006), pp. 149,150.
21. Figley and Nash, *Combat Stress Injury*, p. 314.
22. Mason, "How Does PTSD Affect Families?" under "Principles of Recovery."
23. Matsakis, *Trust After Trauma*, pp. 318,319.
24. Cantrell and Dean, *Hearts On the Homefront, Section Two*, p. 6.
25. Department of Veterans Affairs, "Support and Family Education," Session 13 – PTSD and its impact on the family; section IV, point 7.
26. Mason, "How Does PTSD Affect Families?" under "How Families Can Recover."
27. Matsakis, *Trust After Trauma*, p. 332.

12: How Can I Help My Children?
Making a Safe, Healthy Environment for Your Kids

1. Article by Jennifer L. Price, Ph.D., "Children of Veterans and Adults with PTSD," National Center for PTSD Fact Sheet found at www.ncptsd.va.gov/ncmain/ncdocs/fact_shts/fs_children_veterans.html.
2. Kate L. Harkness, Ph. D., "Transgenerational Transmission of War-related Trauma," in J.P. Wilson & B. Raphael (Eds.), *International Handbook of Traumatic Stress Syndromes* (New York: Plenum Press, 1993), pp. 635-643.
3. The National Child Traumatic Stress Network, article: "Understanding Child Traumatic Stress" found on their web site: www.nctsnet.org.
4. Many observations in this section from Dr. Jennifer Price's article, p. 2 (endnote #1).
5. R. Rosenheck & A. Fontana, "Transgenerational Effects of Abusive Violence on the Children of Vietnam Combat Veterans," *Journal of Traumatic Stress*, 1998, 11, 731-742.
6. L. Cosgrove, M. E. Brady & P. Peck, "PTSD and the Family: Secondary Traumatization," in D. K. Rhoades, M. R. Leaveck, & J. C. Hudson (Eds.), *The Legacy of Vietnam Veterans and Their Families: Survivors of War, Catalysts for Change* (Washington: Agent Orange Class Assistance Program, 1995), pp. 38-49.
7. M. R. Ancharoff, J. F. Munroe & L. M. Fisher, "The Legacy of Combat Trauma: Clinical Implications of Intergenerational Transmission," in Y. Danieli (Ed.), *International Handbook of Multigenerational Legacies of Trauma* (New York: Plenum Press, 1998), pp. 257-275.
8. Patience Mason, *Why Is Daddy Like He Is?* (High Springs, Fla.: Patience Press, 1992), p. 11. Contact: PO Box 2757, High Springs, FL, 32655 or www.patiencepress.com.
9. The National Child Traumatic Stress Network, same article as endnote #3.
10. Don R. Catherall, Ph. D., *Back From the Brink: A Family Guide to Overcoming Traumatic Stress* (New York: Bantam Books, 1992), p. 139,140.
11. "Silence" and "Overdisclosure" entries from Dr. Jennifer Price's article, p. 3 (endnote #1).
12. Annette M. La Greca, Ph.D., Scott W. Sevin and Elaine L. Sevin, *Helping Children Cope With the Challenges of War and Terrorism* – download from 7-Dippity Custom Educational Programs: www.7-dippity.com, p. 6.
13. Bridget C. Cantrell, Ph.D., & Chuck Dean, *Down Range: To Iraq and Back* (Seattle: Word Smith Publishing, 2005), p. 147.
14. Article by Ilona Pivar, Ph.D., "Talking to Children About Going To War," National Center for PTSD Fact Sheet: www.ncptsd.va.gov/ncmain/ncdocs/fact_shts/a117fs_children_war.html?opm=1&rr=rr117&srt=d&echorr=true

15. Neil T. Anderson, D. Min., and Steve Russo, *The Seduction of Our Children* (Eugene, Ore.: Harvest House Publishers, 1991), pp 228-229, 202-203.

16. Dawn Bradley Berry, J.D., *The Domestic Violence Sourcebook* (Los Angeles: Lowell House Publishers, 1995, 2000), p. 138.

17. Don R. Catherall, *Back From the Brink*, p. 158.

18. Annette M. La Greca, et al, *Helping Children Cope with the Challenges of War and Terrorism*, p. 16.

19. There are over 200 Vet Centers in the United States, the U.S. Virgin Islands, Puerto Rico and Guam. The Vet Center was designed to assist and provide counseling for veterans who have served in a combat zone. The services offered include: individual and group counseling for PTSD, reintegration issues, military sexual trauma (MST); marriage and family counseling, addiction information and assessment, assistance with VA benefits and claims, bereavement counseling for families, and much more. To find a Vet Center near your community and how your husband can initiate services, go to www.vetcenter.va.gov or call 1-800-905-4675 (EST) or 1-866-496-8838 (PST).

13: How Do I Get Back to "Normal"?
The Journey to Peace and Stability

1. Quote by Ralph Waldo Emerson in his essay "The Tragic," found in *Unspeakable* by Os Guinness, p. 44.

2. Quote by Elisabeth Elliot in *A Path Through Suffering*, p. 14.

3. Aphrodite Matsakis, Ph.D., *Vietnam Wives* (Baltimore: Sidran Press, 1996), p. 380.

4. Quote by Douglas H. Everett found at www.quoteworld.org.

5. Spoken by Frederick Buechner in a graduation address, quoted in *Windows of the Soul* by Ken Gire (Grand Rapids: Zondervan, 1996), p. 71.

6. Quote by Tad Williams found at www.brainyquote.com.

7. Quote from Zora Neale Hurston found at www.brainyquote.com.

8. Quote by Alan Lakein from www.thinkexist.com.

9. Quote by Jonas Salk from www.brainyquote.com.

Spiritual Solutions for Combat Trauma

By Major General (Retired) Bob Dees, US Army
Executive Director, Military Ministry
a Division of Campus Crusade for Christ International

The reality of war is that everyone gets wounded. Some wounds heal rapidly, but some last for a lifetime. Some wounds can be seen. Some wounds are invisible inside the heart, soul, and spirit of the warrior. These unseen wounds are often the most difficult to heal – they must heal from the inside out.

The Faith and Hope Gap

Posttraumatic Stress Disorder (PTSD) is on the extreme end of the spectrum of trauma-related symptoms and conditions. PTSD was not an official psychological diagnosis until the early 1980s, but it has existed over the history of warfare, being referred to as "Soldiers Heart," "Battle Fatigue" or "Shell Shock" in former conflicts. Today, PTSD along with Traumatic Brain Injury (TBI) is called by many the "signature injury" of the wars in Afghanistan and Iraq.

Government agencies are working hard to help wounded warriors from past battlefields of WWII, Korea, Vietnam and wounded warriors from current conflicts in the Persian Gulf and around the world. In particular, the Armed Forces and the Department of Veterans Affairs, as well as numerous civilian organizations, are working tirelessly to help with the mental wounds of war.

A Department of Defense Mental Health Task Force report found that 49 percent of National Guard members, 38 percent of active duty Soldiers, and 31 percent of Marines are experiencing mental health issues after serving in Iraq and Afghanistan. The Task Force recognized that programs within DoD are not adequately reflecting the increasing demand. The treatment shortfall is partly caused by a lack of resources, but the fear of stigma to military and civilian careers is also a significant hurdle blocking requests for treatment.

In response to the need for more PTSD care, Veterans Affairs is seeking to add 40,000 new mental health hospital beds costing roughly 3 billion dollars, and also on significantly increasing the numbers of available mental health professionals.

The Services are likewise scrambling to reach the capacity needed to handle the PTSD challenge. In spring 2007, the Army surveyed over 100 combat-tested company commanders who indicated that "dealing with combat stress/PTSD among soldiers" is a major area in which they and others need deeper understanding. The Army, seeking to better train its leaders, recently conducted "chain teaching" for all echelons of command regarding PTSD. All the Services are working PTSD issues and related family issues hard and fast.

The reality, however, is that the Department of Veterans Affairs and the Department of Defense simply don't have the capacity or the means to address the magnitude of this national challenge, particularly for the many National Guard, Reserve, and former troops and families who often suffer invisibly because they are not eligible for the same programs as active duty military.

The reality, also, is that wounds of the heart, soul and spirit are not addressed adequately by government services. Despite the valiant efforts of chaplains and many organizations and the commitment of billions of dollars, there remains a serious gap – the faith and hope gap.

For Christians, addressing this gap starts with the premise that God is the true healer and that Jesus Christ is the avenue to experience true recovery from the ravages of combat trauma, particularly those visited on the mind and emotions. For many of our veterans and returning warriors, this will be a long road – but there is hope. In my own life and in the lives of many wounded warriors, I have observed the peace, the calm and the healing that God can bring to war-ravaged souls.

Whether it's the veteran who has lived in the lonely isolation of combat memories for decades, or young warriors just returning from their first combat horrors, the power of God, the power of God's written word, and the community of God's people around our nation can become powerful resources in this healing process. And this healing can certainly extend to military families and many others impacted by these mental, emotional and spiritual wounds of war.

As an example from the Bible, David was honored as a "man after God's own heart" and as a "mighty man of God." Yet, David's Psalms indicate he was also a serious PTSD sufferer. For instance, consider his following lament:

> "My heart is in anguish within me, and the terrors of death have fallen upon me. Fear and trembling come upon me, and horror has overwhelmed me." Psalms 55:4,5 (NASB)

And we read about David's trust in God for his ultimate healing:

> "He will redeem my soul in peace from the battle which is against me." Psalms 55:18 (NASB)

Faith is absolutely a critical factor in resilient recovery from combat trauma, every bit as relevant today as in David's age.

As an organization, Campus Crusade for Christ Military Ministry (www.militaryministry.org) seeks to bring Faith in the Foxhole and Hope on the Home Front, to the Ends of the Earth. It is said that there are "no atheists in foxholes." This is certainly true. Daily, we receive reports from Iraq, Afghanistan and other corners of the earth that testify to the importance, the eternal importance, of "faith in the foxhole." We hear constantly from troops, chaplains and commanders about the power of prayer before dangerous missions, about the value of the Bible to their sense of hope and comfort, and about the healing that comes from faith. They believe wholeheartedly, with David, that God is their "Rock, Fortress, and Deliverer." Psalm 18:18 (NASB)

Whether in peace or in war, American troops (Soldiers, Sailors, Airmen, Marines, and Coast Guardsmen) seek faith to anchor their souls. And families on the home front need the same anchor as they wait in fear and uncertainty. This anchor is available through faith in Jesus Christ.

Military Ministry

At Military Ministry (militaryministry.org), our privilege and responsibility is to assist chaplains and commanders with caring for the spiritual well-being of troops and their families. We do this at our armed forces initial entry training sites (boot camps) and operational locations, on ROTC and academy campuses and on the Internet, with military family seminars and small groups and by publishing and distributing spiritual resources direct and through chaplains, to troops and families. In addition, we seek to help every troop, every leader and every family member hear, receive and draw hope from the life-changing message of Jesus. Only in this way will these ones who selflessly serve us at home and abroad be truly ready, spiritually ready, to face the challenges which will certainly come their way.

In our present time of war and the aftermath of war, Military Ministry is working diligently to provide spiritual solutions relevant and sensitive to the needs of combat trauma and PTSD sufferers. We seek to accelerate the spiritual healing of many thousands of veterans and returning warriors. Hence, we have established the "Bridges to Healing Ministry" to mobilize, equip and support Christians in churches across America creating a "corps of compassion" that will help heal and restore PTSD sufferers, families and caregivers. In the early stages of this Bridges to Healing ministry, we have seen churches and communities in New York, Texas, California and elsewhere capture this vision.

We are also developing relevant Christ-centered content for PTSD sufferers and caregivers. Our new "Church Guide for Ministering to the Military" provides a basic orientation for churches and civic organizations seeking to come alongside our military at such a critical time in our nation's history.

In 2007, we published the Combat Trauma Healing Manual to offer PTSD sufferers a roadmap to for spiritual healing. By combining the latest insights from the medical and psychological communities with the timeless principles of God's Word, this book outlines a step-by-step program that will help PTSD sufferers . . .

- understand their trauma – spiritually, psychologically and physiologically
- adopt therapeutic spiritual disciplines to bring them closer to God
- process their loss and grief
- experience the freeing influence of giving and receiving forgiveness
- rebuild their identity based on what God says about them
- strengthen themselves spiritually against future attacks
- connect with those who will support them in many ways
- define plans to fully reintegrate into society as a strengthened man or woman of God, to include becoming an asset to other trauma sufferers

Also, in the fall of 2008, Military Ministry will publish When War Comes Home, a companion to the Combat Trauma Healing Manual, for military wives.

Military Ministry's partnership with the American Association of Christian Counselors (AACC) is particularly relevant to reversing the PTSD epidemic in our land. The 50,000-plus Christian counselors within the AACC community will have a far-reaching impact in the lives of many military men, women and families. In October 2008, AACC and Military Ministry will deliver a jointly-produced, 30-hour video series and certification program to help prepare professional, pastoral and lay counselors for serving military members and families. Together, Military Ministry and the AACC will join forces to deploy tens of thousands of Christians from thousands of churches in the fight to build bridges between PTSD suffering and God's love and healing power.

MILITARY MINISTRY –
COME JOIN THE FIGHT!

MILITARY
MINISTRY

It is Military Ministry's honor and privilege to serve our troops and their families with spiritual support and the Word of God.

We do this in many ways, but all focus is on the Gospel because "it is the power of God for the salvation of everyone who believes" (Romans 10:16).

With Paul, our "heart's desire and earnest prayer to God is that they [military men, women and families] might be saved." Only in this way will they be truly ready – spiritually ready – to face the challenges which will certainly come their way.

Please read about our ministries below and join us in prayer and in service to those who sacrificially give for us.

Your partner in the gospel,

Bob Dees

Photo by Maj. William Thurmond, courtesy U.S. Army

Bob Dees, Major General, U.S. Army (Retired)
Executive Director, Military Ministry

THE SIX STRATEGIC OBJECTIVES
OF MILITARY MINISTRY

1 Evangelize and disciple enlisted service members at basic training bases and beyond.

> *My faith was nourished through your programs [at Lackland Air Force Base], and I will never forget what the Military Ministry did for me during that difficult time.* – Air Force recruit

Every Sunday, Military Ministry staff and volunteers lead Christian education classes at basic training and operational bases across America. Hundreds make first-time decisions for Christ or openly renew their faith … every week.

2 Develop Christian military leaders at service academies, ROTC campuses and operational locations.

> *I came into Texas A&M as a "young" believer, and through my involvement in Military Ministry, I grew to understand foundational spiritual truths and how to apply them to my life and my mission.* – Army officer

Leadership makes a difference. Military Ministry offers spiritual nurture to future military leaders at service academies, ROTC campuses, and locations around the world – ships, flight lines, foxholes, and at special venues such as the Gettysburg Leadership Conference.

3 Stop the unraveling of the military family with conferences, support groups, spiritual resources and leadership.

You brought us back from the brink ... now we are facing toward Christ instead of away. — *Military Marriage Seminar attendee*

Divorce rates among military families are at epidemic proportions with repeated deployments and the normal challenges of military life taking their toll. The most vulnerable victims of family stress are military children.

Many of the solutions to family unity are spiritual in nature. We work to establish Hope on the Home Front by giving families the faith and knowledge of Jesus Christ.

4 Arm troops in harm's way with spiritual resources.

The Bible in my Rapid Deployment Kit was the one I had, the only one. When we were reading our Bible ... it was a big comfort ... to read before missions. — *Soldier back from Iraq*

I was overwhelmed at the demand for Military Ministry Rapid Deployment Kits. —*Chaplain*

The Word of God has given millions of Soldiers, Sailors, Airmen, Marines and Coast Guardsmen the assurance of God's love as they encounter the toughest conditions our world can offer. Military Ministry teams with chaplains and commanders to provide a spiritual resource network that troops and families can draw upon during tough times. Our goals:

- A Bible in every "foxhole"
- Resources to support chaplains in every service of the armed forces

5 Wage global online evangelism, discipleship and leader training.

I have received Christ in my heart and rededicated my life to Him ... I want to grow and ... start my life off in the right direction. — *A visitor to godlovesairmen.com*

Worldwide outreach to military members everywhere is now possible with the help of new technologies and partners. We are touching thousands of people with the gospel who might never visit a church or be available to hear the good news in person but will surf the Web, even from deployed locations.

6 Change continents for Christ.

I can do my job much more effectively because of the Military Ministry in Kenya. — *Chief of Chaplains, Kenya Armed Forces*

Our vision is to see the militaries of the world lead their nations to Christ. The same strategic principles used in America apply to military ministry around the world. Working through indigenous military leaders, Military Ministry works to recruit, train, equip and deploy military missionaries who will in turn build ministry teams in their countries.

Military Ministry Re-Supply

Help us get the word out about Military Ministry! Re-supply your efforts at www.militaryministry.org or by calling 1-800-444-6006.

- Prayer ministry – submit prayer requests and learn how you can pray for our military.
- Bibles and spiritual development tools –
  - Rapid Deployment Kits: a New Testament, daily devotional and Gospel presentation
  - Spiritual Fitness Kits – Discipleship tools for the new or growing believer
  - Family Readiness Kits – "Hope on the Home Front" inspiration for spouses and children
  - Chaplain's Boxes – A resource sampler for chaplains everywhere
- Posttraumatic Stress Disorder (PTSD) resources — material for individuals and churches
  - *Combat Trauma Healing Manual: Christ-centered Solutions for Combat Trauma*
  - "Bridges to Healing" DVD
  - Training curriculum
  - Church Guide for Ministering to the Military
- Standard Bearer – the Military Ministry news source, online or by mail
- Military Ministry brochures, videos, bulletin inserts
- Ambassador Kits – to help you tell churches or friends in your community about Military Ministry

NEED MORE INFORMATION?
WOULD YOU LIKE TO SERVE THOSE WHO SERVE?
PLEASE SEE THE BACK OF THIS PAGE.
THANKS!

WAYS TO SERVE THOSE WHO SERVE …

Our church wants to learn more about ministry to the military and the Bridges to Healing program. Please contact me at my email address or phone number below.

Church Name _____

Church Website: _____

Please provide more information on:

❏ Prayer ministry
❏ Bibles for our troops
❏ PTSD ministry for my church
❏ Military Marriage Seminars
❏ HomeBuilders® groups for military couples
❏ International ministries
❏ Other: _____

Send me/us the Standard Bearer newsletter

❏ By e-mail to _____
❏ By postal mail (complete address section below)

I/we …

❏ Will pray for the spiritual needs of military couples.
❏ Would like to volunteer our time to minister to military couples.
❏ Would like to provide a financial gift to Military Ministry.
   • To give online, visit www.militaryministry.org and click "Give Online."
   • For additional information on support opportunities, e-mail development@militaryministry.org.

Photo courtesy of U.S. Army, by Spc. Lorie Jewell

Name(s) _____

E-mail _____

Address _____

City, State, ZIP _____

Phone including area code _____

❏ Please call me.

Please complete and clip out this form, then mail it to **Military Ministry, P.O. Box 120124, Newport News, VA 23612-0124.**

Other ways to contact us:
    Phone: 1-757-928-7200 or (toll-free) 1-800-444-6006
    e-mail: info@militaryministry.org
    Web: www.militaryministry.org

 Please remember us during the annual Combined Federal Campaign, CFC # 12040.

The Combat Trauma Healing Manual:
Christ-Centered Solutions for Combat Trauma
by Chris Adsit, published by the Military Ministry Press

The Combat Trauma Healing Manual offers spiritual solutions for struggles with PTSD by helping construct an environment that will give God optimal access to the wounded soul. Designed for individual or group study, *The Combat Trauma Healing Manual* combines the latest insights of the medical and counseling communities with the timeless principles of God's Word. The book outlines a step-by-step program that will help PTSD sufferers...

- understand your trauma – spiritually, psychologically and physiologically
- adopt therapeutic spiritual disciplines to bring you closer to God
- process your loss and grief
- experience the freeing influence of giving and receiving forgiveness
- rebuild your identity based on what God says about you
- strengthen yourself spiritually against future attacks
- connect with those who will support you in many ways
- define plans to fully reintegrate into society as a strengthened man or woman of God

Available from the Military Ministry Online Resource Center at http://resources.militaryministry.org or by calling 1-800-444-6006.

ISBN: 978-1-4196-7820-2   Soft cover, 178 pages   Price: US $15.99, or $10 for active duty military